Monogram Monarch Series

The Focke-Wulf Ta 152

Monarch Three

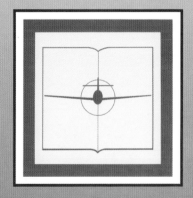

The Focke-Wulf Ta 152

THOMAS H. HITCHCOCK

Illustrated by Thomas A. Tullis
Cover illustration by Gareth Hector

First Edition

ISBN: 978-0-914144-53-3 Standard Edition
ISBN: 978-0-914144-50-2 Deluxe, autographed, leather bound, limited edition

Manufactured in Hong Kong

Monogram Monarch Series Number Three

Library of Eagles

Eagle Editions Ltd.
Post Office Box 580
Hamilton MT 59840 USA
www.eagle-editions.com

*We are interested in hearing from those who have
photographic or other material
for possible inclusion in future publications.*

It is important to note that this book in no way promotes or agrees with the "Nazi" atrocities, ideals and actions perpetrated during WWII and does not reflect the views of the publisher, the author or the illustrators. Rather this book is a presentation of the known historical facts surrounding the development and use of the late war German *Luftwaffe* fighter commonly known as the Ta 152 and some of the men who flew this aircraft.

Contents

During World War II, the *Luftwaffe's* standard fighter aircraft was the Me 109, joined sometime later by the Fw 190. *Luftwaffe* leadership believed that with these two outstanding fighter types, they would be equal and even superior to the enemy. Their opinion was confirmed during the first months of the war; however, later in the conflict, the Allies introduced fighter types which were equal, or even with superior performance to the German fighters. The *Luftwaffe's* leadership strategy was found to be wrong, and solutions were anxiously sought. It was Focke-Wulf (the company) who developed the Fw 190 D-9, which went into action during late 1944, and somewhat narrowed the gap with Allied superiority.

Further development was undertaken by Professor Kurt Tank under the type designation Ta 152 H-0 and H-1; a fighter aircraft was brought into operational service which overshadowed everything so far standard with powered fighter aircraft.

In the early morning hours of 27 January 1945, JG 301 pilots were underway on a LKW truck from Altenow near Luckau to the aircraft facility at Neuhausen near Cottbus. The reason for the ride was to take delivery of Ta 152s for operational service in the *Reichsverteidigung* (Defense of the *Reich*). When the pilots left the hard wooden truck benches, they faced twelve Ta 152s, neatly lined up in three rows. With critical eyes and anxious feelings, the pilots walked between the lined-up aircraft, since the impression of the long protruding engine, the enormous wingspan and the unusually broad propeller blades was not that of a maneuverable fighter. Following a brief technical introduction, the pilots accepted the aircraft for the return flight to Altenow.

At 11:08, I took off for the first time in a Ta 152 from Neuhausen and touched down at 11:28 at Altenow. The first impressions: Acceleration during take-off was so great that my body was pressed into the back rest, and after a few hundred meters only, the Ta 152 lifted off. The climb following take-off was enormous while the large wingspan took some getting used to. All around view and freedom of movement in the cockpit were very good. The landing speed was rather slower than the models flown before and thus again somewhat unusual.

In the course of the following operations with *Reichsverteidigung*, I was able to fully enjoy the flying qualities of the Ta 152 compared to the Me 109 and Fw 190 I had flown earlier. During air combat with various enemy fighter models, and even in low level flight, I never had any feeling of inferiority. I was always impressed by the speed, maneuverability and climbing speed of the Ta 152. For me, the Ta 152 was my life insurance during the hard fighting over the last weeks of the war. Unfortunately, all remaining examples of the Ta 152 eventually ended up on the scrap heap except for one solitary aircraft.

Willi Reschke
Stotternheim, Germany
April 2005

Willi Reschke was born 3 February 1922 at Mühlow in Brandenburg. After completing his pilot training in June 1944, he was posted to I./JG 302 based at Götzendorf near Vienna. He achieved his first success on 2 July 1944, while flying a Bf 109 G-6 by downing two B-24s over Budapest.

In September 1944, after being re-equipped with Fw 190 A-8s, I./JG 302 became III./JG 301. In October 1944 his unit was transferred to Stendal near Berlin. On 1 January 1945, Reschke downed a B-17 for his 22nd aerial victory. He was awarded the German Cross in Gold on 13 March 1945.

Reschke flew a total of 48 combat missions, achieving an impressive score of 27 confirmed victories, of which twenty were B-17s and B-24s. Ofw. Reschke was awarded the coveted Knight's Cross to the Iron Cross on 20 April 1945. One of the Ta 152s flown by Reschke, W. Nr. 150168, is illustrated herein. He was shot down eight times, bailed out four times and was wounded once.

Today, Willi Reschke lives a far quieter life near Erfurt in the German state of Thuringia. He is the author of **Jagdgeschwader 301/302 "Wilde Sau"**, an autobiography of his career in the German *Luftwaffe*.

Oberfeldwebel Willi Reschke posed for this autographed snapshot just after the cessation of hostilities in May 1945. His tunic not only denotes his *Luftwaffe* rank but also displays his awards. These include the *Deutsche Kreuz* (German Cross) in gold above his right pocket, his *Frontflug-Spange für Jäger* (Fighter Pilot's Mission badge) in bronze on top of his left side, his *Eisernen Kreuz* 1. *Klasse* (Iron Cross First Class), his *Verwundetenabzeichen* (Wound Badge) in black and lastly his silver and gray *Luftwaffenflugzeugführerabzeichen* (Air Force Pilot Badge). But, the most revered award is, of course, his *Ritterkreuz des Eisernen Kreuzes* (Knight's Cross of the Iron Cross) worn about his neck and held in place by a black-white-red-white-black ribbon.

His collar insignia consisted of four silver-gray "wings" mounted on a yellow board with the collar itself edged in silver-gray braid. His shoulder boards carried two silver-gray pips over the tunic color, which was in turn, edged in sliver-gray braid offset by yellow piping. The color yellow signified flying personnel. In response to an Allied dictum, his tunic's customary embroidered *Luftwaffe* service eagle containing a swastika, sewn over the right breast, was removed.

Fw 56 A-1, TK+BU, began its career as a civilian sport plane but later served as a military fighter pilot trainer. This example, posted to FFS A/B 4, is shown taxiing. Slightly over 400 of these splendid performers were manufactured.

Fw 159 V2, W. Nr. 933, D-INGA, an experimental fighter which was one of the contenders for an all-important government fighter contract but which lost out to the Bf 109.

This is the story of the German Focke-Wulf Ta 152 and its little known cousin, the Ta 153. The story is supplemented by as many relevant illustrations as possible. Additional contemporary photographs of the Ta 152 exist but are almost always of marginal photographic quality. Genuine wartime images of the Tank fighter are virtually nonexistent. In many instances, German wartime photographs often focus on individuals relegating aircraft as backdrops. By 1945, photographing new frontline fighters by members of the *Luftwaffe* was strictly prohibited. Severe penalties awaited those who choose to ignore such stringent security measures. Additionally, the personal effects of German airmen, such as photo albums, were often lost during the last months of the war due to chaotic and hastily arranged transfers. Often a soldier's personal belongings traveled separately by rail or road vehicles. Often too, these transports were themselves attacked and destroyed by low flying Allied aircraft.

WHAT'S IN A NAME?

The hyphenated name "Focke-Wulf" originated from the surnames of the two young principals who founded the company on 1 January 1924. Thirty-four year old Henrich Focke and twenty-nine year old Georg Wulf joined with a third partner, Dr. Werner Naumann, to establish their fledgling enterprise located in modest offices within a hanger at Bremen airport. Seven years later, on 1 November 1931, thirty-three year old Dipl. Ing. Kurt W. Tank came aboard to lead the company's blossoming design and flight test offices. Previously four years earlier on 29 November 1927, Georg Wulf had tragically lost his life while test flying one of the company's more unusual early aircraft, the canard designed F 19 *Ente* (Duck). Ten years after this event in 1937, Henrich Focke left the firm to pursue his deeply held interest in rotary-winged aircraft. In the meantime, Dr. Neumann quietly continued in his role as the firm's Commercial Director, a title which he held throughout the war. By 1933, Kurt Tank had advanced to become the company's Technical Director and in 1942, he received the prestigious title "Professor" from Braunschweig Technical School.

The designation prefix "Ta" represented the first two letters of Kurt Tank's surname while the number "152" was one of an official sequence of numbers assigned to the Focke-Wulf company by the German Air Ministry.

TECHNOLOGY VERSUS NATIONAL SOCIALISM

During the twenties and thirties, Kurt Tank and his team of dedicated and skilled engineers and designers crafted many advanced and innovative aircraft for the state and civilian aviation market, but each project was heavily dependent upon the nation's aero engine industry. Restricted by the stifling terms of the Treaty of Versailles, German engine makers were officially prohibited from producing and developing aero engines that could conceivably be adapted for offensive military purposes. This meant that by the time the Nazi government gained power, Germany was producing successful small to medium sized air-cooled and liquid-cooled power plants but trailed noticeably behind Britain and the United States in the design and development of large capacity internal combustion aero engines with the possible exception of diesels.

After 1933, when Germany freed itself of Allied restrictions, a great deal of catching up had to be accomplished before an acceptable level of parity could be achieved. Another equally important factor exacerbating Germany's attempts to introduce reliable military high-performance reciprocating internal combustion engines was the state's attitude toward engineering and technology. It is difficult for us in the twenty-first century to comprehend a regime that in time of war routinely favored class position over job qualification. Yet, the relationship between the German officer class and technical engineers was seldom equal. When it came to placing the right person in critical military technical positions, a military line officer was almost always automatically chosen regardless of his academic qualification. Moreover, National Socialism, with its sinister intoned mantra of racial supremacy and mysticism, failed to embrace the idea of a society based upon diversity and technology. This insured that technical considerations always trailed operational

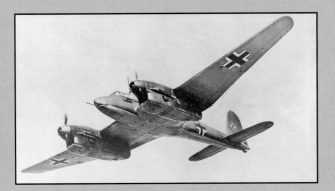

*Fw 187 A-0, W. Nr. 1975, CI+NX, "Yellow 7", carried
a crew of two but never went into series production.*

*If the Ta 183 had been built, it is likely it would have closely
resembled this meticulously crafted, large scale model created
by master modeler Günter Sengfelder.*

dictums. In truth, engineers were essentially classified as civil servants unless, of course, they were fortunate enough to simultaneously hold engineering degrees while serving as a commissioned officer. Thus, it was not surprising that only 30 percent (less than 300 persons!) of the engineering graduates for the eight years leading up to 1941 majored in aero-engine engineering.

CATCHING UP WHERE IT COUNTS

During the war, even a large and well established firm such as Daimler-Benz was never staffed by more than 250 engineers and, of these, only about 15 percent were senior designers. When measured against America's astonishing wartime aero-engine industry, these figures pale by comparison. For example, at the height of the war, the Connecticut based engine maker, Pratt & Whitney alone employed a labor force of over 39,000 men and women.

Unfortunately for Germany's aero engine manufacturers, this shortfall would become painfully evident when, through shortages and reductions in skilled technical manpower, it was belatedly recognized and accepted that a full five to six years' lead time was required before a new world-class engine was ready for series production. This meant that even under ideal conditions, German internal combustion aero engines created in 1941, could not be expected to enter large scale series production before 1946 or 1947.

For the Ta 152, dependent as it was on large capacity engines, the realization that this powerful fighter might not enter service during Germany's most desperate hours was indeed a very bitter pill. Nevertheless, through shear force of will, the German aero engine industry came very close to pulling off the impossible.

A QUESTION OF AVIATION FUEL

By the early thirties aviation gasoline (avgas) had an octane reading of only 75 to 80 which was achieved through a process distillation of high-grade petroleum. German domestic oil was not of this quality but thanks to the lead additive tetraethyl, German avgas could be raised to a maximum of 87 octane. The rights for the production of this additive were acquired from America in 1935, but without high-grade oil, even this additive was not very effective. High octane avgas was essential for high-performance engines, as its antiknock characteristics determined engine compression ratios, and it was the compression ratio which, in turn, determined the engine's power.

In 1935, a significant breakthrough in avgas production occurred in America when it became possible to produce isooctane with a reading of 100 in large quantities. By the beginning of the war in Europe in 1939, American and British aircraft began using the improved fuel. Germany came up with a method to manufacture equivalent high-test avgas, but it was much more complex, cumbersome and expensive to manufacture. As a result of prolonged German neglect in this area, by 1945 the *Luftwaffe* had no fuel equal to what was readily available to the USAAF and RAF.

In sum, because the war lasted far longer than German planners had first imagined, indubitable weaknesses and systemic failures conspired to weaken, not strengthen, Germany's war footing.

THE LABOR POOL

During the last year of the war, Focke-Wulf recorded a large labor force of 11,920 direct employees with a further 17,040 employed in indirect operations. Because the German aviation industry tended to use a large amount of general-purpose (rather than specialized) machinery, a high proportion of skilled labor was required for the workforce. According to the Aircraft Industry Report of the U.S. Strategic Bombing Survey, German airframe plants employed about 450,000 persons in October 1944. About 23 percent or 103,500 were women. The total number employed, both men and women, was only 52 percent of the entire workforce. The remaining 48 percent, or 216,000, was composed of political prisoners, prisoners of war, Jews, and foreign nationals of both sexes. Of the total workforce, some 36 percent, or 162,000, were foreigners, many of which were forced workers.

FIGHTERS PAST, PRESENT AND FUTURE

In the 25 years preceding V-E Day, Focke-Wulf Flugzeugbau GmbH created and produced a wide range of civilian and military aircraft; including sport planes, utility and meteorological aircraft, plus multi-engined transports. In addition, the firm also produced a limited number of single-seat Fw 56 fighters in the 1930s. The firm also produced three unsuccessful prototypes of the Fw 159, a design of mixed construction, employing a parasol wing and an awkward-looking stalky retractable undercarriage. The experience gained with these diverse aircraft proved invaluable enabling Tank to proffer an entirely new all-metal fighter; the twin-engine Fw 187. Although fewer than a dozen Fw 187s were completed, and successfully flown before the war, series production failed to materialize. However, experience gained with the Fw 187 was ultimately translated into the legendary Fw 190 and by extension, the Ta 152.

Kurt Tank believed the future of front-line military aircraft rested with those powered by turbojets. Beginning in 1943, Focke-Wulf evolved a number of advanced fighter designs powered by turbojets. One project of particular interest eventually crystallized into what became the Ta 183 *Huckebein* (being supported by stalky legs). This jet fighter project bore tell-tail Focke-Wulf features which, coincidentally or not, later found their way into postwar military aircraft of the West and East.

A mosaic montage of the Ta 152 H-0 presently in storage at the National Air and Space Museum. It graphically conveys the fuselage's lengthy silhouette plainly revealing successive coats of German, British and American paint. See Epilogue for additional images.

About the Author

Thomas H. Hitchcock, the creator and former CEO of Monogram Aviation Publications, is the author of numerous articles and a dozen published titles pertaining to German aeronautical subjects. His interest in aircraft designed and produced for the German aviation industry spans more than fifty years.

As a youngster during World War 2, his interest in aviation was sparked by the flood of patriotic wartime motion picture films which flowed from Hollywood during the 1940s. Wartime aviation was also glamorized by "Victory in the Air" coloring books, countless paper and balsa models and by the real life exploits of a cousin who flew operational missions with the 82nd Fighter Group while piloting the sensational Lockheed P-38 G Lightning.

Years later, Tom's interest in airplanes prompted him to serve in the U.S. Army's 82nd Airborne division, and eventually his love of flying guided him to flight school where he mastered recreational flying on single-engine Cessna and Piper aircraft.

Tom is also a former educator having a background in history, graphic arts and design, film, photography and audio-visual production. Tom's post graduate work included further training in audio-visual communication where he gained skills that greatly facilitated his 1972 entry into the specialty publishing world; a career which spanned 36 years.

Tom guided Monogram's list of published titles through dozens of historical non-fiction books dealing with technologically significant military aircraft, aircraft colors, camouflage and markings of American, German and Japanese origin. One large hardcover title Tom is especially proud of is Monogram's 1994 book, V-Missiles of the Third Reich. This volume was Monogram's highly successful and only venture into the realm of military missiles and rockets.

In addition to the subject of this title, the Ta 152, Tom continues to research and write about another of his favorite airplanes, the legendary Messerschmitt Bf 109 and its many derivations. Tom is married to Barbara, has two lovely daughters, a stepson and three grandchildren. And he is also an active member of the Cadillac and LaSalle Club, an organization dedicated to the preservation and enjoyment of one of America's finest automobiles.

Barbara and Thomas H. Hitchcock at the Fantasy of Flight, Polk City, Forida.

Introduction

Most students of world history have heard of the German Focke-Wulf 190, and, those with a particular interest in military aviation may have even heard of the Ta 152. Yet, for all their familiarity with this tumultuous period, few really know the Ta 152. The significance of this warplane rests not with its combat record, nor its outstanding performance, nor its development potential, but with the fact it represented the crowning achievement, the apogee of development, for one of the most successful warplanes of the Second World War—the renown Fw 190—a famous fighter plane designed by Kurt Tank and built by Focke-Wulf Flugzeugbau GmbH.

This story begins in 1941 and advances chronically through five chapters and an epilogue. The history of the Ta 152, and its still-born cousin the Ta 153, is set forth in the story which follows and encapsulated within the context of the times each was advanced.

There are several underlining themes throughout the story. One salient argument rippling throughout concerns Germany's lack of a comprehensive and coordinated plan providing for a war lasting more than one or two years. Another complementary topic was Germany's flawed process for the timely introduction of new technology. Each of these mutually dependent themes highlighted the inherent weakness of the dictatorial single-party Nazi regime.

No one in Germany could have anticipated the huge scale of the Allied bombing offensive largely because the world had not previously witnessed anything remotely similar. Now, threatened with attack from the air by fleets of high-flying large multi-engined bombers, the Germans scrambled to find an antidote. The Ta 152 certainly could have addressed this issue, providing its performance lived up to its designer's predictions, and providing enough of these fighters could be quickly manufactured, issued, fueled and manned to make a difference.

Although the U.S. secretly decided against mounting significant high altitude bombing missions over Europe, the *Luftwaffe* was convinced it was a question of where, and not when, such missions would be flown. However, there were compelling factors leading to the American decision. Chief among these was the need to accurately and effectively hit specific strategic targets. To accomplish this with the best hardware then extant, meant daylight missions had to be flown thousands of feet below American heavy bombers' maximum operational ceiling. On average, most combat missions involving B-17s and B-24s, were flown between 17,000 and 20,000 feet (5,182 – 6,096 m), whereas the maximum service ceiling for the B-17G was rated higher than 30,000 feet (10,668 m).

To German air defense planners, news of the phenomenal American four-engine Boeing B-29 was proof positive the Allies were serious about high altitude bombing. With a service ceiling over 32,000 feet (9,754 m), the pressurized B-29 was able to carry impressive bomb loads over great distance. Unknown to the men in Berlin, the B-29 was not earmarked for the European Theater of Operations. In the end, not a single American B-29 ever flew a bombing mission over the German *Reich*. It is therefore ironic then that given the enormous effort, cost and sacrifices that went into the Ta 152 H, by the time the Tank fighter entered service, the need for such a specialized high altitude warplane no longer existed.

ACKNOWLEDGEMENTS

To the author, the German Focke-Wulf Ta 152 has always represented something of an enigma. The history of the Fw 190, from which it evolved, is well known but why was the opposite true for the Ta 152? To answer this and other questions the author began researching this warplane four decades ago. Years later, a great deal of information from a wide variety of sources has clarified much and dispelled many of the myths that have persisted far longer than necessary. Through the relentless pursuit of collecting, organizing and analyzing data, the author is confident the story which follows is the most up-to-date report of the history of the Ta 152 and Ta 153 yet published in the English language. Three aviation historians in particular are singled out for special mention. They include, J. Richard Smith, Jürgen Rosenstock and Dr. Ing. Elmar Wilczek, who were especially helpful in this challenging endeavor. Such was the comprehensive thoroughness of their assistance that without their help, compilation of this work would have been far less meaningful.

In the 1980s, discussions with the late gifted aviation writer and accomplished war bird pilot, Jeff Ethell, lead to the publication of Monogram's Close-Up 24 on the Ta 152. Jeff's skill in taking raw data plus interview transcripts and crafting these into a coherent narrative resulted in a highly personal impression of frontline fighter pilots struggling to stay alive while performing their duty with pride and skill. Many of these interviews are included in this book. In addition, other no less dedicated individuals contributed in ways too numerous to mention here, but each is genuinely deserving of not only an acknowledgement, but also of my heartfelt appreciation and thanks. These special acquaintances and friends include: Jürgen Balke, Dana Bell, Liam Biggs, David E. Brown, Douglas Cole, Jerry and Judy Crandall, Thomas J. Dietz, Charles Garrad, Jean-Michel Goyat, Rainer Haufschild, Dr. Volker Koos, Geoff Lipscombe, Brian Niklas, H. Rinne, *Flugkapitän* Hans Sander (†), Günter Sengfelder, Brian Silcox, Bernard Touvenin, Gen. Harold E. Watson (†) and Robert F. Wray. Last, but by no means least, a special word of gratitude is extended to Willi Reschke, a highly decorated veteran of JG 301, who kindly provided the Foreword.

It was my intention that you derive enjoyment from the story which follows. The degree to which I have succeeded would not have been possible without the help, support and encouragement of all of these kind people, and others, from around our world.

Thomas H. Hitchcock
Sturbridge, Massachusetts
February 2008

*The man behind Focke-Wulf striking a commanding pose next to one of his highly successful designs. Kurt W. Tank, born 24 February 1898, was both gifted and pragmatic. Always in charge, he never doubted his skill as an accomplished pilot who routinely flew his own designs. He is shown here wearing the hat of a Lufthansa pilot with its distinctive blue and gold braid. In the background is Focke-Wulf Fw 200 V1, W. Nr. 2000, D-AERE, Brandenburg, the first prototype of his four-engined airliner better known as the **Kondor** (Condor). After the war, Tank secretly left Germany for South America to accept the challenge of building a jet fighter for the dictator of Argentina, Juan Perón. Tank's sojourn in Argentina, though marked by professional success, failed to fulfill his expectations. Later, he accepted a position in India with Hindustan aircraft where he designed the HAL HF-24, Marut, a sleek, high performance jet fighter that was ultimately produced in modest numbers. He eventually retired and returned to Germany where he died a few years later at age 85 on 10 June 1983.*

Chapter One

1941 - No Resting on Laurels

INTRODUCTION

The development of the remarkable Focke-Wulf Ta 152 and its lesser-known cousin, the Ta 153, had its origins in 1941. It was in that year that the *Luftwaffe* first took delivery of a brand new fighter that would become an exceedingly formidable and versatile warplane. That fighter was the legendary Focke-Wulf Fw 190 *Würger* (Shrike). It was to play a major role in the design and development of both the Ta 152 and Ta 153.

From the very beginning, Kurt Tank had deliberately designed and built the Fw 190 around a radial air-cooled engine. This decision was in sharp contrast to contemporary German fighter design. Neither Heinkel nor Messerschmitt, the other principal producers of German fighter aircraft, favored air-cooled radial-powered fighters. Instead, the usual German practice was to mate a slim liquid-cooled in-line engine within an equally slim airframe. Daimler-Benz and Junkers, the two dominant aviation engine makers in Germany, were both deeply committed to the design and production of liquid-cooled in-line engines. The fact the Fw 190 first flew with a BMW air-cooled radial engine was not by itself proof positive that Tank was enamored with the radial layout. Instead, it demonstrated his brilliance in creating a world-class design around a promising powerplant not likely to be adopted by any other contemporary German fighter.

During the night of 1 January 1941, RAF Bomber Command launched the new year by sending 141 British bombers to attack the Focke-Wulf aircraft factories in Bremen, particularly the facility in the southern suburb of Hemlingen. Other and more frequent raids followed but were directed toward other important strategic targets in and around Bremen. Although the New Year's raid caused considerable damage to aircraft production facilities, it failed to disrupt production of the first examples of Kurt Tank's new fighter. Nevertheless, this and other raids against Focke-Wulf's Bremen headquarters and production centers were sufficient to accelerate company dispersal planning.

THE FIRST AIRCRAFT OF THE ANTON SERIES

The Fw 190 was flown for the first time shortly before the outbreak of hostilities in June 1939, and by the first quarter of 1941, was poised for full-scale production. Although only a handful of prototypes had been built and flown up to the end of 1940, such was the design's potential that a production contract was quickly awarded. In February 1941, the first preproduction machines of the Anton series (A series), the Fw 190 A-0 series, had been completed.

During this period, the 16-month old war in Europe had been going according to plan for Germany with but one

An early production Fw 190, this example, Fw 190 A-0, W. Nr. 0024, SB+ID, built by Focke-Wulf at Bremen. Altogether some 58 examples of the A-0 "preproduction" series were completed between November 1940 and May 1941. Most were primarily development aircraft assigned to test different combinations of equipment and weapons to meet a wide range of operational needs. Many of the later examples served as prototypes for other programs employing different engines and in at least one case, different wings.

exception: The Battle for Britain. All of western Europe was either occupied or under the direct control of Hitler except for Portugal, Spain, Sweden, and Switzerland. These four nations, together with the Republic of Ireland, essentially chose to remain neutral for the duration of hostilities. A defeated France was roughly divided in half after an armistice had been signed the year before. In this, the Germans occupied the northern portion of the nation, including the entire Atlantic coastline. The southern half of France, known as Vichy France, became a collaborative entity, exercising control over France's Mediterranean coastline. Great Britain stood alone against German military might. Many thought it was just a question of time before German troops attempted a direct invasion of England. In fact, had the 1940 Battle of Britain gone differently, and if the *Luftwaffe* had succeeded in breaking the back of the RAF, Operation Sea Lion, as the German invasion was code-named, would probably have been launched. However, history has recorded that the decisive 1940 Battle of Britain thwarted Hitler's plan of quickly neutralizing England.

The Fw 190 was not the only new German fighter to emerge in 1941. In January, the first examples of the greatly improved Messerschmitt Bf 109 F series appeared. Not surprisingly, this new Messerschmitt fighter was similarly plagued by stubborn development problems. However, unlike Focke-Wulf, the Messerschmitt's faults were primarily centered on the airframe. Concurrently with the introduction of the Bf 109 F, Messerschmitt forged ahead with plans to introduce an entirely new pressurized version of the Bf 109.

In March 1941, a special experimental *Staffel* was formed at Rechlin, under the command of Oblt. Otto Behrens, whose task was to facilitate the Fw 190's transition from production line to operational service. Six preproduction aircraft had been quietly delivered to the unit, which included among its staff some personnel drawn from II./JG 26. Early results with the new fighter proved extremely disappointing. Among the more critical challenges facing the unit were the new BMW engines and dealing

Prior to the actual invasion of the British Isles, the German Ministry of Propaganda was engaged in some wishful thinking by releasing photographs, such as this example, purporting to show German armor at the cliffs of Dover. Of course, it was all cleverly staged for the Germans never mounted an invasion.

With its propeller slowly rotating, this brand new Fw 190 A-1/U1, W. Nr. 0110.001, SB+KA, taxis past watchful engineers at Focke-Wulf's Bremen facility. Besides being the first true example of the A-1 series, delivered in June 1941, this aircraft served as a engine test vehicle swapping its standard BMW 801 C-1 for an early example of the BMW 801 D. Simultaneously known officially as the Fw 190 V7, this aircraft was armed with four MG 17 machine guns plus two MG FF cannon and equipped with FuG VIIa and FuG 25 radios. Even at this early date, the thoroughbred qualities of this fighter were unmistakable.

with their propensity for overheating. It was not uncommon for these early BMW 801s to completely fail after only twenty hours of operation. By the end of March, no less than twenty-two brand new Fw 190 A-1s had been delivered to 6./JG 26, commanded by Oblt. Walter Schneider, based at Moorseele in Belgium.

NO RESTING ON LAURELS

Having achieved his objective with official blessing, Tank lost little time resting on his laurels. As good as the Fw 190 was, notwithstanding the labored maturing of its engine, Tank was under few illusions as to the limits of his creation. He fully understood that what was today's superior weapon may become tomorrow's second-class fighter should your opponent produce something better. Moreover, it was axiomatic that an adversary will always exploit new avenues to neutralize and eventually overpower an opponent. In 1941, Germany was, generally speaking, well ahead of its adversaries. The time was right for giant strides and Germany was well positioned for success. Whether or not German industry was capable of maintaining its numerical and qualitative edge at this period in the war, rested almost entirely on government support for technological advances.

NEW AIRCRAFT ENGINES

In 1941, while Focke-Wulf engineers were busy shepherding the BMW-powered fighter from prototype to full-scale production, Tank and his associates were energetically exploring ways to increase the Fw 190's performance mostly through alternative powerplants. Working in conjunction with the three principal engine makers, several design studies were advanced employing engines from Bayerische Motorenwerke (BMW) including their BMW P 8010 – 8035 series, and from Daimler-Benz, the DB 603, DB 609, DB 614, and DB 623 were on the table and, lastly from Junkers, their Jumo 213 and advanced Jumo 222 were studied. However, it was not long before attention focused principally upon five promising powerplants. These included the BMW 801 J, BMW P 8028, Daimler-Benz DB 603, Junkers Jumo 213, and the Jumo 222.

The BMW 801 J, rated at 1,810 hp for take off, was similar to the standard production BMW 801 D-2 but equipped with a large exhaust-driven turbosupercharger mounted aft of the engine at an angle of 20 degrees. It required C3 aviation fuel of 96 octane and was to drive a large four-bladed propeller. With this engine, it was theoretically possible for the Fw 190 to reach an altitude of 32,808 ft (10,000 m) in only 17 minutes. However, installation of this engine presented engineers with a considerable challenge: What to do about the mandatory location of the turbo's exhaust. BMW's Peter Kappus explains:

> Our turbosupercharger development was oriented toward use in multi-engine aircraft and it was not suitable for the Fw 190. The turbo unit, with its intercoolers, was integrated with the BMW 801 engine which meant that it would have exhausted directly in front of the cockpit.

As it was, the infiltration of exhaust gasses and heat into the cabin was a persistent concern even with a normal engine.

During the first half of 1941, BMW had also been working on an entirely new, but complimentary radial engine.

The BMW 801 was a very compact radial engine that was delivered complete with a cowl system already in place. This fine specimen is a BMW 801 MA that was primarily suited for multi-engine application and is on public display at the New England Air Museum, Windsor Locks, Connecticut.

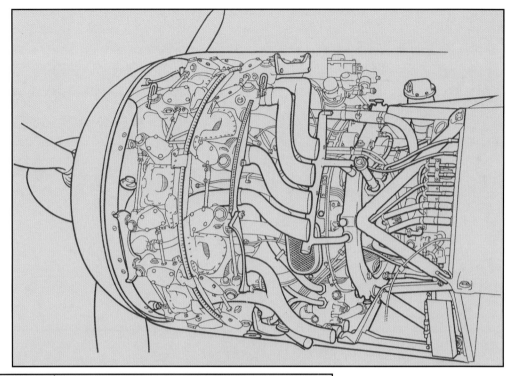

A superb Focke-Wulf period drawing revealing the engine's complex exhaust system as well as the oval, screened port side entry duct for the rear mounted supercharger.

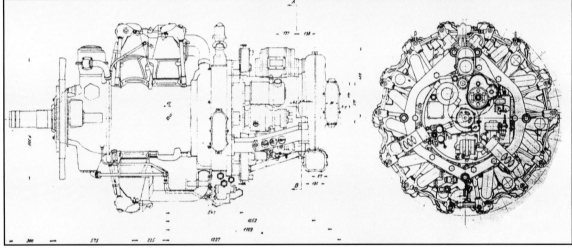

A portion of a large BMW drawing displaying the side elevation and end view of the BMW P 8028 which was a promising development of the BMW 801 A having higher rotation speed with left hand gearing. The project eventually officially became the BMW 801 H-2 but failed to enter series production.

When fitted with a turbo supercharger, the designation became the BMW 801 TJ. This engine was expressly designed to operate at much higher altitudes than the standard BMW 801 D, but BMW had a tough time attaining reliability with this engine. In the end, it proved better suited to multi-engine applications, such as the twin-engined Ju 388. This view of a BMW 801 TJ, photographed in 1987 at RAF St. Athan, clearly shows the engine's rear-mounted turbo with its distinctive exhaust stack protruding above, and to the rear of the mounting assembly. The supercharger's intake can not be seen in this view since it was a long tubular chin type attached beneath the rear.

The radial BMW 802 was a logical development of the BMW 801 which had 18 cylinders, four more than the BMW 801, plus a single-stage, three-speed supercharger.

Recovered after the war at BMW's development facility, is this cowled example of the BMW 802 complete with its 12-bladed cooling fan and propeller spinner. A 4-bladed propeller assembly would have been standard for this engine.

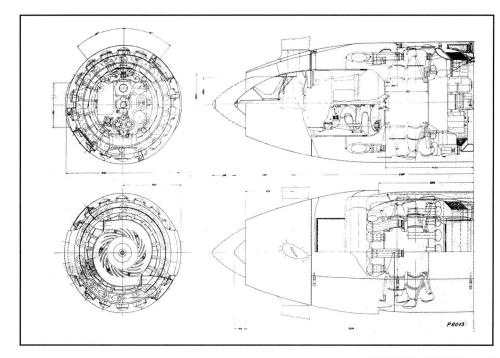

Elevation and section views of the advanced experimental BMW P 8013 a development of the company's P 8010 intended for single-engine fighter application. According to BMW, this engine with its ducted and adjustable spinner was adaptable to contra-rotating propeller configuration. But whether or not any working examples of this powerplant were built and tested before the end of the war is unknown.

Photographed at the Auto and Technik Museum, Germany, is this fine example of the DB 603 A complete with an annular nose cowl enclosing both the oil and coolant radiators. Several different engine mounting rigs were developed depending on the engine's final application. Late in the war, when strenuous methods were advanced to conserve high-strength steel, Focke-Wulf complained that the replacement support arms, having less high-strength steel, caused just enough flexing to upset the engine-mounted cannon's aiming alignment.

It was a 14-cylinder air-cooled twin-row radial. Peter Kappus recalls:

> *...in 1941 the need for better altitude performance led to the initiation of a new engine design of similar overall configuration (to the BMW 801-Ed) with a displacement of 45.5 liters (the BMW 801 was 41.8 liters-Ed) which was designated BMW 804. However, because of limited capacity, this engine was canceled in late 1941.*

Another more promising BMW radial project, the BMW P 8028, based on the BMW 801 H, was a specially boosted supercharged engine. This engine utilized a supercharger mounted to the rear of the engine, with an external centrally-mounted chin air intake with induction cooler.

Meanwhile, the DB 603 had appeared in the autumn of 1936 as a 44.5 liter privately funded venture that was intended to power the company's phenomenal Daimler-Benz T80; a specially built six-wheel vehicle designed to set a new world land speed record. Unfortunately, the finished car, powered by the 3,000 hp DB 603 RS never made the attempt. Instead, it was only briefly run on a dynamometer in 1939. As an aircraft engine, the DB 603 enjoyed only limited Air Ministry interest and little official backing. By 1939, mostly because of development cost over runs and a lack of visionaries within key government positions, the RLM withdrew its meager support for this engine. Then, within a matter of months the Air Ministry revisited the program and early in 1940 reversed itself by authorizing continued development by placing an initial order with Daimler-Benz for 120 examples. Early prototypes of this revamped engine for aircraft use produced approximately 1,750 hp for take off and emergency.

Since 1939, thirty-seven year old *Doktor-Ingenieur* (Dr-Ing.- Academic Doctor of Engineering) August Lichte and his associates at Junkers had been involved in the design and development of the Jumo 213. This engine was a logical development of the firm's earlier Jumo 211, having essentially the same displacement but was substantially larger and heavier. It was equipped with the latest Junkers direct fuel injection in conjunction with a master control module that regulated boost pressure, supercharger intake, magneto advance, and propeller pitch. In its initial form, this engine operated at slightly higher RPMs than the Jumo 211 and produced 1,750 hp for take off. However, in 1940, at the behest of the Air Ministry, this promising engine's development priority had been subordinated to the company's Jumo 222. The result of this action was predictable. The Jumo 213's development timetable was placed on an indefinite hold.

Air Ministry officials enthusiastically endorsed Junkers to develop an ambitious and complex engine having 24 cylinders in six rows. This highly advanced high-performance engine, the Jumo 222, was expected to produce not less than 2,500 hp at take off. At 46.5 liter (2,838 in²) displacement, this engine presented Junkers engineers with many technical challenges. Initially intended as a bomber engine, its promise and size were such that it eventually found application in other aircraft types including single-engine fighters.

In 1938, BMW had decided to abandon its research and development of in-line aircraft engines and instead concentrate on radial powerplants. The firm's 14-cylinder BMW 139 of 1939 had been successfully developed into the BMW 801 which first appeared in 1941, and remained in production throughout the war. Since 1939, the company was also energetically developing more powerful and complex second, and third, generation radials such as the BMW P 8010, 8011, 8013, and the 8035. Some of these projects evolved to a point where they were approved for further development and production. At least two examples each of the BMW 802 and the remarkable BMW 803 were ultimately completed and bench tested.

Amid this plethora of new engines, Kurt Tank faced the not insignificant challenge of choosing the right powerplant for the task at hand, namely improving the Fw 190's performance above 20,000 feet (6,096 m). For Tank and his associates, the primary concern boiled down to the question of engine availability. Based on the manufacturer's sanguine

This unusual three-engine Junkers Ju 52/3m was extensively modified to flight-test a prototype of the DB 623 installed in the nose position driving a large 4-bladed propeller. Note the unusual telescoping exhaust stacks leading back to the port side turbo and the long external exhaust waste pipe attached to the corrugated side of the "Tanta Ju." This engine was essentially symmetrical since it employed twin turbo superchargers, one on each side. Development of the DB 623 began in late 1941 and continued for one year before it was abandoned.

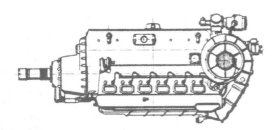

Daimler- Benz DB 603 A – D

General: Twelve-cylinder inverted V liquid-cooled aero engine having a displacement of 44.5 liters and broadly based on the smaller DB 605.

Fuel Requirement: B4 (87 octane)

Length: 2610 mm (8.562 feet)

Height: 1167 mm (3.828 feet)

Width: 830 mm (2.723 feet)

Weight: 910 kg (2,002 lbs.)

Compression Ratio: 7.5:1 left bank, 7.3:1 right bank

Supercharger: Single centrifugal type driven through a hydraulic coupling.

Performance: Take-off and Emergency power 1,750 hp at 2,700 rpm, at 1,40 ata at sea level, 1.620 hp at 2,700 rpm at 1.40 ata at 5,7 km (18,700 ft), Climbing 1,580 hp at 2,500 rpm at 1.30 ata at sea level, 1,510 hp at 2,500 rpm at 1.30 ata at 5,7 km (18,700 ft). Maximum cruising 1,375 hp at 2,300 rpm at 1.20 ata at sea level, 1,400 hp at 2,300 rpm at 1.20 ata at 5,4 km (17,700 ft).

Subtypes: DB 603 A = Series production engine with right hand rotation. DB 603 B = Similar to "A" but with different drive gear ratio. DB 603 C = Similar to "A" but with different drive gear ratio. DB 603 D = Similar to "A" but primarily left hand rotation.

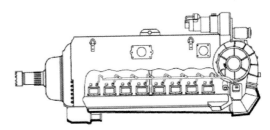

Daimler- Benz DB 609 A – F

General: An experimental sixteen-cylinder inverted V liquid-cooled aero engine having a displacement of 61.8 liters and design features similar to the DB 603. Development halted in April 1943 largely because testing revealed damaging harmonics and vibration which proved too involved and costly to eradicate.

Fuel Requirement: C3 (96-100 octane)

Length: 2935 mm (9.629 feet)

Height: 1180 mm (3.871 feet)

Width: 840 mm (2.755 feet)

Weight: 1,400 kg (3,800 lbs)

Compression Ratio: 8.5:1

Superchargers: Twin (adjoining on each side of the engine) three-speed centrifugal.

Performance: Take-off and Emergency power 2,660 hp at 2,800 rpm at 1.42 ata at sea level. 2,450 hp at 2,800 rpm at 1.42 ata at 6,6 km (21,600 ft). Climbing 2,270 hp at 1.30 ata at sea level. 1,980 hp at 2,500 rpm at 1.30 ata at 8,7 km (28,500 ft). Maximum cruising 1,950 hp at 2,300 rpm at 1.20 ata at sea level. 1,780 hp at 2,300 rpm at 1.20 ata at 8,0 km (26,247 ft).

Subtypes: DB 609 A = Left hand rotation. DB 609 B = Similar to "A" but with different gear ratio. DB 609 C = Similar to "A" but with different prop gear ratio. DB 609 D = Similar to "A" but with right hand rotation. DB 609 E = Similar to "D" with different prop gear ratio. DB 609 F = Similar to "D" with different prop gear radio. No series production for any subtype.

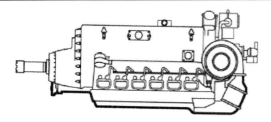

Daimler- Benz DB 614 A – F

General: An experimental twelve-cylinder inverted V liquid-cooled aero engine having a displacement of 44.5 liters and broadly based on the DB 603 G. This engine was abandoned during June 1942 for unknown reasons.

Fuel Requirement: C3 (96-100 octane)

Length: 2670 mm (8.759 feet)

Height: 1130 mm (3.707 feet)

Width: 900 mm (2.952 feet)

Weight: unknown

Compression ratio: unknown

Superchargers: Twin (adjoining on each side of the engine) with dual intercoolers.

Performance: Take-off and Emergency power 2,000 hp.

Subtypes: DB 614 A, B, C, D, E, F of unknown characteristics. No series production of this engine.

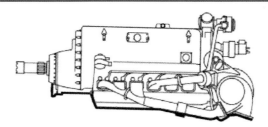

Daimler- Benz DB 623 A – F

General: An experimental twelve-cylinder inverted V liquid-cooled aero engine having a displacement of 44,5 liters and similar to the DB 603 G but equipped with dual turbos. Development of this engine was abandoned in January 1943.

Fuel Requirement: C3 (96-100 octane)

Length: 2738.5 mm (8.985 feet)

Height: 1190 mm (3.904 feet)

Width: 1060 mm (3.478 feet)

Weight: 900 kg (1,984 lbs.)

Compression ratio: unknown

Superchargers: Twin (adjoining symmetrical and parallel on each side of the engine) exhaust-driven turbo superchargers designed by Daimler-Benz and mounted below the engine's centerline.

Performance: Take-off and Emergency power 2,340 hp at 2,900 rpm at 1,50 ata at sea level. 2,125 hp at 2,900 rpm at 1,40 ata at 8,7 km (28,542 ft). Climbing 1,880 hp at 2,700 rpm at 1,30 ata at sea level. 1,830 hp at 2,700 rpm at 1,30 ata at 9,5 km (31,168 ft).

Subtypes: DB 623 A, B, C, D, E, F of unknown characteristics. No series production of this engine.

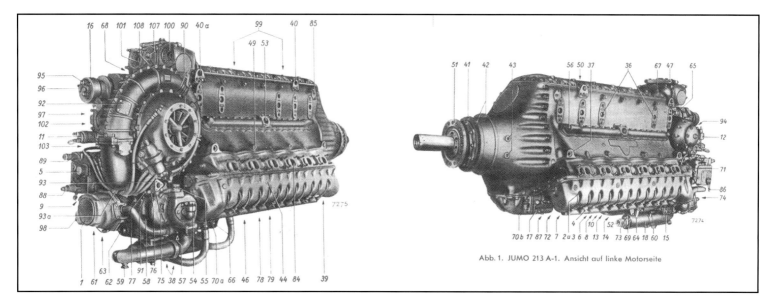

Port and starboard views of the Junkers Jumo 213 A-1 showing the engine's salient features.
This inverted V-12 had an overall length of 7.34 feet (2,266 mm) and weighed 1,815 lb (840 kg).

predictions coupled with recommendations from his staff, Tank's choices narrowed still further to the DB 603 and Jumo 213. Unfortunately for BMW, the possibility of successfully developing a new generation high-performance engine in the short term was almost impossible.

Tank correctly understood that in order to develop "a better Fw 190," within the shortest possible period, every requirement hinged on having the right engine available when needed. He also knew that, more often than not, engine makers were too optimistic when it came to accurately forecasting development timetables. Moreover, the anticipated power derived from many new engine projects failed to materialize. The task of developing a modern high-performance aircraft engine was not a simple exercise. Mechanical complexity, size, weight, fuel requirements, cost, and anticipated maintenance support, contributed significantly to the development cycle. Other concerns allied to metallurgy, raw materials, a labor force, and suitable working conditions were also governing factors.

THE MYSTERIOUS HESS FLIGHT

During this deceptively quiet period in the war, a small but influential segment of the Nazi leadership became intrigued with the novel idea of neutralizing Britain by unconventional means. This select group reasoned that German objectives could be advanced if the war were shortened by first convincing England to cease hostilities and, second, persuading the British to allow the Germans a free hand in the east against the Bolsheviks. It was against this backdrop that lead to Rudolf Hess's top-secret flight to Britain on the evening of 10 May 1941. According to the plan, if Hess could convince the British to stand down, Hitler would indeed have had a free hand in the east. At best, it was a naive and deeply flawed idea. What made it especially brazen was the British Prime Minister's repeated public denunciation of the Nazi government. Winston Churchill had made it abundantly clear that there would be no accommodation with the Hitler regime. Thus, when Hess's mission failed, Hess was marginalized as "insane" by the press in both England and Germany.

From the outset, German aviation industry was infatuated with the promise offered by the Junkers Jumo 222 and, in spite of its protracted development, remained loyal in their support to the bitter end. No ordinary internal combustion engine, the Jumo 222 was a very complex, compact, 24-cylinder engine created to power multi-engine types but also having the potential for single-engine application. Shown here is the early short version, the Jumo 222 A/B-1. This liquid-cooled engine with six equally disposed cylinder banks arranged about its drive shaft gave the appearance of an air-cooled radial, but was in fact liquid-cooled. With a displacement of 46.5 liters and with compression ratios of only 6.5:1, it burned low-grade aviation fuel. With three fuel injection pumps and a two-speed supercharger, the Jumo 222 was designed to produce 2,000 hp for take off.

A line-up of newly produced Fw 190 A-1s at Focke-Wulf's Bremen facility. In the center is W. Nr. 008, SB+KH, followed by W. Nr. 014, SB+KN, and W. Nr. 027, TK+MA. The smaller versions of the national aircraft insignia (crosses and swastika) were only temporary while the aircraft were in their acceptance stage. Final painting of the camouflage and regulation insignia occurred shortly thereafter.

There would be no shortening of the conflict. This fact was underscored seventeen days later when British air and naval forces sank the dreaded powerful German battleship Bismarck. In this dramatic action at sea, stretching over several days, 95 percent of the Bismarck's compliment of 2,206 men were lost. News of the sinking shocked Hitler and finally convinced him that the British could not be won over.

Up to this time, the German Air Force's frontline fighter had been the Messerschmitt Bf 109 E, a small, slim, single-engine fighter powered by a liquid-cooled in-line engine. During this early period of the conflict, the nimble Messerschmitt had proven itself to be an effective yet limited weapon. Nevertheless, with the urgency of war, both sides accelerated the design and development of new and improved warplanes, particularly single-engine fighters.

In June 1941, full-scale production of the refined Bf 109 F-4 series commenced which proved an immediate success. However, another event occurred in June, the importance of which cannot be overstated: Operation Barbarossa. On 22 June 1941, 3 million German troops supported by 2,770 *Luftwaffe* aircraft launched a surprise assault on the Soviet Union over a front that stretched for a thousand miles (1,609 km). To achieve this, the Germans secretly pulled many active units from western Europe, leaving only a token force of two fighter *Geschwadern* deployed against the RAF. The Soviet command was taken by surprise, in spite of warnings from British intelligence and their own agents operating in

Germany. By August, the Germans appeared unstoppable. They were deep into Ukraine, at the outskirts of the city of Uman. Entire Soviet armies were destroyed along with an enormous arsenal of Soviet war materiel, including aircraft.

THE Fw 190 ENTERS THE WAR

Meanwhile in the west during August, the new Focke-Wulf fighter first appeared in action over the coast of the English Channel. It instantly demonstrated its superior performance against the Spitfire V, then the principal British fighter of the RAF. On 7 August 1941, the first Fw 190s were lost. Two Fw 190 A-1s crashed at Moorseele due to engine failures. However, unbeknownst to the British, over the next twelve months, the new fighter exhibited a variety of handling difficulties, primarily as a result of its hurried introduction.

GROWTH AND EXPANSION

By 1939, Focke-Wulf had expanded greatly. An attractive new office complex and satellite factory had been built in Hemlingen, a suburban community located in the southern most district of Bremen. In addition, two additional satellite factories had also been erected in Bremen at Hastedt and Neuenland. Unfortunately for the staff and workers of these plants, each of these facilities proved to be an irresistible military target. Early in the war, the RAF bombed each which

This Fw 190 A-2, W. Nr. 228, DN+CB, is shown here with an operational fighter unit, probably JG 2. Note the collapsed tail wheel.

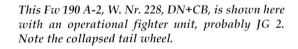

*Perhaps one of the most publicized Focke-Wulf 190s is this example photographed in England shortly after its pilot, Oblt. Arnim Faber landed his Fw 190 A-3, W. Nr. 313, CM+CL, fully intact on 23 June 1942. The official wartime report states Faber's landing was the result of a navigation error, but historians have openly questioned the veracity of this explanation. Faber, a respected officer who served as the **Gruppen Adjutant** of III./JG 2 was made a POW and remained in British custody throughout the war.*

resulted in significant loss of life among Focke-Wulf employees. Most of the casualties were non-combatants including Focke-Wulf's office staff. In response, the company's officers belatedly undertook to disperse its operations to safer locations.

THE Fw 190 A-3 ENTERS PRODUCTION

During August 1941, the improved Fw 190 A-3 entered production, powered by the newly produced BMW 801 D engine. Production commenced at Focke-Wulf Bremen and soon followed at Ago, Arado, and Fieseler plants. A total of approximately 933 examples of the Fw 190 A-2 and A-3 were completed; each subtype being produced in roughly equal numbers up to December 1942. Production continued to gain momentum throughout the remainder of 1941. In addi-

tion to correcting production gremlins within the airframe, BMW was also feverishly eradicating numerous manufacturing faults associated with their new engine. Some of these changes were carried out on the moving assembly line so as not to halt the flow.

LEAVING HARM'S WAY

As a result of the deadly RAF bombing raids against Focke-Wulf facilities at Bremen, Prof. Tank and his colleagues initiated contingency plans calling for the evacuation of all key Focke-Wulf personnel to a less vulnerable locale. The site selected for the firm's new general management and design offices was the quiet bucolic spa community of Bad Eilsen. Located in Lower Saxony about 30 miles (48 km) west of Hanover, the small community of Bad Eilsen is Germany's

A splendid in-flight shot of a factory-fresh Fw 190 A-3 built under license by Arado. This example, W. Nr. 471, KO+PS later suffered 10 percent damage when it crash-landed at Bergen, Norway in July 1942. Note the pilot's head and shoulder armor plate had not yet been fitted when this photograph was snapped.

In 1939, Focke-Wulf contracted for this modern brick and glass office building constructed at Bremen-Hemelingen. Housing hundreds of design and administrative employees, it represented a bold international style of architecture with classical overtones so favored by German architects during this period. Unfortunately, when the war came to Bremen in 1941, so did casualties. During several raids by the RAF, this facility was one that was singled out for attack. The unexpected resulting loss of life caused Kurt Tank to immediately search for a safer location for his design and administrative offices. Right: The main gate at Focke-Wulf's Bremen airport facility. In 1939 this plant became a beehive of activity employing hundreds of workers who daily passed through these gates.

oldest sulphur spa and a favorite health resort. By 21 August 1941, about 2,000 personnel from Focke-Wulf's technical office, research, design, aerodynamic section, static design, construction office, mockup department, graphics and blueprint office, printing division and the company canteen were secretly relocated to Bad Eilsen. To accommodate such an influx, the community's three large palatial hotels, were supplemented by twenty newly erected wooden barracks on the grounds of the Kurpark. In addition, a large barn near a rail line was taken over to serve as the woodworking shop were everything from scale models to full-size mockups were constructed. The largest and most impressive hotel, the Badehotel, was converted to office space that also served as Prof. Tank's primary headquarters. Concurrent with relocation to Bad Eilsen, manufacturing facilities were established farther east to such locations as Cottbus (sometimes spelled Kottbus), Marienburg, Posem-Kreising and Sorau.

Fw 190 VERSUS Bf 109

An interesting demonstration was carried out early in October 1941, in an effort to ascertain the best attributes of Germany's newest fighters. An official mock aerial combat was staged at Rechlin, one of the *Luftwaffe's* major testing facilities, between a standard production Fw 190 A-1 and a randomly selected newly produced Bf 109 F-4, W. Nr. 7314. Test results of this fly-off showed the Fw 190 superior to the Bf 109 in overall performance. The test further showed the Bf 109 to have a noticeable and exceptional acceleration while the Messerschmitt's turning capabilities were also deemed superior. This, however, was offset by the Focke-Wulf's better overall handling qualities with lighter rudder forces. Climbing to an altitude of 32,735 feet (9,977 m) at take off power required 13.5 minutes for the Messerschmitt against

21.25 minutes for the Focke-Wulf. Clearly, this demonstration test underscored the Focke-Wulf's altitude limitation which was directly related to the BMW's falling-off of power above 20,000 feet (6,096 m).

A FALSE SENSE OF INERRANCY

By November 1941, Germany's campaign in the east had proven the skeptics wrong, there were those in Germany who nevertheless expressed anxiety about the wisdom of a two-front war. The whole idea of *blitzkrieg* (lightning war), predicated as it was on overwhelming force, brought to bear against a weak and unprepared foe, left little room for maneuver when events didn't unfold according to plan. The Nazi government and military German High Command had relied upon a relatively quick and decisive war against the British and Russians. For this reason, Hitler was of the opinion that German industry need not invest heavily in new and complex advanced weapons. He reasoned that equipment then in production, or already under development, would be adequate. Thus, in Hitler's view there was no compelling reason to waste time and resources on new projects unless they could be quickly realized. The war would be won without stringent measures. This myopic view of the European conflict, espoused by the German and Italian dictators, would have profound consequences for the Axis powers.

Late in November, deliveries of the new Fw 190 A-2 commenced, the first examples going directly to the second and third *Gruppen* of JG 26. Hptm. Joachim Müncheberg, the *Kommandeur* of II./JG 26, was the first *Luftwaffe* airman to receive the new Fw 190 A-2 series aircraft.

At Bad Eilsen, it had been decided the Fw 190 B series, powered by the BMW 801 D, would be equipped with GM 1 power boosting plus a pressurized cabin while the Fw 190 C

Following the deadly attacks at Hemelingen, the bucolic community of Bad Eilsen was selected as Focke-Wulf's new office center. The stately and elegant Badehotel served as the main headquarters for Kurt Tank and his designers, draftsmen and engineers. Featuring large and spacious rooms, a grand entrance and elegant restaurant it contained hundreds of well-appointed guest rooms. Before the war it was an idyllic spa where one could relax and enjoy the healing qualities of the world renowned mineral baths or, promenade leisurely along the many wide tree lined walkways. But, in 1941 the character of Bad Eilsen changed dramatically. Today, all three hotels serve as health centers.

The master himself at work! Kurt Tank in his office at Bad Eilsen touches his pencil to a Focke-Wulf drawing depicting the tail section of a proposed aircraft project.

The imposing and richly decorated Fürstenhof of Bad Eilsen is shown here surrounded by green lawns and manicured gardens.

The Kurmittelhaus, another fine hotel at Bad Eilsen was one of the three establishments that accommodated Focke-Wulf design and administrative personnel following their relocation in 1941.

series would receive the new Jumo 213. In support of this plan, several Fw 190 prototypes were now dedicated as engine test vehicles.

On 7 December 1941, the Imperial Japanese Navy struck the American fleet anchored in Pearl Harbor. The following day, President Roosevelt declared before Congress that "a state of war now exists between the United States and the Empire of Japan." Three days later, in a speech before the German *Reichstag*, Hitler summarily declared war on the United States. The conflict was now undeniably global.

ALLOCATING DEVELOPMENT PROTOTYPES

As the year came to a close, Focke-Wulf drafted a plan earmarking a number of prototypes to test and evaluate the DB 603 and Jumo 213, the two engines that would later play a

major role in both the Ta 152 and Ta 153. Initially, three prototypes, the Fw 190 V13, V15, and V16, were allocated to the DB 603 program. Then, on 18 December 1941, Focke-Wulf drafted broad parameters for testing and evaluating the Jumo 213. This phase stipulated that two prototypes, the Fw 190 V17 and V18, were to be assembled using the A-0 fuselage, without armament (not to be retrofitted), and with the aircraft's wing moved slightly forward. Each of these prototypes was to be used strictly for engine and handling trials. Added to these were 3 additional Jumo 213-powered aircraft that were to be fully equipped and fitted with the final production fuselage. These prototypes included the Fw 190 V19 to V21 inclusive.

At the close of 1941, the stage had been set. The events of war and politics in 1942 would further accelerate the Fw 190's development and would inexorably lead directly to the Ta 152 and Ta 153.

The standard fuselage for the Fw 190 A-0 formed the basis for most of the early Fw 190 prototypes. They were rugged, easy to service and adaptable to modification. Shown here is a company illustration of the fuselage for the A-1 model, which was essentially identical to the A-0 pre-series. Splendid illustrations such as this were created by Focke-Wulf's staff of skilled technical illustrators. They were incorporated into Focke-Wulf's technical manuals and, with good reason, considered more explanatory than comparable photographs.

Daimler-Benz routinely supplied airframe manufacturers with complete engines and ancillary systems for their newly designed powerplants. In this view a complete DB 603 A with its annular nose radiator is supported by forged steel engine bearer arms.

Three Focke-Wulf prototypes that figure promi-
nently in this story are the Fw 190 V16, W. Nr. 0038,
CF+OW (top), the Fw 190 V17, W. Nr. 0039, CF+OX
(middle), and the Fw 190 V18, W. Nr. 0040, CF+OY
(bottom). The last mentioned machine, W. Nr. 0040,
would evolve through two subsequent major modifications that ultimately directly served the Ta
152 H program. Its long career ended unceremoni-
ously at Reinsehlen airfield in 1945 (see p. 165).

Chapter Two

1942 - Matching the Right Horse with the Right Wagon

INTRODUCTION

On New Year's Day, 1942, the United States, Great Britain, and the Soviet Union jointly declared that there would be no separate peace with Hitler's Germany. Even though the United States had declared a state of war only the previous month, the Roosevelt administration made no secret of America's desire to ensure the total defeat of the Axis powers, in what was now referred to as World War Two. The British, who had been fighting alone in the west for two and a half years, were relieved that America, with her astonishing manufacturing capacity, was finally openly in the conflict. With Hitler's singular act of declaring war against the United States the previous month, the German dictator demonstrated not only his fundamental lack of understanding of the consequences of such a brash act but revealed his supreme overconfidence. In a nutshell, Hitler completely failed to entertain the counsel of his close advisers. He perilously misjudged the Americans and underestimated their will. He derisively minimized the American ability to manufacture war material by declaring that "the only thing the Americans can do well is mass-produce shaving blades."

THE TOOLS OF RESEARCH AND DEVELOPMENT

For several months during this period, Kurt Tank and his design bureau had been developing guidelines designed to facilitate the proper selection of follow-on projects in anticipation of forthcoming Air Ministry orders. These guidelines allocated various prototypes to specific B, C and D series development. Yet, somewhat surprisingly, by April 1942, Focke-Wulf planned the allocation of only one prototype as a true engine and airframe development workhorse; the Fw 190 V19, W. Nr. 0041, CF+OZ. The uniqueness of this machine was such that it received a unique secondary designation, Fw 190 Wb1 (*Wiederentwicklungs bau* 1 – Development construction 1), that was more descriptive of its mission. In addition to the aircraft's Jumo 213 C engine, the primary distinguishing feature of this prototype would be a newly designed wing having a straight leading edge with a surface area of 18,3 m² . But although the new wing incorporated a number of internal structural changes, coincidentally it retained exactly the same surface area of the well-known standard Fw 190 A series. The V19 was also scheduled to test at least two different vertical tailplanes which were similar in design to the type ultimately selected for the Ta 152.

Meanwhile, on 1 February 1942, the RLM's Technical Department (*C-Amt* / C-Office) instituted *Programme Nr.* 21/2 that, among other things, called for the Fw 190 V13 to be equipped with the DB 603. During this period, Focke-Wulf was forced to change the designated engine for the Fw 190 C series from the Jumo 213 to the DB 603. It will be remembered that the Air Ministry had previously afforded a low development priority to the Jumo 213, owing to their enthusiastic support of the highly touted Jumo 222 project. But, since the Jumo 222's development was not living up to expectations, the Air Ministry belatedly reinstated the Jumo 213 as a high-priority engine. However, having withdrawn the Jumo 213 from the planned Fw 190 C series, it was now decided to transfer this engine, whose development had been curtailed, over to the newly proposed Fw 190 D series. The result of this shuffling is shown by the following revised series line-up:

Fw 190 C-1 - DB 603, non-pressurized, armament: 2 x MG 131, 2 x MG 151/20 with provision for two additional MG 151/20 plus a 500-kg bomb or 300-ltr drop tank. FuG 16Z and FuG 25a radio. Prototype: V13

Fw 190 C-2 - As C-1 but pressurized. MG 151/20, MK 103 or MK 108 as engine cannon. Prototypes: V15, V16

Fw 190 D-1 - Jumo 213, non-pressurized, similar to C-1 but equipped with a FuG 16ZY radio, 20.3 m² wing. Development prototypes: V22, V23

Fw 190 D-2 - Jumo 213, pressurized, similar to D-1. Prototypes: V26 and V27

It was further anticipated that both the C and D series were to share a common fuselage, wings, and other systems with the standard Fw 190 A series. Early in March 1942, the Fw 190 V13, W. Nr. 0036, SK+JS, the first Fw 190 fitted with a DB 603, flew successfully for the first time powered by a new DB 603 A-0, driving a 3-bladed metal VDM (Vereinigte Deutsche Metallwerke) propeller having a diameter of 11.5 feet (3,50 m).

Meanwhile, as America reeled under continued military losses and reversals in the Pacific, her military planners were vigorously searching for ways to dramatically bring the war home to the Japanese and, at the same time, generate positive news for the home front. Out of this planning emerged the daring daylight bombing raid over Tokyo, Yokohama, Kobe, and Nagoya. During the early hours of 18 April 1942, under the utmost secrecy, sixteen specially modified land-based twin-engine North American B-25 "Mitchells," lead by Col. James "Jimmy" Doolittle, labored off the flight deck of the carrier USS Hornet while steaming several hundred miles from Japan. The Japanese were caught by surprise and, although this highly publicized feat caused little material damage to Japan, its meaning was not lost upon military planners in Berlin; America possessed the means and the will to boldly bomb targets deep within the enemy's homeland.

With a wing span of 149 feet (45.4 m), the huge Boeing XB-15 of 1938 had a span 45 feet (13.7 m) greater than the B-17. Because its four Twin Wasps did not deliver enough power, its top speed was just under 200 mph (322 km/h). But its range was extraordinary at almost 3,500 miles (5,633 km). Unfortunately series production eluded the XB-15 and it ended its days as the XC-105...a cargo plane.

AMERICA'S BIG STICKS – THE SUPER BOMBERS

Among the four-engine long-range Super Bombers in America's growing arsenal during this period were four noteworthy designs: The Boeing XB-15, the Boeing B-17 "Flying Fortress," the huge Douglas XB-19, and the Consolidated B-24 "Liberator." Each of these new bombers represented "state of the art" design when they debuted between 1937 and 1941, amid much media fanfare. The message conveyed by these new military aircraft was unmistakable; America was building heavy long range bombers having but one purpose. Now that the United States was fully in the real shooting war, German planners within the Air Ministry were gravely con-

cerned that America might build enough of these large high altitude bombers to pose a serious problem for the *Reich's* air defenses. Clearly, counter measures had to be found.

In May 1942, as production of the Focke-Wulf fighter steadily gained momentum, the first aircraft of the new Fw 190 A-3 appeared. Simultaneously, the first examples of the new Messerschmitt Bf 109 G series and the twin-engine Bf 110 G series debuted both powered by the new DB 605. Little time was lost inspecting, flight-testing, certifying, and delivering these fighters directly to front line units. On 10 May, the second Fw 190 prototype equipped with the DB 603, the Fw 190 V15, W. Nr. 0037, CF+OV, flew and, other than its engine, a DB 603 A-1, it was essentially identical to the V13.

There was nothing diminutive about the huge Douglas XB-19 when it first flew in June 1941. Clearly, one of America's true super bombers, with a span of 212 feet (64.7 m) it was powered by four Wright 2,000 hp R-3350-5s, and featured an innovative tricycle undercarriage plus a very heavy defensive armament of machine guns and cannon. In addition, it was capable of carrying an astonishing internal bomb load of 16,000 lbs (7,258 kg). As in the XB-15, series production also eluded this giant and, like the XB-15, it too ended its days as a cargo transport.

A SPECIAL HIGH ALTITUDE FIGHTER

Later in the month, on 20 May 1942, an important meeting was convened at Messerschmitt's Augsburg headquarters among representatives of the *Reichsluftfahrtministerium* – RLM (German Air Ministry), Messerschmitt, and Focke-Wulf. At this time, the RLM's officer outlined the parameters of an urgent new requirement for a *Spezial Höhenjäger* (special high altitude fighter) capable of intercepting high-flying bombers with a secondary mission of reconnaissance. In 1942 parlance, high altitude meant operations above 20,000 feet (6,096 m).

Scarcely ten days later, on 30 May 1942, RAF Bomber Command unleashed Operation Millennium, an astounding 1,000-bomber night raid on the city of Köln. Three nights later, another RAF bombing raid struck the sprawling Krupp steel and munitions works at Essen. Bombing raids of this magnitude, inflicting wide spread damage, were designed to break both civilian morale and inflict destruction upon the German military industrial complex.

Meanwhile, in Bremen, Tank's design bureau had been actively investigating numerous predesign proposals based upon the Fw 190. From these preliminary drafts there emerged complementary but distinct proposals known as *Rechnerische Ankündigung* – Ra (Analytical prospectus) studies (see table page 42) the purpose of which was to define projects for feasibility study. From these rough design proposals, pre-design studies would follow to validate project feasibility and establish development parameters. Eventually, these studies helped pave the way to both the Ta 152 and Ta 153. The purpose of the "Ra" studies was keyed to improving altitude and mission performance through new engines, wings, airframes, and other systems.

The RLM's urgent requirement for a new high altitude fighter was recognized and accepted without hesitation by both Focke-Wulf and Messerschmitt. However, formidable obstacles faced both manufacturers before a decisive winner of the competition could be declared. In 1942, the *Luftwaffe* did not possess a single-seat fighter that could be strictly classified as "high altitude." Achieving this goal with the engines and technology then extant was only feasible by either increasing engine power through turbo supercharging with intercoolers or, boosting the engine chemically in conjunction with high octane aviation fuel (see p. 202). Unfortunately, such solutions usually carried with them the odious byproducts of system complexity coupled with significant increases in deadweight.

In June 1942, the first American B-17s and B-24s arrived in Britain. On 12 June 1942, the United States Army Air Corps launched an ambitious long-range attack from bases in North Africa on the vital Ploesti oil fields operated by Germany's Axis partner, Romania. It was an audacious plan and a predictor of things to come. Two weeks later, Roosevelt met Churchill in Washington, where the two Allied leaders agreed to attack Germany first through North Africa before attempting a direct invasion of "Fortress Europe."

THE Fw 190 A-4 ENTERS PRODUCTION

In June 1942, the improved Fw 190 A-4 entered production at Focke-Wulf, Ago, Arado, and Fieseler. This variant was similar to the A-3 model but switched from the FuG 7a radio to the improved FuG 16Z. It was also planned to equip

Liberally coated with a Black distemper for night operations, this Fw 190 A-4/U8, W. Nr. 7155, NN+MS, "Yellow H", flown by Ofw. Otto Berchtold, of 7./SKG 10, landed by navigation error at West Malling before dawn on 17 April 1943. The aircraft was equipped with Modification Construction Set U8, which enabled it to carry two underwing drop tanks for extended range bombing missions. Berchtold was taken into custody and spent the remainder of the war as a POW.

this variant with GM 1 power boosting, but apart from a single prototype (Fw 190 V24), no other A-4s with this feature were completed. Total production of the versatile Fw 190 A-4 amounted to approximately 900 examples.

SELECTING THE RIGHT ENGINE

At the heart of Focke-Wulf's planning was the persistent question pertaining to new aircraft engines and whether or not they would measure up to expectation. Specifically, interest focused on the 44,5-liter (2,716 in²) Daimler-Benz DB 603 and the 35-liter (2,136 in²) Junkers Jumo 213. Both 12-cylinder, liquid-cooled, inverted V engines were equipped with single-stage superchargers, and each of these powerplants would soon play a major role in the development of the Ta 152 and Ta 153.

In a secret memorandum dated 9 July 1942, *Obering-enieur* (Senior Engineer) Willi Kaether, Focke-Wulf's highly skilled chief technical officer, outlined the firm's latest prototype development program keyed to the DB 603 and Jumo 213:

DB 603 Three prototypes, the Fw 190 V13, V15, and V16 are to be assembled using A-0 fuselages and used for engine and handling tests.

Six aircraft in the definitive version, two without armament and pressurization, for immediate completion.

V19 and V20 are to be non-pressurized, without armament, of Dural construction. Factory to prepare for conversion from Jumo 213 to DB 603.

V21 to be the definitive pressurized and armed version made from Dural.

V25, V26, V27 Definitive version with armament pressurized but in aluminum-zinc alloy.

One test engine for Daimler-Benz (supplied) plus three spare engines to be held for testing.

Jumo 213 Two prototypes, the Fw 190 V22 and V23 to be built as the definitive version with pressurization and armament. Construction to be in aluminum-zinc alloy.

Also to be built is one pressurized test airframe made from aluminum-zinc alloy.

V28 as static test with one wing, without ailerons and flaps and made from aluminum-zinc alloy.

The Daimler-Benz DB 603 A was a 60° inverted V-12 liquid-cooled engine that displaced 44.5 liters (2,716 cu-in), weighed 2,002 lb (910 kg), had a single stage supercharger, and delivered 1,750 hp at 2,700 rpm for take off. By comparison, the Rolls-Royce Merlin 61, was a 60° V-12 liquid-cooled engine which powered the Spitfire Mk 9 and the North American P-51 (with a Packard-built Merlin 61) and displaced only 27 liters (1,647 cu-in), with a 2-speed, 2-stage supercharger that produced 1,290 hp at 3,000 rpm for take off. The DB 603 A had a power-to-weight ratio of 0.87 whereas that for the Merlin 61 was slightly less at 0.79.

Up to this time, the Fw 190 V18, W. Nr. 0040, CF+OY, had been the first prototype equipped with a Jumo 213. However, it is unclear whether the V18 ever flew with this engine. Presumably, it was primarily intended as a non-flying instructional mockup rather than a full-fledged flying test bed.

Saturday, 18 July 1942, was an especially important date for Messerschmitt's flight-test division. At 08:40 hours on this day, company test pilot Fritz Wendel successfully flew the first Me 262 off Leipheim's main runway powered solely by turbojets. Wendel was ecstatic in his praise of the Me 262 V3. Later that same day, Messerschmitt test pilot Karl Baur sat in the cockpit of another brand new Messerschmitt fighter; the Me 309 V1, W. Nr. 001, GE+CU. After completing his preflight checks, he pushed the throttle forward, beginning his take off roll and soon rotated off the runway. But, after only a few minutes in the air, Baur was forced to return to the base owing to an alarming and unexpected rise in coolant temperature. This prototype was the first Messerschmitt fighter powered by one of the new DB 603s. Messerschmitt and the RLM had high expectations for this attractive advanced single-seat high-performance aircraft. Classified as a "normal" fighter, the Me 309 was tied to the Air Ministry's requirement for a standard escort day fighter, and was expected to enter production later in the year, to ultimately replace the Bf 109.

In compliance with the Air Ministry's May requirement for a new high altitude fighter, Focke-Wulf prepared a detailed general information report on 23 July 1942, outlining plans to equip those DB 603-powered Fw 190 prototypes with exhaust-driven turbo superchargers.

Daimler-Benz	Leistungsblatt			DB 603 A,D B 4

Höhe km	Leistungsstufe	PS	U/min	Ladedruck ata	Kraftstoffverbrauch g/PSh	l/h
0	Start- und Notleistung	1750	2700	1,40	235 + 10	565
0	Steig- und Kampfleistung	1580	2500	1,30	220 + 10	480
0	Höchstzul. Dauerleistung	1375	2300	1,20	215 + 10	410
5,7	Notleistung	1620	2700	1,40	235 + 10	520
5,7	Steig- und Kampfleistung	1510	2500	1,30	220 + 10	450
5,4	Höchstzul. Dauerleistung	1400	2300	1,20	215 + 10	410
5,0	Dauersparleistung	1170	2000	1,05	205 + 10	330
10,0	Notleistung	950	2700	0,85		

Untersetzung: A u. D 1:1,93

Vergleichsgewicht: 910 kg + 3 % für DB 603 A, 970 kg + 3 % für DB 603 D

Abzuführende Wärmemenge bei Steig- und Kampfleistung:
a. aus Schmierstoff max 65 000 kcal/h am Boden
   " 40 000. " in Volldruckhöhe
b. " Kühlstoff " 380 000 " " "

Sonstige Vermerke:
DB 603 A = rechtslaufend
DB 603 D = linkslaufend

Merkmale und Eignung:
Neues Grundbaumuster. Durchschußmöglichkeit. Je 1 Zündkerze auf Außen- und Innenseite der Zylinderblöcke. Clachleuder anbaubar.

Unterschriften: DAIMLER-BENZ A.G. Stgt-Untertürkheim BAL / RLM GL/C-E3

Mappe Leistungsblätter Ausgabe: 501 / Lft 10.43.

Information

Secret!

RE: Fw 190 with exhaust gas turbine and as high altitude fighter

1. A decisive improvement of high altitude performance of the DB 603 powered Fw 190 (V13 version) can be obtained by installing an exhaust gas turbine, as research has shown. Service ceiling of this version would be approximately 2,000 m higher than that of the currently best high altitude fighter. The Fw 190 would thus have the high altitude performance needed to combat high altitude daylight bombers, so far immune from attack standard fighters, as the front and RLM demand so urgently.

Today, an RLM order for 6 prototype aircraft was received (by us). A decision regarding series production will follow. The urgency of this new venture is self-evident. KB 1 will commence design work today with selected staff, work to be distributed as far as possible (practical). In order to meet the deadlines as per para 3, special (emergency) measures to be introduced in the factory.

The new DE (Dringende Entwicklung = urgent development) priority schedule will apply, apart from the SS classification.

A BMW or Hirth turbine will be fitted. Clarification latest early next week. Messrs Klauer and Gross are on their way to Stuttgart and Berlin respectively to discuss the installation problem with Hirth, DB and BMW. They have instructions to return with mock-ups of the turbines.

2. The V13 will be modified as a high altitude fighter. Since V13 is scheduled to go to Rechlin for engine trials, the 2 completed prototypes V15 and V16 will be converted, 4 additional aircraft to be newly built. Due to the shortage of time, the 4 extra aircraft are to be completed in the V13 version, they will be modified as required. As to the powerplant of these 4 aircraft, the complete cowling, including the oil and water cooler flap mechanism, will have to be redesigned due to the larger front radiator. Engine bearer assembly and control lever system will remain unchanged. The 4 aircraft as above are to be ordered immediately from the factory.

To reduce work, only the last 2 of the total of 6 conversions will be fitted with armament.

All 6 aircraft will have the new large 20.3 sq. m wing, which will be designed (converted) in France. Chatillon has already been instructed accordingly. Should the larger wings not be available in time, turbine testing can be made with the standard wing.

3. Design documentation and deadlines

In order to save time, design drawings for the modifications of the 6 test aircraft will be as simple as possible. A list of modifications will be submitted to the factory on 28 July 1942. In the KB, Herr Pfost will

be responsible for prompt action. Full construction details to be supplied to the factory during the period from mid-August to 25 Sept. 1942.

The first converted aircraft to be ready to fly on 15 Nov. 1942.

The factory should submit proposals for the completion of the remaining 5 aircraft to Herr Tank.

The 2 ½ months available for conversion require adoption of special measures similar to the KB's. The KB has less than 2 months for redesign and clarification of development problems. The situation in the air war demands that the above schedules must be kept strictly, as promised to the RLM.

4. Design

Design work is subject to the following rules and distribution of jobs:

I. General

As a basic rule for the design, production aircraft of fuselage types V13 and V19 must be suitable for modification. As an example, the turbine assembly with coolers and air scoop has to be designed for installation in both versions without modification.

II. Exhaust and turbo charger ducts in engine area and cowling. Responsibility of Herr Gross

Execution of sealed exhaust pipes as per research report No. 1525. Special consideration of most favorable gas glow conditions within the exhaust system. According to DVL tests, badly designed exhaust gas flow pipes may result in losses of up to 160 hp. Visit to DVL for exchange of information probably on Saturday 25 July 1942. Flexible connectors for the pipes will be supplied by BMW or Hirth (BMW version with piston rings). Compressor air ducts from the engine separation points will have the largest possible diameter. Diameter and shape of ducts are of equal importance for the prevention of pressure loss.

Herr Gross is also responsible for the engine covers between front fuselage and front radiator. The oil cooler has to be fitted below the engine as on the V13 (as opposed to the V19), since the increase of the front radiator leaves no space for the oil cooler in front.

III. Exhaust and turbo charger ducts from Frame No. 1 to turbine junction. Responsibility of Herr Hische.

The exhaust pipes will have circular diameter. Exhaust gas temperature 800 degrees C approximately, internal pressure approximately 2 atü, speed approximately 100 m/sec. Pipes insulated against fuselage by an alloy sheet having air gaps on both sides. To prevent heat losses, pipes are covered by sheeting (Distance from circular pipe about 5 mm).

Compressor air pipes: Light alloy, diameter approximately 200 mm, internal pressure about 1.0 atü. Design Department will submit a draft for the fairing between wing surface and exhaust gas ducts on leading edge by 28 July 1942.

IV. Turbine Installation. Responsibility of Herr Klauer

Herr Klauer's responsibilities include turbine installation, turbine lubricating system (oil tank capacity 4 to 5 ltrs), compressor intercooler, and turbine control system. The turbine will be mounted on a removable fuselage panel, loads being transferred from the panel to the fuselage structure. The turbine can easily be removed for service when the lower fuselage cover with air scoop and radiator is opened.

Turbo charger air cooler area approx: 10 sq dm

Water cooler area   approx: 14 sq dm

Should the turbine have no fittings (connections) for the compressor water cooler pump, provision for the installation to be made on the airframe.

V. Lower fuselage covers with water cooler and air scoop. Responsibility of Herr Lochow.

All covers to be quickly and easily removable (including quick release connection of compressor air and cooling water pipes) to ensure fast replacement of turbine. The compressor air scoop is to be provided with a shutter to prevent foreign matter (stones) from entering. Function to be similar to the tropical air filter scoop, preventing accumulated foreign matter from entering when opening the shutter. During take-off, air will be supplied via louvres (gills) near the compressor air duct behind the radiator. Whether an air scoop as on the Fw 200 would be more suitable than gills has yet to be clarified. Cooling air discharge is regulated by hydraulically adjustable and thermostatically controlled gills (VDM standard as on V19). Dr. Wendland to clarify urgently whether there is a danger of radiator freeze during winter flying below the critical altitude due to insufficient heating from the turbine despite closed radiator gills.

VI. Radio. Responsibility of Herr Großmann

FuG 25 will not be fitted for the time being. Relocation of radio between Frame No. 8 and pilot's seat. Access after removal of seat respectively from above. Master compass to be relocated.

VII. Fuselage. Responsibility of Herr Quast

Easy access to and quick replacement of turbine by removal of the lower load-bearing fuselage panel required. Pressure cabin bulkhead to be moved from Frame No. 7 to Frame No. 8 due to radio installation. (Factory to provide for this modification with the 4 new aircraft of the V13 type). Transfer of bulkhead from 7 to 8 and simultaneous relocation of radio to be introduced earliest with V19 production aircraft in the new subseries to ensure that V19 production aircraft can be retrofitted for turbine operation. Due to lack of time, V19 production drawings will initially show the bulkhead in the old position.

VIII. Front radiator for DB 603. Responsibility of Herr Oetker.

Front radiator to be enlarged from 48 to approximately 67 sq dm., therefore new engine front section and cooling gills. Dr. Wendland to indicate definite radiator size by 27 July 1942. The 4-blade propeller of VDM design will be fitted. Should the new radiator and propeller not be available in time, initial V15 test flights can be made with the 3-bladed propeller and the old radiator in extreme emergency.

Due to the new size of the water cooler, it may be necessary to delete the two MG 131 fuselage guns. Herr Manigold will clarify whether only two MG 151 or additionally two wing-mounted MG 151 or MG FF are to be used.

IX. Controls. Responsibility of Herr Voges

The only modifications are those relating to the turbine.

X. Mock-Up

Herr Quast will be responsible for the mock-up of the rear fuselage. Deadline for the wooden mock-up: 31 July 1942.

5. Technical Field Service will make out all orders necessary for the completion of the above work – broken down into subsections as required – immediately. Deadline 25 July 1942.

Bad Eilsen   23 July 1942

(Kaether, Technical Director)

The Fw 190 C series program received a setback on 30 July 1942, when the V13 crashed while landing at Wenzendorf Airfield. The aircraft was a total write-off. This accident temporarily left the flight-test crew with only one DB 603-powered aircraft (the V15). But, within a week of this incident, a new prototype joined the program. Flying for the first time on 2 August 1942, the Fw 190 V16, W. Nr. 0038, CF+OW, was essentially identical to the previous aircraft. This machine was destined to continue flying for two years, having been transferred to Daimler-Benz for engine development duties.

On 17 August 1942, the Americans launched their first major bombing attack in Europe when a dozen B-17s successfully bombed the railway marshaling yards at Sotteville near Rouen from an altitude of 23,000 feet (7,010 m) without loss. It proved deceptively easy, but in the end, the mission was instructive for both sides. On the eastern front, on 20 August, the German army crossed the Don River where it bends east toward the Volga River and was now only some 40 miles (63 km) from Stalingrad.

Oberingenieur *Willi Kaether was Focke-Wulf's chief technical officer who oversaw the technical development of many variants of the Fw 190 as well as the Ta 152 and Ta 153.*

THE "Ta" PREFIX EMERGES

In September 1942, at the behest of the Air Ministry, Focke-Wulf commenced preliminary design of a two-seat night and bad weather fighter constructed largely of wood. By this time, Kurt Tank (with the departure of Heinrich Focke in 1938) became Focke-Wulf's chief executive officer and technical director. In this capacity, Tank formally petitioned the Air Ministry to authorize that henceforth all Focke-Wulf creations should automatically carry the prefix "Ta" instead of "Fw." Largely because of his esteemed reputation, his request was readily granted. In October 1942, with RLM approval of the new Focke-Wulf night fighter, it became known officially as the Ta 211. The Air Ministry number "211" was chosen only because it was a previously unassigned relatively low number within the RLM's designation system.

However, almost immediately, considerable confusion arose within this project since, by sheer coincidence, the airframe and the intended engines both bore the RLM number 211. Aircraft were frequently listed in official documents by their airframe 8-number, i.e., 8-211, which signified the complete Ta 211. Similarly, engines were officially known by their

9-number, i.e., 9-211, which signified the Jumo 211. As a consequence, Tank requested that the RLM withdraw the '211' and assign another number of their choosing. The Air Ministry readily concurred and accordingly issued Tank a batch of three consecutive numbers, 8-152, 8-153, and 8-154, to be used at his discretion. Previously, Klemm Leichtflugzeugbau GmbH, known for their elegant small single-engine touring and sport planes, had been issued "8-numbers" 151 to 155 inclusive. But, up to this time, this small firm had only succeeded in using one of the five producing a single example of the Klemm 151. The RLM's practice of reassigning unused numbers reflected a change in policy whereby every unused "8-number" would eventually be reassigned if not taken up by the original grantee. The RLM also took this opportunity to pull the unused number 8-155 from Klemm, and soon transferred it to Messerschmitt. Thus, it came to be that the new Focke-Wulf night fighter project, formerly known as the "Ta 211," now officially became the Ta 154. Prof. Tank was now poised to assign Air Ministry numbers 8-152 and 8-153 to new projects as the need arose.

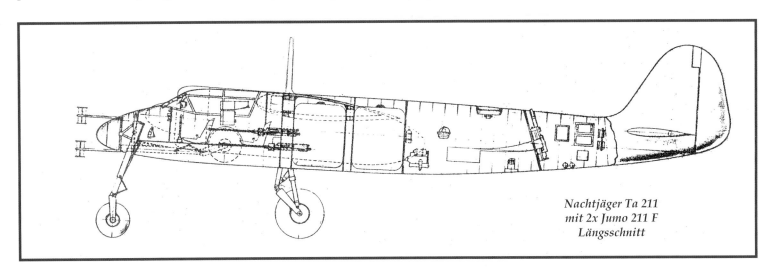

Nachtjäger Ta 211
mit 2x Jumo 211 F
Längsschnitt

*When Kurt Tank received Air Ministry numbers 8-152 through 8-154, the first design to appear was the Ta 154. Shown here is the first newly completed night fighter prototype, the Ta 154 V1, W. Nr. 100001, TE+FE, whose airframe was almost entirely made of wood, leading pilots to affectionately refer to it as the **Moskito** in recognition of the highly successful all-wood British Mosquito.*

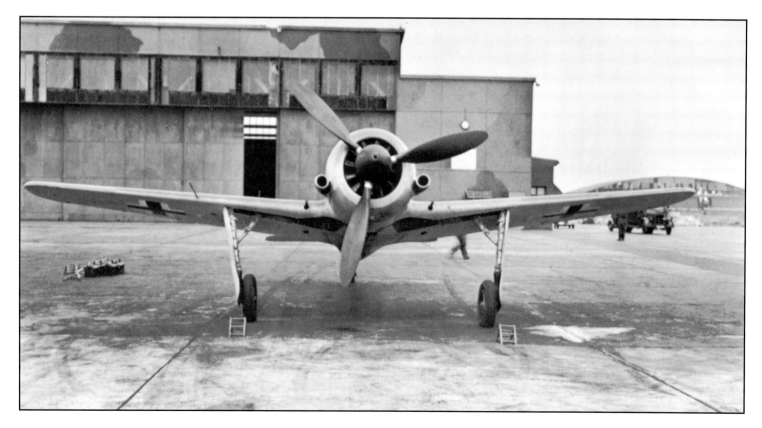

*One of the three Fw 190s converted to **Höhenjäger 1** specifications by the removal of armor plate and all weapons excepting the two wing root cannon. Known as the Fw 190 A-3/U7, these aircraft were equipped with externally-mounted twin supercharger air scoops which unsuccessfully sought to significantly boost the aircraft maximum speed through ram effect.*

HÖHENJÄGER 1

Late in September 1942, Focke-Wulf's work into the realm of high altitude flight had assumed the utmost importance and urgency. To meet this challenge, Focke-Wulf had commenced flight-testing three specially modified Fw 190s as part of their *Höhenjäger 1* (high altitude fighter 1) program. Identified as Fw 190 A-3/U7 machines, these aircraft consisted of *Werknummern* 528, DJ+AB; 530, DJ+AD; and 531, DJ+AE. But before the program could be launched, W. Nr. 530 was transfered, its place taken by W. Nr. 531, DJ+AE. All three *Höhenjäger 1* aircraft were lightened by the removal of their armor plate, cowl machine guns, and outer wing weapons, thereby limiting armament to only two MG 151/20 mm cannon mounted in the wing roots. One of the distinguishing features of these fighters was the twin supercharger air scoops mounted externally on either side of the cowling, the purpose of which was to boost supercharger pressure by ram effect. The maximum speed increase with these measures amounted to only about 15 mph (24 km/h).

Concurrent with the quest for greater altitude, Focke-Wulf also earmarked numerous test aircraft for the proposed Fw 190 B series, to study pressurized cabins in conjunction with the application of GM 1 power boosting. Initially, it was proposed that no less than a dozen aircraft would participate in the B series program, but later this was amended to nine aircraft. Of these, only five were to be pressurized although all retained the standard 18,3 m² wing with the exception of Fw 190 B-0, W. Nr. 0049, TI+IN. This particular aircraft was slated to receive the new 20,3 m² wing prior to being transferred to BMW. This plan was later revised whereby only the Fw 190 V45, W. Nr. 7347, RP+IU and V47, W. Nr. 530115, DO+RO, actually received the larger wing. One highly visible outcome of B series testing involved the design of a suitable high altitude canopy. These experiments eventually produced a double-walled "blown" canopy later adopted by the Ta 152.

THE JUMO 213 IS AIRBORNE

On 26 September 1942, the Fw 190 V17, W. Nr. 0039, CF+OX, the first flying prototype fitted with a Jumo 213 took to the air, piloted by the firm's chief test pilot Hans Sander. This aircraft was essentially an engine test bed built on a standard A-0 airframe, but equipped with an early Jumo 213 A-0 driving a narrow-chord 3-bladed metal propeller.

To the south in Augsburg, Willi Messerschmitt and his design bureau had been exceedingly busy for several months laboring over a wide range of projects. One of these was a proposal to meet the Air Ministry's high altitude fighter requirement. Known internally within the Messerschmitt works as the Me 109 ST (*Spezial Tragwerk* – Special Wing Structure), it was offered in two distinct but complementary versions, both of which envisioned the use of a new laminar flow wing mated to standard Bf 109 fuselages.

The second version, *Ausführung B*, called for a high altitude fighter initially powered by the new DB 605, but also capable of accepting either the DB 628 or the Jumo 213, depending upon availability.

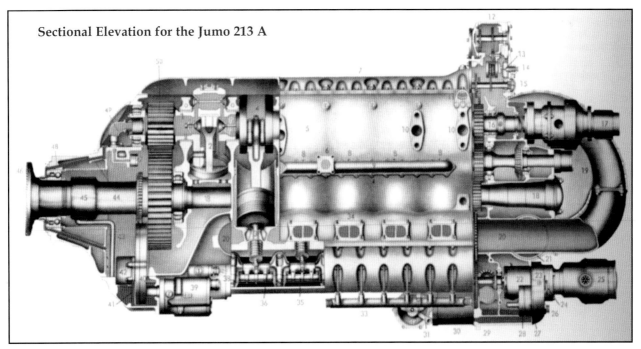

Sectional Elevation for the Jumo 213 A

Jumo 213 A Basic Engine Specification
Type: Twelve-cylinder inverted V liquid-cooled, under pressure, with direct fuel injection and having a displacement of 35 liters.
Fuel Requirement: B4 (87 octane)
Length: 2,437 mm (7.996 feet)
Height: 1,095 mm (3.593 feet)
Width: 776 mm (2.546 feet)
Weight: 920 kg (2,028 lbs)

Compression Ratio: 6.5:1
Specified Propeller: Wooden variable-pitch Junkers VS 111
Supercharger: DVL designed two-speed, single-stage
Performance: Take-off and Emergency 1,776 hp at 3,250 rpm at sea level. 1,600 hp at 3,250 rpm at 5,486 m (18.000 ft). Using MW 50 power boosting, Take off power can be increased to 2,240 hp for short periods. Maximum cruising power 1,220 hp at 2,700 rpm at 5,182 m (17.000 ft).

The Messerschmitt Bf 109 V31, W. Nr. 5642, SG+EK, was an early production Bf 109 F-1 and is shown here modified by an experimental inward retracting undercarriage as part of the Me 155 development program. Whereas the standard outwardly retracting undercarriage of the Bf 109 was attached directly to the aircraft's fuselage, the Me 155 was to switch to the inward retracting format similar to that previously employed by the first four Me 209 prototypes.

ENTER THE Me 155

By autumn 1942, the "Me 109 ST" had progressed to a point where it could become a serious contender for the RLM's high altitude fighter specification. At this juncture, Messerschmitt unilaterally redesignated the project, "Me 409," as a logical continuum stemming from his Bf 109 and prewar Me 209. Unfortunately for Messerschmitt, the Air Ministry was not well disposed to the designer's stated preference. Instead, acting on a precedent set a short time before, the RLM's GL/C office assigned this project the unused "8-number" 155. Thus, the new Messerschmitt design officially became the Me 155.

On 1 October 1942, the Me 262 V2, the second jet-powered prototype, was successfully flown for the first time. By now it was clear that Messerschmitt's design and manufacturing plate was exceedingly full. In addition to several multi-engine projects, mass production of the Bf 109 G and Bf 110 G series, Messerschmitt was simultaneously dealing with the Me 309 and the revolutionary jet-powered Me 262. Production of the Me 309 was slated to commence immediately upon satisfactory completion of its testing program. Aircraft

Production Plan 22E called for a production rate of not less than 240 machines per month.

At first, in fulfilling Air Ministry requirements, two versions of the Me 155 were proposed: The Me 155 A carrier-based fighter, and the Me 155 B, a dedicated high altitude fighter designed around the DB 628. This new engine was essentially a DB 605 A equipped with a two-stage mechanical supercharger, with the large circular low-pressure first stage being mounted around, and driven from, the engine's reduction gear. Development of this unorthodox and complex engine had begun earlier in the year, and appears to have been created exclusively for Messerschmitt-designed high altitude fighter projects.

To relieve his already overcommitted design bureau, and to hasten development, Messerschmitt transferred the Me 155 B to Paris. The work was entrusted to a newly recruited design staff, operating under German supervision, and formed from the SNCAN (*Société Nationalede Constructions Aéronautiques du Nord*) consortium. While the French with the Germans supervising the work were laboring over the Me 155, Daimler-Benz was having a difficult time bringing their complex DB 628 to an acceptable level of reliability. Until this

The newly completed Me 309 V1, W. Nr. 001, GE+CU, as it first appeared in July 1942, just prior to commencement of its flight-test program. A larger airplane than the Bf 109, it was powered by the heftier DB 603. As a consequence of landing mishaps coupled with the machinations of rival political factions, the whole Me 309 program ultimately collapsed before the type could be thoroughly tested or approved for production.

could be accomplished, the Me 155 B's future was decidedly uncertain.

Messerschmitt's design bureau was acutely aware that without the DB 628, the Me 155 B would never meet the RLM's *Spezial Höhenjäger* requirement. Messerschmitt therefore concluded that nothing short of a complete and radical redesign was required. The new design must be formulated around an exhaust driven turbosupercharger operating in concert with an engine already in series production. In taking this course of action, it was understood that work already invested in the Me 155 B would now come to nothing, that is, unless a serendipitous event occurred.

Messerschmitt's engineering division had by this time labored mightily in their efforts to develop the Me 309 into a full-fledged *Höchleistungsjäger* (high performance fighter) that would become a worthy successor to the firm's Bf 109. But Messerschmitt also knew that things were not going well with the Me 309 and its future was anything but assured. At this juncture, in what must have been a burst of insight, he instructed his staff to investigate the possibility of adapting the abandoned Me 155 B to take the same engine as the Me 309, i.e., the DB 603. If this possibility proved feasible, then Messerschmitt would almost certainly have his high performance fighter regardless of the outcome of the Me 309's testing program.

Within a short period, the verdict was in. The DB 603 could be successfully grafted onto the Me 155's fuselage, providing that a *"ring kühler"* (annular nose radiator) installation

was used. This approach would allow the new fighter to use the same laminar flow wing and undercarriage but eliminate the need for underwing radiators originally intended for the Me 155 B.

THE Me 209 CHANGELING

Concurrently, Messerschmitt's *Projektbüro* had sketched the parameters of a new *Höhenjäger* known as project Me P 1091. This new concept study called for a special high altitude airframe powered by a standard DB 605 A, but boosted by a TK 15 (9-2279) exhaust driven turbo. This project, with exceptionally long wings, would require a complex system of intake and exhaust piping, intercooler, aftercooler, and wastegate discharge. Over time it would eventually evolve into an entirely new design known as the Me 155 B-1.

Meanwhile, although Messerschmitt would undoubtedly have preferred that his "revised Me 155 B with DB 603" bear the designation "Me 409," he resisted the temptation of bringing this to the attention of the Air Ministry. Instead, he wisely chose to list this new creation simply as the "Me 209 II." By this brilliant political move, Messerschmitt assuaged RLM trepidations and nullified any accusation that this fighter project was an entirely new design.

Thus, the RLM GL/C 8-number '209,' which had been assigned previously to an unsuccessful prewar Messerschmitt fighter, of which only four prototypes (Me 209 V1 – V4) were completed, was reinstated. Messerschmitt's devious plan had

The Me 209 V1, W. Nr. 1185, D-INJR, was flown for the first time on 1 August 1938, powered by a DB 601 ARJ. Months later, on 26 April 1939, Fritz Wendel broke the world speed record in the Me 209 V1, but for propaganda purposes, it was identified as the "Me 109 R," an entirely false and misleading designation. Shown here is a large-scale meticulously crafted model by master modeler Günter Sengfleder.

The Me 209 V4, W. Nr. 1188, D-IRND, later as CE+BW, was flown for the first time on 12 May 1939, but by 1940 interest in the type had already begun to wane due largely to the aircraft's unremarkable performance and tricky handling characteristics. Flight-testing was halted in 1941 when it was belatedly recognized the type was completely unsuited as a single-seat fighter replacement for the Bf 109. At that point, and at the behest of the Ministry of Propaganda, it was repainted with a large graphic undulating serpent and the simulated tactical number '14' adorning its fuselage, presumably giving rise to the false notion the type was in active service with the **Luftwaffe.**

worked. The Air Ministry gave their support to the project and awarded Messerschmitt a contract to build two flying prototypes in the shortest possible time. Thus, in the space of one year, a project that had begun as a simple development of the Bf 109 had become a true changeling, progressing from Me 109 ST, Me 409, Me 155 B, to Me 209 II. Moreover, these various projects did not include other curious but unsuccessful cousins such as the Me 155 A (carrier fighter) and the Me 155 TL (twin-jet fighter).

While this political maneuvering was unfolding, hundreds of miles away on the eastern front, German troops were locked in a deadly struggle at Stalingrad. On 9 November, Hitler told the Party's faithful …"Stalingrad is ours except for a few enemy positions still holding out." The next day, two days after the Americans and British launched Operation Torch (the invasion of North Africa), French Admiral Darlan, representing the Vichy government, agreed to an armistice with the Allies and ordered his forces to stand down. An enraged Hitler immediately ordered the *Wehrmacht* (Armed Forces) to occupy Vichy France while simultaneously nullifying his agreement with Marshal Pétain.

MORE JUMO PROTOTYPES

Meanwhile, in Bremen, while Messerschmitt was wrestling with his Me 155 B, other Jumo-powered Focke-Wulf 190 prototypes had been completed or were under construction. The 9 July 1942, plan, calling for six prototypes to be fitted with DB 603s, had been revised. Now, five months later, all of these eight aircraft were to be equipped with Jumo 213s.

Two views of the Fw 190 V20, W. Nr. 0042, TI+IG, an engine development vehicle outwardly quite similar to the Fw 190 V19. Had it survived, it might have flight tested several new and promising engines including the highly advanced BMW 803. Initially it was completed with this unusual lower cowl, designed to hide the engine's hot exhaust, an idea driven by night ops consideration. The Jumo 213 CV's hot exhaust dumped directly into a long "stove pipe" before exiting from a single orifice on either side near each wing root's leading edge. Airflow originated from the annular nose radiator and forced aft by the aircraft's forward velocity. Flown for the first time by Hans Sander on 24 November 1943, this non-pressurized prototype was constructed around a basic Fw 190 A-0 fuselage. It was completed without armament but carried standard electronics consisting of the FuG 16Z and FuG 25a sets. In addition, its 18.3 m² wing incorporated an electro hydraulically operated undercarriage.

Each of these aircraft, with the exception of the V28, was to be fitted with a Jumo 213 C. These eight prototypes are summarized in the table below.

Aircraft	W. Nr.	Stkz	Cabin	Electronics	Qualifications
Fw 190 V20	0042	TI + IG	Non pressurized	FuG 16z, FuG 25a	Engine test aircraft
Fw 190 V21	0043	TI+IH	Pressurized	FuG 16z, FuG 25a	Dural. Armed, definitive
Fw 190 V22	0044	TI+II	Non pressurized	FuG 16z, FuG 25a	For Fw 190 D-1
Fw 190 V23	0045	TI+IJ	Non pressurized	FuG 16z, FuG 25a	For Fw 190 D-1
Fw 190 V25	0050	GH+KO		FuG 16z, FuG 25a	Engine weapon test aircraft
Fw 190 V26	0051	GH+KP	Pressurized	FuG 16z, FuG 25a	For Fw 190 D-2 definitive
Fw 190 V27	0052	GH+KQ	Pressurized	FuG 16z, FuG 25a	For Fw 190 D-2 definitive
Fw 190 V28	0053	GH+KR			Static airframe for destruction testing

Of these aircraft the V20, V22, and V23 were each under construction by the end of 1942. The others were completed during 1943: The V21 in March, V25 in April, V26 in May, V27 and V28 in June 1943. It is worth noting that five of these prototypes (V20, V21, V25, V26, and V27) were originally scheduled to receive DB 603s, in conjunction with the definitive Fw 190 C series. However, because of the urgency of the Jumo program, this earlier plan was shelved indefinitely.

The new alignment called for another batch of five prototypes (V29 – V33 inclusive) to be built, each with DB 603s. To hasten construction, each of these DB 603-powered test aircraft was to be assembled using older A-0 airframes. Thus, in spite of appearances, by late 1942, production of the DB 603-powered C series had not been deferred or abandoned, construction of its development prototypes had been merely pushed farther ahead. These aircraft are also summarized on page 47.

In the meantime, production plans for the Fw 190 D series were well advanced, but totally dependent upon the timely delivery of the Jumo 213. Junkers were seen by many at Focke-Wulf as dragging their feet. This engine's continued unreliability was hampering everything. Junkers production estimates had to be continually advanced, which in turn caused the aircraft manufacturer to continually revise its own delivery schedules. Nevertheless, everyone at Focke-Wulf was convinced that sooner or later all of the major objections associated with the Jumo 213 would be overcome, and once in service, their faith in this powerplant would be vindicated.

The first of three views of the Fw 190 V20 photographed soon after it had been modified by the substitution of its novel exhaust flame suppression feature (see page 39 caption) for a conventional cowl and exhaust system. In addition, this prototype also received its new rear fuselage extension and vertical fin. It was flown in this configuration by chief test pilot Hans Sander on 4 August 1944.

Plans to further modify this prototype, Fw 190 V20 by switching its Jumo 213 C for a DB 603 L, thus becoming the Fw 190 V20/U1 for participation in the Ta 152 C program, were dashed when this aircraft was 70% damaged in an Allied bombing attack on Langenhagen the day after chief test pilot Hans Sander's last flight, on 5 August 1944.

Focke-Wulf Ta 153 A-1
With Jumo 213A – 16 July 1943

ENTER THE Ta 153

It was during the summer of 1942 that Kurt Tank finalized proposals for an entirely new fighter design keyed to the RLM Technical Office's requirement for what was termed a high-performance *Begleit Tag Einheitjagdflugzeug* (Standard Escort Day Fighter) with enhanced altitude performance. This B.T.E. project was initially formulated around the Jumo 213 A but other engines of similar size were viewed as viable alternatives.

Tank assigned the new project the RLM 8-number "153" from among the three numbers he had earlier received. Thus, the new fighter design officially became the Ta 153. This project was to embody all the progressive development changes that had been attained up to this time. The similarly powered Fw 190 D series, while complementary, were still based upon the older Fw 190 A-0 airframe. The Ta 153's generalized overall description, contained within Focke-Wulf design study Ta 153 Ra-1, was formulated around design study Fw 190 Ra-4. The project's armament package was envisioned as exceptionally heavy, consisting of no less than six 20 mm cannon augmented by one 30 mm cannon firing through the spinner. The Ta 153 was also to be fitted with a new wing having an area of 20 m² (215.3 ft²) housing the hydraulically operated undercarriage with larger 740 x 210 main wheels.

Perhaps the most salient feature was the Ta 153's new fuselage. Although at first glance it appeared similar to Fw 190's structure, in fact it was to be entirely new construction incorporating a longer rear fuselage as a purposeful part of the airframe. It was determined that the aircraft's lubricants were to be contained aft of fuselage seam 1, and in addition, to an entirely new fuselage, a new internal fuel tank was to be incorporated. Finally, a new tailplane design was planned with the vertical fin having a subtle new contour of increased surface area. The Ta 153 Ra-2 design study was similar but centered around a long span wing of 22,5 m² and equipped with the DB 603 G or any of the progeny of this engine, including the DB 623, DB 624, DB 626, and the DB 627. Soon, the provisional designation Ta 153 Ra-1, utilizing the Jumo 213A, gave way to the type's primary designation Ta 153 A-1. Actual on-the-job engineering and equipment expenditure for the Ta 153 was estimated to be about 20 percent, or 60,000 hours. Total construction hours were estimated at 320,000 hours. Based upon established 1942 Focke-Wulf mission-driven precedents, it is likely the Ta 153 series subtypes were structured as follows:

> Ta 153 A-1 (Ta 153 Ra-1) Normal fighter, Jumo 213 A or Jumo 213 C
> Ta 153 B-1 high altitude long wing fighter, Jumo 213 A or Jumo 213 C
> Ta 153 C-1 Normal fighter similar to the Ta 153 A-1 but with DB 603 G
> Ta 153 D-1 (Ta 153 Ra-2) high altitude fighter like B-1 with DB 603 G

One of the more unusual features of the Ta 153 was its exhaust flame suppression system, designed to eliminate all traces of the flame emitted from the engine's exhaust stacks. This feature was primarily intended for aircraft assigned to night operations but presumably it could have had the same effect for bad weather operations. At least two prototypes flight tested the system, the Fw 190 V20 and V21, with mixed results. The device consisted of a long "stove pipe" fitted closely over the aircraft's exhaust stack row, which directed the exhaust flow aft to egress from a single large exhaust port on either side of the aircraft's nose (see pages 37, 47). Because of its size, and corresponding engine cowl drag, the idea was eventually dropped.

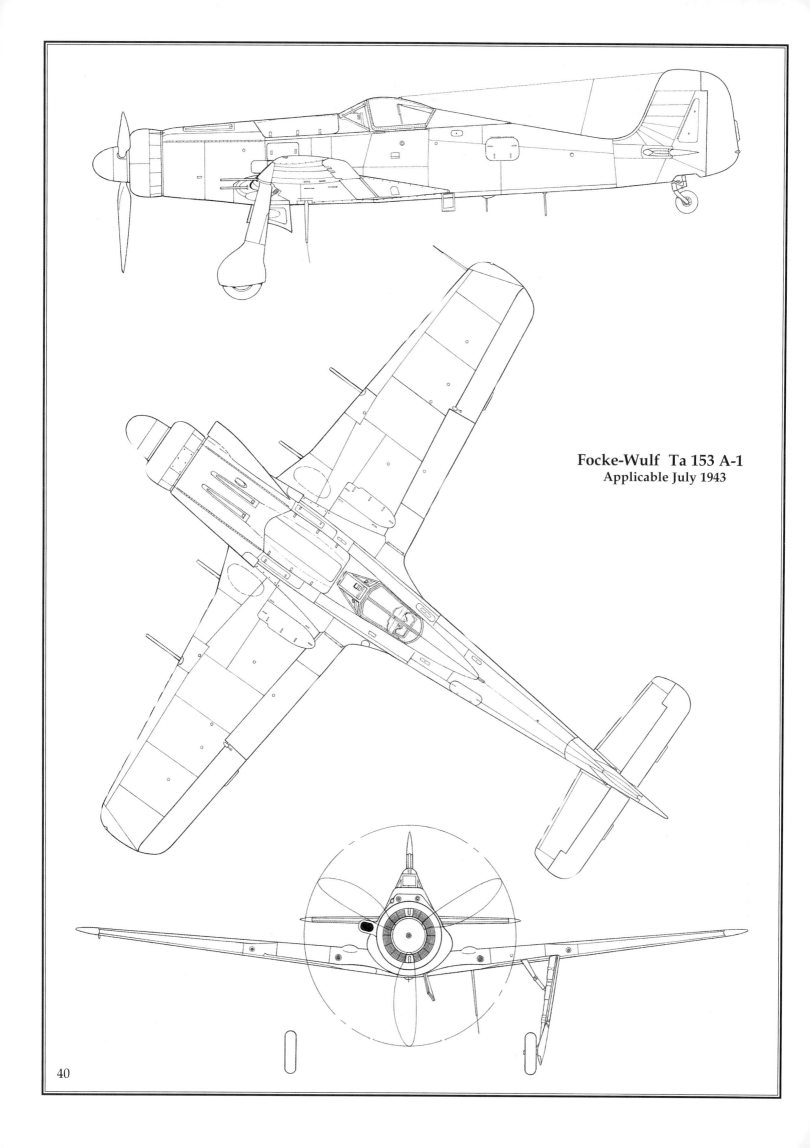

Focke-Wulf Ta 153 A-1
Applicable July 1943

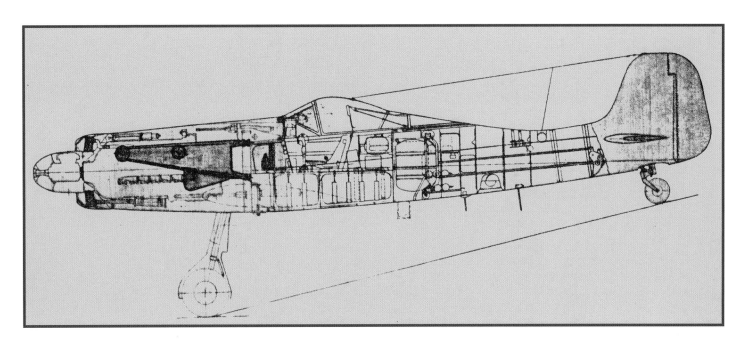

A sectional elevation of the Fw 190 V17 shows the prototype equipped with the blown canopy and a single piece engine support arm. Although production aircraft with in-line engines utilized cast and forged support arms, other options were explored in which conservation of high alloy metal and simplification of manufacture were of concern.

The Jumo 213 A was a 35 liter (2,136 cu in) twelve cylinder, inverted V, liquid-cooled engine, which enjoyed a favorable power to weight ratio of 0.88. The generally similar Jumo 213 C had provision for an engine-mounted cannon designed to fire through the propeller shaft.

DB 603 G

Side elevation and end view of the new and enlarged supercharger employed by the DB 603 G. The G engine was generally similar to earlier versions of the DB 603 but delivered increased performance derived in part from C3 fuel of 96 octane and higher compression ratios (8.3:1 left bank, 8.5:1 right bank). The G engine's supercharger also ran faster which increased the engine's critical altitude. The engine was slightly heavier and longer and had provision for accepting either the Messerschmitt Me P 6 or P 8 propeller assemblies.

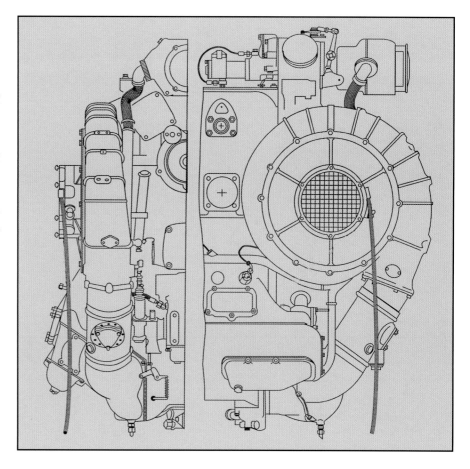

Fw 190 Design Studies *Rechnerische Anküngigung* (Ra) — Analytical Prospectus

The following eight design studies were first formulated 8 June 1942 and revised on 7 August 1942, 25 May 1943, 1 July 1943, 3 August 1943, 5 August 1943, 7 September 1943 and 10 March 1945. The purpose of these studies was to establish, in broad terms, the parameters for further development.

Fw 190 Ra-1   Fighter study based upon the experimental Fw 190 Wb-1 (Fw 190 V19). Suggested engine was the Junkers Jumo 213. Empty weight estimated at 4,360 kg (9,612 lbs). Wing area: 18.3 m² (196.9 ft²). Hydraulic Undercarriage.

Fw 190 Ra-2   Ground-attack study equipped with the BMW 801 D and having an empty weight of 4,260 kg (9,392 lbs). This project study was developed into the Fw 190 A-3/U3 and the *Schlachtflugzeug* 1 which eventually became the Fw 190 F-1.

Fw 190 Ra-3   A high altitude fighter study equipped with the BMW 801 D without a turbosupercharger. Having an empty weight of 3,700 kg (8,157 lbs) it was to have cabin pressurization, an extended wing of 20.3 m² (218.5 ft²) and electrically operated undercarriage.

Fw 190 Ra-4   Fighter study having a lengthened fuselage, a Junkers Jumo 213 and an empty weight of 4,500 kg (9,921 lbs). It was to also be equipped with the 20 m² (215.2 ft²) standard wing, a new enlarged 1.77 m² (19.1 ft²) tail, larger main wheels (740 X 210) armed with 7 guns (1 x engine cannon, 4 wing cannon, 2 cowl weapons) and the new blown canopy. This study served as a template for the Ta 153 Ra-1.

Fw 190 Ra-5   Fighter design study that was to serve as the basis for the proposed Fw 190 A-10 powered by the BMW 801 F having a standard Fw 190 A series fuselage. Empty weight was at 4,400 kg (9,700 lbs). Standard 20 m² wing, tail to be 1.77 m², undercarriage to be hydraulic, and main wheels were 740 x 210.

Fw 190 Ra-6   Fighter study for the Fw 190 H equipped with the 22.5 m² (242.2 ft²) wing, 1.77 m² tail, lengthened fuselage and 700 x 175 main wheels. Its armament called for 3 aircraft guns while the study's powerplant could have been either the Daimler-Benz DB 603 G, Jumo 213 E or the DB 632. Empty weight was 4,600 kg (10,141 lbs). This design study later served as the basis for the Ta 152 Ra-2.

Fw 190 Ra-7   Fighter study powered by the BMW 801 F and similarly equipped as the Ra-5 but with the normal 18.3 m² wing armed with the 4 aircraft guns and was valid for the Fw 190 A-8 and Fw 190 F-8 series.

Fw 190 Ra-8   Fighter study similar to the Fw 190 V17 but able to accept either the Jumo 213 A, E or F, or the DB 603 E or L and having a lengthened fuselage, standard 18.3 m² wing with 700 x 175 main wheels and electrically operated undercarriage. With an estimated empty weight of 4,250 kg (9,370 lbs), it incorporated an enlarged tail of 2.10 m² (22.6 ft²) and armed with 3 or 4 guns. This design study served the development of the Fw 190 D-9 through D-15 as well as the Ta 152 A.

Daimler-Benz DB 624 A

General: A highly unusual experimental twelve-cylinder inverted V liquid-cooled aero engine based on the DB 603 G-M but having dual superchargers plus a turbo operating as a two-stage system depending on altitude. Development of this complex engine extended over two years, but was eventually abandoned in April 1944.

Fuel Requirement: C3 (96 – 100 octane)
Length: 3,065 mm (10.055 feet)
Height: 1,337 mm (4.386 feet)
Width: 1,210 mm (3.970 feet)
Weight: 970 kg (2,139 lbs.)
Compression Ratio: unknown
Superchargers: Essentially a combined setup of supercharger and turbocharger. The first stage consisted of two superchargers operating in sequence with the starboard unit blowing into the port unit. The second stage was the turbocharger which was activated at high altitude. While operating at low altitude, the superchargers, operated by hydraulic coupling, but for high altitude operation, the exhaust-driven turbo with intercooler and aftercooler was mechanically driven.
Performance: Take-off and Emergency power 2,220 hp at 2,900 rpm at sea level. 2,100 hp at 2,900 rpm at 14,6 km (47,900 ft). Climb and Combat 1,850 hp at 2,700 rpm at 15,0 km (49,212 ft).

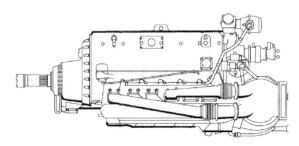

Daimler-Benz DB 626 A – F

General: An experimental twelve-cylinder inverted V liquid-cooled aero engine based on the DB 603 G with dual turbo superchargers and an induction cooler. Development of this high altitude engine was reportedly halted in November 1942.
Fuel Requirement: C3 (96-100 octane)
Length: 2,702.5 mm (8.867 feet)
Height: 1,155 mm (3.789 feet)
Width: 1,138 mm (3.734 feet)
Weight: 900 kg (1,984 lbs.)
Compression ratio: unknown
Superchargers: Twin adjoining units mounted below the engine centerline and operated by twin exhaust-driven turbos.
Performance: Take-off and Emergency power 2,075 hp at 2,900 rpm at sea level. Emergency power 1,960 hp at 2,900 rpm at 5,1 km (16,732 ft.). Climb and combat performance 1,700 hp at 2,700 hp at 6,0 km (19,685 ft.).
Subtypes: DB 626A = Left hand rotation. Other versions unconfirmed but could correspond to DB 609 subtype characteristics.

Daimler- Benz DB 627 A – B

General: An experimental twelve-cylinder inverted V liquid-cooled aero engine based on the DB 603 G with twin superchargers and an aftercooler. Development of this engine was stopped in March 1944.
Fuel Requirement: C3 (96 – 100 octane)
Length: 2,765 mm (9.072 feet)
Height: 1,230 mm (4.035 feet)
Width: 945 mm (3.100 feet)
Weight: 1,020 kg (2,249 lbs.)
Compression Ratio: unknown
Superchargers: Twin adjoining two-stage mechanical superchargers with the first stage two-speed unit on the right side while the second stage with hydraulic coupling was on the left side. Up to about 5,5 km (18,045 ft.) the 2nd stage unit's rpm is controlled barometrically. As altitude increases both supercharger units act in a reciprocal way to ensure the correct boost pressure is balanced for the specific altitude.
Performance: Take-off and Emergency power 2,000 hp at 2,700 rpm at 1,50 ata at seal level. Emergency performance 1,325 hp at 2,700 rpm at 1,40 ata at 11,5 km (37,730 ft.). Climb and Combat performance 1,240 hp at 2,500 rpm at 1.30 ata at 11,2 km (36,746 ft.).
Subtypes: DB 627 A = Right hand rotation, gear ratio .518:1. DB 627 B = similar to "A" but with a gear ratio of .483:1.

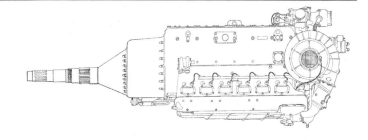

Daimler- Benz DB 632 A - D

General: An experimental twelve cylinder inverted V liquid-cooled aero engine based upon the DB 603 N with a modified supercharger and equipped with gearing to accommodate contra-rotating propellers. Development extended from August 1943 through February 1944 when it was abandoned in favor of the DB 603 L. Note side elevation drawing is provisional.
Fuel Requirement: C3 (96-100 octane)
Length: 3293 mm (10.804 feet) [approximate]
Height: 1203 mm (3.947 feet)
Width: 1008 mm (3.307 feet)
Weight: 1,000 kg (2,200 lbs.)
Compression Ratio: 8.3: 1 left bank, 8.5:1 right bank
Supercharger: Two-stage unit similar to the DB 603 L.
Performance: Take-off and Emergency 2,400 hp at 3,200 rpm at 1.65 ata at sea level. 1,625 hp at 3,200 rpm at 1.65 ata at 8,2 km (27,000 ft.). Climb and combat performance 1,790 hp at 3,000 rpm at 1.32 at sea level. 1,500 hp at 3,000 rpm at 1.30 ata at 8,2 km (27,000 ft.). Maximum cruising 1,075 hp 2,700 rpm at 1.20 ata at sea level, 1,350 hp at 2,700 rpm at 1.20 ata at 7,7 km (25,200 ft.).
Subtypes: DB 632A – D with different gear ratios.

ENGINE DEVELOPMENT AIRFRAMES

In an effort to determine the feasibility of pairing specific engines with the Fw 190, Focke-Wulf engineers and draftsmen first tried to determine if various engine options, then under consideration, would actually fit and function within the Fw 190's existing airframe. To standardize their findings, it was decided to use the Fw 190 V19, alias Fw 190 Wb1, as their test example.

Engine options included: BMW 801J, BMW P 8028, DB 603, DB 609, DB 614, DB 623, DB 624 plus the Jumo 213 in several variations. Most were ultimately found to be completely unsuited because of space, weight, complexity or center of gravity considerations. These included the BMW 801J, DB 609, DB 614, DB 623 and the DB 624. This thinning out process brought Focke-Wulf's apparent options down to the BMW P 8028 (which was developed into what eventually became the BMW 801H), DB 603 and Jumo 213.

But in addition to these finalists, several additional engines, such as the Jumo 222 and BMW 802 were under development, although not grouped within the control study involving the Fw 190 V19 (Wb1), they nevertheless held sufficient promise as to be included in future Focke-Wulf testing studies.

Eberhard-Dietrich Weber, the august Focke-Wulf scholar, who extensively researched the entire Fw 190 history, has stated that six additional prototypes were proposed for the purpose of testing new engines when they became available. Dipl-Ing Weber's list includes unusual Fw 190 prototype designations. For example, the suffix '41' would appear to indicate each of these test vehicles was to embody the same airframe characteristics of *Werknummer* 0041, the Fw 190 V19.

This list includes the following examples:

Fw 190 V20/41 - A rebuilt V20 to test the feasibility of installing the BMW 803 in a single-seat fighter.
Fw 190 V21/41 - Was to eventually test the Jumo 222 within the Fw 190 V21's airframe.
Fw 190 V23/41 - A project using the V23 as flying test bed for the BMW P 8028, alias BMW 801 H.
Fw 190 V34a/41 - Presumably a re-engined V34 modified to test the BMW 802.
Fw 190 V35a/41 - Presumably a re-engined V35 modified to test the BMW 801 E.
Fw 190 V36a/41 – Presumably a re-engined V36 modified to test the BMW P 8013.

This tantalizing list includes the 18-cylinder BMW 802 and 28-cylinder BMW 803, two advanced BMW engines offering great potential but for a variety of reasons, failed to progress beyond prototype status before the end of the war. Whether or not either engine could have been successfully integrated into the comparatively small airframe of the Fw 190 is questionable. Certainly this is true for the BMW 803 whose overall length of just over 12 feet would appear to have made the challenge all but impossible.

Left: This Focke-Wulf performance graph dated 7 August 1943, titled Horizontal Speeed at Cruising Altitude, lists five so-called "Normal Fighters" including the Fw 190 with a standard wing and powered by a BMW 801 D using C3 fuel; a Fw 190 with an enlarged wing (20.0m²) powered by a BMW 801 F with C3 fuel; two Ta 153s also with 20.0 m² wings and powered by a DB 603 G or Jumo 213 both using C3 fuel; and a Ta 154 with a standard 32.4 m² wing plus two Jumo 213s using B4 fuel. All aircraft with armament. The chart shows the DB 603 G to be the highest performer with the Jumo 213 with C3 fuel of 100 octane to be the second best.

HORSES IN THE STABLE: *HÖHENJÄGER* 2

During this period, Willi Kaether and his engineers had reached the same conclusion as Messerschmitt regarding the need for an immediate and effective turbosupercharger power system if they were to field a suitable and practical high altitude fighter. Accordingly, Focke-Wulf initiated the second stage of their plan to produce a successful contender for the high altitude fighter requirement. Known as the *Höhenjäger* 2, this program called for five test aircraft, each based upon the non-pressurized Fw 190 V18/U1, fitted with a DVL-Hirth developed TK 11 A (9-2281 having a rated altitude of 11,000 m – 36,089 ft) exhaust-driven turbosupercharger. In addition, each was to have a pressurized cabin and FuG 16Z and FuG 25a electronics. In addition, the wing span of each of these five prototypes would be increased by 6.3 ft (1,920 mm) to 40.4 ft (12,300 mm) with an area of 23,5 m² and powered by a DB 603 S ("S" *Sonder* – Special). The five test aircraft assigned to the *Höhenjäger* 2 program included the V29, V30, V31, V32, and V33. As mentioned previously, each of these aircraft, with the exception of the V18/U1, were initially earmarked for a definitive C series and were to be completed with DB 603 A engines driving Schwarz 4-bladed propellers. The exception, the V18, was originally to be equipped with a Jumo 213, although it is doubtful it ever flew with this engine prior to being re-engined with a DB 603 A plus turbo and emerging as the Fw 190 V18/U1. It was also equipped with FuG 7a and FuG 25 electronics. While this machine served as a template for the five *Höhenjäger* 2 prototypes, it was never officially part of this program.

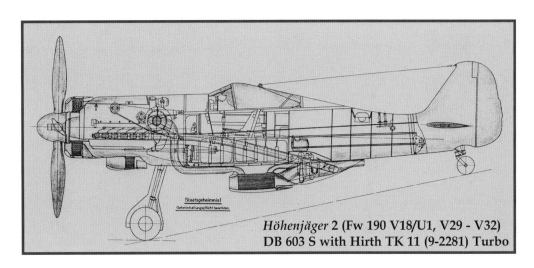

Höhenjäger 2 (Fw 190 V18/U1, V29 - V32)
DB 603 S with Hirth TK 11 (9-2281) Turbo

THE DEATH KNELL TO THE Me 309

By early November 1942, the Me 309 V1 had been transferred to the *Luftwaffe*'s experimental testing facility at Rechlin, where on 22 November 1942, it was flown by *Luftwaffe* test pilot Heinrich Beauvais in simulated combat against a current production Bf 109 G. The test revealed that the Messerschmitt Bf 109 G could turn inside the Me 309. Beauvais's report states:

> ...that the Me 309 would present problems for the average pilot and, when fully equipped, it was only 50 km/h (31 mph) faster than the Bf 109 G.

His report concluded by saying, "...and there seems to be no real advantage to introducing such a fighter when a superior aircraft will soon be available." Beauvais did not elaborate as to the identity of this "superior" aircraft but presumably he was referring to the Fw 190 C-1/C-2 and/or the Fw 190 D-1/D-2.

The Fw 190 V21, W. Nr. 0043, TI+IH, was similar to the V19 and V20, but it was considered the definitive engine development prototype. It was not only pressurized, and constructed of Dural, but at some stage was to have been equipped with armament comprised of two cowl-mounted MG 131s, two MG 151s in the wing roots plus an engine-mounted MG 151 cannon. Provision for optional outer wing cannon (MG 151) was also planned. This prototype, completed in the autumn of 1943 and following cabin pressurization tests in November, was flight-cleared a few months later and flying for the first time on 13 March 1944. It was powered by a Jumo 213 CV and fitted with the novel exhaust flame suppression system and was also intended to flight-test new advanced engines including the Jumo 222.

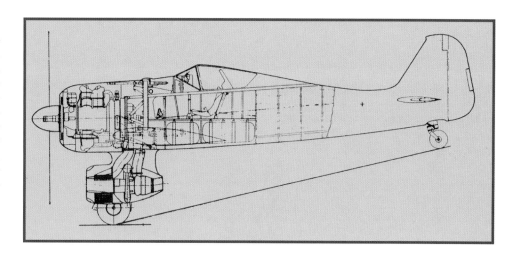

One of the more radical ideas for improving altitude performance was this January 1943 proposal utilizing an externally-mounted turbosupercharger suspended beneath the aircraft's fuselage. This called for a pressurized aircraft having a new 20.3 m² wing with a loaded weight of 8,818 lb (4,000 kg). Its armament was only two wing root MG 151/20s. The fuel load totaled 138 gal (525 ltr) of C3 fuel. A complicated system of ducting would have connected the under slung turbo to the BMW 801 D which would have driven a 4-bladed prop (diameter 11 ft (3,40 m).

A week later, on 29 November 1942, the Me 309 V2, W. Nr. unknown, GE+CV, the second prototype, was successfully flown for the first time, but upon touch down the aircraft's nose wheel leg unexpectedly and suddenly collapsed causing extensive damage to the prototype's airframe. Unfortunately for the unlucky Me 309, the damage was such that this aircraft was completely written off. Almost predictably, and in spite of rigorous testing, landing gear failures were the ever-present bane of many Messerschmitt designed aircraft.

In December 1942, the Fw 190 V19, W. Nr. 0041, CF+OZ, flew for the first time. This engine development aircraft, a companion ship to the V17, was only the second Fw 190 to be flown with the Jumo 213 C. Simultaneously known as the Fw 190 Wb-1 (*Weiterentwicklungs bau* 1 – Development construction 1), it was also built around an Fw 190 A-0 airframe. In addition to its role of flight-testing new engines, it also served as a development vehicle for a new wing having a straight leading edge and new vertical tailplane of increased surface area. During the first two months of flight-testing the Jumo-powered V17, pilots complained about the aircraft's directional instability. This defect was primarily the result of altering the aircraft's original center of gravity by installing an engine having a greater overall length than the original BMW radial.

To correct the problem, engineers decided to compensate this increase in forward length by adjusting the center of gravity through lengthening the rear fuselage. This additional stretch was achieved by inserting a 500 mm (19⅝ inch) parallel box section between the tailplane and the rear fuselage and relocating some internal items. The V17 and V19 were the first Focke-Wulf fighters to feature this distinctive alteration which later became a standard trademark of the Ta 152.

THE Fw 190 A-5 ENTERS PRODUCTION

Easily recognized by its lengthened engine mounting, this version entered production in December 1942. The factories at Bremen, Kassel, Marienburg, Oschersleben, Sorau, and Warnemünde were responsible for series manufacture of this important variant. More than 1,700 examples were eventually completed.

As 1942 came to a close, the war's course was changing. By 13 November German forces in North Africa were trapped between two advancing Allied armies. On 22 November, the Red Army completed its encirclement of Stalingrad and on Christmas Day, the Reds successfully halted von Manstein's Stalingrad offensive. The fate of the entire German Sixth Army was sealed.

The Fw 190 A-5 was one of the great workhorses of the **Luftwaffe** *proving amenable to many varied roles. Shown here is an Fw 190 A-5/U12, W. Nr. 813, BH+CC, equipped with no less than six 20 mm MG 151/20 cannon. Conceived as a specialized close-support fighter, but because of its high wing loading, it was not widely embraced by the* **Schlachtgruppen** *who demanded their fighter-bombers be far more agile than this variant.*

Chapter Three

1943 - Thinking out of the Box

INTRODUCTION

On New Year's Day, 1943, the war news flowing into Berlin was not encouraging. The massive Soviet offensive to retake Voronezh on the Don succeeded and, the battle for Stalingrad dragged on toward its inevitable conclusion. In North Africa, the specter of defeat of the *Afrika Korps* was becoming a very real possibility. Vital supplies and reinforcements were being destroyed before they could reach their destination. At sea, the hard-fought submarine war in the North Atlantic was continuing with mounting U-boat losses. Meanwhile, German fighter aircraft production during 1942 had increased by 40% over the previous year. It was now crystal clear that the war could not possibly be won as easily, or decisively, as Hitler had planned. Indeed, if Germany was to prevail, military planners recognized that the losses sustained the previous year, could not be allowed to continue. It was a tall order even for a nation still solidly behind its Führer.

THE *KÄNGURUS* ARRIVE

Early in January 1943, Focke-Wulf's conversion shop at Adelheide had completed modifying the first prototype equipped with a turbo. Now known as the Fw 190 V18/U1, it was fitted with a DVL-Hirth TK 11 exhaust-driven turbosupercharger enclosed within a large pouch structure in the lower fuselage. This ventral housing, with its distinctive appearance, gave rise to the aircraft being affectionately known as the *Känguruh* (Kangaroo). The V18's original Jumo engine was removed and replaced by a specially adapted DB 603 A (DB 603 S) driving a wooden Schwarz 4-bladed propeller. Following completion of the modifications, known as *Umrüst-bausätze* 1 (Modification construction set 1 - U1) this aircraft was flight cleared on 14 January, and flown for the first time eleven days later on 25 January 1943.

With the Fw 190 V18/U1 serving as a template, conversion of the five official *Höhenjäger* 2 prototypes, utilizing Fw 190 A-0 airframes, to *Känguruh* configuration followed with the last being completed in April. These aircraft include:

Prototype	Werk Nr.	Stkz Code	Completed
Fw 190 V29	W. Nr. 0054	GH+KS	Mar 43
Fw 190 V30	W. Nr. 0055	GH+KT	Mar 43
Fw 190 V31	W. Nr. 0056	GH+KU	Apr 43
Fw 190 V32	W. Nr. 0057	GH+KV	Apr 43
Fw 190 V33	W. Nr. 0058	GH+KW	Apr 43

During 1943, extensive flight testing of the *Höhenjäger* 2 revealed a number of shortcomings primarily pertaining to the turbo and cabin pressurization systems. Although the Hirth turbines were well designed, they suffered failures due to the turbine's steel alloy having inadequate strength when subjected to sustained high exhaust temperatures. Cabin pressurization was another source of frustration requiring continual spot fixes. Nevertheless, when all systems were functioning properly, the Kangaroos' service ceiling approached 40,000 feet (12,192 m). At first, all five prototypes were to retain the standard A series wing, but this was soon amended whereby each received the new 23,5 m² wing plus new vertical tailplanes of increased area based on a design first evaluated on the V17 and V19. Previously, the V18 and V32 had also been fitted with new vertical tailplanes of even greater surface area (see p 60).

EXIT THE Me 309, ENTER THE Me 209

On 20 January 1943, to almost no ones surprise, the Air Ministry's Technical Office Chief (RLM GL/C-Chef) issued orders canceling the Me 309 in favor of the Me 209, in spite of the fact the new Me 209 prototype had yet to be built or flown. However, Messerschmitt's design bureau had finished preliminary design of the Me 209 II's laminar flow wing, which was essentially identical to that chosen for the Me 155 B. Production plans were made to fabricate the wing and the landing gear as soon as possible. The latter had, in the meantime, been tested successfully on the Bf 109 V31, W. Nr. 5642, SG+EK.

In February 1943, Messerschmitt's Regensburg plant began series production of a small number (50) of the pressurized fighter Bf 109 G-3; a model that would soon play a key role in the new Me 209 program.

During this period, in February 1943, Messerschmitt commenced production of the new standard day fighter Bf 109 G-6. This subtype, which was eventually produced in larger numbers than any other, remained in production up to the end of the war.

Ta 152 – THE PRAGMATIC HYBRID

By March 1943, Dipl-Ing Kurt Tank realized the Air Ministry's enthusiasm for the Ta 153, which he had considered the definitive Fw 190 inspired high performance single-engine fighter, had waned. In truth, the RLM's hesitancy was well founded. The Ta 153 would have required a multiplicity of entirely new construction forms, jigs and tooling, requiring additional materials and man hours. Prof. Tank was also well aware that the Ta 153's prime competitor, the Me 209 (alias Me 155 B), was heavily derived from production Bf 109s. In fact, Tank knew that approximately 65% of the Me 209's airframe components were standard Bf 109 G items. This realization

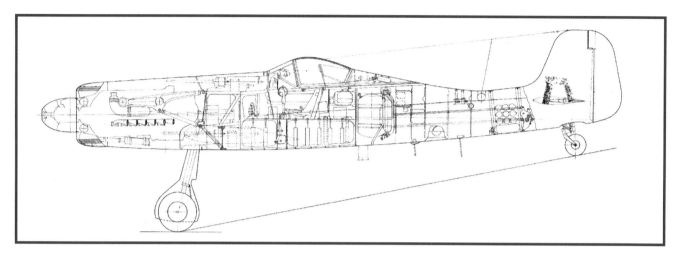

One of the earliest drawings of the Ta 152 H is this elevation, nr. 10 13 291-01, from 28 April 1943, indicating the placement engine ancillary equipment was quite similar to the layout favored by the Fw 190 D-9.

was of grave concern to Tank because the Ta 153 was unabashedly an entirely new build aircraft, except for certain select components such as the undercarriage, cockpit and canopy. Tank also knew full well that the RLM could not turn a blind eye to this reality, especially in view of the worsening war situation and the urgent need to concentrate on proven designs requiring minimal retooling.

To solve this dilemma, early in March 1943, Tank and his designers took a pragmatic step to ensure Focke-Wulf would become the winner of the High Performance Escort Day Fighter requirement. They correctly concluded that a workable alternative could be achieved by exchanging the Ta 153's entirely new fuselage for one derived from a standard production Fw 190 A series paired with the rear fuselage extension section. This new "hybrid" design would also retain the Ta 153's Jumo 213 A engine, undercarriage and tailplane with only minor alterations to the latter. With these changes, the Ta 152's wing span and surface area of 11,500 mm (37 ft 8.75 in) and 20.0 m² (215.3 ft²) was slightly reduced for the Ta 152 resulting in the new wing having a span and surface area of 11,000 mm (36 ft 1 1/8 in) and 19.6 m² (210.9 ft²). In this composite form, Tank bestowed the new hybrid fighter design with the official designation "Ta 152." For all intents and purposes, Kurt Tank had "taken a page from Messerschmitt's book," because no less than 65% of the resulting Ta 152 originated straight from existing standard Fw 190 hardware and components.

To further define the plan, new Focke-Wulf analytical design studies were quickly drafted. The first, Ta 152 Ra-1, included the possibility of using one of several engines including, but not limited to, the Jumo 213 A, Jumo 213 E and Jumo 213 J as well as the DB 603 E and DB 603 G. The Ta 152 Ra-2, which itself was based upon Fw 190 Ra-6, incorporated a long span wing associated with the projected Fw 190 H having a surface area of 22,5 m². In addition, various engines were proposed including the Jumo 213 E, Jumo 222 A, DB 603 G and the newly promoted DB 632. The latter engine was a progressive development of the DB 603 N equipped with a modified supercharger and other advanced features such as coaxial

contra-rotating propellers. The Ta 152 Ra-3 design study was a fighter design probably linked to the Jumo 222.

By early April 1943, the various analytical design studies, combined with project proposals, had evolved into three primary Ta 152 mission categories; (1) the Ta 152 A series *Normaljäger* (Standard Day Fighter), (2) the outwardly similar Ta 152 B series *Schlachtflugzeug* (close-support fighter) and (3), the long span Ta 152 H series *Höhenjäger* (high altitude fighter). To further simplify matters and to increase the likelihood of a favorable government development contract, preliminary engine assignments specified the Jumo 213 A for each of the three Ta 152 subtypes.

KURT TANK'S DARK HORSE, THE Fw 190 H

Sometime during the first quarter of 1943, the precise date is unknown, Focke-Wulf finalized design of a little-known high altitude fighter project easily recognizable by its extended wing having an area of 22,5 m² (242.2 ft²) with a straight leading edge. This new project, built around a Fw 190 B series airframe, with cabin pressurization, was to be powered by the DB 603 G employing GM 1 power boosting. Briefly known as the Fw 190 A-9, this new variant evolved from design study Fw 190 Ra-6. But, by mid April 1943, as a result of Focke-Wulf's rationalization program, this project's designation was changed to Fw 190 H-1. The intent of this rationalization policy was to simplify and standardize. Accordingly, it was further decided the entire Fw 190 A series was to be exclusively powered by the BMW 801. The series letter 'H' was henceforth linked to the *Höhenjäger* mission. Somewhat later, the Fw 190 A-9 re-emerged as a development of the standard Fw 190 A-8 powered by the BMW 801 F. Interestingly, by the time the Fw 190 A-9 actually entered series production, its designated engine had changed once again to include the hybrid BMW 801 TS/TH.

As originally conceived, the anticipated all-up weight of the Fw 190 H-1 would have been 4,600 kg (10,141 lb) and would have been armed with three cannon consisting of two MG 151/20 located in the wing roots plus an engine-mounted

The Fw 190 H-1 was to use a wing which was essentially a stretch version of an experimental wing designed in early 1943 and planned for the Fw 190 V19, also known as the Fw 190 Wb 1 (Weiterentwicklungs bau 1 – Development construction 1). Although this wing had the same surface area (18,3 m²) as the standard Fw 190 A series, its design was quite different including its almost straight leading edge. The Fw 190 H-1 wing plan would have increased surface area to 22,5 m²

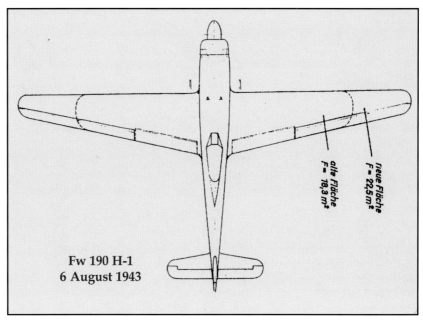

**Fw 190 H-1
6 August 1943**

MK 108. The "H" was to also incorporate the lengthened fuselage, larger 700 x 175 main wheels and a wing plan employing a straight leading edge. This wing was essentially identical to that earmarked for the experimental Fw 190 V19 (aka Fw 190 Wb-1) but featured extended tips increasing the span to 14.8 m (48.6 ft). The horizontal tailplane remained unchanged from the Fw 190 A series having a span of 3,650 mm (11 ft 11¾ in) with a surface area of 2,82 m² (30.4 ft²).

In addition to the DB 603 G, several additional engines were also under active consideration as alternative powerplants for the Fw 190 H; primarily the Jumo 213 E and the unconventional DB 632. However, by this period in 1943, Daimler-Benz's faith of their newly proposed DB 632, featuring co-axial contra-rotating propellers, remained completely theoretical since no development examples of this intriguing engine had yet been assembled or bench tested.

Events were now moving quickly, and by the end of April 1943, the promising Fw 190 H-1 had been all but abandoned. Soon, it was about to be totally eclipsed by "a new and improved Heinrich" known as the new Ta 152 H.

Me 209 PRODUCTION PLANNING

By mid March the third Me 309 prototype, Me 309 V3, W. Nr. unknown, GE+CW, was successfully flown for the first time in spite of the fact the RLM had canceled the entire Me 309 program. By this time too, the RLM's Technical Office was convinced the proposed Me 209 offered significant advantages over the Ta 153—chief among these was the previously mentioned component commonality with a type currently in series production. On 26 March 1943, State Secretary Milch instructed Messerschmitt to bring Me 209 pre series (Me 209 A-0) production forward by eight to nine months without interfering with Me 410 and Bf 109 production. Normally, this should have posed few problems, especially since the Me 209's fuselage was nearly identical, apart from the wing attachment points, to that of the newly produced Bf 109 G-3. In addition to the DB 603, the Me 209's new components included the nose with cowling, wings, main undercarriage and tailplane. These new items had to be fabricated and were heavily based upon design work undertaken earlier in Paris on the Me 155 B.

During the first two weeks of April 1943, Messerschmitt was busy assembling a design staff in preparation for series production of the Me 209. In contrast, the Air Ministry had still not determined or announced the priority level for the Me 262, which resulted in fewer people being employed in this program than that for the Me 209.

Meanwhile to the north, on 17 April 1943, the Focke-Wulf factory at Hemlingen-Bremen was pounded by 115 B-17s of the 8th U.S. Army Air Force. Because German resistance was particularly stiff the raid proved costly for the Americans. *Luftwaffe* fighters and Flak engaged the bombers and successfully downed 14 percent (16 aircraft) of the attacking force.

HÖHENJÄGER Me 209 A-4 IS SUBMITTED

Concurrently with these preparations, Messerschmitt's *Projektbüro* had drafted the parameters for a new high altitude fighter variant of the Me 209. These were submitted to the RLM's Technical Office on 23 April 1943. Known as the Me 209 A-4, this project was to be powered by the DB 628. This Messerschmitt project was crafted to meet the RLM's still outstanding requirement for a high altitude fighter. The design called for the insertion of a new wing center section which significantly increasing the aircraft's overall wingspan. Unfortunately, the Me 209's laminar flow wing and inward retracting undercarriage did not lend itself to expansion. Therefore, Messerschmitt substituted the Bf 109 G wing, suitably modified, to accept a new center section.

GALLAND AND PETERSEN FAVOR THE Me 262

On 15 May 1943, the Me 262 V4 was flown for the first time. This prototype was the last Me 262 equipped with the traditional "tail dragger" tricycle undercarriage. A few days later, this prototype was demonstrated before the General of the Fighters, Adolf Galland, who became an instant and enthusiastic supporter of the jet. Soon thereafter, Galland and *Oberst* Edgar Petersen, head of the *Luftwaffe's* experimental stations, together drafted a one-page letter to the RLM in which they advocated canceling the Me 209 altogether in favor of the Me 262.

HÖHENJÄGER Bf 109 H

At this time, Messerschmitt's prototype assembly shop was busy putting the finishing touches to the high altitude Bf 109 V49, W. Nr. 16281, SP+LB. This machine was created by pulling a standard Bf 109 G-3/U2 from the assembly line and modifying it to flight-test an early example of the high altitude DB 628 (DB 628 V8); the same engine originally earmarked for the Me 155 B. When, on 18 May 1943, the V49 took to the air powered by this long-awaited engine, Messerschmitt was gratified but not overly optimistic for its series production. Spurred on by advances made with the V49, Messerschmitt continued developing the standard Bf 109 G for high altitude operations. Now known as the Bf 109 H and finalized in May 1943, it featured an extended wing that was virtually identical to the newly designed structure destined for the Me 209 A-4. In addition, it was hoped to fit a more powerful version of the DB 628 to this new model. By 21 May 1943, detailed drawings for various components of the Bf 109 H had been completed.

On 25 May 1943, at a conference held in Berlin at the Air Ministry's GL Office of Air Armaments, Messerschmitt was invited to begin series manufacture of the Me 262 by producing no less than 100 by the end of the year. Later in the afternoon, Erhard Milch, Secretary of State for Aviation, telephoned Göring and requested…"we drop the Me 209 and put the Me 262 in its place." Göring agreed knowing that Galland was solidly behind the decision. Six days later, on 31 May, at a special meeting hosted by Junkers at Dessau and attended by the *Reichsmarschall*, the RLM's Technical Office and the *Luftwaffe*'s Testing Centers (E-*Stelle*), Göring agreed to a temporary suspension of the Me 209 in favor of the Me 262.

LOSS OF THE Fw 190 V31

Tragically, two weeks later, on 29 May 1943, the Fw 190 V31 was being ferried from Bremen to Langenhagen by Focke-Wulf test pilot Werner Bartsch, when the aircraft's engine began loosing power necessitating an emergency landing near Kaltenweide. In the ensuing wheels-up landing, the prototype cartwheeled. Although the accident totally destroyed this third *Höhenjäger* 2 prototype, Bartsch escaped serious injury.

A month after the first flight of the Bf 109 V49, the second DB 628-powered experimental prototype, the Bf 109 V50, W. Nr. 15338, assembled from a standard Bf 109 G-5/U2, was completed. Powered by another early example of the DB 628 (DB 628 V20), it joined the program in mid June. Although development of the DB 628 was progressing, the pace was agonizingly slow and, almost no one at Messerschmitt believed this engine would ever live up to expectation. By this time, Messerschmitt was all the more convinced the future of high altitude fighter design rested solely with a proven series-built Daimler-Benz powerplant, e.g., the DB 603 or DB 605, operating in concert with an exhaust-driven turbosupercharger.

Unfortunately, the small fuselage of the Bf 109 simply did not permit the installation of an exhaust-driven turbo with its attendant delivery and exhaust piping. On 26 June 1943, Messerschmitt published a *Kruzbeschreibung P 1091 Höhenjäger m.TK 15*, which was a short description of the Me P 1091 equipped with a fuselage-mounted TK 15 (9-2279) turbosupercharger. The report called for a single-seat stretch fighter having a very long wing spanning 21,000 mm (68.9 ft) with an area of 39 m² (419.8 ft²)

THE Fw 190 A-6 APPEARS

Appearing during June 1943, the Fw 190 A-6 fighter subtype was a progressive development of the Fw 190 A-5/U10. The distinguishing feature of this series was the outer wing cannon, which was upgraded from the MG FF/M to the faster firing MG 151/20. Over 1,000 examples of the A-6 were produced by Ago, Arado and Fieseler before this series was overtaken by the Fw 190 A-7 in December.

In the meantime, Hitler had become deeply concerned over development and production problems associated in bringing new fighters into service within the shortest possible time. To personally resolve this issue the *Führer* took the unprecedented step of bringing the nation's leading aircraft manufacturers together on 27 June 1943, for a special secret meeting at his Alpine Berghof on the Obersalzberg. Neither Milch nor Göring were present. Hitler surprised them by stating that the *Luftwaffe* knew nothing of this meeting. It was clear that Hitler was looking for answers from the men who were quite familiar with the present state of the aircraft industry. When Messerschmitt's turn came, he vigorously defended the Me 209 and railed against what he felt was Milch's ill-advised decision regarding this aircraft, vis-à-vis, the jet powered Me 262. Hitler listened intently but did not betray his considered opinion.

THE QUICK SOLUTION DICTUM

Eight days later, another important meeting was convened at Focke-Wulf's Bad Eilsen headquarters on 5 July 1943. The Air Ministry had become alarmed, perhaps as a direct result of Hitler's special conference, because the two principal fighter makers were taking too much time to field new service-ready fighters.

To address these issues, representatives from the Air Ministry's Technical Office met with officials from Focke-Wulf and Messerschmitt to discuss the status of each firm's special high altitude and high-performance fighter projects. Following the presentations, Air Ministry officials instructed both firms to quickly submit proposals in what was termed a *Schnellösung* (quick solution) to these unfulfilled contracts. The RLM further stipulated that both firms were expected to produce proposals based upon current production types with as little design change as possible.

In order to fulfill the RLM's request for a quick solution high performance escort fighter, Focke-Wulf 's choices came down to two options; the Fw 190 D or the Ta 152 A. For Messerschmitt, the choice was made somewhat simpler. He essentially had only one official choice; the newly designed Bf 109 H. Unofficially, he could just as easily have offered the Me 209, had it not been for Galland's assertion that the Me 209's

performance would be inadequate and, if Milch in his sublime ignorance, had not canceled the project.

During this July meeting, the Technical Officer also discussed the Special High Altitude Fighter requirement. Focke-Wulf pointed to their *Höhenjäger* 2 program and discussed the potential offered by their Ta 152 H project. However, there were many frustrations associated with the *Höhenjäger* 2 program and, up to this time, very little had actually been achieved with either the Fw 190 H or the Ta 152 H. Significantly, apart from the Fw 190 H's relationship to the Fw 190 B series and the wing of the Fw 190 V19, there is no record of any Focke-Wulf development aircraft having been assigned specifically to the Fw 190 H.

By 25 August 1943, Focke-Wulf with RLM approval, decided to restrict the Fw 190 H to the DB 603 G and to apportion the "standard Jumo 213" (Jumo 213 A) as the designated powerplant for the Ta 152, which Focke-Wulf now officially refered to as a "simplified version of the Ta 153."

HERR MESSERSCHMITT, CAN YOU BUILD AN *EXTREMER HÖHENJÄGER*?

Messerschmitt continued with his commitment to the high altitude Me 209 H. However, up to this time German airmen, air defense forces and military planners felt they had been lucky. The Allies had not yet committed their dreaded four-engined bombers to massed high altitude missions, but most German defense planners believed such attacks were inevitable. It was just a question of when and where. The Air Ministry had earlier provided Messerschmitt with a detailed 3-stage road map in meeting ever increasing high altitude operational goals. The third stage called for interceptors capable of operating between 40,000 and 56,000 ft (12.0 – 17.0 km).

Against this backdrop, the RLM's Technical Office (C-Amt) Chief surprised Messerschmitt by giving him verbal suggestions that he should investigate the possibilities of obtaining better ceiling performance than those currently offered, even if this meant additional equipment and support personnel. Whether by coincidence, or by design, Messerschmitt had the perfect solution...his ultra high altitude study, Me P 1091.

*In June 1943, it was in this spacious meeting room at Hitler's **Berghof** on the Obersalzberg that the **Führer** secretly conferred with the leaders of the nation's aviation industry. The meeting was an unusual step in an effort to obtain a clear first-hand picture of the challenges facing each producer.*

Two views of the Fw 190 V53, W. Nr. 170003, DU+JC, after it had been repaired following damage sustained in the 5 August 1944, raid on Langenhagen. Note hastily installed replacement cowl panels. This prototype, equipped with a Jumo 213 C, served as a template for the Fw 190 D-9 equipped with auxiliary apparatus R1 which, in addition to its standard two MG 131s and two wing root MG 151/20s, also carried a similar cannon in the outer wings. Later, it was modified to serve as a weapons prototype for the Ta 152 B-5 which called for two 30 mm MK 103 cannon to be installed in the wing roots. In the meantime, the two outboard 20 mm MG 151/20 cannon had been removed. In this modified form it was redesignated Fw 190 V68 and was flight-cleared, and possibly flown for the first time, on 13 December 1944.

THE DORA 9, A CASE FOR MAKING THE RIGHT CHOICE

For Kurt Tank, choosing the right high-performance quick solution fighter boiled down to the Fw 190 D primarily because its intended wing was straight from the standard production Fw 190 A series whereas the Ta 152 A's wing and undercarriage, though complimentary, were entirely new. Up to this time, several development prototypes were flying which, collectively, represented the definitive D series. These included the Fw 190 V17/U1, the Fw 190 V19 and V20. The plan was to produce the Dora as a non-pressurized fighter but, instead of assigning the first production model the designation Fw 190 D-1, it was decided to begin the Dora series with "D-9" in accord with the firm's designation rationalization policy begun on 19 April 1943. Inasmuch as the Fw 190 D-9 airframe was essentially identical to that of the Fw 190 A-8/A-9, commencing the series with "Dora-9" was both logical and expedient. With cancellation of the D-1 and D-2 series, their development prototypes (V22, V23 for the D-1; V26, V27 for the D-2) were reassigned. The Fw 190 V22, W. Nr. 0044, TI+II, and V23, W. Nr. 0045, TI+IJ, were non-pressurized examples constructed from aluminum-zinc alloy and completed with Jumo 213 Cs for participation in the Dora 9 program. The Fw 190 V26, W. Nr. 0051, GH+KP, and V27, W. Nr. 0052, GH+KQ, made from aluminum-zinc alloy, would swap their

Jumo 213 Cs for DB 603s and participate in weapon development trials.

Unfortunately for Messerschmitt, with the imminent official cancellation of the Me 209 and apart from *Höhenjäger* prototypes Bf 109 V49 and V50, both having wings of normal span, he lacked a clear-cut Bf 109 H development prototype. Undaunted, within ten weeks his design and fabrication shops had hurriedly produced the Bf 109 V54, W. Nr.15708, PV+JB, from a standard Bf 109 G-5/U2. Up to this time, Messerschmitt still held out hope that Milch's cancellation order for the Me 209 would be reversed. On 30 July 1943, Hugo Hügelscheffer, of Messerschmitt's *projektbüro* dispatched a conference addendum to *Herr* Begandt of Focke-Wulf comparing and contrasting the Me 209 to Focke-Wulf's Ta 153. Not surprisingly, the findings favored the Me 209. It is worth noting that Messerschmitt's reference line on the document included "Fw 190 D" in parentheses. Perhaps in this way, Messerschmitt was also attempting to link the Me 209 to the *Schnelllösung* specification.

Nevertheless, the RLM wisely chose the Fw 190 D-9 as the winner of the competition and, in early August 1943, awarded the production contract to Focke-Wulf. Then, in early August 1943, an example of how dictatorships can quickly cut through bureaucratic red tape occurred when, on Hitler's order, the Me 209 was suddenly and without discus-

Bf 109 HV54

The Bf 109 HV54, W. Nr. 15708, PV+JB, was an unsuccessful contender for the quick solution fighter requirement awarded to Focke-Wulf for their greatly superior Dora 9. The pressurized fuselage of this Messerschmitt prototype originated from a Bf 109 G-5/U2 equipped with GM 1 power boost while the vertical tailplane and wing center section were entirely new components. The STKZ code, PV + JB, has also been recorded as "PV +IB" within official documents.

GEWICHSVERGLEICH Ta 153 (Fw 190 D) – Me 209

In order to arrive at a potentially comparable result, the comparison was based on the following:

1) Flying weights based on the weight comparison by Focke-Wulf as of June 22, 1943.
2) The Jumo 213 Standard Engine was selected by Focke-Wulf for both aircraft for reasons of better comparison. Due to the Me 209's unfavorable fuel tank shape, an extra 35.3 lb (16 kg) were added to the type.
3) Me 209 equipment was used. For the Ta 153, an extra weight of 28.7 lb (13 kg) for hydraulic flaps operation and electrically controlled hydraulic valves was entered.
4) For armament, the same equipment status as Me 209 standard was used for both types, resulting in extra weight value for the Ta 153's ammunition container (in the Me 209, this container is situated inside static fuselage assembly).
5) For both aircraft, the fuel, lubricants and ammunition supply were the same.

Remarks:

The Ta 153 is not pressurized, while the Me 209 is to have a high altitude cockpit. According to Focke-Wulf, the Ta 153 could be pressurized but with a 33 lb (15 kg) weight increase. Since the Ta 153's design already provides for pressurization, conversion is therefore minimal. Behind the fuel tank, the Ta 153 has no light armor. Including this would add another 27 to 33 lb (12 – 15 kg). The difference in flying weights, according to the enclosed table, would therefore increase from 286.6 lb (130 kg) to 350 lb (159 kg).

WEIGHT COMPARISON TA 153, Me 209

	Me 209	Ta 153
Airframe according to 22 June 1943 list	1157 kg	1279 kg
Jumo 213 Engine forward of bulkhead	1388	1388
Propeller	265	265
Engine aft of bulkhead	110	110
Fuel tank weight Me 209	16	-
Equipment	177	177
Fw 190 extra weight for electric hydraulics and hydraulic flap operation	-	13
MK 108 (engine cannon)	83	83
Ta 153 extra weight for ammunition container	-	11
70 rounds for MK 108	41	41
Two MG 131 (cowl weapons)	78	78
Ammunition 2 x 300 rpg	51	51
Two MG 151/20 in wing roots	120	120
Ammunition 2 x 200 rpg	84	84
Intermediate gear with gun	10	10
Pilot	100	100
Fuel supply	420	420
Lubricants	45	45
Flying weight without pressure Cockpit and light metal armor	4145	4275
Flying weight including pressure cockpit	4145	4304
	(9,138 lb)	(9,489 lb)

sion, reinstated with his blessing. Messerschmitt had clearly presented a convincing case during his visit to the *Burghof* in June.

Willi Messerschmitt had once again out-foxed his old antagonist Milch. Little time was wasted in ordering construction of a Me 209 prototype. In order to speed the process, Messerschmitt pulled a standard Bf 109 G-3/U2, W. Nr. 16289, SP+LJ, from among the fifty G-3s produced, and commenced modifying its airframe. On 15 August 1943, the RLM issued its "Modified Production Program 223" calling for series production of the DB 603 G-powered Me 209 beginning in July 1944 and running through September 1945. It forecast the production of 91 Me 209s in 1944, with an additional 3,230 by the end of September 1945.

Me 155 B-1 EXTREME HIGH ALTITUDE FIGHTER

Once the Air Ministry's Technical Office had given Messerschmitt the green light to develop a high altitude fighter that would be in a class by itself, the resourceful designer immediately began drafting the preliminary specifications for an entirely new aircraft with an old designation. Given the identifier Me 155 B-1, the new design bore little or no resemblance to the earlier Me 155 B (aka Me 209). Instead, it was patterned after the Me P 1091 having an exceptionally long narrow-chord wing matched to a stretch fuselage large enough to house an exhaust-driven turbosupercharger.

On 13 August 1943, an important meeting was held at the RLM to once again discusses the relative merits of the Me 209 and Ta 153, and to establish the framework whereby one of these two fighter designs would be produced. The following is a translated transcript of this meeting:

A) Aircraft

1.) Me 209 / Ta 153

GL/C Chef (*Oberst* Dr. Ernst Pasewaldt): Since full comparative performance calculations show only minor performance differences between Ta 153 and Me 209, the decision has to be taken as to which of the two aircraft is to go into series production. However, the bottleneck in assembling capacity and operational facilities demand restriction to only one type. Also, the factories scheduled for the other model will later convert accordingly. Additionally, improvements will have to be introduced to the current types.

C-E 2: As calculated, the Me 209 is 4.4 to 7.5 mph (7 to 12 km/h) faster than the Ta 153, which is 260 lb (118 kg) heavier. Comparative flight tests are not available (first prototype for the Ta 153 only flew recently, Me 209 prototypes due from September 1943); no outstanding superiority of either model is to be expected. Also possible development and adaptability of the two are similar.

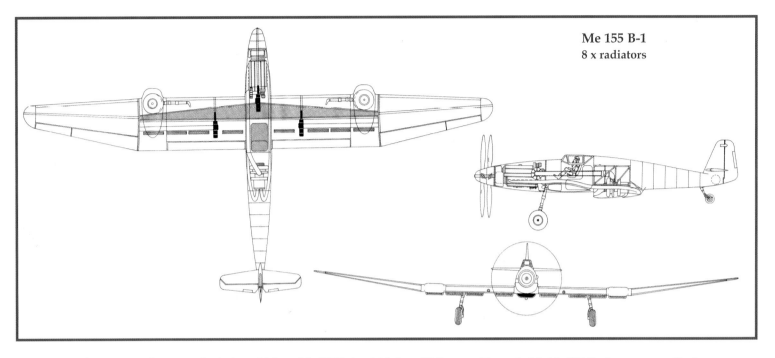

Me 155 B-1
8 x radiators

This 3-view of Messerschmitt's ambitious Me 155 B-1, which bore little resemblance to his Me 155 B, shows a complicated high altitude fighter design employing a turbosupercharger and an array of no less than eight underwing cooling radiators. This project was ultimately handed over to Blohm & Voss who greatly simplified and refined the concept.

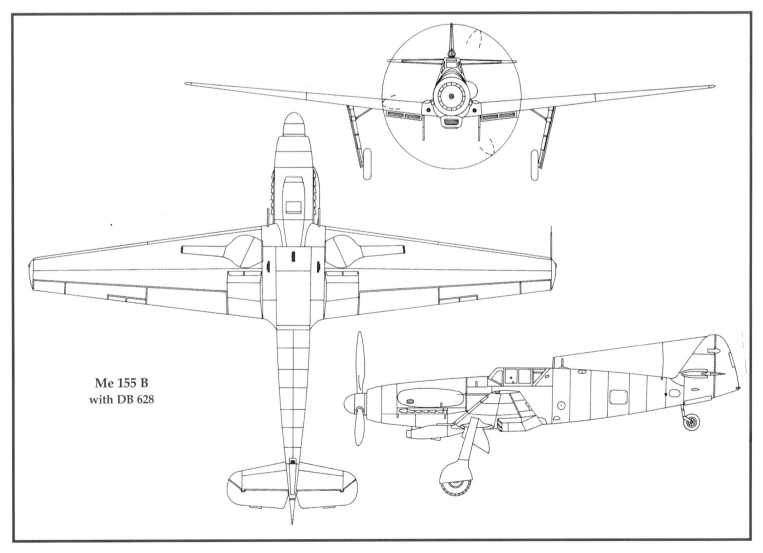

Me 155 B
with DB 628

C-B 2: As to procurement, only one model has to be insisted upon. Manufacturing deadlines within the companies are more or less similar. According to them (full production start March 1945), realization was only possible once an alternative has been selected. The expenditure with the Me 209 is decidedly less. Conversion of the present Fw 190 factories to Me 209 would result in much reduced change over losses than conversion of the current Bf 109 factories to the Ta 153. The Luther and Gotha factories could, at present, easily convert to either the Ta 153 or the Me 209.

C-2 Manufacturing: The Me 209 assembly rigs are 50 percent finished, but for the Ta 153, they would have to be completely newly made. Production requirements for the Me 209 would involve only half the effort. Attention is drawn to the high, light metal requirement of the current Fw 190.

Prof. Tank: Conversion effort for the Ta 153 is not as high as originally imagined because, in any case, between the current Fw 190 and Ta 153, the improved Fw 190 with the BMW 801 E is to be introduced, involving 50 percent high conversion. Apart from the forward movement of the engine and modifications to the fuselage, the undercarriage and wings are to be the same as for the Ta 153.

General of the Fighters (*Generalmajor* Adolf Galland): As to armament, the Ta 153 is superior to the Me 209 because – complement being similar – it has two MG 151s on top of the engine in place of the two smaller MG 131s. To avoid any risk, we demand combat tests of both types.

K. d. E. (Aircraft Test Establishment): We also think both types are necessary in order to maintain the chance of more performance variations, see inset at right.

Prof. Messerschmitt: Reports that as demanded by the General Field Marshal [Milch – ed.] on 10 August 1943, agreement with Prof. Tank has been reached for greatest possible cooperation. Accordingly, the Me 209 is to be made jointly

and, in cooperation with Focke-Wulf, performance data to be check over again.

Prof. Tank: Points out that the Ta 153's ailerons will differ from the Fw 190's, without setting problems, as they have

	ME 209	TA 153
Ailerons	ok – same as Bf 109	(Fw 190, very sensitive to setting and precise manufacture)
Pressure cabin	planned (better visibility than Bf 109)	not planned
Undercarriage	wide track for both	
Main wheels	740x210 (700x175 possible)	only 740x210
Standard Armament	1 x MK 108 (re MK 103 see below)	1 x MK 108 or 103
Upper fuselage	2 x MG 131 or 151	2 x MG 151
Wing roots	2 x MG 151	2 x MG 151
Employment	- similarly demonstrated - fast 2-seater by adopting Bf 109 trainer version	
Armor	light metal sectioned armor in front of fuel tank	otherwise similar
Assembly rig mods	60% compared to Bf 109	100% compared to Fw 190
Manufacturing hours per aircraft	(109 7,100)	(190 8,300)
Prototypes	V1 – Sep 1943	Already flown

Kurt Tank had high hopes for the BMW 801 E (aka BMW 801 TG and TH) which was similar to the standard BMW 801 D but fitted with different supercharger gear ratios and other internal modifications. It was expected to produce 2,000 hp at 2,700 rpm for take-off and 1,340 hp at 2,400 rpm at 1.3 ata at 19,000 ft (5,791 m), but whether or not it actually entered series production is unclear. One late war report indicates it was at one time earmarked for the Fw 190 A-9.

At first glace the Ta 153 A-1 might be mistaken for the Dora 9, but in fact it was an entirely new design predating the Fw 190 D series. Unfortunately for the Ta 153, rapidly changing operational needs coupled with intense political intrigue conspired to kill the project before a prototype could be built. This rendering shows the aircraft as it would have appeared in contemporary **Luftwaffe** *fighter camouflage and national aircraft insignia.*

already been tested. Moreover, rearward visibility in the Fw 190 and the Ta 153 is much better than in the Bf 109 and Me 209. Not to be forgotten is the stronger armament of the Ta 153, which permits fitting of the MK 103 engine cannon and both MG 151s in the fuselage including sufficient ammunition.

Mr. Kaether: (Focke-Wulf's Chief Technical Officer): For an immediate improvement, a new Fw 190 with a DB 603 or standard engine Jumo 213 could be developed with only 10 percent extra input for new or adapted assembly rigs. The fuselage would be lengthened by about 10 inches (400 mm) and the spar girder redesigned. The fuselage, wings and vertical and horizontal tail surfaces would remain unchanged (also no change in profiles). Performance would be only slightly inferior to the Ta 153 in climb (about 16 ft/sec – 5m/sec), otherwise would remain similar.

K.d.E. and Staff Engineer Schwarz: Raised objections to this proposal because of performance figures.

Gen. Director Dr. Karl Frydag (Director of the Main Committee for Airframes): Has serious doubts that the conversion effort will be correctly stated.

General of the Fighters: Demanded a fighter aircraft of improved performance as quickly as possible, which – if not the Ta 153 – should be according to the last proposal.

Tech Officer for the *Reichsmarschall:* Agrees with General of the Fighters and stresses the fact that, apart from a Fw 190 development, the main effort should not be directed at the Me 209.

The *Generalfeldmarschall:* (GFM Erhard Milch): Sharply points out to Mr. Kaether the responsibility he has taken with

this proposal, by which the matter under discussion, was put into a completely new perspective. Taking it for granted that a Bf 109 replacement will have to come in any case, and that the high investment for assembly rigs in the large license factories at Regensburg, Erla and WNF, does not permit alternatives.

The *Generalfeldmarschall* orders:

a) **Work on the Me 209 has to be started immediately within the scope previously agreed**.

   Me 262 is not to suffer from this measure, whether capacity-wise or operationally.

   According to the statement by Focke-Wulf, that the changes to assembly rigs and/or rigs will not amount to more than 10 percent, at the most 15 percent of the rigs and material requirements of the current Fw 190 production, and that an improved Fw 190 would be available much earlier, with similar performance and armament as the Ta 153, the *Reichsmarschall* (Göring) decides further:

b) **Ta 153 is dropped**.
   In order to be able to convert soonest, Fw 190 series production factories and the Luther and Gotha works, which so far have not given any definite type production, Focke-Wulf will have to produce definite and binding production and planning schedules by 17 August 1943 for the new Fw 190.
   The *Generalfeldmarschall* is pleased about the beginning cooperation between Messerschmitt and Focke-Wulf, and hopes that it will remain so in all circumstances.

Tech Officer of the *Reichsmarschall*, General of the Fighters, GL/C Chef and the K.d.E. underwrites the directive.

c) The Fighter Engine

It was stressed once more that the "new Fw 190" will have to adopt the "Standard Fighter Engine" Jumo 213/DB 603 (standard function plane!). Director Schilo points out that heretofore Focke-Wulf had reported that considerable effort would have to be spent on rig making, this being the reason for the practically completely new Ta 153 fuselage.

Director Schilo (Director of Aircraft Engines) has reservations against an engine cowling diameter of 42 in (1050 mm) since it would be insufficient to improve high altitude operation, and thinks that 48 in (1,200 mm) cowling advisable for the fitting of piping etc. Apart from this, a 44 in (1100 mm) version is to be built. Both are to fly about August/September 1943.

Profs. Messerschmitt and Tank state that a 1,200 mm engine cowling would fit both the Me 209 and Ta 153, however both would prefer the smaller engine cowling for performance reasons. On the Me 209, the larger engine cowling would require further increase in fin and rudder.

General of the Fighters does not believe it necessary to design the engines for the most unfavorable conditions.

In this case the radiator should have a device for fast evaporation. At higher altitudes, a large radiator would be much more economical, since otherwise one would have to fly with radiator flaps wide open.

d) DB 605 with DB 603 supercharger for Bf 109

General of the Fighters asks that the DB 605 for the Bf 109 should be fitted with the DB 603 supercharger. This would result in a considerable performance increase, especially at altitude, the more since GM 1 could then be used. This conversion would be around 500 monthly.

C-E 3: Apart from a small spacer and, possibly a minor adjustment to the supercharger impeller, still under test at Daimler-Benz, standard DB 603 superchargers will be fitted to DB 605 engines. Trial installation by VfH (*Versuchsstelle für Höhenflüge* – High Altitude Flight-Test Station).

The *Generalfeldmarschall* insists on most immediate start of this improvement. CB-3 is therefore to be involved initially. Prof. Messerschmitt will now prepare construction and rig documentation.

The foregoing provides a glimpse into the decision making process that, for political reasons, frequently impeded the rapid development and production of new and superior aircraft. It is not an indictment of the designers, engineers or servicemen, because these individuals did their best within

The Fw 190 V35, W. Nr. 816, BH+CF, photographed at Rechlin, was created from an Fw 190 A-5 airframe. It embodied armament found on production Fw 190 A-7 fighters most notably the four 20 mm MG 151/20 cannon supplemented by two cowl-mounted MG 17s. In this condition, its production designation bore the Modification Construction Set "U9," i.e. Fw 190 A-5/U9. This test prototype, one of a trio equipped with an early example of the BMW 801 F complete with its obligatory 14-blade cooling fan. This engine was originally earmarked for the Fw 190 A-10 (Nov. 1943), but later it was also planned for the A-9 (June 1944). The BMW 801 F was derived from the BMW 801 E and, reportedly rated at 2,400 hp for take-off.

the system's politically-biased framework. Willi Kaether's only contribution and astute observation before this important assemblage perfectly reflected the bureaucratic systemic handicap under which important decisions were handled.

The assertion that a "prototype of the Ta 153" had already flown, is misleading since this reference can only really refer to the Fw 190 V17 and V19, both of which flew the previous year and, were primarily engine development aircraft not directly associated with a specific aircraft series. However, it is equally possible Tank was thinking ahead to the Fw 190 V32, which at this time was still linked to the doomed *Höhenjäger* 2 program, but was scheduled to undergo significant changes at Daimler-Benz later in December. Prof. Tank's comments about the BMW 801 E are also misleading as this engine was never widely employed by the Fw 190 and differed from the ubiquitous BMW 801 D by its many internal improvements and changed supercharger gear ratios.

In addition, the accompanying table gives the 20 mm MG 151 as an upper fuselage (cowl) weapon for the Me 209 and Ta 153. Whereas this weapon installation was possible within the Ta 153's structure, but its inclusion within the Me 209 was highly questionable. Further on, Dir. Schilo's comments regarding the necessity for a new engine cowling, and the related discussion about installing the supercharger of a DB 603 onto the smaller DB 605 are noteworthy. This installation ultimately resulted in the DB 605 AS engine (the "S" for *Sonder* – Special), but again, due to a lack of leadership and urgency, it would take another year before this important, and relatively simple, modification found its way onto production fighters!

U.S. ARMY AIR CORPS MOUNTS MISSION 84

Tuesday, 17 August 1943, saw the U.S. Army's 8th Air Force execute Mission 84; the twin daylight bombing raid on Messerschmitt's Regensburg facility and the ball bearing works at Schweinfurt. Not only was the raid the deepest penetration yet made into Germany, it was also the largest by the 8th Bombing Command and a crucial test of the American policy of daylight precision bombing.

For the attack, 315 Boeing B-17s dropped 724 tons of high explosive bombs, causing extensive damage. At Regensburg, every important building was hit or damaged. At Schweinfurt, there were 80 high explosive hits on the two main bearing plants. American losses numbered 60 aircraft lost, or almost 20% of the attacking force. Approximately 175 American P-47s and 96 RAF Spitfires provided penetration support with another similar sized group providing withdrawal support. However, escort was only possible for part of the mission due to Allied fighter range limitation.

For over a year, *Luftwaffe* air defense planners had worried over the threat posed by America's long-range high altitude 4-engined bombers. In 1943, German planners were convinced America would attack the *Reich* using fleets of the high-flying super bombers. It was feared that such aircraft, flying at altitudes in excess of 25,000 feet (7,620 m), would not only place them beyond the range of effective Flak defenses, but would also make them invulnerable to interception. The

fact that the Regensburg-Schweinfurt raid was flown between 17,000 – 20,000 feet (5,182 – 6,096 m) came as a surprise and undoubtedly contributed to high American losses. Although the service ceiling for the B-17 was rated well above 30,000 feet (9,144 m), flying at lower altitudes assured better bombing results.

After the raid, Göring was incredulous when advised that plant management officials at Schweinfurt had made so little effort to decentralize their highly specialized industry. In sum, although the raid had been costly for both sides, it was clear that new methods of attack and defense would be required to avoid further losses. In the weeks and months following the raid, American planners took time out to develop an improved strategy. The most obvious remedy was the realization that, if present bombing altitudes were to be maintained, heavy bombers required continuous fighter escort to and from the target area. In addition, less complicated missions would be mounted relying more on tight formations and improved gunnery techniques than on stealth and deception. German planners also learned from the hard lessons of August. The Germans realized that on a moment's notice, the enemy could opt for increased bombing altitudes. Should this eventuality occur, it was understood that many of the *Luftwaffe*'s current frontline fighters would simply not be equal to the task.

On 20 August 1943, another conference was held at the Air Ministry in which an impassioned discussion took place about the relative merits of the Me 209 compared to the jet-powered Me 262. In response to the statement that the *Führer* himself had personally reinstated the Me 209, Milch's adjutant expressed his opinion that replacing the Me 209 with the Me 262 was correct. "But what a decision!" Milch agreed succinctly. "A clear course of action!"

Throughout September 1943, while Focke-Wulf was making preparations for full-scale production of the Dora 9, Messerschmitt was busy building the first prototype of the new Me 209, which by this time had officially become identified as the Me 209 V5. It will be recalled that the original Me 209 (V1 through V4), which bore no relationship to the new version, was built and flown before the war. Shortly thereafter, in early October 1943, Focke-Wulf sought RLM approval for priority development of the Ta 152 A, but Tank's request was once again deferred.

Ta 152 ANTON, BERTHA, EMIL AND HEINRICH ARE ESTABLISHED

By this time, Focke-Wulf had finalized their line-up of short and longspan subtypes for the Ta 152. These included the Ta 152 A series known as normal fighters, the B series classified as heavily armed close-support aircraft, the E series photo reconnaissance version and the high altitude fighter version, the H series. Initially, each of these was to be powered by a common engine; the Jumo 213 A. However, as back-up, Focke-Wulf had also provided for the possibility of using the Daimler-Benz DB 603 G in one or more of these subtypes. According to Focke-Wulf documents, the normal day fighter A series would be produced as Ta 152 A-1 and Ta 152 A-2 each

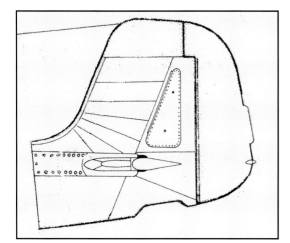

Variations on a theme by Focke-Wulf aerodynamicists. The vertical tailplane shown left, embodied a design selected for the Ta 153 (see page 39). On the right, is the wide chord fin design evaluated on the Fw 190 V32/U1 (see p 80).

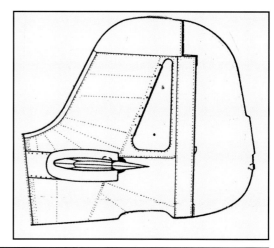

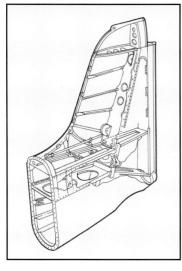

Illustrated is the standard fin design selected for production Ta 152s. Two versions were offered; one made of aluminum (shown) and another of wood (see p 107). Of these, the metal assembly was preferred because of its lighter weight. Ostensibly, wooden components were substituted in an effort to conserve metals, but in reality the decision was primarily driven by the need to decentralize manufacturing.

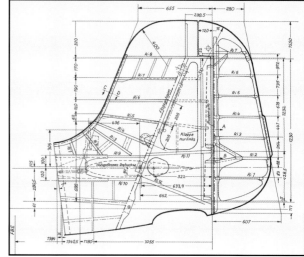

powered by a Jumo 213 A engine driving a 3-bladed VS 9 propeller. But, since Jumo 213 A lacked provision for the engine-mounted cannon, the engine of choice actually fell to the slightly different Jumo 213 C, which had this capability.

The Ta 152 A-1 was also to have been equipped with the exhaust flame suppression cowl system originally planned for the Ta 153 and experimentally tested on the Fw 190 V20 and V21. This equipment was normally found on twin-engined night fighters, where night time concealment was an important requirement, but by advancing this feature to the Ta 152, it was thought the fighter could double equally well for either day or night operations. Standard offensive armament was to have consisted of a 30 mm MK 103 engine-mounted cannon (70 rounds), or if this were not available in time, a MK 108 of similar caliber (85 rounds), augmented by four 20 mm MG 151/20 synchronized cannon. These were distributed as two cowl weapons with 150 rpg plus two wing root cannon with 175 rpg. This array of large caliber weapons could be further augmented, as circumstances warranted, by two additional cannon mounted in the outer wings. The wing was borrowed from the Ta 153, which itself was only slightly modified from the planned standard production A-8/D-9 wing, and outfitted with an hydraulically retractable undercarriage having 740 x 210 main wheels.

The Dural and steel fuselage was to have been adapt-ed from the newly devised Fw 190 A-8 complete with the obligatory 500 mm rear fuselage extension. However, a fair amount of revision was necessary for the aircraft to successfully accommodate the extra length demanded of the engine-mounted MK 103 as well as the two MG 151/20 cannon mounted above the cowl. A newly designed forward fuselage extension of 772 mm (30 in) was firmly secured to the A-8's pre-existing firewall. In conjunction with this forward adjustment, the wing with its corresponding attachment points, was to be moved forward 420 mm (16½ in). In addition, because of the new location of the wing spars, the length of the forward fuselage fuel tank was shortened slightly. The second fuselage fuel tank remained unchanged and, just aft of this was an 85 ltr (22.5 gal) insulated cylindrical tank containing GM 1 power boosting chemicals. In addition, provision for fitting a centrally mounted under fuselage ETC 503 (*Elektrische Trägervorrichtung für Cylinder bomben* – an electrically operated carrier for cylindrical bombs, model 503) was incorporated. The aircraft's enlarged metal fin, first evaluated on the Fw 190 V19 and, having an area of 19.1 ft² (1,77 m²), was assigned to the Ta 152.

The Ta 152 A-2 variant, evolved concurrently with the A-1, was essentially identical apart from its cowling. This model, favored by the RLM, dispensed with the bulky drag-inducing exhaust flame suppression feature opting instead for a Jumo 213 E cowl system. In all other respects, the Ta 152

A-2 was identical to the A-1 series. The A series was eligible for three auxiliary apparatus options known collectively as *Rüstsätze*. These are summarized in Appendix 3.

Complementing the normal fighters were the heavily armed close-support aircraft (*Schlachtflugzeug*) of the B series. Because the weight of seven cannon and their ammunition was considerable, the B series was not envisioned as a pure fighter. Instead, this type of warplane whose take off weight was approximately 500 lb (240 kg) greater than the A series was primarily designed for the close-support mission of attacking and destroying enemy ground targets.

Ta 152 B-1 was to have been externally very similar to the Ta 152 A-2, and initially powered by a Jumo 213 C, encased within a 9-213 E cowling, driving a Junkers VS 9 variable-pitch propeller. In accord with the aircraft's mission, the series was to have been equipped with a mix of 20 and 30 mm cannon. In this subtype, the engine-mounted weapon was to be the MK 108 (with 100 rounds but later reduced to 85-90 rounds) while the fuselage cowl weapons consisted of two MG 151/20 cannon (175 rpg). Wing root armament was also composed of two MG 151/20 cannon (175 rpg) augmented by two optional outboard MG 151/20s (140 rpg) as the B-1/R1 or, two MK 108s (55 rpg) as the B-1/R2 or, lastly two MK 103s (40 rpg) as the B-1/R3 contained in underwing packs known as gondolas.

The Ta 152 B-2 series was virtually identical to the B-1 apart from its engine-mounted cannon. In this model, the MK 108 was replaced by the newer MK 103 with 80 rounds. In addition, two MG 151/20s (140 rpg) were the preferred outer wing cannon options (B-2/R1). Thus, its armament was set at six 20 mm cannon plus one 30 mm engine-mounted MK 108. Like the B-1, the B-2 was eligible for an under-fuselage ETC 501 bomb rack.

The Ta 152 B-3 series would have been powered from the beginning by a Jumo 213 E and armed with three MK 108s, one engine mounted cannon plus two in the wing roots. The centrally-mounted bomb rack was upgraded to the ETC 503 but in all other respects, including its VS 9 propeller, it would have been very similar to the B-2 version.

The Ta 152 B-4 model was similar to the B-3 but characterized by armament consisting of three MK 103s; one as an engine-mounted cannon and the other two located in the wing roots.

As with the A series, the B series was also eligible for the three auxiliary apparatus items summarized in Appendix 3. Although a production contract for the Ta 152 A and B series had failed to materialize during this period, Focke-Wulf was prepared to inaugurate a small number of "preproduction" aircraft e.g., Ta 152 A-0 and/or Ta 152 B-0 had the RLM granted Tank's request. Preproduction aircraft were generally considered working-in machines allowing the manufacturer and services to iron out any production bugs prior to the type entering full-scale production. Typically, preproduction aircraft numbered five to twenty machines depending on their complexity and service considerations.

Throughout the summer and into autumn 1943, following RLM ambivalence toward the Ta 152 A series, Focke-Wulf continued lobbying for the B series in the belief this model would suit current battlefield requirements if ordered into production. The RLM believed the venerable Fw 190 F series, dedicated to the fighter-bomber role, would suffice well into 1944. Consequently, no final decision regarding production of either the A or B series was made during the course of 1943.

To the south, BMW had in the meantime, evolved a new and improved 14-cylinder air-cooled radial design known as the BMW 805. Designed with a rated altitude of 11,000 m (36,089 feet) it was viewed as a logical successor to the firm's BMW 801.

As part of the original Air Ministry requirement for high performance fighter aircraft, the Technical Office stipulated that the aircraft must be capable of undertaking the role of photoreconnaissance. That the Ta 152 was selected for this mission was in compliance with this requirement. The letter "E" was chosen for the Ta 152 reconnaissance series for ease of recognition since it closely corresponded to the BMW 801 powered Fw 190 E, which was to fulfill the same role but failed to enter series production.

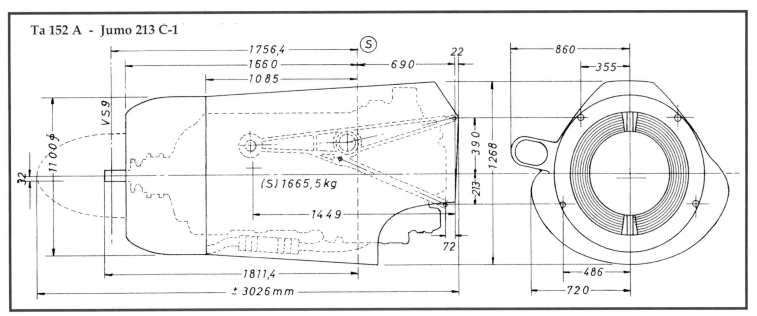

Ta 152 A - Jumo 213 C-1

Ta 152 A Fuselage

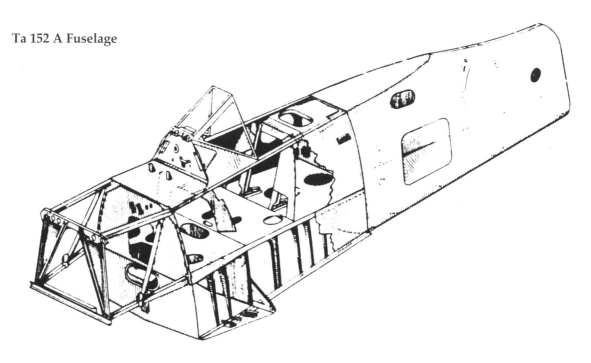

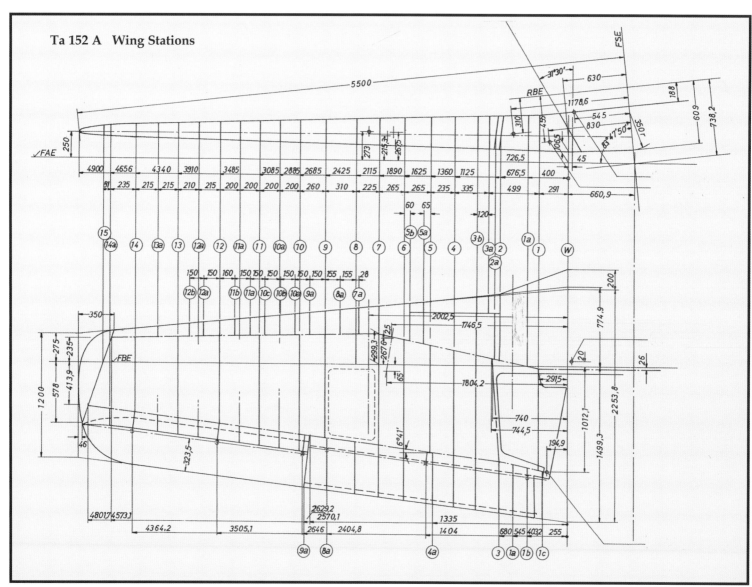

Ta 152 A   Wing Stations

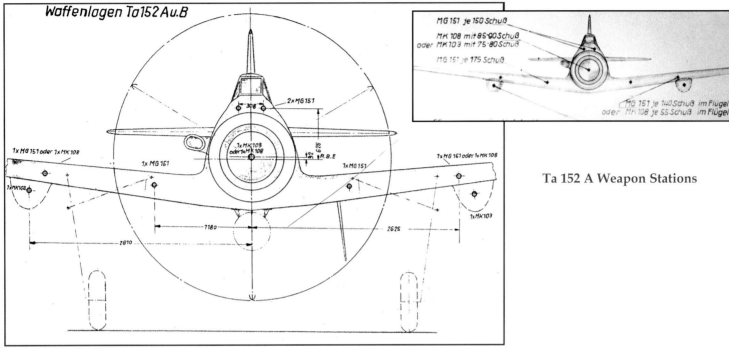

Ta 152 A Weapon Stations

Ta 152 A Metal
Horizontal Stabilizer
Stations

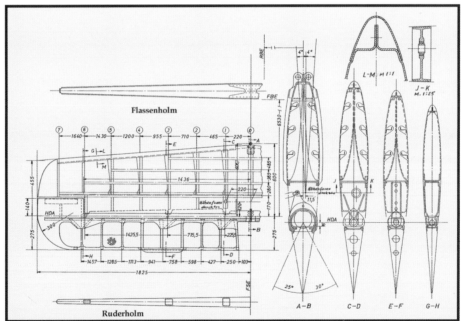

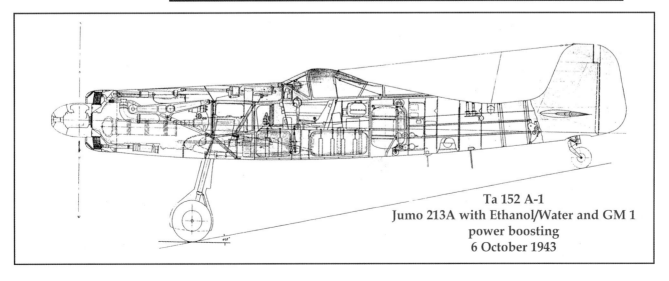

Ta 152 A-1
Jumo 213A with Ethanol/Water and GM 1
power boosting
6 October 1943

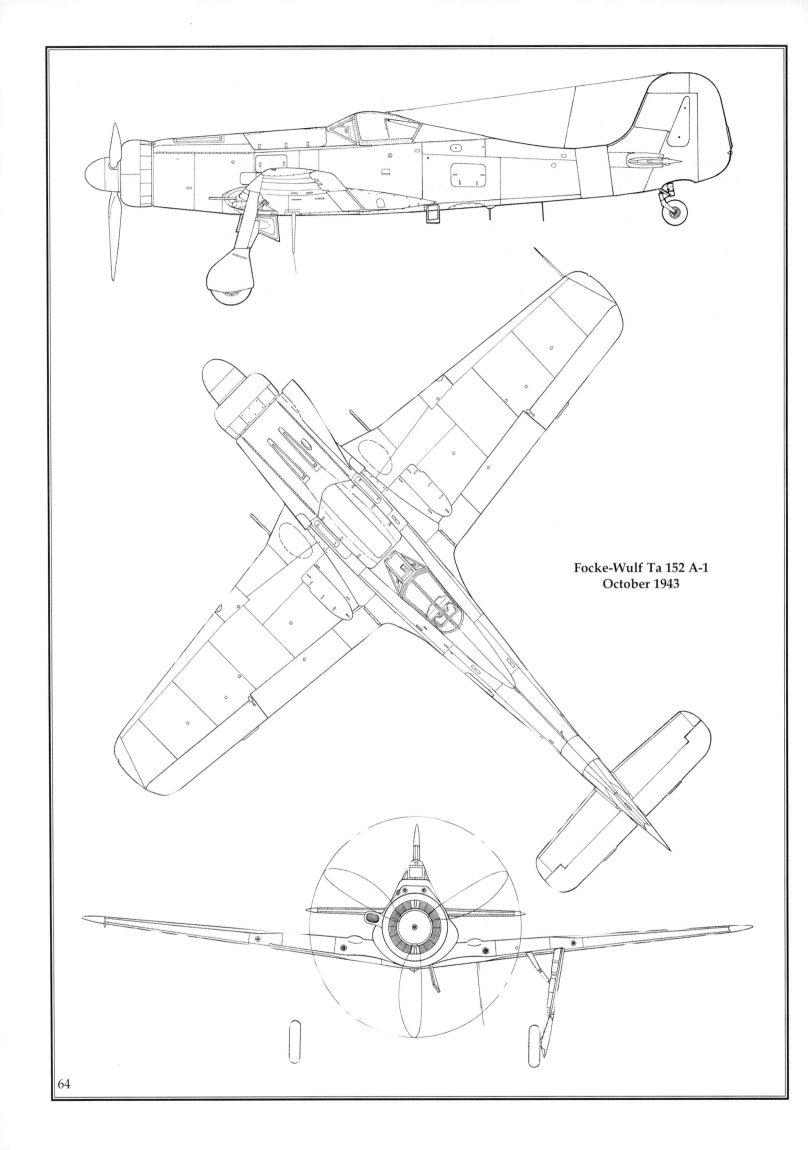

Focke-Wulf Ta 152 A-1
October 1943

64

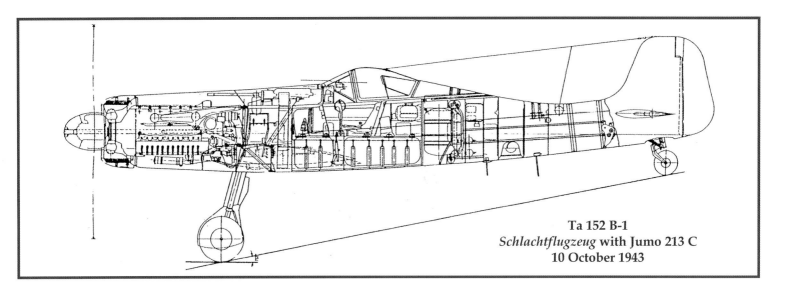

Ta 152 B-1
Schlachtflugzeug with Jumo 213 C
10 October 1943

One of the bolt-on weapons employed by several German fighters during 1943 was the WGr 21, an air-to-air rocket mortar having a body diameter of 21 cm. Shown here being loaded aboard an Fw 190 A-8/R6, the installation configuration would have been the same for the Ta 152. When first used in combat, these early missiles achieved some success, in spite of their unpredictable flight trajectories, against tight American bomber formations. But by 1944, they were largely withdrawn and seldom used thereafter. The main reason, besides the rocket's inherent limitations, was the vulnerability of aircraft fitted with this device. They were slower, less maneuverable, and obligated to approach their targets close-in and level.

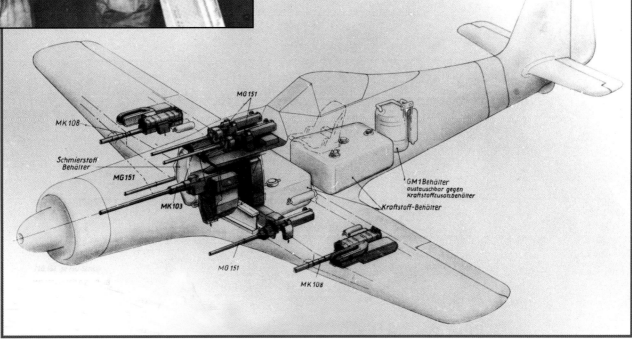

Ta 152 B-4/R2   ARMAMENT
1 x MK 103 engine cannon, 30 mm with 75-80 rounds
2 x MG 151 cowl cannon, 20 mm with 150 rpg
2 x MG 151 wing root cannon, 20 mm with 175 rpg
2 x MK 108 outer wing cannon, 30 mm with 55 rpg

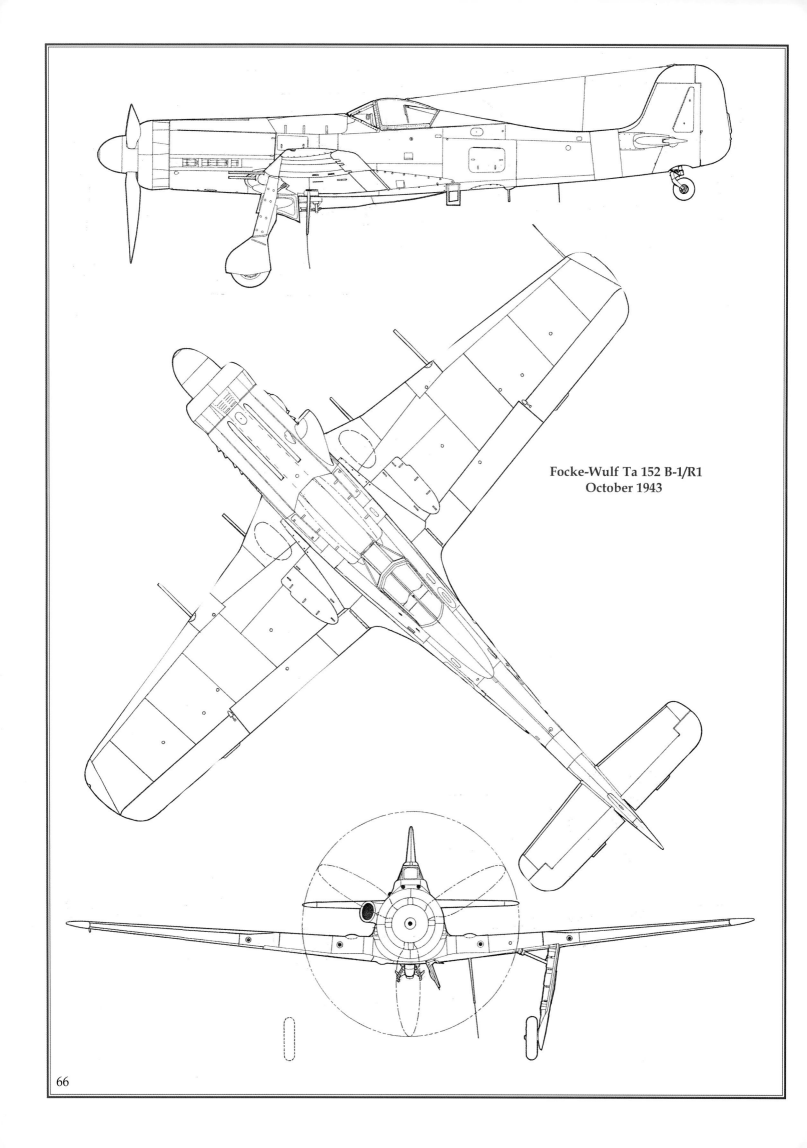

Focke-Wulf Ta 152 B-1/R1
October 1943

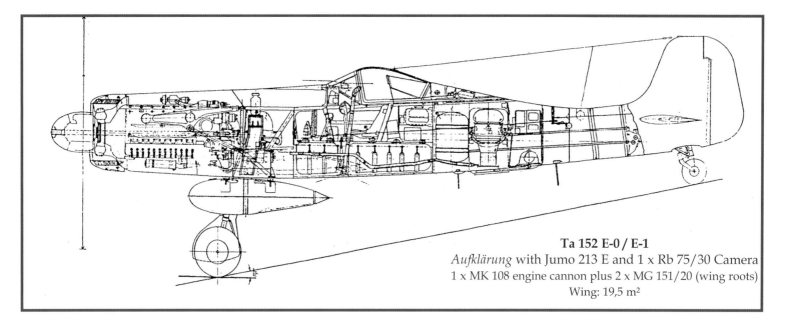

Ta 152 E-0 / E-1
Aufklärung with Jumo 213 E and 1 x Rb 75/30 Camera
1 x MK 108 engine cannon plus 2 x MG 151/20 (wing roots)
Wing: 19,5 m²

The preproduction Ta 152 E-0 and production Ta 152 E-1 series reconnaissance fighters would have been outwardly similar to the Ta 152 B series but armament would have been restricted to one MK 108 engine-mounted cannon (with 85 rounds) plus two MG 151/20 wing root cannon (with 150 rpg). However, there were various internal changes necessitated by the installation of a fairly heavy camera aft of the rear cylindrical fuel tank. To offset the additional weight of a camera and its equipment, and to restore the aircraft's center of gravity, it was decided to relocate the heavy compressed air and oxygen bottles from the rear fuselage filler section to the port and starboard wing roots. Additionally, for ease of accessibility to the camera and its equipment, an over-size camera

access hatch was to be cut into the port side of the rear fuselage replacing the smaller standard hatch. The aircraft's electronics included a FuG 16ZS radio (vhf 40,4-42,3 MHz German Army band) but this was to be eventually upgraded to FuG 15ZY "Christa" when available, and the FuG 25a IFF (Identification, Friend, Foe) radio was relocated farther aft.

Visually aligning and aiming the aircraft to its target area was achieved by means of a *Gerät* 67G periscope. Several periscope mounting arrangements were advanced, ranging from the complex (see p 70) to the simple straight-through (see below) installation. A diverse array of aerial reconnaissance cameras was available to the E series and, depending on the mission, the right camera for the required task would be car-

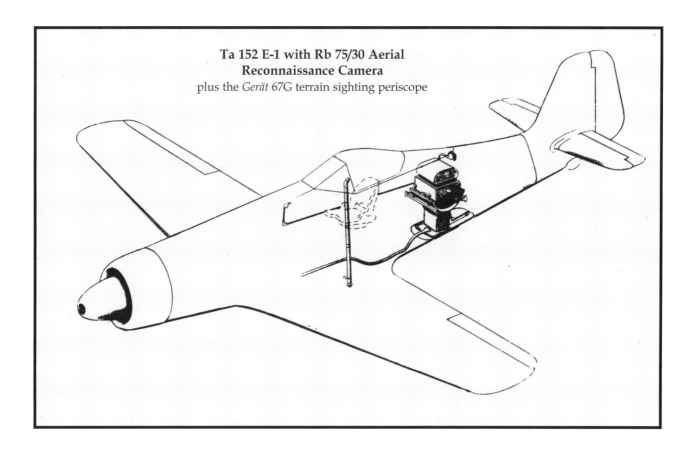

Ta 152 E-1 with Rb 75/30 Aerial Reconnaissance Camera
plus the *Gerät* 67G terrain sighting periscope

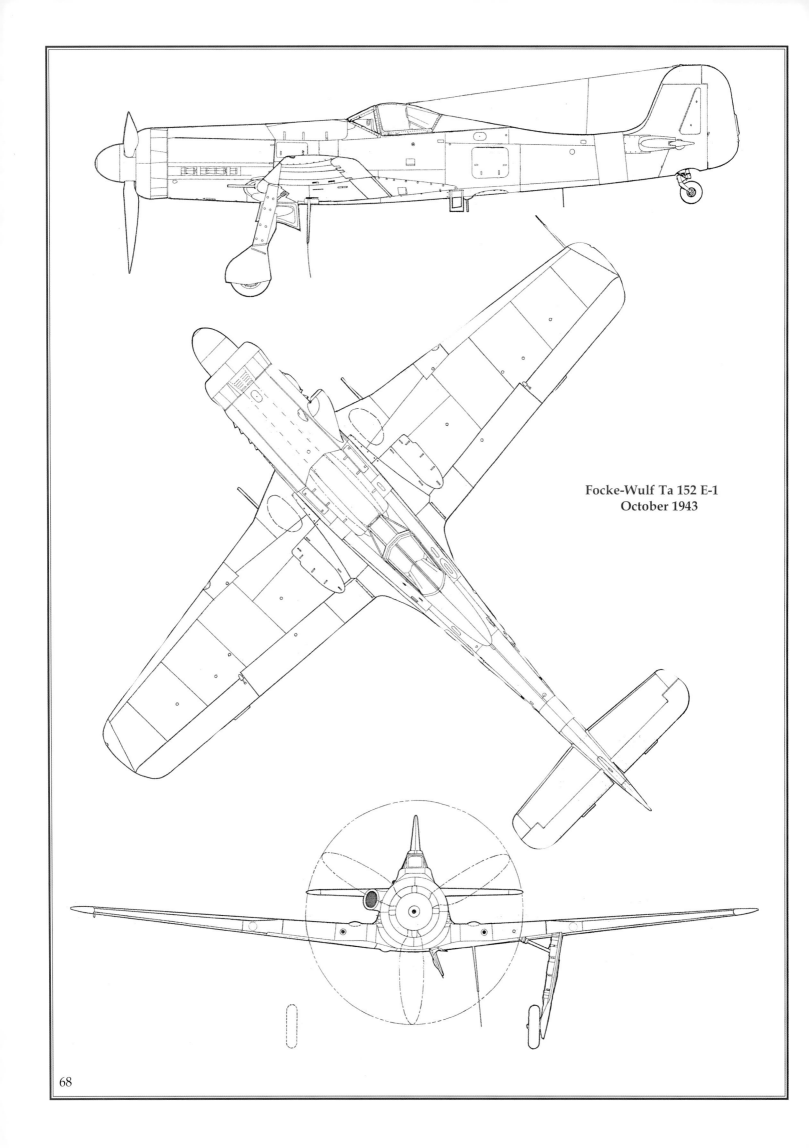

Focke-Wulf Ta 152 E-1
October 1943

68

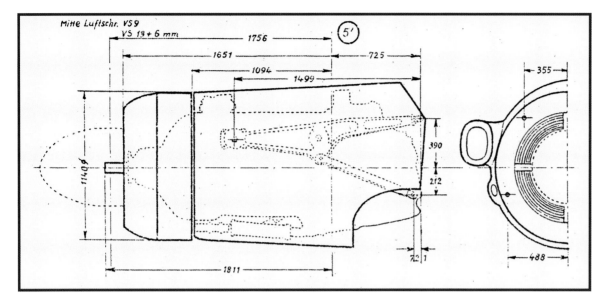

Jumo 213 E (9-8213FE)

ried. These included the following *Reihenbildkamera* – Rb (automatic photo camera):

- One Rb 75/30 – Standard equipment camera
- One Rb 50/30
- One Rb 30/18
- One Rb 50/18 – Standard for the Ta 152 E-1/R1
- Two Rb 20/12 x 2
- Two Rb 40/12 x 2
- Two Rb 12.5/7 x 9
- Two Rb 32/7 x 9

The size and function of these cameras varied widely depending on their capability. The simple and descriptive German designation system identified the camera's focal length and exposure size in centimeters. Thus, the Rb 75/30 camera had a focal length of 75 cm (29.5 in) and produced an exposure size of 30 cm (11.75 in). As a rule, the larger cameras

were used at higher altitudes, while the small models, often used in pairs and mounted obliquely, recorded images at lower altitudes. The Ta 152 E-1 would have also mounted a small, forward facing, Robot II camera in the leading edge of the port wing. This small camera (see p 87) replaced the BSK 16 gun camera, took single 2,4 x 2,4 cm (1 in sq) images from high altitudes down to approximately 2,000 m (6,562 ft). This Robot was sighted through the aircraft's gun sight and actuated by a button on the throttle. The Ta 152 E-1/R1 was planned as a field-modified low-altitude tactical reconnaissance aircraft in which its Rb 50/18 camera was to be mounted obliquely (but almost horizontally to port) in the rear fuselage. Because of the camera's great length, which exceed the limits of the fuselage, it was necessary to fit a rather large aerodynamic blister to cover the protruding portion (see below).

The designated engines for the Ta 152 E-1 were the Jumo 213 E, or the Jumo 213 E-1 each with the high pressure MW stowed in the rearmost cylindrical fuselage fuel tank. Alternatively, a Jumo 213 E-2 could be employed with its MW

A simplified general arrangement drawing showing the Rb 50/18 aerial reconnaissance camera and Robot II camera installation planned for the Ta 152 E-1/R1. Because of the Rb 50/18's size and location within the rear fuselage, it was not possible to contain the whole within the confines of the airframe. Instead, a rather large awkward looking bulge would have been grafted onto the fuselage. This auxiliary equipment, and resulting alteration, would have normally been undertaken at unit level.

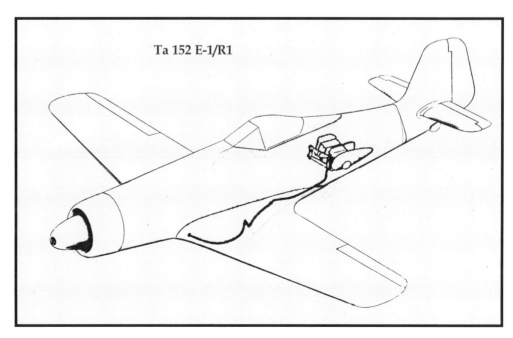

Ta 152 E-1/R1

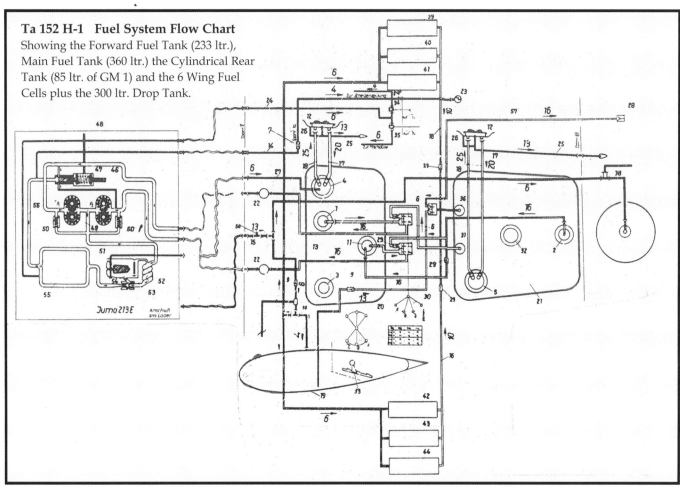

Ta 152 H-1   Fuel System Flow Chart
Showing the Forward Fuel Tank (233 ltr.),
Main Fuel Tank (360 ltr.) the Cylindrical Rear
Tank (85 ltr. of GM 1) and the 6 Wing Fuel
Cells plus the 300 ltr. Drop Tank.

The fuel system, shown above, was applicable for the Ta 152 H-1, H-2, H-11 and H-12. It was similar to, but different from, the system of the Ta 152 H-0 and H-10. The difference between the two systems was six wing fuel tanks. The Ta 152 H-0 and H-10 were not equipped with wing-mounted fuel tanks and thus their fuel flow system was slightly different. All versions of the Ta 152 were designed to accept the 300 liter auxiliary fuel tank. Although the Ta 152 H was always intended to be simultaneously equipped with MW and GM 1, in reality early examples of the Ta 152 H-0 carried neither. The first aircraft to be fitted with GM 1 was the eleventh Ta 152 H-0, W. Nr. 150011 while the first machine to have built-in MW was the first Ta 152 H-1, W. Nr. 150158. For those aircraft without wing fuel tanks, i.e., the H-0 and H-10, MW was contained in the 300 liter drop tank but, with the first Ta 152 H-1, the MW was pumped into the port inboard wing fuel tank. GM 1 was always contained under pressure in a liquidized form in the rear fuselage cylindrical tank. Pressure was maintained by two pressurized air bottles stowed in the rear fuselage just ahead of the tailplane.

External and internal views of the experimental periscope target sighting device expediently crafted for the photoreconnaissance version. This awkward looking apparatus was soon supplanted by a straight through tube type (see page 67) and finally by the preferred cowl-mounted sighting type (see page 87).

supply either stowed in the rear fuselage tank or within the wing fuel tank located in the inner portion of the port side. To extend the aircraft's range, a further change to the fuel supply was offered. In this instance, the MW power boosting fuel, normally carried within the airframe, was relocated to a 300 ltr (79 gal) drop tank carried under the fuselage. This freed-up the rear cylindrical fuselage fuel tank to be adapted to carry 115 ltr (30 gal) of B4 aviation fuel (see schematic on page 70). The designated propeller for the Emil was a wooden three-bladed Junkers VS 9. GM 1 power boosting was not proposed for the Ta 152 E series.

As 1943 drew to a close, the Air Ministry had made no final decision concerning the future of the Ta 152 reconnaissance fighter. Instead in the interim, other single-seat fighter aircraft already in production, were modified to fulfill the mission. Primarily, this responsibility fell to various production models of the Focke-Wulf Fw 190 A and the Messerschmitt Bf 109 G.

By now, the Fw 190 H-1 had been officially abandoned, but not before its fuselage, by now upgraded to the Fw 190 A-7 pattern with rear extension, and outfitted with a pressurized cockpit plus GM 1 power boosting system, had been transferred to the Ta 152 H. As to the question of which engine should power the initial production model of the Ta 152 H, it was decided that either the DB 603 G or the Jumo 213 E, depending on availability, should replace the provisional Jumo 213 A. But the possibility that other engines would come up for consideration was a certainty. Such advanced powerplants as the DB 603 L, DB 603 N, Jumo 222 A/B-3, and the French Hispano-Suiza HS 24Z were on the table and the subject of much debate.

Lastly, since the Ta 152 was to adopt the Ta 153's innovative wings (both short and long span versions), the Ta 152 H adopted the design advanced by the Ta 153 Ra-2. This wing, unlike that chosen for the Fw 190 H-1, was specifically designed for optimal performance at high altitude.

By 25 October 1943, Messerschmitt had finalized plans to produce the Me 209 A-4 high altitude fighter. This version represented Messerschmitt's *Höhenjäger Stufe* I (High Altitude Fighter Stage I) powered by a high performance DB 628 A. However, in the event this engine was not ready in time, backup engines such as the DB 605 A or AS engine with oxygen power boost would be substituted. Meanwhile, Focke-Wulf had been actively pursuing and refining their vision of the ideal high altitude fighter. The aerodynamicists at Bad Eilsen had been conducting advanced airflow experiments in an effort to determine the optimum shape for a long span high-performance wing. These experiments resulted in a wing that would ensure great stability and control throughout all flight regimes.

FOUR MORE NEW PROTOTYPES ARRIVE

On 3 November 1943, the Me 209 V5, W. Nr. 16289, SP+LJ, Messerschmitt's contender for the High-Performance Day Escort Fighter requirement was flown for the first time. Although brief, the first flight was successful without any serious handling difficulties. Chief Messerschmitt test pilot Fritz Wendel found the aircraft's DB 603 A functioned properly through various flight regimes. Nine days later, on 12 November 1943, the prototype was re-engined with one of the early examples of the more powerful DB 603 G. At about the same time, Messerschmitt rolled out another prototype in compliance with the Air Ministry's "Quick Solution" dictum. This aircraft, the Bf 109 HV54, W. Nr. 15709, PV+JB, had been hurriedly assembled by using a standard production Bf 109 G-5/U2 as a basis for the new Bf 109 H series prototype.

Then, on 23 November 1943, Focke-Wulf's chief test pilot Hans Sander successfully flew the Fw 190 V20, W. Nr. 0042, TI+IG, powered by a Jumo 213 CV (W. Nr. 1001570010). This prototype, while not associated with any specific series *per se*, was instead employed solely as an important engine development aircraft.

THE Fw 190 A-7 APPEARS

This Fw 190 A-7 was introduced in late November 1943 and was characterized by an armament upgrade; two MG 131 machine guns in the cowl position replaced the smaller caliber MG 17s. The A-7 also employed simplified electrical

Had the Ta 153 actually been built, this is the competitor it would have been up against, the Me 209 V5, W. Nr. 16289, SP+LJ. Which machine was the better of the two? A question not easily answered! Both aircraft possessed obvious strengths and weaknesses but since a fly-off was never flown, the question remains moot.

circuits without shielding, a new Revi 16b gun sight and a slightly larger tail wheel. Production of this subtype commenced at Focke-Wulf, Ago and Fieseler with a production run of approximately 800 examples.

Finally, on 7 December 1943, the Air Ministry gave Prof. Tank the go-ahead to proceed with construction of five prototypes for the Ta 152 H. These aircraft were to be assembled at Focke-Wulf's Cottbus factory and would be representative of the Ta 152 H-0, or preproduction series, of the high altitude fighter. To accelerate Ta 152 H series development, it was decided to immediately pull two aircraft from the ineffectual *Höhenjäger* 2 program and transform them into H series short-cut engine and airframe testing vehicles.

The first, Fw 190 V32, W. Nr. 0057, GH+KV had been flown to Daimler-Benz at Echterdingen in November where its *Känguruh* equipment and DB 603 S were removed and replaced by an early example of the DB 603 G with a new Schwarz 4-bladed prop. In addition, its 18.3 m² wing was replaced by a new wing having an area of 23.5 m². Concurrently, Fw 190 V33, W. Nr. 0058, GH+KW, was also recalled and modified to accept a newly produced Jumo 213 E with a three-bladed VS 9 prop. But it was the first prototype to have the new 23.5 m² area negative twist wing which was to become standard for the Ta 152 H-0/H-1. During this period, both prototypes also received the new obligatory 500 mm rear fuselage parallel box extension and other specialized equipment.

As the end of the year neared, Focke-Wulf once again approached the Air Ministry seeking development priority for their Ta 152 A. By Christmas 1943, Kurt Tank had all but abandoned the Ta 153 and, instead, had focused his firm's energies toward the successful introduction, and phasing-in, of the Ta 152 A and B. But, there was a problem. The RLM's Technical Office stood solidly behind the Dora 9 and was extremely reticent to deviate from its endorsement. Although Tank had given the Air Ministry what they had demanded in July (a quick solution fighter), he openly viewed the Fw 190 D-9 as "only a stop-gap measure, until the improved Ta 152 appeared."

TWO MORE MESSERSCHMITTS FOR CHRISTMAS

As 1943 came to a close, Messerschmitt's prototype division was going full-tilt producing two additional aircraft just prior to Christmas. Both were completed against the Air Ministry requirement for a high performance escort day fighter (Me 209 V6) and their subsequent demand for a quick solution fighter (Bf 109 HV55). The first, the Me 209 V6, W. Nr. 410528, was flown for the first time on 22 December 1943. This was followed by the Bf 109 HV55, W. Nr. 15709, PV+IC which was completed on 23 December 1943, but not flown before the end of the year.

The Fw 190 V44, W. Nr. 855, utilized the airframe of a Fw 190 A-7 but was primarily used for a variety of range enhancing tests including the use of slipper-type auxiliary fuel tanks mounted above and aft on one (shown) or both wings. Note the extended pilot foot ladder. Normally this gravity activated aid was retracted by the ground crew pushing it upward just prior to take-off.

Chapter Four

1944 - Asset Management

INTRODUCTION

With the arrival of 1944, the war in Europe had been raging for over four years with no early end in sight. The Allied bombing offensive against Germany was having a measurable effect. For German planners within the Air Ministry, all production stops were pulled and yet many felt, with good reason, that even this would not be enough. New technological advances would have to be rushed into production as rapidly as possible. Short cuts had to be implemented wherever possible and new sources of fuel and labor would have to be developed rapidly. In addition, German air-defense planners were still dreading the arrival of America's high altitude super bombers.

END OF THE ROAD FOR THE Ta 153 AND Me 209

Early in the new year, the politically charged question of new aircraft procurement was revisited by the RLM's Technical Office. The long-standing dilemma surrounding the unresolved high performance Escort Day Fighter requirement finally came to a head on 13 January 1944. On this day, the Air Ministry made the bold decision to override Hitler's order issued the previous August, by simultaneously canceling both the Ta 153 and the Me 209. This time there would be no reversal. The order stood. Tank was instructed by the Air Ministry to concentrate on the Fw 190 D-9, in fulfillment of the Quick Solution mandate and to forge ahead with the Special High Altitude Fighter project, the Ta 152 H. He was also frustrated that no definite decision had been reached regarding the future of the Ta 152 A. It had been deferred indefinitely in spite of evidence supporting the performance superiority of the Ta 152 A over the similarly powered Fw 190 D-9.

Messerschmitt was not particularly happy either. Embittered by the Air Ministry's cancellation of his Me 209 A, and their selection of the Fw 190 D-9 over his Bf 109 H, he nevertheless continued selectively working on both. By this time however, regardless of the merits of these piston-engined fighter projects and their relevance to the war effort, they were on the verge of being eclipsed by the nascent German jet program.

Prof. Tank's assertion that the "Dora 9" was really only a "stop-gap" led him to vigorously lobby on behalf of the Ta 152 A. However, the RLM's Technical Office held the view that, apart from certain refinements exhibited by the Ta 152 A, there was no compelling difference between this new design and the Dora 9. In view of the *Luftwaffe*'s urgent need, the Air Ministry was, of course, correct in their analysis. Whatever justification existed for the Ta 152 A had simply been overtaken by events.

Although no Fw 190 prototypes were officially assigned to the Ta 152 A series, a trio of development aircraft was nevertheless involved in testing various features ulti-

mately intended for the Ta 152 A. These development aircraft included the Fw 190 V19, V20, and V21. It will be remembered that each of these engine development prototypes was originally scheduled to receive the DB 603 but this plan was rescinded allowing each prototype to be completed with the Jumo 213. All three prototypes were assembled from Fw 190 A-0 airframes and served exclusively as Jumo 213 development vehicles. Additionally, each of the three prototypes was also scheduled to test the newly designed exhaust flame suppression system that had been earmarked for Ta 153. Plans to install this equipment eventually migrated to the Ta 152 A. The primary rationale for this system was to aid nocturnal operations by shielding the pilot from the distracting bright flash created by the engine's hot exhaust. The design called for a long oval "stovepipe" to be attached over the Jumo's exhaust ports. This in turn was to be encased within a newly crafted smooth-surface outer cowl. The engine's hot exhaust gases were forced to the rear of the "stovepipe" by air passing first through the nose radiator and then channeled aft where it was discharged through a single egress located on either side of the cowl. Unfortunately, the system came with a speed penalty. While not large, it was nevertheless sufficient to warrant deletion of this feature for single-engine Focke-Wulf fighters.

The V19, V20, and V21 were also equipped with new tailplanes, rear fuselage extensions, and main undercarriage covers. Since the V21 was pressurized, it was also equipped with the new blown-type canopy. The wings of all three aircraft were standard Fw 190 A series but each incorporated hydraulic undercarriage actuation replacing the previous electric system.

Early in 1944, the Air Ministry issued instructions that all Ta 152 production efforts must be focused on the long span high altitude fighter with work on the heavily armed close-support series relegated to a lesser priority. Indeed, the Ta 152 B-1 was still not forecast to enter series production before September 1945! Concurrently, it was further decided that development of the Ta 152 E-1 photoreconnaissance fighter should proceed even though its production date was not yet finalized.

THE Fw 190 A-8 ENTERS PRODUCTION

During February 1944, the Fw 190 A-8 fighter entered production on Focke-Wulf's Bremen and Fieseler's Kassel assembly lines. This version of the legendary BMW 801-powered fighter was ultimately produced in larger numbers than any other variant, with some 2,300 being completed before the end of the war.

LAUNCHING THE Ta 152 HEINRICH

Since the end of 1943, Focke-Wulf's design bureau, with RLM approval, determined that the first Ta 152 H series

An American officer views a dozen brand new Fw 190 A-8s inside one of the damaged assembly halls of the Ago Flugzeugwerke (AGO – Aktiengesellschaft Otto / Joint Stock Company Otto) at Oschersleben soon after its capture. The missing roof is indicative of bomb damage. During 1943 and 1944, hundreds of 8th Air Force heavy bombers visited this factory no less than six times. The last raid was carried out on 11 April 1945 by medium and light bombers of the 9th Air Force. This factory was to have been the site of Ta 152 C-1 production but, even though Ago continued producing the Fw 190 A-8, (Werknummern in the 739000 block), up until the last hour, production of Ta 152 never materialized.

prototypes would not be new-build aircraft. Instead, to hasten development, it had been decided to transfer two *Höhenjäger* 2 prototypes directly to the Ta 152 H program. Both aircraft were modified by the removal of their *Känguruh* turbos and engines. The first, the Fw 190 V32, received a new 23.5 m² wing (without negative twist) and a newly produced DB 603 G engine driving a different Schwarz four-bladed wooden propeller. In this form it emerged as the Fw 190 V32/U1. Completed early in 1944, it was transferred to Focke-Wulf's testing facility at Langenhagen where its designer, Kurt Tank, was among those who put the new fighter through its paces.

The second machine, the Fw 190 V33, W. Nr. 0058, GH+KW, was more extensively modified at Focke-Wulf's Adelheide shops. In addition to fuselage and cockpit changes, this aircraft was to receive an early example of the Jumo 213 E engine plus the definitive 23.5 m² long span H series "twist" wing. However, development gremlins with the Jumo 213 E were taking longer to eradicate than expected and construction of the new "twist" wing, with its unique profile, also fell behind schedule. In its final form this prototype would henceforth be known as the Fw 190 V33/U1. On 16 February 1944, Jumo 213 testing was further set back when the Fw 190 V19 (aka Fw 190 Wb-1) was destroyed in a landing accident.

In the meantime, Daimler-Benz had been making sufficient progress with their new DB 603 L that Focke-Wulf ear-marked the Fw 190 V18/U1 as a test vehicle for this engine.

The V18/U1 was to be another H series test machine with the same alterations earlier carried out with the V33/U1.

USAAC BOMBING MISSION HITS MESSERSCHMITT HARD

On 25 February 1944, some 680 B-17s and B-24s from the U.S. Army Air Corps Eighth Air Force attacked Regensburg, Augsburg, Fürth, and a ball bearing plant in Stuttgart. This air attack was devastating and, among the aircraft losses was the second Bf 109 H series prototype, the Bf 109 HV55. In addition to the complete destruction of this aircraft, severe damage was inflicted on vital Me 209 A-4 components. This carefully planned bombing mission was mounted in conjunction with the Fifteenth Air Force's simultaneous attack on Regensburg and represented a major attempt to disrupt the delivery of new German fighters.

During this period, the *Luftwaffe* Planning Staff was astonished to learn that American Thunderbolts and Mustangs, equipped with fuel-laden auxiliary drop tanks, were now flying long-range fighter escort missions deep into Germany. Allied heavy bombers finally had their much-needed fighter escort all the way to the target and return. German defense strategy had not anticipated this new capability, which in their ignorance they had assumed to be impossible and were therefore greatly unprepared to meet this challenge.

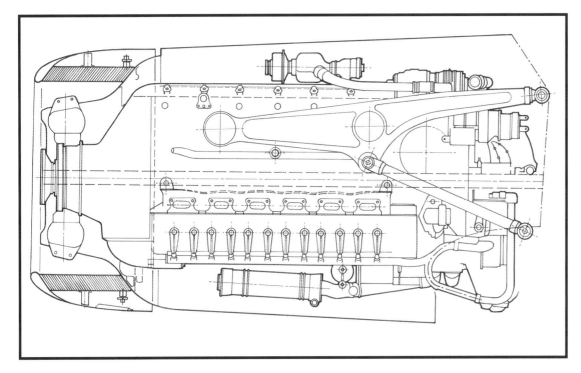

A simplified general arrangement elevation drawing of the port side of the Jumo 213 E, showing its engine bearer arm and ancillary equipment found within a Ta 152 cowl. The dotted lines running through the engine's center locates the hollow shaft for an engine-mounted cannon. The semi-complete circle next to the engine bearer arm represents the engine's supercharger intake located on the engine's starboard side.

This unusual Fw 190 A-8 or A-9 appears to have been equipped with a more powerful supercharged version of the BMW 801, perhaps a BMW 801 E or P 8035? Note the intake located near the wing root. It is also unclear if this particular aircraft was a prototype or production fighter.

THE *JÄGERSTAB* TAKES OVER

On 1 March 1944, an organization known as the *Jägerstab* (Fighter Staff) was established under the leadership of Albert Speer and Erhard Milch with Otto Saur as its executive officer. This new organization was tasked with overseeing future production of all fighters (both single and twin-engined types), fighter-bombers, dedicated ground-attack types, and short-range reconnaissance aircraft. The organization wielded immense power in pursuit of its mission. In keeping with its directive, the *Jägerstab* was responsible for coming to the aid of any aircraft factory that had been targeted by the Allies, and to take whatever measures were deemed necessary to ensure that future air attacks would result in as little damage and loss of life as possible.

As a byproduct of the extraordinary powers enjoyed by this organization, the *Jägerstab* eventually established itself as a primary partner in aircraft production planning.

THE Ta 152 BERTHA REVISITED

As recounted in Chapter 3, the proposed, short span Ta 152 B was a heavily-armed close-support fighter-bomber capable of carrying no less than seven aircraft cannon. Up to this time, the Air Ministry had shown only lukewarm interest in this particular design, largely because the RLM held the notion that fighter-bombers currently in production would be adequate. Nevertheless, Focke-Wulf continued refining the Ta 152 B based upon the latest operational situation. In this regard, on 24 March 1944, the planning department at Bad Eilsen clarified existing B series designations and established

new applications pending RLM approval. These were delineated thus:

1.) <u>Ta 152 B-1</u>	Jumo 213 C within an E cowling MK 108 engine cannon.
<u>This series starts first:</u>	
2.) <u>Ta 152 B-2</u>	Jumo 213 C with an E cowling MK 103 engine cannon
3.) <u>Ta 152 B-3</u>	Jumo 213 E MK 108 engine cannon
4.) <u>Ta 152 B-4</u>	Jumo 213 E MK 103 engine cannon

5.) The designation for aircraft having MG 151/20 cannon as the outer-wing weapons:

e.g., <u>Ta 152 B-1/R1</u>

With MK 108 as the outer-wing weapons:

e.g., <u>Ta 152 B-1/R2</u>

When the B-2, resp. B-3 or B-4, production begins is to be announced by a special committee [RLM ed.] after clarification of the weapons situation and engine delivery situation (the memorandum of 30 Dec 43 is overtaken with this).

It is not generally known, but early in 1944, Focke-Wulf was investigating the possibility of adapting the projected French Hispano-Suiza HS 24Z to the Ta 152. This large 24-cylinder, 72 liter engine, had been under protracted development in occupied France. Its cylinders were arranged in a vertical H-form and connected to co-axial shafts which drove two large contra-rotating propellers. Not completed until after the war, it was capable of developing 3,600 hp at 2,800 rpm for take-off and requiring aviation fuel of 100 – 130 octane. Shown here is the sole surviving example, now on public display in Paris at the Musée de l' Air. The engine employed two side-by-side single stage superchargers mounted to the rear of the block with each supplying 12 cylinders. The engine measured almost 11 feet long (3,341 mm), with a height of 4.6 feet (1,414 mm), a width of 3.7 feet (1,138 mm) and weighed a hefty 3,527 lbs (1,600 kg). Remarkably, its power-to-weight ratio was an ideal 0.98. Even if this remarkable powerplant had been available in time for the Ta 152, it is difficult to imagine how it could have been incorporated into the Ta 152's modest airframe.

Next page: A Ta 152 performance chart comparing the power output using three different engines with, and without, GM 1 power boosting

Kurve Nr.	Flugzeug Muster	Fluggewicht	Fläche	Motor	Motor-beanspruchung	Drehzahl	Ladedruck	Kraft-stoff	Bemerkungen			
–	–	kg	m²	–	–	U/min	ata	–	Motor	Rumpf	Flügel innen	Flügel außen
1	Ta 152	4600	19,5	Jumo 213 A-1	Start-und	3200	–	B4	1×Mk 108 (1+60Schuß)	2×MG 151 (2×175)	2×MG 151 (2×150)	2×Mk 108 (2×60)
2	Ta 152	4635	"	DB 603 G	Not-	2700	1,5/1,4	C3	"	"	"	"
3	Ta 152	4700	"	Jumo 213 E	leistung	3200	–	C3	"	"	"	"

Focke-Wulf Flugzeugbau G.m.b.H. Abt: Flugmechanik L

Horizontalgeschwindigkeit über der Flughöhe

Leistungsvergleich Ta 152

Motorleistungsangaben für: Jumo 213 A-1 nach Bl. Jumo 9-213-2030 13 vom 27.7.43.
DB 603 G nach Bl. DB 9-603-2115 vom 30.1.43.
Jumo 213 E nach Bl. Jumo 9-213-2028 13 vom 20.X.43.

Bei GM1 erhöht sich Fluggewicht um ΔG = 150 kg

DB 603 G
GM1 – ΔN = 320 PS
GM1 – ΔN = 280 PS
Jumo 213 E
Jumo 213 A-1
GM1 – ΔN = 135 PS
275 PS
415 PS

H (Km)
13
12
11
10
9
8
7
6
5
4
3
2
1
0

500   550   600   650   700   V (Km/h)

n J. 152.000 ~001

Datum: 4.9.43.

Bearbeiter: James

Ta 152 H-0	Preproduction series originally set at 115 aircraft but later scaled back to 40 examples (see Appendix 2) which were built at Focke-Wulf at Cottbus. Pressurized high altitude fighter with 23,5 m² wing. Standard engine and armament were the Jumo 213 E (Powerplant number 9-8213FH) driving a Junkers VS 9 wooden propeller (Part number 9-21036 C-0) and one engine-mounted MK 103 and two MG 151 cannon in the wing roots. Series lacked wing fuel tanks and the first aircraft with GM 1 was the 11th machine (W. Nr. 150011). No internal tankage for MW but two examples carried this power boosting fuel in a 300 ltr. drop tank mounted on an ETC 503 B-1 carrier. Eligible for *Rüstsätze* (Auxiliary apparatus): R11
Ta 152 H-1	Primary series pressurized high altitude fighter. Approximately 17 aircraft completed (see Appendix 2) by Focke-Wulf at Cottbus. Similar to the H-0 but having the definitive wing containing six fuel cells, of which the inboard port tank carried MW 50 power boosting fuel. GM 1 power boosting was contained in the rear fuselage cylindrical tank. Hydraulic flaps and undercarriage. Later, the VS 9 propeller would have been replaced by the wooden four-bladed VS 19 (Part number 9-21019 B-1). Main wheels were size 740 x 210, while the tail wheel was size 380 x 150. Electronics: FuG 16Zy, FuG 25a. Eligible for *Rüstsätze* (Auxiliary apparatus): R11, R21, R31
Ta 152 H-2	Pressurized high altitude fighter project identical to the H-1 but equipped with the improved FuG 15 Z and FuG 15 Zy "Christa" radio replacing the FuG 16Zy radio. Development of the FuG 15 began in the autumn of 1942, but two years later, with reliability issues unresolved and less than 200 examples manufactured, its operational deployment was stalled indefinitely. Production of the H-2 series was initially planned for Erla and Gotha beginning 1 March 1945 but, by 16 January 1945, this subtype had been canceled. Eligible for *Rüstsätze* (Auxiliary apparatus): R11
Ta 152 H-3	Provisionally: A pressurized high altitude fighter project based on the H-1 but powered by the Daimler-Benz DB 603 G (powerplant number: 9-8603 F) driving a three-bladed VDM propeller. In 1944 this series was deferred indefinitely.
Ta 152 H-4	Provisionally: A pressurized high altitude fighter project based on the H-2 with the promised FuG 15 Zy radio, and powered by the DB 603 G. Subtype deferred indefinitely after the DB 603 G program was canceled during 1944.
Ta 152 H-5	Provisionally: A pressurized high altitude fighter project based on the H-1 but powered by the Junkers Jumo 222 E driving a wooden four-bladed VS 19 propeller. To be fitted with a new 23,7 m² laminar profile wing without internal fuel tanks or MW 50. Armament was to consist of 2 x MG 151/20 (150 rpg) cowl cannon plus two MG 151/20 cannon (175 rpg) in the wing roots. An under-fuselage ETC 504 munitions rack was also planned. Production deferred.
Ta 152 H-6	Provisionally: A pressurized high altitude fighter project similar to the H-5 but equipped with a new 23,7 m² laminar profile wing with provision for internal storage of 240 liters of B4 aviation fuel and MW 50 carried in the fuselage. Electronics were to be the FuG 16 Zy, FuG 25a and FuG 125 "Hermine". Armament consisted of the 2 x MG 151/20 (cowl) plus 2 x MK 103 (55 rpg) cannon in the wing roots. Production deferred.
Ta 152 H-7	Provisionally: A pressurized high altitude fighter project similar to the H-1 but fitted with a Junkers Jumo 213 J engine. Unfortunately, Junkers only succeeded in producing six examples of this potent engine from January 1945 up to the war's end. The Jumo 213 J had a displacement of 37,5 liters (slightly larger than the Jumo 213 E's 35,0 liters), 4-valves per cylinder, double overhead cams and a two stage, three-speed supercharger with induction cooler of the Jumo 213 E. It was capable of 2,600 hp at 3,700 rpm at take-off and emergency at sea level. It produced 2,000 hp at 3,700 rpm at 8,1 km (26,600 ft).
Ta 152 H-8	Provisionally: A pressurized high altitude fighter project similar to the H-3 but powered by a DB 603 L or LA engine. Two prototypes, the Ta 152 V27, W. Nr. 150030, and the Ta 152 V28, W. Nr. 150031, were to be completed in 1945 with DB 603/B1/TEA (DB 603 Es) engines equipped with the MK 103M engine-mounted cannon. Although these two prototypes were "officially" referred to as development aircraft for the Ta 152 C-3, in reality they bore little resemblance to the short wing C-3 apart from their engine cannon. Instead, they were hybrids whose true series identity was apparently purposely masked from the RLM because of the emergency fighter program prohibition against the introduction "new" aircraft.
Ta 152 H-9	Provisionally: A pressurized high altitude fighter project similar to the H-8 but equipped with the FuG 15 Zy radio and powered by a DB 603 L or LA engine (resp. powerplant numbers 9-8603/B1/TL and 9-8603/B1/TLA). Because deliveries of the FuG 15 radio could not be guaranteed, this subtype was deferred indefinitely. As with the H-8, the Ta 152 V27 and V28 would have served as development prototypes.
Ta 152 H-10	High altitude photoreconnaissance fighter based on the Ta 152 H-0 (without wing fuel tanks) and was the result of a designation rationalization policy whereby the designation of the identical Ta 152 E-2 was dropped in favor of the Ta 152 H-10. The E-2/H-10 specification called for any one of several possible cameras including the Rb 20/30, Rb 50/30 or the Rb 75/30 aerial reconnaissance camera. Since there was no internal provision for MW power boosting, a 300 liter drop tank carrying B4 fuel or MW was an optional alternative. Production with Mimetall at Erfurt canceled 15 March 1945 in favor of the H-11. Eligible for *Rüstsätze* (Auxiliary apparatus): R11
Ta 152 H-11	High altitude photoreconnaissance fighter similar to the Ta 152 E-2 / H-10 but based on the Ta 152 H-1 (with wing fuel tanks) and capable of carrying the same camera options as the H-10. Production of the first machines at Mimetall Erfurt had reached an advanced stage by the war's end. Eligible for *Rüstsätze* (Auxiliary apparatus): R11
Ta 152 H-12	High altitude photoreconnaissance fighter based on the Ta 152 H-2 (with FuG 15 radio) and equipped with the same camera options as the H-10. This subtype was deferred indefinitely after the similarly equipped H-2 was canceled on 15 December 1944.

Ta 152 H Auxiliary Apparatus (*Rüstsätze*) Equipment
(Applicable for Jumo 213 equipped aircraft)

R11 - Bad weather fighter fitted with LGW K23 fighter directional control; FuG 125 "Hermine", VHF radio beacon signal receiver; heated windows and PKS 12 autopilot. The entire Ta 152 H-1 production was to be quipped with R11 from the first aircraft.

R21 - Special version with high pressure MW 50 in the port wing inboard fuel tank, PKS 12 autopilot and FuG 125 "Hermine". Besides the standard Jumo 213 E stage, the Jumo 213 E-1 or EB versions were optional alternatives as production moved forward. GM 1 power boost was not installed. This equipment package was originally planned for March, April and May 1945.

R31 - Modification to address center of gravity concerns. The designated engine for this version was the Jumo 213 E-1 with high-pressure MW 50 injection or the similar EB engine the pressurized air bottles for the GM 1 power boosting system were removed from the engine bay while the necessary propellant pressure was now generated by the E-1 engine in place on the air bottles, ballast of steel plates were added. The 85 liters of GM 1 was unaffected and remained in the usual location aft of fuselage seam 8.

In addition to the above listed equipment options, a few novel anti-bomber weapons were planned or, under test, for eventual use by the Ta 152 H including: (a) wing-mounted vertically firing SG 500 *Jägerfaust* (Fighter's Fist) projectiles. Five of these 50 mm projectiles were installed vertically, in rifled barrels arranged in a line parallel to the fuselage and contained within the wing in the space normally occupied by the center fuel cell. The shells were fired by means of a photo-cell trigger when flying under a bomber. (b) Similar to the SG 500 installation, was a device known as the *Rohrbock* 108 (Barrel Ram) which was comprised of two MK 108 gun barrels set vertically in the same location and manner as the SG 500 but fired by the pilot using a specially modified gun sight as the fighter flew beneath a bomber. Each of the two barrels per wing held only one 30 mm round. (c) Two X-4 (Ru 344) air-to-air wire-guided rockets mounted on underwing pylons and launched from a safe distance beyond a bomber's defensive fire. Their flight path was somewhat controlled by the pilot using a small joystick control whose signals were transmitted through a spool of wire that unwound when the missile was launched.

Ta 152 E-2 HIGH ALTITUDE RECONNAISSANCE FIGHTER

In accordance with the 1942 Special High Altitude Fighter specification, which called for a secondary mission requirement of aerial reconnaissance, it was predetermined that a short-range high altitude reconnaissance fighter version of the Ta 152 H would be developed. The result was the Ta 152 E-2. It will be recalled that the proposed Ta 152 E-1 was to be a short span (19,5 m² wing) reconnaissance fighter fitted with any one of a number of aerial reconnaissance cameras, standard armament, and powered by a Jumo 213 E driving a VS 9 propeller. For the time being, the Ta 152 E-1's priority level was relatively low pending issuance of an RLM construction order.

Apart from its wing, the Ta 152 E-2 was very similar to the E-1. It was to carry the same armament and electronic equipment as the Ta 152 E-1, but patterned after the H series with the long span (23,5 m²) wing. Unlike the E-1, the Ta 152 E-2 was to carry both GM 1 and MW power boosting systems in essentially the same manner as the Ta 152 H-1. Like the E-1, the E-2 was to be equipped with an ETC 503 rack for an under-fuselage auxiliary fuel tank. This 300 ltr tank could alternatively be fueled with MW 50 or B4 aviation fuel depending on the aircraft's mission. The designated powerplant was the Jumo 213 E driving a wooden three-bladed Junkers VS 9 propeller. Aerial reconnaissance cameras Rb 75/30, Rb 50/30, and Rb 20/30 were the preferred cameras of choice and were to be installed in the field. In addition, to aid the pilot in identifying the mission target, each aircraft was to be fitted with a *Durchblickfernrohr* 67G periscope system employing a straight-through tube extending vertically from the cockpit, through the floor to exit the fuselage underside. However, this rather complicated solution, which further compromised the airtightness of the pressurized cabin, was dropped in favor of a field installed ZFR (*Zielfernrohr* – Telescopic Sight) sight embedded in the top cowling at the windshield. These sights were generally not suited for gunnery use, but instead served to assist the pilot in locating and approaching his objective well in advance of target over flight.

Both the Ta 152 E-1 and E-2 were deferred only until production of the Ta 152 H had begun. In this respect it was anticipated that the first preproduction example would be flight ready in September with production commencing jointly at Ago's Oschersleben (Ta 152 E-1) factory and the Mimetall Erfurt North (Ta 152 E-2) plants in February 1945.

The singularly attractive Fw 190 V32/U1, W. Nr. 0057, GH+KV, as it appeared, unarmed, during the winter of 1943-1944. It is shown here following removal of its disappointing **Höhenjäger 2** equipment, including the so-called Kangaroo turbo pouch. At this time, the original 18.3 m² wing was removed and replaced by a new long span wing having an area of 23.5 m² but without negative twist. In addition, it was also ferried to Daimler-Benz where it received an early example of the DB 603 G, without turbo, plus the newly approved rear fuselage extension. Many historians have claimed the V32/U1 in this new form was really a shortcut to the Ta 153. This is only partly true. The fact is, by the time the V32/U1 emerged from Focke-Wulf and Daimler-Benz workshops, the Ta 153 had already been canceled. However, it is equally true, that had the V32/U1 flown with the DB 603 G six months earlier, it could indeed have been legitimately con-

strued to be a prototype for the Ta 153. Before the end of the war, the Fw 190 V32/U1 would undergo two additional successive modifications. In September 1944, its Daimler-Benz engine was exchanged for a new Jumo 213 E plus VS 9 prop, emerging as the Fw 190 V32/U2. In October 1944, it exchanged its long span wings for those originally earmarked for the stillborn Ta 152 V25. This final wing had the same surface area, but was built to Ta 152 H-1 standards, incorporated negative twist and having provision for internal fuel storage. Then early 1945, it was once again returned to the workshops to be fitted with a prototype of the remarkable MK 213 engine-mounted cannon. Finally, in April 1945, it ended its days abandoned at Reinsehlen airfield. Whether or not it was purposely destroyed at Reinsehlen, a fate suffered by other German aircraft on this field (see page 165), remains open to speculation.

RESHUFFLING Ta 152 H PROTOTYPES

By March 1944, Focke-Wulf decided to modify the two remaining *Höhenjäger 2* aircraft to H standards in order to expedite construction of Ta 152 H prototypes adding these to the three already allocated. This meant the first five Ta 152 H series prototypes were essentially rebuilt examples of existing hardware. Thus, Focke-Wulf's early plans to build the first five prototypes (Ta 152 V1 – V5) at Sorau, having *Werknummern* 110001 – 110005, as new build aircraft were effectively canceled. In their place were the following prototypes:

Prototype	Werk Nr.	Stkz	New designation
Fw 190 V33	W. Nr. 0058	GH+KW	Fw 190 V33/U1
Fw 190 V30	W. Nr. 0055	GH+KT	Fw 190 V30/U1
Fw 190 V29	W. Nr. 0054	GH+KS	Fw 190 V29/U1
Fw 190 V18/U1	W. Nr. 0040	CF+OY	Fw 190 V18/U2
Fw 190 V32/U1	W. Nr. 0057	GH+KV	Fw 190 V32/U2

In order to bring these aircraft up to Ta 152 H standards, each required extensive modification. This process called for the removal of their existing engines, oil and cooling systems, turbos and wings (excluding the V32). It was anticipated that all five aircraft would be modified, cleared for flight and ready for testing between June and September 1944.

FOCKE-WULF WEIGHS ENGINE OPTIONS

During the first half of 1944, Focke-Wulf worked closely with representatives from the aero engine industry exploring suitable powerplant options for the Ta 152 in general, and specifically the Ta 152 H. Even though the Jumo 213 E was the designated engine of choice for the first production model, a variety of other engines were seriously considered. Among the high performance powerplants under discussion were the BMW 801 R, the DB 603 G, DB 603 N, DB 603 L, the Junkers Jumo 213 J, Jumo 222 A/B-3, Jumo 222 E/F and the French Hispano-Suiza HS 24Z. The latter powerplant project had caught Prof. Tank's attention because it, like the projected DB 632, was a powerful high performance engine equipped with coaxial contra-rotating propellers. In addition to these engines, BMW advanced their P 8035 primarily based upon the company's BMW 801 E but equipped with a variable speed turbo. In theory accommodating this engine within the Ta 152's airframe would have been relatively straightforward but undoubtedly would have negatively impacted the aircraft's center of gravity which, in turn, would have necessitated further engineering man-hours and obligatory airframe modification.

The other engine offered by BMW was the firm's newly proposed hybrid BMW 801 R. Peter Kappus explains:

When it became clear that no production facilities could be made available for the all new BMW 805, it was decided to try instead to equip the BMW 801 E with as many of the advanced design features of the BMW 805 as possible. The resulting version was known as the BMW 801 R. It was rated at 2,000 hp at sea level and 1,400 hp at 11,000 m (36,089 ft). Like the BMW 805, it had a two stage, four-speed supercharger, inter and after coolers and even automatically controlled variable intake guide vanes for the cooling fan.

All of this equipment resulted in an engine whose overall length of 2,741 mm (8 ft 11⅞ in) was 735 mm (29 inches) longer than the standard BMW 801! But, when compared to the liquid-cooled Jumo 213 E, the BMW unit was longer by only 304 mm (12 in) and, against the DB 603 G, its overall length was greater by a mere 61 mm (2⅜ in). Flight calculations of a Ta 152 C, powered by the BMW 801 R, indicated its maximum speed would have been in the area of 442 mph (711 km/h) at 38,400 ft (11,704 m) while the aircraft's climb rate would have been very respectable, reaching an altitude of 36,000 ft (10,973 m) in 11.7 minutes.

Of the three engine possibilities from Daimler-Benz, it was decided to concentrate on the DB 603 G and DB 603 L. As recounted earlier, the Fw 190 V32/U1 had been equipped with an early example of the DB 603 G. This engine, outwardly similar to the DB 603 A and D, incorporated a number of performance enhancing features and special equipment. These included increased compression ratios (8.3:1 left bank, 8.5:1 right bank) reliance upon C3 aviation fuel, a faster running supercharger and having a greater critical altitude. At 2,700 rpm it developed 1,900 hp for take off. This engine employed a VDM 9-13030 V1 propeller assembly and was also capable of accepting the Messerschmitt Me P 8 reversible pitch propeller.

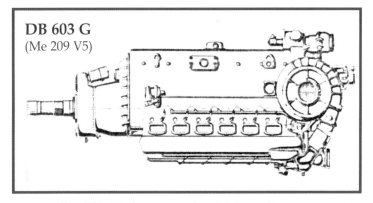

DB 603 G
(Me 209 V5)

The DB 603 L was another high performance engine generally similar to the DB 603 E but utilizing certain altitude enhancing features. To flight-test this new engine, in conjunction with the Ta 152 H program, it was initially planned to modify the Fw 190 V18/U1 for this task. The DB 603 L employed a new two stage supercharger of increased diameter with intercooler and equipped with automatic propeller control. In addition, the DB 603 L's take off power was rated at 2,000 hp at 2,700 rpm. The DB 603 L also required C3 aviation fuel of at least 96 octane.

Development of the high performance DB 603 N lagged behind the DB 603 L, upon which it was based. Its cylinders were redesigned, resulting in a slight increase in engine rpm. One of the unusual features of the 'N' engine was its ability to use various arrangements of supercharger gearing. It had a mechanically driven low gear supercharger

and hydraulic coupling for high gear. Using C3 fuel, it was rated at 2,830 hp at 3,000 rpm for take off with a service ceiling of 36,089 ft (11,000 m).

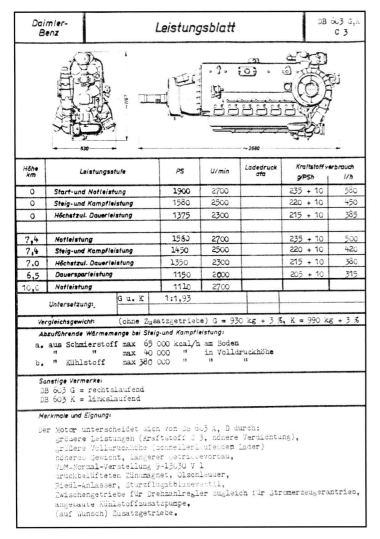

Ta 152 H-0 TO H-12

The Ta 152 H series chart on page 78 lists six known and confirmed subtypes plus seven additional marks (Ta 152 H-3 through H-9) of the Heinrich series for which no official record has been discovered. The author believes this stated series delineation, though speculative and based upon circumstantial evidence, is undoubtedly very close to Focke-Wulf's definitive series lineup. Nevertheless, it should be noted that the allocations for the H-3 through H-9 are provisional. The author's arrangement of the DB 603 G, Jumo 222 E/F, Jumo 213 J, and DB 603 L within the chart is predicated on precedent and an established timeline. Placing the Jumo 222 E/F within the lineup is more ambiguous because this engine continued to enjoy the Air Ministry's favor over a long period in spite of its protracted development history. In contrast, the DB 603 L, which appeared late in the war, was an engine which enjoyed a decidedly definite future.

During the first half of 1944, Daimler-Benz was actively engaged in the development of their DB 603 G and DB 632

A; two engines contained within the original Ta 152 Ra-2 prospectus. But whereas the DB 603 G was planned for series production, the complex DB 632 A, with its co-axial contra-rotating propellers, was not. The DB 632 was essentially an advanced development of the DB 603 N which, in turn, incorporated features from the DB 603 L.

On 21 July and 5 September 1944, hundreds of U.S. bombers attacked targets in the Stuttgart area, including Daimler-Benz, with deadly precision. Whether coincident or not, during this time period plans to mass produce the DB 603 G were unexpectedly abandoned.

Development of the advanced Junkers Jumo 213 J began in the autumn of 1942, but it was not until January 1945 that Junkers produced a working prototype. This 37,5 liter engine was characterized by having 4 valves per cylinder and a two stage, three speed supercharger with intercooler. It was to utilize B4 fuel in conjunction with MW 50 power boosting and capable of developing 2,600 hp at 3,700 rpm at sea level. By the war's end Junkers had only succeeded in producing less than ten examples of the Jumo 213 J.

The Junkers Jumo 222 was an exotic powerplant that had been under continuous development for seven years. It was a highly ambitious project, offering the promise of truly outstanding performance unlike anything then currently available. But, in the end, only 286 test examples of this remarkable engine were manufactured, and the type ultimately failed to enter series production. Nevertheless, the RLM and aviation industry placed great expectations with this engine which they believed would eventually deliver its designed performance.

Essentially, the Jumo 222 was a 24-cylinder multi-bank liquid-cooled radial. It had six banks with four cylinders, each arranged equally about a central crankshaft. Kurt Tank was an enthusiastic supporter of this engine which he planned to install in the Ta 152 H, the preferred variant being the Jumo 222 E. The 'E' engine had right hand rotation while the 'F' had left hand rotation. The Jumo 222 E/F was generally similar to the Jumo 222 AB-3 (also with right and left hand rotation) and was intended for high altitude operation. The 'E/F' engine carried a displacement of 55,5 ltr and featured a two stage supercharger with aftercooler. Using B4 aviation fuel of 87 octane, the Jumo 222 E/F was officially rated at 2,500 hp at 3,000 rpm for take off and 1,680 hp at 2,700 rpm at 36,000 ft (10,973 m). The RLM's Technical Office eventually decided that unless the Jumo 222 E/F could routinely produce 3,000 hp, the project should be dropped. Although Junkers tried to boost performance, it remained elusive. Using MW 50 power boost, at least one example did succeed in developing 2,900 hp. Hans Sander recalled, "I flew the 222 with 2,000 hp in the Fw 191 (a twin-engine bomber-Ed), but we never did get much more out of it." In fairness, test pilot Sanders's experience with the Jumo 222 in the experimental Fw 191 occurred over a year earlier during the spring of 1943, fitted with Jumo 222 A/B-2 engines.

The Ta 152 H with the Jumo 222 E would have incorporated a number of new components complementary but distinct from other H series variants. Up front, a large wooden four-bladed Junkers VS 19 propeller, having a diameter of

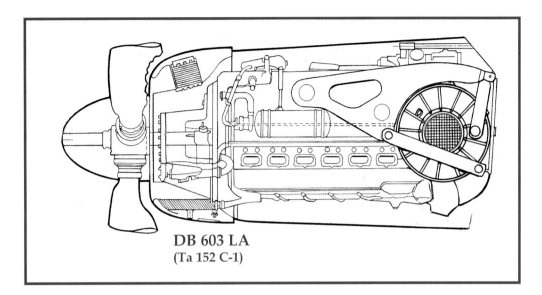

DB 603 LA
(Ta 152 C-1)

3,600 mm (11 ft 9¾ in), would have been installed. Apart from the engine cowling, the aircraft's fuselage and tailplane would have been virtually identical to the Ta 152 H-1. Provision for MW 50 power boosting was included, but not GM 1. The aircraft would have been equipped with the advanced EZ 42 gun sight, 740 x 210 main wheels, and electronics consisting of FuG 16ZY, FuG 25a plus FuG 125 "Hermine." Surprisingly, Prof. Tank planned to use an entirely new wing of laminar flow airfoil. This new wing was 760 mm (30 in) shorter than the H-1's wingspan, and only maintained its laminar profile from the wing root outward to the attachment point of the landing gear. A Ta 152 H equipped with the Jumo 222 E would have been a very high performance fighter with pull-out loads of six Gs. Fully loaded, the maximum take off weight, would have been 12,820 lb (5,815 kg), or 1,092 lb (495 kg) heavier than the take off weight for the standard Ta 152 H-1.

Two armament options were planned for the Ta 152 H with the Jumo 222 E. The first option included two MG 151/20 cannon mounted in the cowl having 150 rpg plus two similar weapons at the wing root position, each having 175 rpg. The second option would have swapped the wing root cannon for the larger caliber MK 103 having only 55 rpg. In addition, a fuselage mounted ETC 504 bomb rack could have been fitted. Depending on availability, the aircraft's standard Revi 16 B gun sight could have been replaced with the new EZ 42.

With the proliferation of Ta 152 series and model designations during this period, Focke-Wulf instituted a designation rationalization policy with regard to its aerial reconnaissance fighters. It will be recalled that the Ta 152 E series (E-0, E-1, E-2), was an outgrowth of the stillborn Fw 190 E recon-

naissance fighter which had been advanced in compliance with the original RLM requirement specification for the Ta 152 H. The Ta 152 E-0/E-1 series was short span versions powered by the Jumo 213 E, but the proposed Ta 152 E-2 and Ta 152 E-2/R11 were long span versions based on the Ta 152 H-0.

The RLM's confidence in the Ta 152 E-2/R11 is illustrated by the fact that no less than 230 examples were to be built by Mimetall between March and July 1945. But, apart from obligatory internal changes for the requisite cameras, the Ta 152 E-2 and E-2/R11 were, for all intents and purposes, identical to the Ta 152 H-0 and H-0/R11 respectively. Therefore, as part of Focke-Wulf's rationalization policy, it was decided to contain the Ta 152 E-2 program and designation under the H series umbrella. Thus, the Ta 152 E-2 was henceforth redesignated Ta 152 H-10. Simultaneously, the Ta 152 H-11 was established as a reconnaissance version of the Ta 152 H-1 while the Ta 152 H-12 reconnaissance fighter was similarly based on the Ta 152 H-2.

Ta 152 C, CONTENDER FOR THE STANDARD ESCORT DAY FIGHTER?

In March 1944, Focke-Wulf proposed a short span (19,5 m² wing) nonpressurized fighter having the fuselage and tailplane of the Ta 152 H, but powered by the promised DB 603 L. Known as the Ta 152 C-1, it was to be essentially a Ta 152 A without the flame suppression feature, but fitted with a revised wing and powered, at least initially, by a Daimler-Benz engine in lieu of the Jumo. Like the Ta 152 A, the Ta 152 C series was to have been heavily armed with a battery of no

The DB 603 L was equipped with a two stage supercharger with aftercooler designed to lower the temperature of the fuel/air mixture. This engine was rated at 1,820 hp at 2,700 rpm for take off and required C3 fuel. The DB 603 LA engine (A – Änderungs – Alteration) was simpler and was to precede the DB 603 L. The LA engine dispensed with the aftercooler but achieved cooling of the supercharger's compressed fuel/air mixture by MW 50 injection. However, the MW was only to be used for take off and brief periods of war emergency power owing to the high rate of consumption. This engine was alternatively known as the DB 603 LM (M – Methanol).

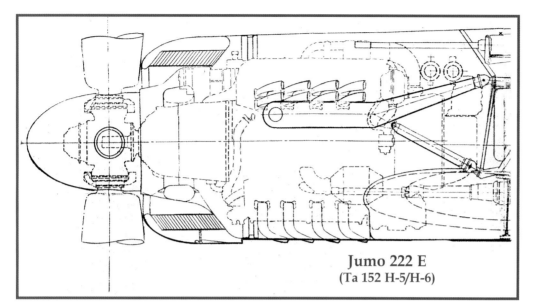

Jumo 222 E
(Ta 152 H-5/H-6)

*General Specification for the Junkers
Juno 222 E*

<u>Type</u>: *Twenty-four cylinder star pattern
six bank liquid-cooled high performance
engine of 55.5 liters with a two stage
supercharger and aftercooler*

<u>Length</u>: *ca 2,753 mm (9.03 ft)*; <u>Height</u>: *ca
1,242 mm (4.08 in)*; <u>Width</u>: *1,160 mm (3.81
in)*; <u>Weight</u>: *2,476 kg (5,459 lbs) [includes
the complete cowled engine]*

<u>Performance</u>: *Take-off and Emergency
2,500 hp at 3,000 rpm at sea level, 1930 hp
at 3,000 rpm at 8,992 m (29,500 ft). Climb
2,220 hp at 2,700 rpm at sea level or 1,680
hp at 2,700 rpm at 11,811 m (36,000 ft).*

less than six 20 mm cannon plus one 30 mm MK 108 (later MK 103) engine-mounted cannon. In addition, the outer wing MG 151/20 cannon could be replaced by MK 108s. Production of this model was forecast for the end of July 1944. Officially classified as a *Normaljäger* (Normal Fighter) it nevertheless represented the definitive Standard Escort Day Fighter the *Luftwaffe* had long been seeking. Not as high flying as the Ta 152 H, the C series was expected to operate efficiently between 19,685 ft (6,000 m) and 32,808 ft (10,000 m). By the middle of March, the RLM authorized the release of a "dozen new DB 603 L engines for use in the Ta 152 and Ta 154 programs."

Ironically, only one of these engines was earmarked for the Ta 152 program and, within this framework, it was relegated to the development of suitable engine fairings. It is also ironic that a DB 603-powered Ta 154 never existed. However, a progressive development of the *Moskito* (Mosquito), known as the Ta 254 B, was to utilize the DB 603 L. Though eventually approved for production, the Ta 254 B series (B-1 to B-3) progressed no further than a wooden mockup. The apparent anomaly surrounding this engine's distribution priority appears to suggest a certain degree of subterfuge on the part of Focke-Wulf.

Meanwhile, Focke-Wulf at Bad Eilsen had received blueprints and performance projections from Munich for the BMW 801 R (correctly identified as the BMW 801 TR – *Triebwerksanlage* / Power Installation complete with mounts and exhaust stacks). It is unknown if BMW succeeded in fabricating any working examples of this new engine, apart from mockups. Nevertheless, a new version of the short wing Ta 152 C series, powered by the BMW 801 R, was allocated and slotted into the Ta 152 production lineup.

During this period in March 1944, the *Luftwaffe's* Technical Office conducted comparison studies contrasting the twin-engined, single-seat Dornier Do 335 with the Ta 152. The subject of inquiry was the unorthodox but highly promising creation from Oberpfaffenhofen, the Do 335 *Pfeil* (Arrow) and whether it was preferable to the Ta 152. The Do 335 was a large airplane. As a single-seat fighter, it sat unusually high upon a fully retractable tricycle undercarriage, and was unique in its engine arrangement. Having a DB 603 in the nose and tail, it was capable of maintaining flight on only one engine, and was arguably the fastest propeller driven aircraft of the Second World War. The Technical Report determined that the Do 335 would be 18.5 to 54.1 mph (30 to 87 km/h)

Shown here on public display at the Deutsches Museum in Munich, is an example of the Junkers Jumo 222 E/U2. This particular engine was acquired by American forces at the end of the war and ultimately given to the National Air and Space Museum. It has recently been returned to Germany for long term display. This 1944 engine was equipped with a two-stage supercharger and aftercooler and primarily intended for high altitude operations. This engine was also earmarked for several German aircraft types including the Ta 152 H and the **Hütter Hü 211.** *The Jumo 222 E/F was officially rated at 2,500 hp at 3,000 rpm for take off driving a large wooden 4-bladed Junkers VS 19 propeller having a diameter of almost 12 feet. Unfortunately for the Germans, the engine failed to live up to expectations and series production never materialized.*

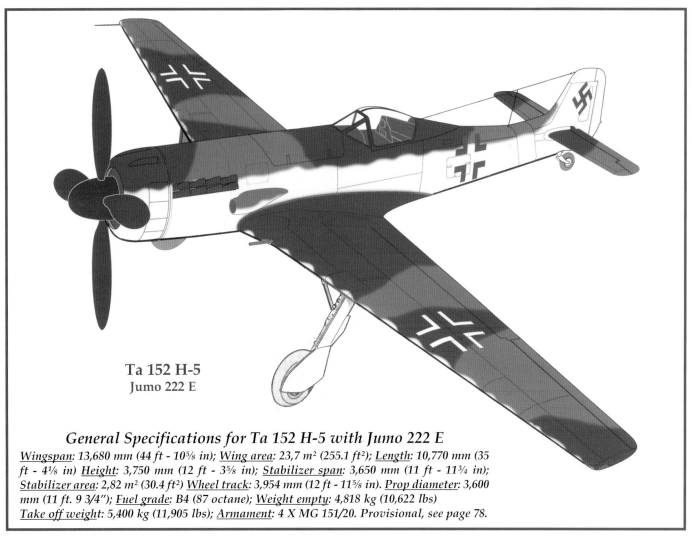

Ta 152 H-5
Jumo 222 E

General Specifications for Ta 152 H-5 with Jumo 222 E

Wingspan: 13,680 mm (44 ft - 10⅝ in); *Wing area:* 23,7 m² (255.1 ft²); *Length:* 10,770 mm (35 ft - 4⅛ in) *Height:* 3,750 mm (12 ft - 3⅝ in); *Stabilizer span:* 3,650 mm (11 ft - 11¾ in); *Stabilizer area:* 2,82 m² (30.4 ft²) *Wheel track:* 3,954 mm (12 ft - 11⅝ in). *Prop diameter:* 3,600 mm (11 ft. 9 3/4"); *Fuel grade:* B4 (87 octane); *Weight empty:* 4,818 kg (10,622 lbs) *Take off weight:* 5,400 kg (11,905 lbs); *Armament:* 4 X MG 151/20. Provisional, see page 78.

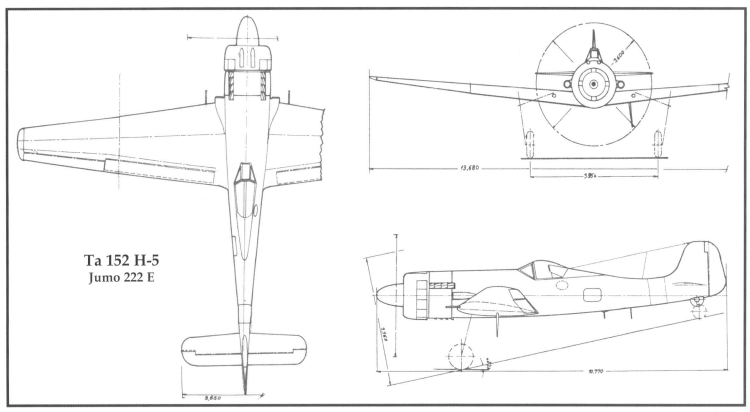

Ta 152 H-5
Jumo 222 E

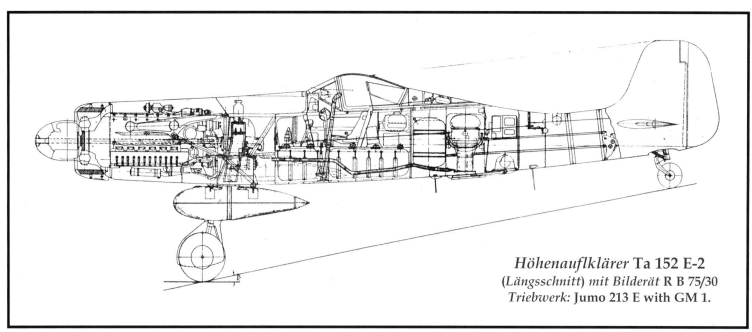

Höhenauflklärer **Ta 152 E-2**
(*Längsschnitt*) *mit Bilderät* R B 75/30
Triebwerk: **Jumo 213 E with GM 1.**

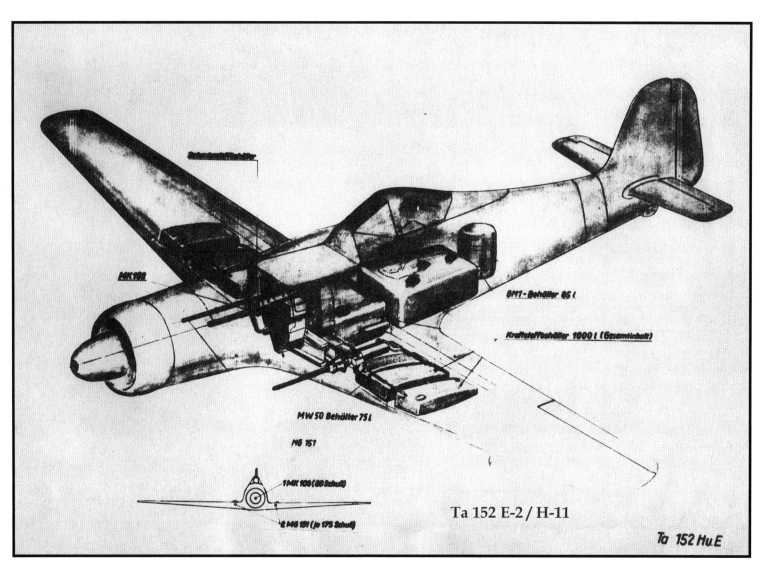

Ta 152 E-2 / H-11

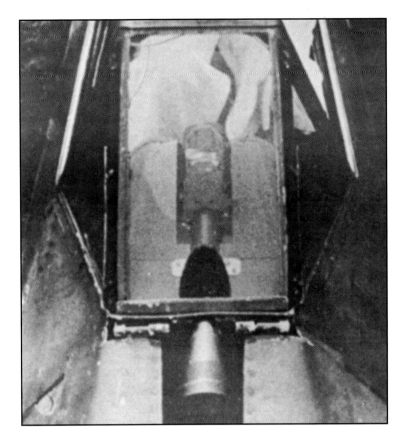

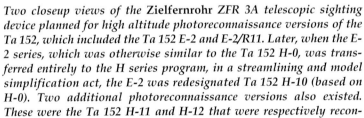

Two closeup views of the **Zielfernrohr ZFR 3A** telescopic sighting device planned for high altitude photoreconnaissance versions of the Ta 152, which included the Ta 152 E-2 and E-2/R11. Later, when the E-2 series, which was otherwise similar to the Ta 152 H-0, was transferred entirely to the H series program, in a streamlining and model simplification act, the E-2 was redesignated Ta 152 H-10 (based on H-0). Two additional photoreconnaissance versions also existed. These were the Ta 152 H-11 and H-12 that were respectively recon-

naissance versions of the H-1 and H-2. However, since the Ta 152 H-2 had earlier been canceled, so too was its photorecon version, the Ta 152 H-12 and, when production of the Ta 152 H-0 ceased in early 1945, plans to produce the Ta 152 H-10 were also shelved, leaving only the Ta 152 H-11 (see p 97) as the remaining high altitude photoreconnaissance version eligible for the ZFR telescopic sight. The two images shown here depict an Fw 190 A-8 equipped with the ZFR system.

Another piece of camera equipment routinely carried by the Ta 152 was the small Robot single frame camera. Rigidly mounted inboard on a special tray located in the port wing's leading edge, and accessible through a pop-up hinged cover, the Robot camera was activated

by the pilot depressing a switch mounted on the throttle. The resulting photographs were not necessarily high resolution, but were of sufficient quality for trained photo interpreters to gain vital information on selected ground targets.

The first Dornier Do 335 prototype in flight running on both front and rear engines. A large airplane, but exceedingly fast, its performance was evaluated against the Ta 152. Below: A perspective illustration of Messerschmitt's high altitude fighter the Me 209 HV1 as it would have appeared upon completion. It utilized parts from several Messerschmitt fighters.

faster than the Ta 152 at all altitudes with the same armament of a single 30 mm and two 20 mm cannon. Of course, the primary difference between these two designs was the fact that the Dornier was substantially more complex, required two engines, and therefore, more man-hours to construct. Piloting skills required for successfully handling the Do 335 would also have been more exacting. Take off and landing techniques required more than just a single familiarization flight in order not to damage the aircraft's cruciform tailplane. Finally, although the Do 335 was ordered into limited production, fewer than seventy were completed before the war's end.

THE *JÄGERSTAB* AND EASTER 1944

In keeping with the *Jägerstab*'s mandate to aid aircraft factories in their efforts to better prepare defenses, this organization issued orders directing that blast pens were to be provided for aircraft while similar blast walls were to be built around valuable machine tools. They further directed that fireproof walls were to replace all wooden structures, and proper storage facilities had to be provided for all flammable materials. In addition, factories were instructed to deploy their own fire brigades at a safe distance to ensure their survival in an attack. On April 4 and 5, the *Jägerstab*'s leaders, Speer and Milch, paid a surprise visit to four major Focke-Wulf factories located at Cottbus, Marienburg, Posen (now Poznan, Poland), and Sorau (now Zary, Poland). These sites were selected primarily because it had become known that Focke-Wulf's compliance with *Jägerstab* regulations was frequently spotty at best.

As a result of this inspection, a round-the-clock work schedule was immediately instituted to ensure complete compliance. Good Friday and Easter holidays were summarily canceled. The factory labor force was understandably disappointed but understood the gravity of the situation and energetically obeyed the order.

Four days later on Easter Sunday, 9 April 1944, 399 B-17s and B-24s bombed aircraft factories and airfields in Germany and

Poland. Singled out were the Focke-Wulf plants at Marienburg and Posen. A total of 98 heavy bombers attacked Marienburg while 33 Flying Fortresses dumped their bombs on Posen. Cottbus and Sorau were spared this time. As a direct result of the *Jägerstab*'s intervention, actual bomb damage was approximately only 50 percent of what the factories might otherwise have sustained.

A MAKESHIFT MESSERSCHMITT?

Earlier in the year, Messerschmitt had hoped to get his new high altitude Me 209 A-4 airborne no later than February 1944. However, the Allied bombing attack on Regensburg had damaged or destroyed vital components intended for this fighter, thereby jeopardizing the whole program. It will be recalled that this high altitude fighter project was to have been powered by a 1,685 hp DB 628. After the attack, and recognizing the urgency attached to the project, Messerschmitt's *projektburo* decided to expedite matters by assigning the undamaged Me 209 V5 to the high altitude program, which, it will be recalled, had been marginalized earlier by the Air Ministry. This plan required modification of the

Me 209 HV1

American daylight heavy bombing raids during April and May 1944 were costly for both sides; nevertheless the attacks seriously disrupted German aircraft production. Focke-Wulf plants at Cottbus and Sorau were hard hit. The scene in this photograph was repeated many times throughout Germany. German air defenses were formidable including well equipped and trained Flak batteries that frequently exacted a heavy toll of attacking bombers. Occasionally, losses were as high as 8 percent of the attacking force.

Me 209 V5's airframe. Re-christened Me 209 H-1, in a clear attempt to link the project's series letter with the aircraft's stated mission, reconstruction of this first high altitude prototype proceed rapidly.

The Me 209 H-1 had been formulated around an engine derived from the DB 603 known as the DB 627 B. This 2,000 hp powerplant was broadly based upon the DB 603 G but equipped with a two stage mechanical supercharger plus intercooler. However, because Daimler-Benz felt this engine's power output was only slightly better than the DB 603 G, and in view of the firm's already stretched resources, in March 1944, management prudently decided to halt further development of this high altitude engine. This decision compelled Messerschmitt to stick with the slightly less powerful (1,900 hp) but simpler DB 603 G.

In addition to a new engine, cowling, and propeller, a more efficient cooling system was designed, reminiscent of the layout fielded by the British Mosquito. This consisted of radiators buried in the leading edge of the new wing's center section. Unfortunately, the short span laminar flow wing of the Me 209, which incorporated inward-retracting landing gear, did not lend itself to long span extension. To solve this problem, and without spending valuable time or expense developing an entirely new wing, Messerschmitt adapted the 43.5 ft (13,260 mm) long span wing of the Bf 109 H, with its outward retracting gear to fit the Me 209 H.

AIR RAID SIRENS WAIL IN COTTBUS AND SORAU

On 11 April 1944, the Eighth Air Force launched 830 B-17s and B-24s in three separate formations, to attack aircraft production centers in northern Germany. The Focke-Wulf assembly plants at Cottbus and Sorau were among the heavi-

ly defended targets singled out for special attention by the bombers. During this period, the workers at Focke-Wulf's Cottbus assembly plant, located approximately 65 miles (104 km) southeast of Berlin, were busy producing new Fw 190 A-8s and Fw 200 Cs. The Sorau facility was located in Silesia approximately 50 miles (80 km) east of Cottbus, and was engaged in the assembly of new Fw 190s while simultaneously manufacturing components for the four-engined Fw 200. Over the next eight months, both assembly sites were to emerge as important Ta 152 production centers. German air defenses surrounding these production centers were formidable. This Allied bombing mission resulted in their heaviest single day losses of the war. Sixty-four American bombers, or 8 percent of the attacking force, failed to return. Bomb damage to Cottbus and Sorau was considerable, but thanks to the *Jägerstab*, much less than it would have been the previous month.

On 19 April 1944, during one of Hitler's important planning conferences, the question of Ta 152 production was raised. Göring stated that Xaver Dorsch, the chief of the *Todt* Organization, should be placed in charge of building bomb-proof factories and that these should be dedicated to the production of jet-powered Me 262s. When Milch and Saur both reminded the *Reichsmarschall* that the Me 262 was in fact to be assembled in the underground Mittelwerk complex at Nordhausen, Göring quickly retorted that …"in that case the Ta 152 could go into the bomb proof factory."

Throughout April and May 1944, Messerschmitt's workshops labored long hours over the first Me 209 H prototype. Gradually the workers forged the product into a finished airplane.

To the north on 29 May 1944, the air raid sirens once again wailed in Cottbus and Sorau. As if to underscore Allied

The Fw 190 V33/U1, W. Nr. 0058, GH+KW, was the first Ta 152 H prototype. Because no photographs of this machine are known to exist, this representation is undoubtedly very close to the actual aircraft. The day after its maiden flight, the prototype was being flown from Adelheide to Langenhagen when an in-flight emergency forced a landing near Vechta. The ensuing crash-landing damaged the aircraft beyond repair. After logging only half an hour, the unexplained loss of this critical development prototype was a heavy blow to the program.

determination to cripple or eliminate German aircraft production, the Eighth Air Force again hurled over 800 B-17s and B-24s deep into the *Reich* to pound aircraft assembly plants at Cottbus, Sorau, Leipzig, Posen, and Posen-Krzesiny. American losses during this attack totaled 34 heavy bombers. As a result of these combined raids, over 50 percent of the Focke-Wulf assembly lines were seriously disrupted or destroyed. Within a relatively short time however, determined German reconstruction measures, directed by the *Jägerstab*, succeeded in bringing aircraft production up to an astonishing 60 percent of its former capacity.

On 3 June 1944, the *Jägerstab* published their comprehensive list of aircraft selected for production. Under "Fighters" this list included the Ta 152 A and Ta 152 H, while the Ta 152 E was listed under *Nahaufklärer* (short-range reconnaissance). It is worth noting that the Ta 152 A had been repeatedly deferred since January 1944. The list also included a vast array of aircraft intended for everything from multi-engine bombers to engineless assault gliders. Clearly, almost every base was covered, predicated on the assumption that both offensive and defensive operations were to continue as before. However, events were about to occur that would change everything.

On Tuesday, 6 June 1944, Departure Day (D-Day), the long anticipated joint American - British landing in France, was finally launched. The German High Command's worst fears were soon realized when the Allied beachhead held against German attempts to throw the Allies back. Several hundred miles from these momentous events, Messerschmitt had completed the Me 209 HV1, and the prototype was at last ready for flight-testing.

In view of the Allied foothold in Europe, on 30 June 1944, Hitler issued an order giving the highest possible priority to the construction of day fighters and other types deemed essential to the defense of the *Reich*. Heavy combat aircraft were canceled and new aircraft development was to be drastically restricted. This was formalized the following day when *Blitzprogramm* 1.7.44 (Lightning Program 1 Jul 1944) was published. Absent from this list was the Ta 152; however, there was provision for a *Höhenjäger* under the "Development" classification. A week later, on 8 July 1944, Production Program 226 was approved. This plan, replacing Program 225 of 1 December 1943, was developed by the *Jägerstab* and established the parameters for aircraft production for the foreseeable future. Program 226 called for a vast increase in the total production of all aircraft types, especially fighters and interceptors. Monthly production goals for single-engine day fighters included 2,600 Fw 190s and Ta 152s plus 500 Bf 109s. In conjunction with these figures, the *Jägerstab* conference of 6 July 1944, included telling comments concerning this agency's perception of the Ta 152:

> Now we come to the important second fighter aircraft, the Fw 190. Output of this fighter version must be increased from 540 in June to 710 in July and then 955, 1200, 1288 and 1725. Production will reach its peak in December and then this type will be promptly converted into the Ta 152. Output will have to be drawn to 100 aircraft by next June and production will be wound up altogether in December. At present, output of the ground-attack version is 395 and this should increase to 495 this month and then to 500, 600 and finally 650.

Two company portraits on this page of the Fw 190 V30/U1, W. Nr. 0055, GH+KT, reveal salient features of this, the second Ta 152 H prototype. Completed in August 1944, it had logged just over ten hours when it suffered an engine fire seventeen days after its first flight. Although the fire had not spread, the aircraft was destroyed

while on final approach to Adelheide. This machine, like the first, had been completed to Ta 152 H-0 standards but without armament or the twin power boosting systems. The loss of the first two Ta 152 H prototypes so early in their flight-testing seriously hampered the already over-stressed and rushed Ta 152 H development program.

Wilhelm Schaaf (formerly with BMW) interjected:

> *I should just like to say that the Ta 152 is apparently no more than an unimportant development of the 190. However, it will require an enormous expenditure on a new plant which must be set up as it must be put through other processes owing to its having a different engine. We are confronted by a very great problem in this matter.*

Such comments not only serve to underscore undisguised bias, but also blatant ignorance as to the true significance of a new warplane, based on existing equipment, having markedly superior performance.

THE FIRST FOCKE-WULF SPECIAL HIGH ALTITUDE FIGHTER

While Messerschmitt was busy completing his Me 209 HV1, the Focke-Wulf prototype construction shops to the north at Adelheide were nonetheless busy. The first official Ta 152 (Ta 152 H) prototype completed was the Fw 190 V33/U1, W. Nr. 0058, GH+KW. It was flown successfully for the first time on 12 July 1944, powered by a newly produced Junkers Jumo 213 E driving a wooden three-bladed Junkers VS 9 propeller.

This aircraft was generally completed to Ta 152 H-0 standards, including cabin pressurization, but dispensed with

wing armament and GM 1 nitrous-oxide power boost equipment. In spite of considerable experimentation that was conducted primarily with the Fw 190 B-0 series, the pressurization system never really worked as planned. Its low pressure of 2.34 lb/ft² (.23 kg/cm²) was disappointing. To correct this, the pressure relief valve was eliminated, but this measure compromised pilot safety. Test pilot Hans Sander recalled "that the Fw 190 and Ta 152s were not really designed to be 'air tight.' They leaked like a sieve and the Rooh compressor did not deliver much air."

From the beginning, the Ta 152 H was to have been heavily armed with no less than five cannon—two cowl-mounted 20 mm MG 151/20 cannon augmented by two additional MG 151/20s in the wing roots, plus a 30 mm MK 108 engine-mounted weapon. As events unfolded however, it was decided to defer the two cowl-mounted cannon owing to critical center of gravity considerations.

This page: Having a wingspan of slightly over 47 feet (14,440 m) helped ensure the Ta 152 H's effective control throughout the entire flight envelope. The front view of the Fw 190 V30/U1, clearly shows the rather large spinner aperture, which was omitted on production machines (see drawing p 98/99). Note the lack of armament and the wide chord wooden Junkers VS 9 propeller blades. This aircraft carried all of its fuel within the fuselage, but full production models would have had six interconnected supplemental wing tanks.

The Ta 152 H's wing, it will be remembered, was entirely new and differed significantly from the Fw 190's wing. Having a high aspect ratio and span of 47.4 ft (14,400 mm), with an area of 252.9 ft² (23.5 m²), it was of mixed construction. Steel had long been planned for both the Fw 190 and Ta 152; specifically for use in wing spars and skinning despite a 15 to 25 percent weight penalty. But, more importantly, the wing's design was unusual in two additional respects. First, the all-steel front spar extended only just outboard of the landing gear attachment points. The rear spar ran the full span with additional stiffness coming from close-set ribs and numerous lateral stringers to reinforce the stressed skin. Second, since the aircraft was a high performance and highly maneuverable fighter, the wing was designed to ensure that airflow separation at high angles of attack did not occur at once over the entire wing. To achieve this, Focke-Wulf aerodynamicists created a wing with a 2.5 to 3 degree negative twist

from the wing root trailing edge outboard to the flap-aileron junction. Since the aileron's angle was less, airflow separation was delayed, thereby enabling prolonged control during combat conditions.

Thursday, 13 July 1944, was not fortuitous. On that morning, following its maiden flight, this first prototype developed an early in-flight emergency while being ferried from Adelheide to the Focke-Wulf's experimental shops at Langenhagen. This necessitated a hurried forced landing at Vechta that ended badly, resulting in significant structural damage and rendering the aircraft a complete loss. The identity and fate of the prototype's test pilot is unknown. This accident prompted *Oberst* Edgar Petersen, commander of *Erprobungsstelle* (Test Center) Rechlin, to file a report five days later expressing strong doubts about the dangerously low quality level that had resulted from efforts to rush the Ta 152 H into production. In particular, *Oberst* Petersen sited the air-

Kurt Tank's superlative "quick solution" fighter, the Dora 9. This Fw 190 D-9, W. Nr. 500570, "Blue 12", of II./JG 6, was manufactured by Mimetall at Erfurt. Its pilot landed and surrendered to Americans occupying Fürth airfield near Nürnburg on 8 May 1945.

*Jack Woolner enjoys a quiet moment at Fürth with a fellow officer beside Fw 190 A-8, W. Nr. 961118, "Red 5",
of 2./JG 6. This particular Focke-Wulf fighter was manufactured by Norddeutsche Dornier at Wismar.*

Two views of the third Ta 152 H prototype, the pressurized Fw 190 V29/U1, W. Nr. 0054, GH+KS, photographed soon after it joined the test program. First flown on 24 September 1944, it was first evaluated three days later at the **Luftwaffe** flight-testing center at Rechlin. Over the next few months the prototype demonstrated its thoroughbred characteristics for the first time attaining impressive speed and altitude scores. However, the aircraft also exhibited many of the vices and shortcomings that proved so difficult to correct and eradicate and, in some cases, even followed the type in production. This prototype was to test a ZFR telescopic device which was to become standard equipment for the Ta 152 E-2, H-10 and H-11 (see p 87). The ultimate fate of this particular prototype remains unknown.

craft's dangerous aft center of gravity, which would not be corrected for production machines unless a longer testing period was accepted. Petersen recommended H series production actually be delayed for safety reasons and, that the first dozen aircraft off the assembly line be strictly allocated for exhaustive testing.

Hans Sander remembered very well the difficulties in test flying at this point in the war.

> *It was impossible in those times to get more flying hours for testing the Ta 152, taking into account the situation in Germany – people hungry, cold and without enough sleep. This was compounded by low-level strafing by Thunderbolts, Lightnings and Mustangs. In addition, bombing attacks on Berlin (flying over Langenhagen) and on Langenhagen itself, resulted in frequent Fliegeralarm warnings. There were also commercial difficulties – spares and equipment had to be delivered by railway, bicycles and on foot. For two months we lived on the water from the fire extinguishing reservoir. The Jägerstab demanded the promised number of aircraft to be delivered – in consequence they were received but without full equipment and only one acceptance flight was authorized due to low fuel reserves.*

July 1944 was an especially painful month for BMW and their plans to produce the hybrid BMW 801 R — an engine intended for the Ta 152 C. Over a two week period beginning on 12 July, the U.S. Army's Eighth Air Force mounted four major bombing raids against BMW's aero engine works at Munich. An indication of this target's importance can be measured by the magnitude of these maximum effort raids; between 577 and 1,117 heavy bombers per mission. By 23 October 1944, when 500 heavy bombers from the Fifteenth AF paid a return visit to BMW's Munich plant, the company had been so heavily damaged that all hope of producing the BMW 801 R was abandoned.

On 16 July 1944, Messerschmitt's *projectburo* had finalized production drawings for the Bf 109 H-2 despite the fact that this aircraft series was rejected by the RLM in favor of the Fw 190 D-9. One of the early prototypes for the Dora 9, the Fw 190 V53, W. Nr. 170003, DU+JC, which had flown for the first time on 12 June 1944, sustained 5 percent damage less than two months later. On 5 August 1944, the V53 escaped with minor damage while in Langenhagen during one of the astonishing Eighth Air Force's "Thousand Plane" bombing missions that devastated the Magdeburg-Brunswick-Hannover area. This Dora prototype was quickly repaired and destined to serve some months later as an armament development aircraft primarily for the Ta 152 B and C series (see Chapter Five).

THE SECOND Ta 152 H PROTOTYPE CRASHES

The second conversion, completed almost three weeks after the first prototype, Fw 190 V30/U1, W. Nr. 0055, GH+KT, was rolled out at Adelheide and flown for the first time on 6 August 1944. Virtually identical to the first machine, it was the subject of several portrait photographs taken by the company's official photographer. Barely two weeks later, on 23 August, company test pilot Alfred Thomas was making a high altitude test from Langenhagen when the engine suddenly caught fire. Thomas instinctively cut power and, as the fire had not spread, he banked the aircraft toward the runway dead stick, and lost altitude too quickly, catching a wing on final approach. Thomas perished in the ensuing violent crash that totally destroyed his aircraft. Clearly not an encouraging beginning for the new Tank fighter. In less than two months, both prototypes were lost under unforeseen circumstances. Nevertheless, preparations for series manufacture of the Ta 152 H went forward quickly at Cottbus.

Continued complaints about the Jumo 213 E's reliability brought about a desperate but effective solution. Hans Sander recalled "Junkers Motorenwerke locked its best engineering team in the factory for four weeks and did not allow them to see their families until the troubles were rectified. Fewer engine failures were experienced thereafter!"

MESSERSCHMITT SUFFERS ANOTHER SETBACK

The only flyable Bf 109 H prototype, the HV54, remained in development even though several notable *Luftwaffe* test pilots remained highly critical of the aircraft's handling characteristics. In fact, Messerschmitt was still forging ahead with plans to place the Bf 109 H-2/R2, the reconnaissance version, in series production. Meanwhile, the whereabouts and condition of Messerschmitt's other prototype, the Me 209 HV1, the Ta 152 H's chief competitor, remain a mystery. No official record of this aircraft's fate is known to exist. Perhaps during this period, as a direct result of a bombing attack on the Daimler-Benz works, further work on their DB 603 G and plans to produce this engine were summarily canceled.

On 1 August 1944, the *Jägerstab* was disbanded and its function and responsibilities were taken over by the Technical Office of Speer's *Reichs* Ministry of Armaments and War Production. Otto Saur was promoted and placed in charge of the Technical Office, the vast responsibilities of which included armament production for the entire *Wehrmacht*. With this move Milch had been effectively marginalized.

PRODUCTION OF THE DORA 9 BEGINS

In spite of the two devastating American springtime bombing raids, carried out against Sorau's aircraft production facilities, the first Fw 190 D-9s began rolling off the replenished Sorau assembly line in late August 1944. Production of this "stop-gap" Dora 9 quickly gained momentum. Thus, in little more than a year from issuance of the Air Ministry specification for a *Schnellösung* fighter, the first production examples were poised to enter service with the *Luftwaffe*.

ADDITIONAL EYES IN THE SKY

By August 1944, plans to produce the dedicated short-range reconnaissance version, the Ta 152 E-0 and E-1, had crystallized. It was decided that two airframes were to be

Before Reinsehlen airfield was occupied by Canadian troops, German personnel disabled and destroyed several aircraft, such as the Fw 190 V18/U2, W. Nr. 0040, CF+OY, shown here.

modified at Sorau and although these were originally intended for the Ta 152 C-1 series, they were instead reassigned as *Normalaufklärer* (normal reconnaissance fighters) for the planned Ta 152 E-1 series. In compliance with this series specification, these prototypes were each to be powered by the Jumo 213 E. The two prototypes, the Ta 152 V9, W. Nr. 110009, and the Ta 152 V14, W. Nr. 110014 were reworked at Sorau to accept their Jumo 213 Es. From surviving records, it is uncertain whether either prototype was initially fitted with DB 603s (as specified for the C-1) before switching to the Jumo 213 E.

A third Ta 152 airframe was selected to serve as prototype for the Ta 152 H-10 *Höhenaufklärer*. This Sorau prototype, the Ta 152 V26, W. Nr. 110026, was to function as a production template to be immediately delivered to Mimetall. The Ta 152 V26, equipped with both GM 1 and MW power boosting systems, was supposed to be flight cleared by 6 February 1945, but this was eventually pushed ahead to March 1945. During this period, the RLM ordered 20 examples of the Ta 152 H-10, which were to be built by Mimetall at Erfurt north. Production data was to be finalized by October 1944, with production commencing in May 1945.

ENTER THE FOCKE-WULF 190 A-9

Outwardly almost identical to the A-8, the improved Fw 190 A-9, equipped with a more powerful BMW 801 TS (or

TH) radial engine, appeared on Focke-Wulf's Cottbus assembly line in September 1944. The basic fuselage structure for this variant was considered essentially interchangeable with the Fw 190 D-9 and Ta 152. The BMW 801 TS was another hybrid engine manufactured from components of the BMW 801 D and F models but capable of developing 2,000 hp for take off. Approximately 870 examples of the A-9 were manufactured before the end of the war, many by Focke-Wulf at Cottbus and Aslau, by Norddeutsche Dornier at Wismar, and Arado at Tutow.

AUTUMN BRINGS Ta 152 H PRODUCTION PLANS AND NEW PROTOTYPES

By mid-August 1944, the planning department at Bad Eilsen had established that all aircraft within the Ta 152 H-0 series, the preproduction model, would be completed with GM 1 power boost equipment but delivered without wing fuel tanks or provision for MW power boosting. Because of the urgency attached to the H series and recognizing that considerable flight-testing was a foregone necessity, in September 1944 the Air Ministry took the unprecedented step of authorizing construction of 115 examples of the Ta 152 H-0. This unusually large quantity is astonishing, especially when compared to the usual industry practice of producing only ten to twenty preproduction aircraft. With such a large number of 0 series fighters it was hoped the type could enter flight-testing and operational service more rapidly than would otherwise be possible. It also bought time for the various manufacturers who were responsible for the untested wing fuel bags, stocking up on power boosting parts and supplies and procuring the latest electronic navigation aids.

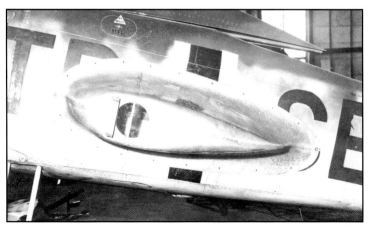

Left: A closeup of the oblique reconnaissance camera housing tested on Fw 190 D-9, W. Nr. 210002, TR+SB and planned for the Ta 152.

Two American servicemen pose with an incomplete Ta 152 H-11 discovered at the Mimetall factory located at Erfurt Nord. The Ta 152 H-11 was a specialized photoreconnaissance version of the Ta 152 H-1. When, in March 1945, the H-10 was canceled in favor of the H-11, it coincided with the RLM's early cancellation of the Ta 152 H-0 contract (the H-10 was based on the H-0). Note the slightly enlarged fuselage access hatch in the top image. The increased size was necessary to facilitate installation and removal of the aerial reconnaissance camera mounted to the fuselage.

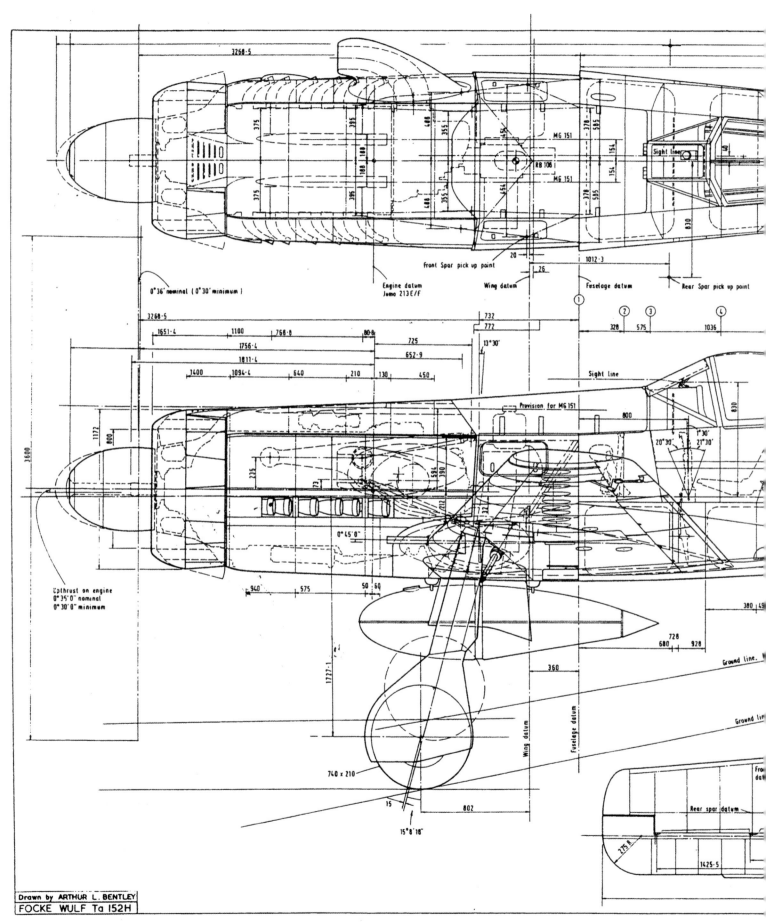

Drawn by ARTHUR L. BENTLEY
FOCKE WULF Ta 152H

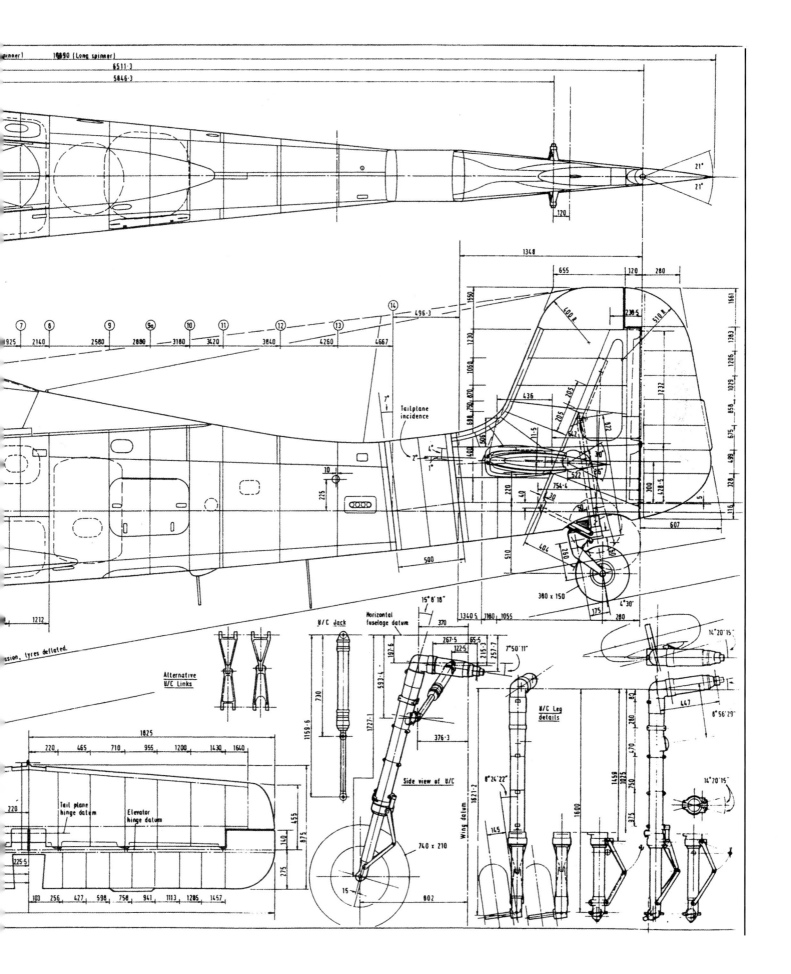

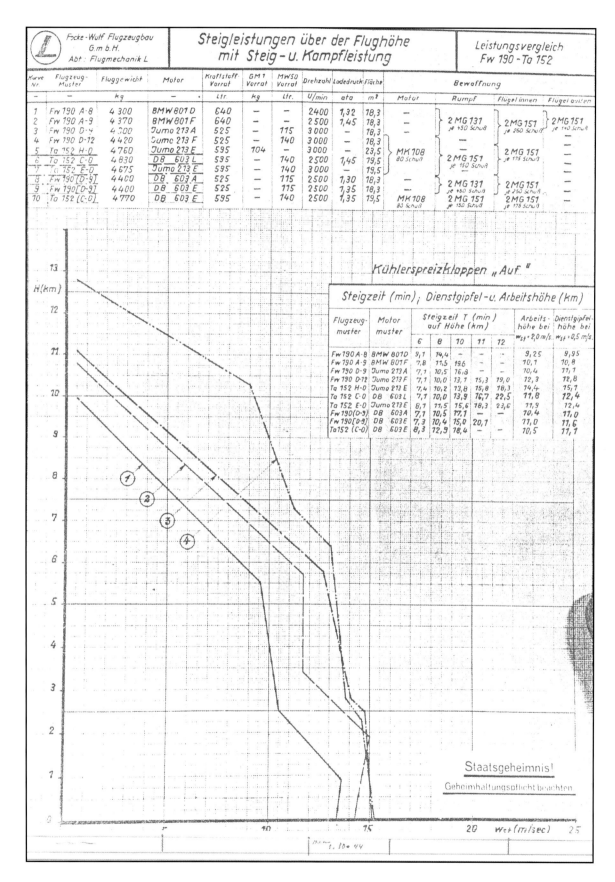

This performance graph dated 1 October 1944, deals with Climb Rates to Cruise Altitude as well as Climb and Combat Performance. Four rates are plotted: (1) Fw 190 A-8 with BMW 801 D, (2) Fw 190 A-9 with BMW 801 F, (3) Fw 190 D-9 with Jumo 213 A and (4) Fw 190 D-12 with Jumo 213 F. Rates for various other Fw 190 fighters and the Ta 152 are recorded only in the tables.

The third Ta 152 H-0, W. Nr. 150003, CW+CC, officially photographed in December 1944, soon after completion at Focke-Wulf's Cottbus facility, south of Berlin. It was flown by Chief Test Pilot Hans Sander, who is shown in the cockpit in the image below.

From the beginning, the primary production fighter would be the Ta 152 H-1/R11. This mark would have been equipped with the specified standard equipment, including dual power boosting systems as well as the LGW K23 fighter directional control, FuG 125 "Hermine" VHF radio beacon signal receiver, heated windows, and the PKS 12 autopilot. It was planned to build no fewer than 945 examples in the first eight months of 1945. This plan called for Focke-Wulf to complete 690, Erla to build 150 while Waggonfabrik Gotha would produce 105 aircraft.

Meanwhile, during this period in September 1944, the conversion shops at Adelheide finished their work on the Fw 190 V29/U1, W. Nr. 0054, GH+KS, the third Ta 152 H prototype. Outwardly similar to the two previous machines, it was flight cleared on 23 September and flown successfully by Hans Sander for the first time on 23 September 1944.

While this activity was proceeding, work on the fourth and fifth Ta 152 prototypes also continued at Adelheide. The fourth prototype, the Fw 190 V18/U2, W. Nr. 0040, CF+OY, was initially scheduled for completion in September 1944, but this soon proved to be overly optimistic. Despite the fact that this prototype was equipped with the distinctive *Känguruh* turbosupercharger installation, as the Fw 190 V18/U1, it was classified a development aircraft and technically not part of the *Höhenjäger 2* effort. Nevertheless, it was conscripted into the Ta 152 H program and was completed and flight cleared on 18 October 1944. The following day, it was flown for the first time as the Fw 190 V18/U2. Generally similar to the previous H series prototypes, it had also been further modified to accept a ZFR (telescopic sight) within a sighting trench that had been cut out just ahead of the windshield. This alteration was in conjunction with the Ta 152 H-10 (reconnaissance fighter) requirement.

Simultaneously, an early production Sorau-built example of the Fw 190 D-9, W. Nr. 210002, TR+SB, was modified to test the feasibility of an awkward-looking oblique camera mounting planned for the Ta 152 E-1/R1. This aircraft was test flown by Hans Sander on 25 September 1944, but it is doubtful any further aircraft were similarly modified.

During this period, considerable interest arose in the operational deployment of pilot ejection seats for the Ta 152 as a result of advances made by Focke-Wulf, Heinkel, and others. A year earlier, Focke-Wulf engineers experimented successfully with a pneumatically driven system installed in the Fw 190 V9, W. Nr. 0022, SB+IE, ex-A-0/U4. Although the pneu-

Three further views of the newly completed Ta 152 H-0, W. Nr. 150003, CW+CC. It was one of the two H-0s tested at Rechlin in December 1944 with a wooden tail replacing the original metal assembly shown here. For the H-0, the 300 liter drop tank was to be filled with MW 50 since there was no provision for internal accommodation for this special fuel. In February 1945, this aircraft was handed over to JG 301 and its ultimate fate is unknown.

matic seat worked well, the system was far too heavy for practical application. As a result, additional experiments were carried out using propellant charges in self-contained cylinders attached to the seat itself. This system was much lighter and took up far less space. However, it is unclear why this important pilot safety feature failed to appear on production aircraft.

THE FIRST Ta 152 H-0s APPEAR

On 2 November 1944, *Erprobungskommando* 152 (Experimental Detachment 152) was formed at Rechlin under the command of 29 year old Hptm. Bruno Stolle. A decorated ace with 35 victories, Stolle had previously served as *Kommandeur* of I./JG 11 before taking on the task of working in the new Tank fighter at the *Luftwaffe*'s secret flight test center.

By early November 1944, the Ta 152 H assembly line at Focke-Wulf's Cottbus facility, south of Berlin, was declared ready. The sense of urgency and resulting haste surrounding the entire Ta 152 program is reflected in how quickly the Ta 152 H entered production. Incredibly, only a mere 30 hours 52 minutes flying time had been logged by the prototypes before production commenced. This situation was exacerbated when the third Ta 152 prototype, Fw 190 V29/U2, W. Nr. 0054, experienced an engine failure and sat out of commission at Langenhagen from 2 through 27 November 1944.

Following a flight from Adelheide to Langenhagen on 19 November 1944, the fourth Ta 152 prototype, Fw 190 V18/U2, W. Nr. 0040, was ferried to Cottbus two days later for pilot familiarization, so urgent was the need to get some semblance of a Ta 152 training program started. On 24 November however, the aircraft was declared unserviceable and remained under repair for almost two weeks. Finally, on 10 December 1944, with the aircraft once again flight cleared, Focke-Wulf test pilot Bernhard Märschel successfully flew the aircraft without incident.

A Very Close Shave *Mein Herr*!

Kurt Tank, a designer who insisted on flying his own creations, flew an early Ta 152 H to 45,920 ft (14,000 m) and succeeded in reaching a speed of 463.6 mph (746 km/h) at 42,640 ft (13,000 m). But it was late in 1944 when this performance was life saving. Tank was caught by P-51s while taking off from Langenhagen for a staff meeting at Cottbus. Just after he lifted off in one of the first Ta 152 H-1s [sic] equipped with MW 50 power boost, the tower warned him: "*Achtung! Achtung! Vier Indianer am Gartenzaum!*" (Attention! Attention! Four Indians at the garden fence!). Glancing over his shoulder, he saw four Mustangs rapidly overtaking him. Tank shoved the throttle forward to War Emergency power, kicking in the methanol/water injection at the same time. The P-51s never caught the new fighter, which disappeared safely into the haze. Such was the outstanding performance of the Ta 152 as demonstrated by no less a pilot than the designer of the aircraft himself.

The foregoing dramatic narrative written by the late Jeffrey Ethell formed the introduction to Monogram Close-Up 24. It tells of a well-known event occurring on an unknown date near the end of 1944. Based on this narrative, it is not possible to identify the precise date or Ta 152 H flown by Tank. The only clue rests with the presence of MW 50 power boost. Inasmuch as the two surviving Fw 190 prototypes lacked power boosting and, since no Ta 152 H-1s were completed in 1944, Tank must have been piloting one of the early Ta 152 H-0 machines sometime after 24 November. Although the preproduction H-0 series lacked internal stowage of MW liquid, standard for the production H-1, nevertheless any of these H-0 aircraft manufactured up to the end of 1944, could have theoretically been equipped with a fuselage-mounted drop tank containing the MW 50 with its requisite plumbing, valves, and switches. According to surviving Focke-Wulf documents, only two H-0s were so equipped - W. Nr. 150003 (shown opposite page) plus one other machine. Ultimately, both of these were scheduled for transfer to Rechlin for testing and evaluation. Therefore, it is almost certain Prof Tank was flying one of these power boosted aircraft on the fateful occasion recounted above.

Had Kurt Tank not been flying an aircraft equipped with MW power boost, his survival would have been far less certain. The Ta 152 H was a rugged airplane, but whether or not it could have withstood the concentrated fire of the Mustang's half dozen .50 caliber machine guns is a question Kurt Tank was never asked to answer.

An ironic anecdotal footnote to this incident concerned Milch's cautionary command admonishing Tank never to fly an aircraft in wartime without armament. However, since Milch had said nothing about ammunition, Tank, a civilian, was perfectly happy to fly a fighter equipped with weapons but lacking munitions.

Port view of the Junkers Jumo 213 E-1 (equipment number 9-8213F-1), a 35 liter (2,136 cu in) liquid-cooled, inverted V-12 derived from the Jumo 213 A, but equipped with a three-speed two-stage supercharger and induction cooler. It produced 1,750 hp at 3,200 rpm for take off using B4 fuel of 87 octane. This particular example was photographed at the former Champlin Fighter Museum located in Phoenix, Arizona; it is now owned by Paul Allen. Note the location of the three engine ID plates riveted to the block just beneath the forward engine bearer arm. The primary plate (center) is shown on page 105.

Starboard side view of the Jumo 213 E-1 showing the special cut out on the engine bearer arm which straddled the engine's supercharger air intake venture. This particular engine, manufactured by Vereinigte Flug-motorenwerk GmbH (United Aircraft Engine Works), at Leipzig-Tauchau bore the maker's code "MNR." This firm produced approximately 1,600 Jumo 213s in 1944 plus another 650 in 1945 for a total of approximately 2,250. In addition, up to another 1,000 engines were built up to March 1945 but not tested or accepted for service use.

*Closeup of the ID inscription on one of the three wooden propeller blades, of the NASM's Ta 152 H-0 and was part of the complete Junkers VS 9 propeller assembly. The top line lists the **Baugruppen** equipment number, 9-30372.11, followed by the part's serial number, W. Nr. rlb 25158. This **Baugruppen** number indicates that this blade was intended primarily for the Fw 190 D-12 and D-13, but was also available for use on the first 100 Ta 152 Hs (i.e. H-0 preproduction series). Later, when the 4-bladed VS 19 propeller was to be employed by the Ta 152, using the same Jumo 213 E engine, its blade's ID would have listed **Baugruppen** equipment number 9-30337.17.*

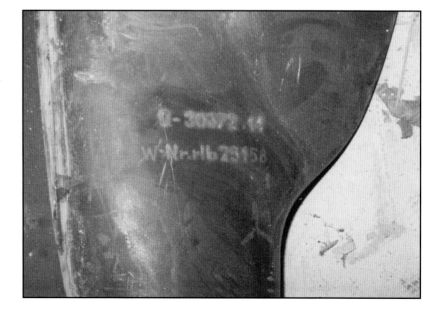

GERMAN ENGINE NOMENCLATURE

In an effort to simplify the allocation of aero engines to specific airframes, the German aviation industry adopted a system in which the engine and subtype, e.g. Jumo 213 E, was made airframe specific by its *Triebwerk* designation, e.g. 9-8213 FH. The term *Triebwerk* has a literal translation of "Powerplant" but in practice it included not only the engine itself but the appropriate propeller assembly, engine bearer arms and all ancillary equipment including the complete engine cowling. The *Triebwerk* part number prefix '9' denoted an engine application item. This was followed by a four-digit number in which the '8' denoted a group number while the next three digits called out the maker's engine model number. And lastly, the alphanumeric suffix referred specifically to the applicant's designated airframe. The following examples are typical:

Junkers Jumo 213 Variants

Triebwerk	Engine	Application
9-8213 B2	Jumo 213 A-1	Ju 188 A-1
9-8213 E1	Jumo 213 AG-1	Fw 190 D-9
9-8213 D1	Jumo 213 E 1	Ju 388 J-3
9-8213 FB	Jumo 213 E	Ta 152 B-5
9-8213 FE	Jumo 213 E 1	Ta 152 E-1
9-8213 FH	Jumo 213 E-1	Ta 152 H-1
9-8213 H1	Jumo 213 F-1	Fw 190 D-11

Daimler – Benz 603 Variants

Triebwerk	Engine	Application
9-8603B	DB 603 E	Ta 152 C-0
9-8603F	DB 603 G	Ta 153 C-1
9-8603B1/TEA	DB 603 E	Ta 152 C-3
9-8603C1	DB 603 EB	Fw 190 D-14
9-8603C2	DB 603 LA	Fw 190 D-15
9-8603B1/TLA	DB 603 LA	Ta 152 C-1
9-8603B1/TL	DB 603 L	Ta 152 C-2

This maker's identification plate, riveted to the port side of the NASM's Junkers Jumo 213 E contains information that, to the uninitiated, might appear to have little or no meaning. To German suppliers, mechanics and technical support groups however, it contains information necessary to ensure that the engine's service career is fulfilled. The first line, Gerät-Nr. (equipment number) represents the Triebwerk identification. This German term, 'Triebwerk', refers to more than just the bare engine, but also includes the complete engine and propeller assembly as a single entity, thus avoiding mismatched components. The number '9' standing alone signifies this is an aircraft engine related item. The next digit, '8' indicates that this device is engine specific while the following three digits, '213' reveal the RLM three digit block number for this engine which, in this case refers to the Junkers Jumo 213. The capital letter 'F' and '1' further define this device as a Jumo 213 E, or E-1, applicable to the Ta 152 E-1 and Ta 152 H-1 airframes (see chart above).

The second line, Werk-Nr. (works number, or serial number) contains additional essential information. The five digits are believed associated with the batch or control number while the remaining five digits are sequential indicating this engine was the 71st example manufactured in this batch.

The third line, Hersteller: (Maker, or Manufacturer), contains the three-letter code assigned to this company by the Ministry of War production. The code can appear in either capitals or lower case. In this example, MNR is the code for Vereinigt Flugmotorenwerk GmbH (United Aircraft Engine Works), of Werk Leipzig C1 (Leipzig-Tauchau).

At first glance, such a system of numbers and letters might appear to be unnecessarily complicated for an already regimented industrial platform but, in reality the German model avoided the possibility of placing the wrong engine, with the wrong equipment, in the wrong airframe.

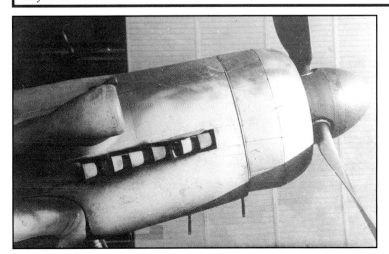

The complete cowled nose from one of the five Ta 152 H prototypes fitted with one of the early four-piece propeller spinners.

The freshly completed Ta 152 H-0, W. Nr. 150005, CW+CE, shown being prepared for calibration of its master compass on a compass swing. Completed and flown for the first time in early December 1944, it was soon dispatched to Junkers at Dessau to take part in various engine development tests but, as far as is known, it was never flown operationally. Note the propeller spinner's shape and length differ slightly from prototype aircraft (see pgs 94, 98).

In the middle of November the first preproduction aircraft, Ta 152 H-0, W. Nr. 150001, CW+CA, was rolled out. Soon thereafter, Hans Sander flew this aircraft for the first time on 21 November 1944, making an unscheduled but successful off-field landing. A few days later, Sander flew the second preproduction Ta 152 H-0, W. Nr. 150002, CW+CB, which was followed four days later, on 3 December 1944, by Ta 152 H-0, W. Nr. 150003, CW+CC, equipped with MW 50 power boost. On 8 December 1944, Ta 152 H-0, W. Nr. 150005, CW+CE, was delivered to the main Junkers facility at Dessau. The next machine, Ta 152 H-0, W. Nr. 150004, CW+CD, equipped with the K23 autopilot and a FuG 125 radio, was fer-ried to Langenhagen on 17 December 1944. In spite of Focke-Wulf's original plan, it was not possible to include GM 1 power boost into the assembly line. When Ta 152 H-0/R11, W. Nr. 150011, CW+CK, was completed, it was the first machine actually equipped with GM 1. The next aircraft, Ta 152 H-0, W. Nr. 150012, CW+CL, which appeared during the last week in December, was probably the last preproduction machine completed during 1944. After acceptance, most of these early aircraft were promptly delivered directly to EK 152 at Rechlin for testing and evaluation.

Meanwhile, Hptm. Stolle wasted little time putting the newly delivered Ta 152 H-0s through a disciplined flight-testing program. Stolle and his pilots found the new Tank fighter to be a fine performer, although due to the increased wingspan, they did not seem to roll as fast as the standard Fw 190. At an altitude of only 1,500 ft (500 m) and an indicated air speed of 292 mph (470 km/h), full aileron deflection produced a complete roll in 4.9 seconds. Stolle attempted to discover the limits of the aircraft's performance, once reaching an altitude 39,400 ft (12,000 m) over Rechlin. Only a lack of oxygen prevented him from flying higher.

The Ta 152 H-2 was to have been identical to the H-1 except for its radio. The standard radio for most fighters of the period was the FuG 16ZY; however, the intention was to replace this with the new FuG 15ZY "Christa" as soon as possible. But the RLM correctly concluded that minimum supplies of this modern radio were not likely in the foreseeable future and accordingly canceled the Ta 152 H-2 (and by association, the Ta 152 H-12) on 15 December 1944.

Meanwhile, back in Adelheide work on the fifth Ta 152 prototype, Fw 190 V32/U2, W. Nr. 0057, GH+KV, continued slowly. This machine was one of the first aircraft to be modified to accept the newly developed and remarkable aircraft cannon known as the MK 213. In addition this prototype was scheduled to receive the definitive H-1 wing with its integrated four fuel cells plus GM 1 contained in the rear fuselage. However, when it was flight cleared on 20 December 1944, powered by a Jumo 213 E, its original wing had still not been exchanged.

On 23 December 1944, Fw 190 V18/U2, W. Nr. 0040, was once again involved in a mishap. While taking off, the aircraft suddenly veered to the right after the pilot had released the throttle, causing damage to the right wing's gear retraction cylinder. During repairs, the wooden tailplane, planned for production aircraft, was installed and shake tests initiated. A mere seven minutes into the test, the plywood sheathing on the horizontal stabilizer fell apart. Focke-Wulf was using wooden tail assemblies that were outsourced from one of many woodworking shops spread throughout Germany. Thereafter, careful gluing, using specially developed adhesives with superior bonding qualities that didn't compromise the longevity of the wood, became imperative.

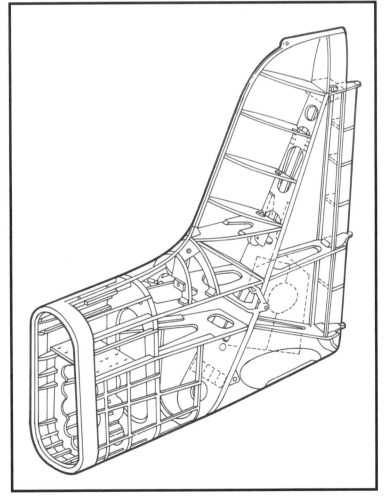

Focke-Wulf illustration on the right, of the optional wooden tail assembly retrofitted to two H-0 aircraft, W. Nr. 150003 and 150010. The use of such wooden components gave the mistaken impression the Germans were running low on aluminum. Instead, the main idea was to bring as many large and small industries into the manufacturing cycle as possible including Germany's sizable woodworking industry. On the left is a closeup of the wooden fin's open triangular access hatch on NASM's Ta 152 H-0.

Focke-Wulf Ta 152 H-0

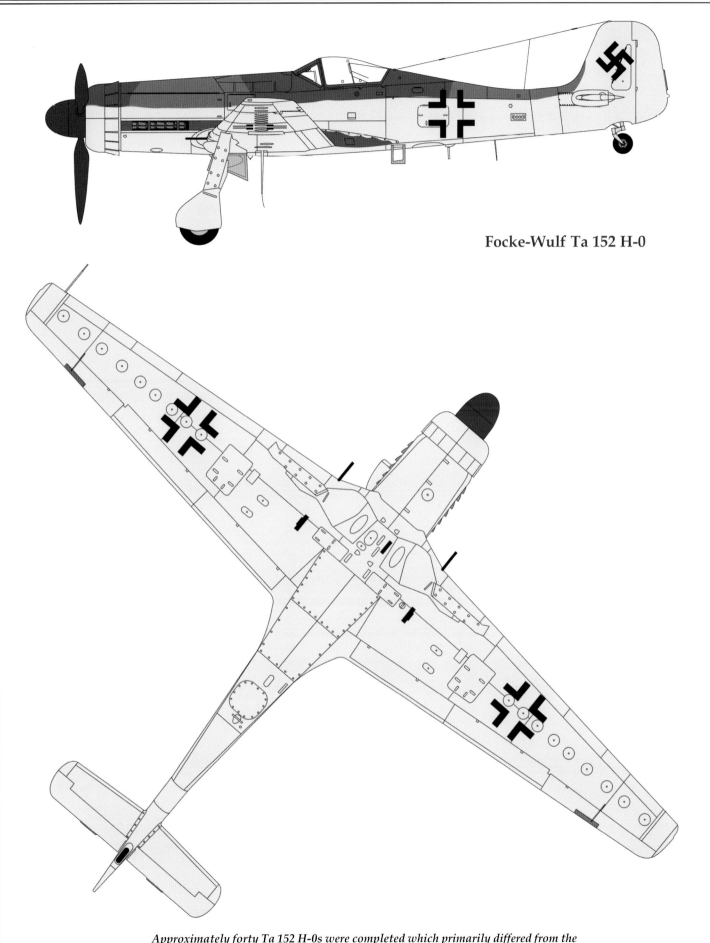

Focke-Wulf Ta 152 H-0

Approximately forty Ta 152 H-0s were completed which primarily differed from the full production Ta 152 H-1 in that all internal fuel was contained within the fuselage. Unlike the Ta 152 H-1, no fuel or power boost was carried within its wings. Additionally, there were slight differences between the two versions in the number and location of certain access hatches located inboard on the wing under surfaces.

THE NATIONAL AIR AND SPACE MUSEUM'S TA 152 H-0

The Focke-Wulf Ta 152 H-0 shown below, opposite, and on pages 170 – 175, represents the sole surviving Ta 152, which is currently in indefinite storage with the Smithsonian Institution's National Air and Space Museum (NASM). The precise identity of this aircraft remains unconfirmed. Seemingly all external traces of the aircraft's *Werknummer* have been lost. Normally, for Ta 152 H-0 aircraft, the last four digits of the six-digit *Werknummer* would have appeared at the top of the fin. In 1973, the author, together with museum staff, thoroughly examined this aircraft's wooden tail for traces of the serial number beneath several layers of paint. None was found. Moreover, preliminary examination of the fuselage failed to reveal an identification plate, a small rectangular metal tag positioned on the port side near the fuselage access hatch. Alternatively, a small triangular metal tag was attached midway along the rearmost inside vertical surface of the fin next to the rudder (see p 189). Such tags recorded the aircraft's six-digit *Werknummer* (e.g. 150010), factory ID code (naz) and subtype (8-152 H-0).

German military aircraft were further identified by their *Stammkennzeichen* (stkz - primary identification code). This coding system consisted of a four-letter code unique to a particular aircraft. Until the last months of the war in Europe, newly produced military aircraft routinely carried this temporary code across both sides of the rear fuselage and spread across the underside of the wings. For the Ta 152 H-0s produced at Cottbus, this stkz code sequencing began with CW+CA (W. Nr. 150001) and sequentially extended through 26 letters to CW+CZ (W. Nr. 150026).

In 1944, for security reasons, the RLM ordered manufacturers to omit all external reference to the stkz code apart from test and experimental aircraft. Careful examination of original photographs on pages 111 and 175 reveal traces of overpainting of the stkz, which suggests the last letter of the four-letter code was 'J.' If this possibility is correct, it would mean the NASM's aircraft was W. Nr. 150010, CW+CJ. This possibility is further made plausible by the fact W. Nr. 150010 was only the second of two 'H' aircraft to have had its original metal tailplane exchanged for a newly produced wooden unit. Added to this is the fact that most aircraft assigned for testing and evaluation at Rechlin were exempt from the code restriction and routinely displayed their stkz during their tenure at this installation.

Therefore, although compelling evidence strongly suggests the NASM's Ta 152 H-0 is W. Nr. 150010, corroborating information is lacking. Positive identification must therefore be deferred until conclusive confirming data is recovered.

The color photograph on page 175 clearly reveals traces of the aircraft's service with JG 301 as evidenced by the 900 mm wide rear-fuselage bands of Red and Yellow. There is also faint evidence that the aircraft once carried the tactical number "Yellow 4" prior to the "Green 4" being applied.

In the summer of 1945, soon after the Ta 152 H-0 arrived at Wright Field, near Dayton, Ohio (now Wright-Patterson AFB), the U.S. Army Air Corps' Air Technical Service Command allocated Foreign Equipment number FE-112 to the aircraft. FE-112 was then moved to the Foreign Aircraft Evaluation Center headquarters at Wright Field, for maintenance and eventual flight-testing.

During the latter part of May 1946, the aircraft was under restoration at Wright Field, but progress was very slow. Three months later FE-112 was still awaiting its restored

In 1948, the department of the Air Force became a separate service branch, and with this change came the repainting of "FE" numbers to "T2" (T2 representing AF Intelligence) numbering. Here the redesignated T2-112 rests at the Air Force's facility at No. 803 Special Depot, Orchard Place, Park Ridge, Illinois (now O'Hare International Airport).

engine. Owing to budget cuts and the advent of more advanced technology, especially jet powered aircraft, work on the Tank fighter essentially came to an end. In 1948, the department of the Air Force became a separate service branch. With this change came the repainting of "FE" numbers to "T2" (T2 representing AF Intelligence) numbering. It is unlikely flight-testing of this fighter occurred prior to the aircraft's move to the Air Force's facility at No. 803 Special Depot, Orchard Place, Park Ridge, Illinois (now O'Hare International Airport). The photograph on page 110 shows the aircraft inside one of the main buildings at Park Ridge.

The Ta 152 H-0 languished at Park Ridge throughout the 1950s and was eventually turned over to the proposed National Air Museum in 1960. Although the NAM failed to materialize, the aircraft was retained by the Smithsonian Institution's Paul E. Garber Restoration Facility of the NASM at Silver Hill, Maryland. As of this writing, no restoration plans have been established for this aircraft.

*Two views of the Ta 152 H-0 now belonging to the NASM at rest at Newark Army Airfield, September 1945, prior to its flight to Wright Field, Ohio. Beneath the British insignia and surrounding paint may be seen traces of the aircraft's original German primary identification code and tactical number '4'. Unfortunately, photographs of this aircraft while still in its original **Luftwaffe** insignia and markings do not appear to exist.*

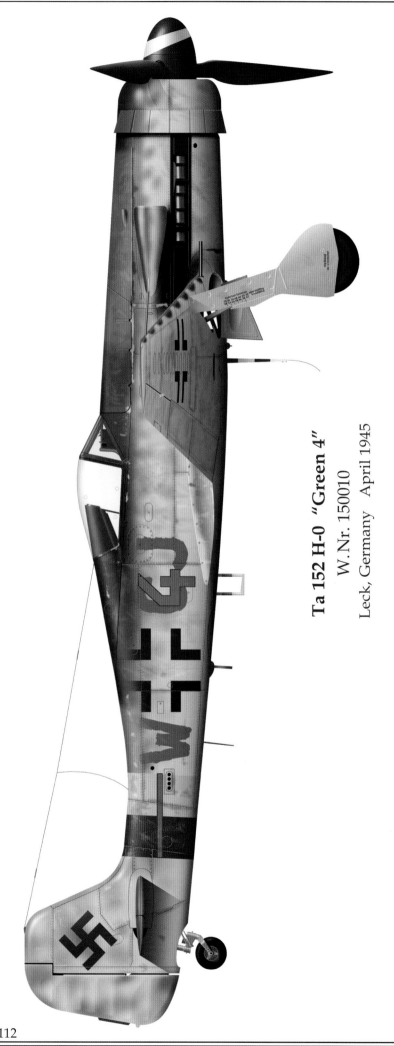

Ta 152 H-0 "Green 4"
W.Nr. 150010
Leck, Germany   April 1945

NOTABLE FEATURES
- Pressurized canopy with pellets and hooks on base of canopy
- Small White square in lower portion of windscreen for heating element
- All antennas intact
- No ETC rack or drop tank

COLORS

UNDERSURFACES	RLM 76 Light Blue
UPPERSURFACES	RLM 82 Bright Green/RLM 83
	Dark Green, Black exhaust panel;
	RLM 70 Black-Green
PROP BLADES	
SPINNER	Black with White spiral

NATIONAL MARKINGS

FUSELAGE	B4 800 mm Black outline crosses
	H3 500 mm Black *Hakenkreuz*
WINGS	Upper: B6 1000 mm White outline crosses
	Lower: B4 1000 mm Black outline crosses

STENCILING
Standard; Red and Yellow fuselage bands with Green horizontal bar over bands; *Stammkennzeichen* CW + CJ partially showing, Green '4' on top of markings

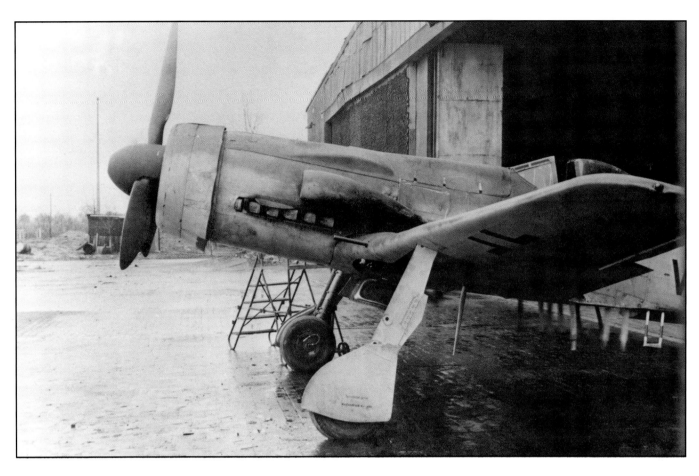

THE FIRST Ta 152 *CÄSAR* APPEARS

On 3 December 1944, the first prototype for the long anticipated 'C' series, Ta 152 V6, W. Nr. 110006, VH+EY, was finally flight cleared and nine days later on Tuesday, 12 December, it was successfully flown for the first time by Bernhard Märschel at Adelheide. As recounted earlier, the designated engine for the first examples of the 'C' series was the Daimler-Benz DB 603 L. However, since the L engine was not yet available, this first true Ta 152 C series prototype was completed using the DB 603 EV21 (twenty first E series prototype built to the DB 603 EC standards) W. Nr. 01300145 with-

out revised engine cowling and the engine-mounted MK 108. From 6 December 1944, when the aircraft had first been flight cleared, until its maiden flight six days later, it was subjected to continuous engine testing. Then, shortly before Christmas 1944, the troublesome DB 603 EV21 was replaced by the DB 603 EV24. In this condition Hans Sander test flew the aircraft at Langenhagen during which no engine complaints were registered.

Although the Ta 152 V6 was the first true ground-up Ta 152 prototype, it was not the first aircraft enlisted on behalf of the Ta 152 C series. This honor went to the Fw 190 V21, which was previously employed as a dedicated engine devel-

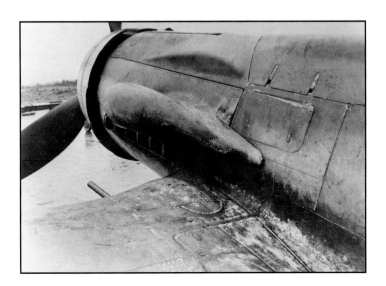

Above and left are the only known photographs of the first genuine new build Ta 152 prototype, the Ta 152 V6, W. Nr. 110006, VH+EY, shown here at Adelheide prior to installation of its main fuselage fuel tank. Note the dangling tank restraining straps beneath the fuselage. This aircraft was first flown on 12 December 1944, by Bernhard Märschel. It was powered by the DB 603 EV21, W. Nr. 145. It was also the first Ta 152 C-0 built to C-1 standards except for its engine and the absence of wing fuel tanks. Shortly before Christmas 1944, its troublesome DB 603 EV21 was replaced by the improved DB 603 EV24, and by June 1945, it was planned this engine was to be exchanged for the new DB 603 LA. The closeup of the wing root and supercharger intake at left, shows how snugly the new integrated engine cowl was fabricated to closely conform to the airframe, but the smoothness was interrupted by the top bulge, in the upper right corner. This was required due to the large size of the cowl-mounted MG 151/20 cannon while the curving bulge above the supercharger scoop covered the large radius of the engine bearer support arm which itself had to clear the supercharger.

Aside from its somewhat smaller wing (18.3 m²) the Fw 190 V21/U1, W. Nr. 0043, TI+IH, was very close to being a pure Ta 152 C prototype. This development aircraft had first flown with a Jumo 213 C as the Fw 190 V21 (see p 45), however once testing with this engine had run its course in the summer of 1944, the aircraft was assigned to the DB 603 L program. The original plan called for the engine conversion to be carried out at Focke-Wulf's Adelheide conversion shops, but repeated delivery delays resulted in an interim engine to be installed. Conversion work finally began in autumn 1944 using a DB 603 E. The aircraft was cleared to fly on 3 November 1944, with its first flight commencing a week later on 10 November 1944. This prototype lacked armament and the definitive 'C' series wing, but otherwise it was very close to the Ta 152 C-0 requirement.

opment aircraft and which had participated extensively in the Jumo 213 program. However, due to the urgency of the DB 603 L engine, the Fw 190 V21 , it was transferred to the Ta 152 C program. In this capacity, it was scheduled to receive one of the early L-engines, but since these were not ready in time, the V21 was re-engined with the DB 603 EV17, W.Nr. 01300525 officially becoming the Fw 190 V21/U1, and in this guise it was flown for the first time on 10 November 1944 on a transfer flight originating from Adelheide to Langenhagen. A week later, on 19 November, it was ferried from Langenhagen to Daimler-Benz's Echtrdingen facility in order to be retrofitted with the sixteenth test example (V16) of the DB 603 LA. This aircraft retained the standard Fw 190 A series wing but switched from electric to hydraulic undercarriage retraction. It is unclear whether or not this final engine swap would have altered its designation. With this definitive engine, the addition of an engine-mounted MK 108 cannon, plus underwing attachment points for the WGr 21 air-to-air rocket, this prototype would have closely resembled the Ta 152 C.

Because of the worsening military situation in the east, plans to produce the first few Ta 152 C prototypes at Sorau were shelved. Instead, it was decided that Focke-Wulf's prototype construction facility located at Adelheide-Delmenhorst airfield, just west of Bremen, would build the first three Ta 152 C-series prototypes.

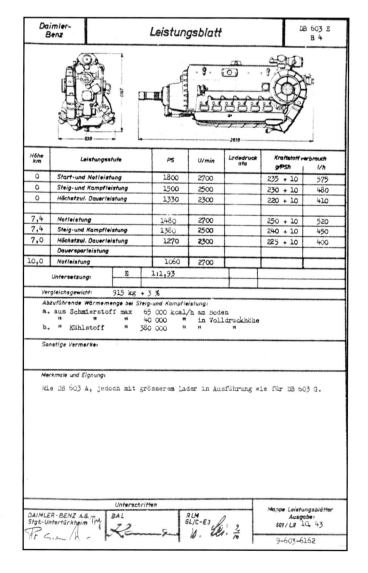

Right: The Daimler-Benz specification sheet for the DB 603 E, using B4 aviation fuel rated at 87 octane, and dated October 1943, gives an overview of this engine's performance.

A striking portrait of the newly completed Ta 152 V7, W. Nr. 110007, CI+XM, at Adelheide early in December 1944. This aircraft, like the V6, was fitted with a DB 603 E (V20, W. Nr. 147) with MW 50 power boost, but was later scheduled to receive a DB 603 LA engine in April 1945. Wing fuel tanks, intended for the production version, Ta 152 C-1, were not installed in this prototype. It was built as a Ta 152 C-0/R11 machine equipped with FuG 16 and FuG 125 radios plus the LGW K23 fighter directional control. Flight cleared on 5 January 1945, it was flown for the first time by Bernhard Märschel on 8 January 1945. Seventeen days later the aircraft was flown to Siemens, for installation of the K23 and, on 27 January 1945 it was flown to Focke-Wulf's test facility at Langenhagen where Hans Sander flew it for the first time.

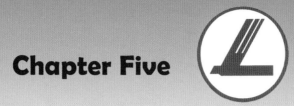

Chapter Five

1945 - Too Late to Make a Difference

INTRODUCTION

At dawn on New Year's Day 1945, under cover of foul weather, the German Air Force launched a massive surprise counteroffensive along the western front. Known as Operation *Bodenplatte*, the surprise attack inflicted substantial damage, but in the end was little more than a "speed bump" to British and American forces. Under the circumstances, the *Luftwaffe*'s fighters and fighter-bombers performed well, but were unable to sustain their initiative. German losses, incurred from this date onward, could never be made up. By January 1945, anyone in Germany old enough to bear arms saw that the war in Europe was inexorably grinding to its inevitable conclusion. No amount of new piston engine fighters, V-weapons, jet fighters or rocket-propelled interceptors could reverse Germany's fortunes. Yet, the Hitler government, backed by fanatic misplaced loyalty, resolved to fight to the last man and bullet.

Beneath a mantle of white, and operating in sub-freezing temperatures concurrent with all sorts of acute shortages, German factories, both large and small, working in harsh conditions, continued producing aircraft components for a dying industry. Without fear from bombing, with adequate fuel reserves, and having flight training worthy of the name, the situation might not have been so desperate. However, reality was far worse. Even though Allied forces had not yet penetrated Germany proper, the *Reich's* industry, now on a "total war" footing, was in shambles. The will to continue was largely driven by the state's threat of severe penalties for those who failed to "do their duty." Factories bombed on Monday were immediately cleared of debris and, wherever possible, resumed operation by Friday, frequently without roofs and other basic amenities. Even with drastic decentralization measures, there were severe bottlenecks impeding the flow of matériel. Moreover, with vast numbers of unskilled workers entering the manufacturing labor pool, many of whom were forced labor, quality control became an inescapable issue.

When British forces occupied Leck airfield close to the Danish border, one of the interesting aircraft they encountered was this Ta 152 H-0, W. Nr. 150004, "Green 6" Stab/JG 301. It was assigned for transfer to England as AM 11, but as events unfolded, AM 11 went instead to W. Nr. 150168 (see photo page 173). "Green 6" was later transported by road to Schleswig where it was eventually scrapped early in 1946.

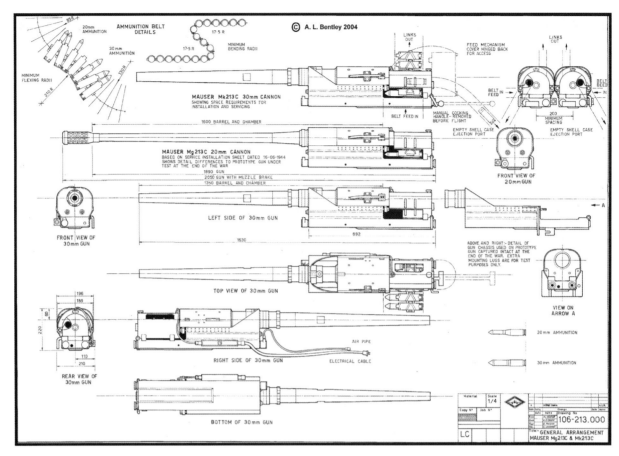

Ta 152 H-1 PRODUCTION BEGINS

Following the completion of the last examples of the Ta 152 H-0 preproduction series in January 1945, production at Focke-Wulf's Cottbus facility transitioned to the manufacture of the Ta 152 H-1. Almost all of the H-0s completed at Cottbus during the last quarter of 1944 and early 1945, participated in testing and evaluation programs, most being carried out by EK 152 based at Rechlin. The number of completed H-0 machines is known to have totaled at least 40 aircraft and possibly more. Out of the original contract order for 115 preproduction machines, the balance, amounting to approximately 75 additional aircraft, was summarily canceled once it was determined that production supplies for the H-1 series were finally at hand.

The Ta 152 H-1 was outwardly virtually identical to the H-0 but internally had provision for additional fuel tanks in the wings. Five of the wing tanks carried the usual B4 aviation fuel while the sixth tank (left inboard) was dedicated to MW 50 power boost but could alternatively be filled with B4 aviation fuel. The H-1 also carried another tank, located aft of fuselage seam 8, that contained 22.5 gal (85 liters) of GM 1 power boosting chemical.

The first full production Cottbus-built H-1 aircraft Ta 152 H-1, W. Nr. 150158, was completed late in January 1945. Additional production aircraft followed rapidly. It will be remembered that the fifth Ta 152 prototype, the Fw 190 V32/U2, W. Nr. 0057, originally scheduled for completion in late 1944, was to embody all the hallmarks of the Ta 152 H-1. Since this aircraft's debut had been seriously delayed, partly

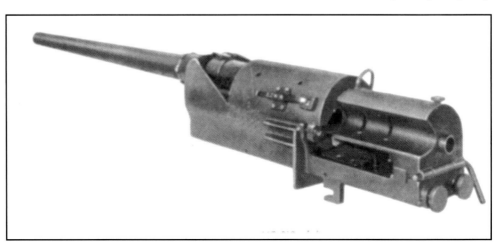

An overall view of the Mauser MK 213. This remarkable gas operated revolver cannon was to be installed in the wing roots of the Fw 190 V32/U2, but whether or not this was actually carried out before the war's end is undocumented.

This historically significant photograph of no less than six Ta 152 H-0s, was reportedly taken at Alteno airfield just south of Berlin during February 1945. These aircraft formed part of 11./JG 301 as evidenced by their Yellow tactical numbers in conjunction with narrow Yellow horizontal bars superimposed over the Yellow/Red tail bands denoting III./JG 301. Note that at the time this photo was taken none of these aircraft yet employed the required White spiral spinner motif. On the right is W. Nr. 150007, "Yellow 7" later transferred to the **Stabsschwarm.**

because of the devastating bombing attack on the wing assembly facility at Posen eight months earlier, it was decided to accelerate this prototype conversion. With cancellation of the Ta 152 H-2 a few weeks earlier, the designated prototype for this series, the Ta 152 V25 was without an assignment. Therefore, in early January, Focke-Wulf's Planning Department ordered the transfer of the Ta 152 V25's wings directly to the Fw 190 V32/U2. It will be recalled that the Fw 190 V32/U2, completed in 1944 with a Jumo 213 E and VS 9 propeller, was equipped with complementary but distinctly differing long span wings lacking the characteristic high performance "twist" of production Ta 152 Hs. Adding to the late arrival of this prototype was the job of installing the aircraft's experimental armament system. In addition to the standard wing-mounted MG 151/20s, it held the distinction of being one of the first German aircraft fitted with the experimental and highly advanced MK 213 (aka MG 213). Focke-Wulf had had this advanced weapon under active planning since mid-1943. In September 1944, Focke-Wulf engineers inspected two prototypes of the MG 213 A for installation in the Ta 152. Installed as an engine-mounted gun, this 20 mm gas-operated revolver cannon, produced by Waffenfabrik Mauser, was loaded and unloaded automatically and capable of firing an astonishing 1,200 rounds per minute.

Tests showed the installation caused no deficiencies except in the ejection of spent shell cartridges. However, luckily for the Allies, this weapon never entered production. Mauser produced approximately 18 prototypes of the MG 213 A cannon, plus another ten under construction by war's end. It is believed the Fw 190 V32/U2 was ferried directly to the *Luftwaffe's* Tarnewitz *Eprobungsstelle*, located at the Baltic Sea, for weapon testing with the MG 213 A. Unfortunately, the final disposition of this particular Ta 152 prototype and its

weapons remains unclear although it is alleged to have been abandoned at Reinsehlen airfield in April 1945.

OPERATIONAL TESTING OF THE Ta 152 H BEGINS

On 9 January 1945, *Erprobungskommando* 152, still headquartered at Rechlin, had its tenure extended through to 1 April, and at the same time the *Kommando* was expanded and reconstructed. From this point on it was to exist as a *Gruppenstab* with a *Stabskompanie* and five *Staffeln*, of which four were to be assigned to operations and the fifth was to carry out technical testing. On 10 January 1945, an order from the General Quartermaster of the *Luftwaffe* came through I. *Jagdkorps*, stipulating that the III. *Gruppe* of JG 301 was to carry out preliminary transition training on the Ta 152 H at Rechlin.

Five days later, on 15 January, the unit's directive was amended when it was decided that all operational testing would also be carried out by III./JG 301. This unit was temporarily led by acting commander Hptm. Karl-Heinz Dietsche but he was replaced by *Major* Guth who remained at this post until the end of the war. Based at Alteno, III./JG 301 was primarily equipped with Fw 190 A-9s. A total of twelve Ta 152 Hs were on strength with the *Kommando der Erprobungsstellen* (KdE Detachment of the Experimental Station) which, on 23 January 1945, became the *Stabsstaffel* of JG 301. On this date, the *Oberkommando der Luftwaffe* issued the following order:

> *Instead of the planned expansion of E-Kommando Ta 152, III./JG 301 will be equipped with the Ta 152 H as an operational test unit. In addition, the Gruppe will retain its former aircraft type [Fw 190 A-8 – Ed.] in combat until further notice.*

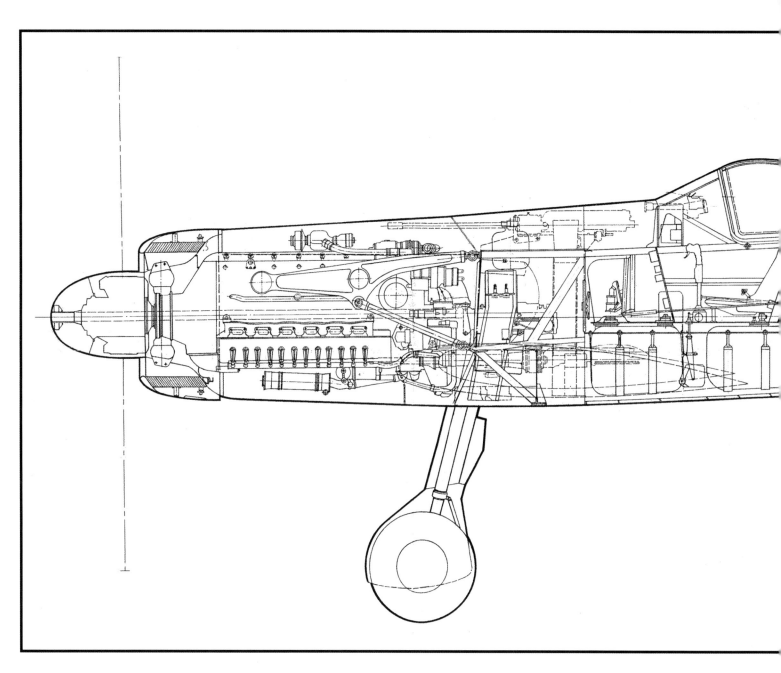

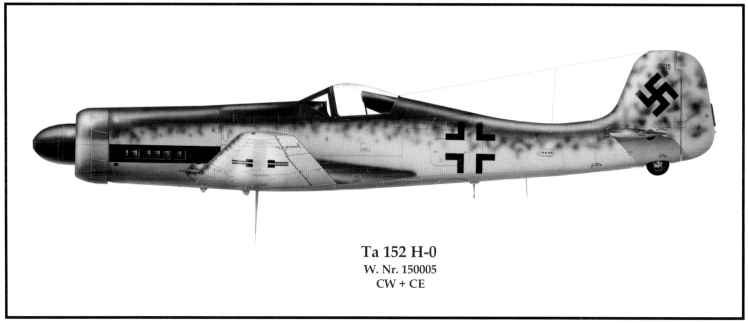

Ta 152 H-0
W. Nr. 150005
CW + CE

Ta 152 H-0, W. Nr. 150005, CW + CE completed during December 1944, and promptly delivered to the aircraft's engine provider, Junkers located at Dessau. So far as is known, the aircraft was retained at Dessau and probably ended its career as an engine test vehicle without having been flown operationally.

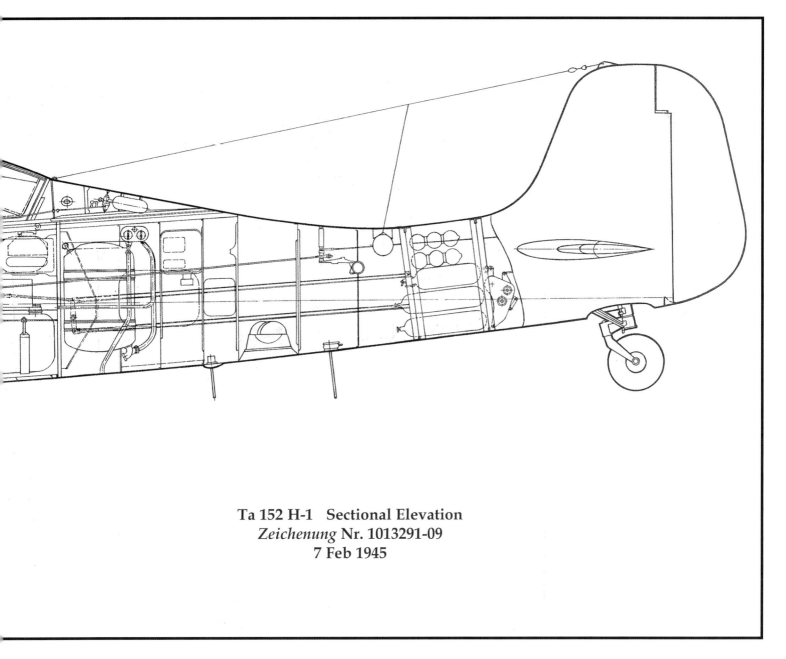

Ta 152 H-1   Sectional Elevation
Zeichenung **Nr. 1013291-09**
7 Feb 1945

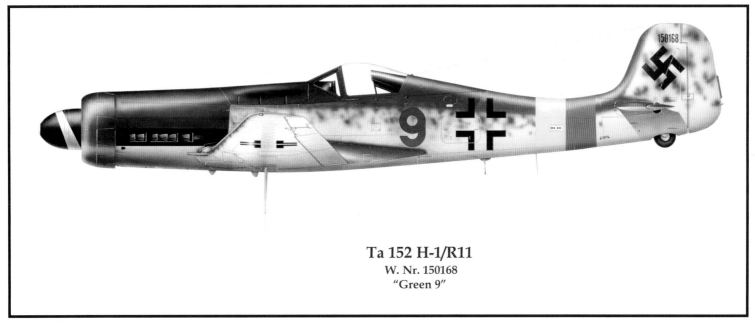

Ta 152 H-1/R11
W. Nr. 150168
"Green 9"

*Ta 152 H-1/R11, W. Nr. 150168, "Green 9" was flown operationally by Willi Reschke with **Stab JG 301** prior to its eventual capture at Leck airfield by British forces. Note this impression is complete apart from the hybrid Bright Green horizontal bar that ran across the Yellow and Red fuselage band, (see page 160).*

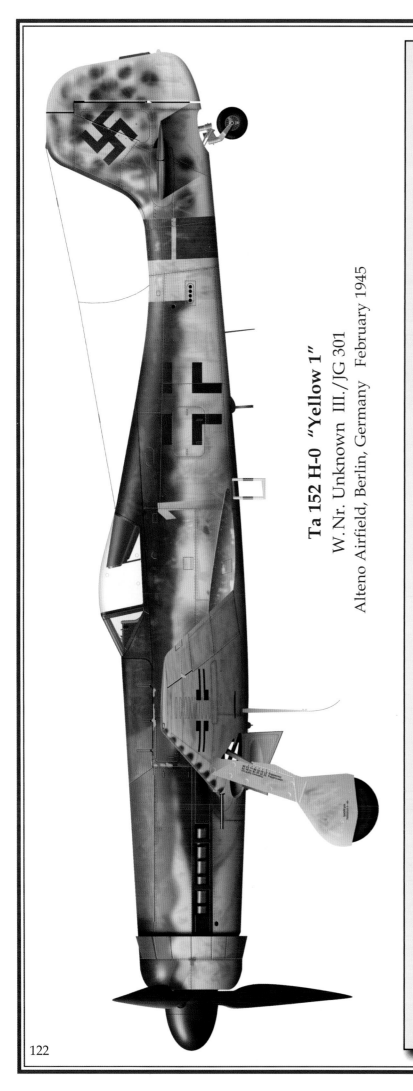

Ta 152 H-0 "Yellow 1"
W.Nr. Unknown III./JG 301
Alteno Airfield, Berlin, Germany February 1945

Three of six Ta 152 H-0s, located at Alteno airfield just south of Berlin during February 1945. These aircraft formed part of 11./JG 301 as evidenced by their Yellow tactical numbers in conjunction with narrow Yellow horizontal bars superimposed over the Yellow/Red tail bands denoting III./JG 301.

NOTABLE FEATURES

- Pressurized canopy with pellets and hooks on base of canopy
- All antennas intact
- No ETC rack or drop tank

COLORS

UNDERSURFACES	RLM 76 Light Blue
UPPERSURFACES	RLM 82 Bright Green/RLM 83 Dark Green, Black exhaust panel; note sawtooth camouflage on upperwing extends onto the underwing
PROP BLADES	RLM 70 Black-Green
SPINNERS	At the time the reference photo was taken, the White spirals had not yet been applied

NATIONAL MARKINGS

FUSELAGE	B4 800 mm Black outline crosses
	H3 500 mm Black *Hakenkreuz*
WINGS	Upper: B6 1000 mm White outline crosses
	Lower: B4 1000 mm Black outline crosses

STENCILING

Standard; Red and Yellow fuselage bands with Yellow bar over bands

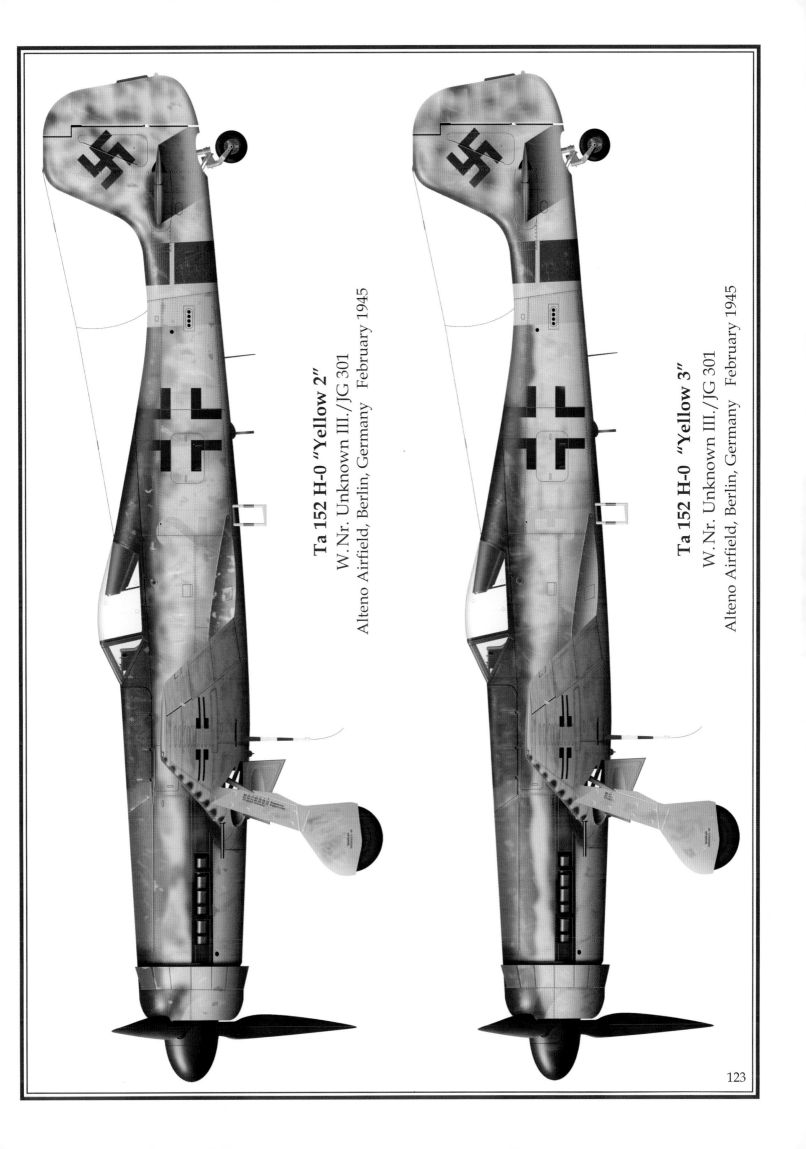

Ta 152 H-0 "Yellow 2"
W. Nr. Unknown III./JG 301
Alteno Airfield, Berlin, Germany   February 1945

Ta 152 H-0 "Yellow 3"
W. Nr. Unknown III./JG 301
Alteno Airfield, Berlin, Germany   February 1945

123

INCIDENT AT COTTBUS-NEUHAUSEN

Hptm. Stolle, who had been aggressively trying to expedite pilot training on the new Tank fighter, eagerly paid a visit to the Focke-Wulf factory at Cottbus early in January. When he arrived, he was surprised to see at least twenty complete Ta 152 Hs parked in front of the factory. Following his tour, Stolle immediately contacted his commanding officer, *Oberst* Petersen, and asked whether these machines could not at once be given to JG 301, which at that time was based primarily at Sachau. Petersen agreed, whereupon the aircraft were quickly moved from the factory proper to a satellite airfield at Cottbus-Neuhausen while they were readied for *Luftwaffe* acceptance.

The majority of JG 301's pilots had been assigned to the unit in September/October 1944, after a rest leave from the "Wilde Sau" units, JG 300 and JG 302, which had been disbanded. Pilots going into III./JG 301 came primarily from the old I./JG 302. Those scheduled for conversion training traveled to Cottbus in a wood-burning LKW (light personnel truck). There to meet the young pilots was Hptm. Stolle who would guide them through their initial training and turn over what aircraft had been certified by BAL (*Bauabnahme Luft* – Construction Acceptance Air) to JG 301. During this inspection phase, it was discovered that all of the fighter's aileron push rods were easily bent by hand, a situation Stolle believed was the result of sabotage. All of the rods were subsequently replaced.

Cottbus-Neuhausen was a grass airfield, some six miles (10 km) southeast from the center of Cottbus and served as a holding field for the Ta 152 Hs until the aircraft could be checked, certified and released to the *Luftwaffe*. Before this could occur however, fate intervened. On Tuesday, 16 January 1945, over 550 heavy bombers of the Eighth Air Force, accompanied by 13 Fighter Groups, took off to attack targets in central Germany. Two of these Fighter Groups, searching for so-called "targets of opportunity," happened upon *Luftwaffe* air activity over Cottbus-Neuhausen. The Groups' P-51s and P-38s attacked the field, destroying unprotected aircraft as they sat in their dispersal pens. Among the German aircraft destroyed in this attack were most of the brand-new Ta 152 Hs. This incident was a heavy blow to the aspirations of Hptm. Stolle and the young pilots of JG 301.

DOWN BUT NOT OUT

During this transition period, former *Feldwebel* Rudi Driebe, a pilot with the 10th *Staffel* of III./JG 301 who had been posted on 22 December 1944, recalled the events.

We were re-equipped in January 1945 at Alteno near Luckau [Spreewald, near Berlin], and received about 24 to 26 aircraft. Quite a number of these were lost during conversion training due to crash landings and other causes. The remaining Ta 152s were then taken over by the Stabsschwarm of the Geschwader.

To my knowledge, only one mission was ever flown by the Ta 152 [during that period] during an air raid on Berlin. The Geschwader suffered heavy losses on that day and only the Ta 152s returned safely. If the Ta 152 had seen action a year earlier, things would have looked bad for the P-51.

Immediately after the British acquired Ta 152 H-1/R11, W. Nr. 150168, "Green 9" Stab/JG 301, its original German insignia were largely obliterated as RAF painters applied roundels and their familiar Red, White and Blue fin flash.

For conversion training we first received two aircraft of the Ta 152 H-0 series. Handling in the air was quite okay. However take off was troublesome. When retracting the gear after take off, the right leg came down again by about one-third and could be retracted again only by briefly pushing the stick down hard so that the leg locked into the wing by centrifugal force. As a result of this, shortly after take off, our aircraft would make a brief but vigorous bow. Very often this remedy was not successful on the first attempt, so that handling during this phase of the flight was very difficult. This fault was remedied with the Ta 152 H-1 and there were no further complaints.

During dogfights the P-51 would turn very sharply and fire its guns almost immediately. Initially, during the first turn, the Ta 152's turn radius would be larger than the P-51's, but would then become smaller. Thus, if one survived the first attack of a Mustang in a dogfight, it was quite possible to line up behind the Mustang during the following turns. During January 1945, some of the comrades from the Stabsschwarm did this successfully.

This small turn radius was due to the wide prop blades and the 2,400 hp of the Jumo 213 engine. It may sound fantastic, but I flew a 'lazy eight' over our home base at Stendal within the field's boundaries. This would have been impossible with the Fw 190."

Rudi Driebe's statement attributing 2,400 hp to the Jumo 213 is a bit optimistic. The Jumo 213 E, which powered most of the Ta 152 H-1s, produced 1,730 to 1,870 hp, depending on equipment and special features. Only the projected Jumo 213 S was reportedly capable of producing 2,400 hp, but this advanced development failed to enter production before the war's end. Driebe concludes by describing the aircraft's performance:

During a training flight, I dived the Ta 152 from 23,000 ft (7,000 m) to about 621.4 mph (1,000 km/h) – more I didn't dare! I recovered from the dive in 1,970 ft (600 m) using the electrical elevator trim and – without touching the throttle – climbed to 7,000 m again. Result: blackout from the last third of the dive to nearly 7,000 meters. But my Ta 152 flew undisturbed 'like a plank' – it was intoxicating!"

REACHING FOR THE STRATOSPHERE

On 20 January 1945, Ofw. Friedrich Schnier, a *Luftwaffe* pilot seconded to Focke-Wulf as test pilot, took off from Langenhagen in Focke-Wulf Fw 190 V29/U2, W. Nr. 0054, the third Ta 152 prototype, in an attempt to determine the aircraft's absolute ceiling. He recalled to Hans Sander:

Before I made this record altitude flight, I had made several flights with other types of aircraft up to an altitude of about 36,080 ft [11,000]. But for this flight, I was requested to climb to the aircraft's absolute ceiling altitude. The current altimeter and barographs in German

aircraft at that time only indicated a maximum of 39,360 ft [12,000 m]. Therefore, an Italian barograph with a range of 45,920 ft. [14,000 m] was installed in W. Nr. 0054, and then checked before and after the flight.

The initial climb was quite normal. Every 3,280 ft [1,000 m] I radioed, in code, the requested values – air speed, altitude, manifold pressure, temperatures, etc., and the blower gear (there were three). At 32,800 ft [10,000 m] altitude I was reminded to inflate the sealing tube of the cockpit canopy, but the result was not satisfactory. Due to leakages the cockpit altitude was not much lower than the atmospheric altitude; however, I can't really remember the exact difference. It was designed to maintain a pressure of 300 gr/cm².

From 36,080 ft [11,000 m] on, I got pains and itching in the elbows and the knees, and I had the sensation that my movements became still. Voice procedures became difficult. At 39,360 ft [12,000 m] I radioed, 'Altimeter pegged (at the limit), will continue to climb with the help of the speed and climb indicator.' Slowly, I climbed higher, having only a visual indication that I got higher than ever before. My vision narrowed to a projector sized view. The sky took on a color of midnight blue and then black, going through the horizon in all nuances of blue to blinding white.

My right arm and hand no longer responded to my mental commands so I continued flying left handed. The aircraft became sloppier and sloppier, barely responding to rudder movement. After stalling twice in the thin air, and when it became more and more difficult to hold or gain altitude, I gave up. As requested, while descending, I made some speed runs at different altitudes, radioing the measured values down to the flight observers.

After landing almost at nighttime, I was received heartily by the technicians who had followed my flight by radio. Then the barograph was checked. Everyone was delighted – it had worked with readings almost to the upper border of the recording strip. Evaluation indicated an absolute altitude of 44,785 ft [13,654 m]."

Because Schnier carried a barograph in his aircraft, this achievement stood as the record altitude for the Ta 152 H, even though others, like Kurt Tank himself, had noted even higher ceilings.

Schnier also made some full throttle dives with the aircraft from 34,440 ft (10,500 m) to determine what today would be called the aircraft's critical Mach number, or the speed at which control was marginal or lost. He remembers getting the aircraft up to Mach 0.96 with violent rocking, but this seems incredibly high.

As W. Nr. 0054 went through the test program it suffered asymmetrical flap retraction and having the right gear failing to lock up. The cause of the latter was traced to the small inner fairing door jamming against the wheel well before the wheel was fully retracted. The entire fairing had to be refabricated. No sooner had this condition been corrected, than the right gear once again failed to lock up. This time, it was traced to the hydraulic system, cutting off after the left

wheel (which came up faster) was in its well. A temporary solution was achieved by increasing the hydraulic pressure to 140 atü, which was far too high for production aircraft.

By 30 January 1945, the total flying time for all of the H series prototypes amounted to only 49 hours 42 minutes. Not surprisingly, problems with the first production aircraft surfaced continually. The right landing gear often failed to lock up. During taxi and braking, the right landing gear leg would fail since both the down and up hydraulic lines were pressurized. When the high pressure air emergency extension system for the landing gear and flaps was activated, it burst the hydraulic reservoir because the compressed air forced its way past the weak check valve and into the tank. Moreover, adjustments to lessen aileron control forces were next to impossible because, each time the ailerons were removed for the adjustment, the reference marks were obliterated.

Rechlin's test pilots also had their share of difficulties regulating the Jumo 213 E. A total of four attempts was made at high altitude flight and each time the supercharger failed to engage. It was determined that the problem centered on the supercharger's third gear speed which, due to under-strength gearing, frequently failed to engage. These and other problems associated with the 'E' engine were eventually resolved through numerous *Änderungs Anweisungen* (Alteration Orders) implemented under the auspices of specialist Junkers field representatives.

> **Rechlin summarized the Fw 190 V29/U2's flight characteristics as follows:**
>
> 1. A change in trim of the pitch axis through the use of flaps was tolerable.
>
> 2. Stall behavior not pleasant, but judged as permissible.
>
> 3. Stability around pitch axis is weak; tendency to drift. With cooling flaps open, instability around yaw axis – aircraft pulled to the right. Elevators barely sufficient for three-point landing, even with full up trim (the Fw 190 horizontal stabilizer angle could be adjusted easily with limit stops on the top and bottom – the Ta 152 had a fixed stabilizer with only adjustable elevator tabs.)
>
> 4. Flight performance: Speeds and combat performance not up to theoretical values, especially above 36,080 ft (11,000 m). Climb rate suffered by 3.28 ft (1 m) per second throughout performance envelope, but reached expectations on subsequent test.

WORKLOAD PLAN FOR 1945 FROM BAD EILSEN

On 20 February 1945, the Construction Office at Focke-Wulf's Bad Eilsen headquarters issued an important document (reproduced on pages 128-129) outlining the firm's personnel requirement for the design, development (*Muster-*

bau), and production (*Serienbau*) of Fw 190 and the Ta 152 up to the end of 1945. The plan also delineated the firm's intent to develop current production Fw 190 and Ta 152s into specialized variants.

Inclusion of the Ta 152 A, B, and E within the series construction program (yellow field) is especially noteworthy since it projects production of these three marks, in parallel with the Ta 152 C and H series, at least up to the end of 1945.

Ta 152 B-5 HEAVY FIGHTER

Operation *Bodenplatte*, conducted over New Year's Day, underscored the importance of effective ground attack aircraft. Up to this time, the most modern German single-engine fighter-bomber in production was the Focke-Wulf Fw 190 F. Classified as *Schlachtflugzeug* the F series embodied the immense versatility of the Fw 190. The Fw 190 F-8 (based upon the A-8) proved to be a significant ground-support fighter-bomber capable of carrying a wide range of ordnance and was still powered by the BMW 801.

When originally conceived in 1943, the mission of the Ta 152 B series was defined as that of a *Schlachtflugzeug* and, in this role four versions were initially forecast: The Ta 152 B-1 through B-4 (see Chapter 3). However, by mid-1944, Focke-Wulf had still not received a firm production order for the 'B' series. Then, in early January 1945, the Air Ministry returned to the B series by upgrading its priority to fulfill the mission of a *Zerstörer*. The result of this endeavor was the Ta 152 B-5. This model was essentially based upon the proposed Ta 152 C-3, but powered by a Jumo 213 E-2 having an induction cooler and high-pressure MW injection. Alternatively, a Jumo 213 EB, without the induction cooler, but retaining high-pressure MW was considered an acceptable alternative engine.

The heavily armed Ta 152 B-5 heavy fighter aircraft was to have been armed with two 20 mm cowl-mounted MG 151/20 cannons plus three 30 mm MK 103 cannons; one as a *Motorkanone* and one in each wing root. The MK 103 was a potent weapon, yet Focke-Wulf had never tested the feasibility of incorporating this cannon as a synchronized wing root weapon for single-engined warplanes. Previously, Focke-Wulf had rigorously flight-tested the MK 103, mounted underwing beyond the propeller arc, as a ground-attack anti-armor weapon. However, in this configuration, test results were not especially encouraging. Besides having poor flight characteristics, aircraft with the MK 103 failed to demonstrate effectiveness against select ground targets. In particular, the cannon's ammunition proved incapable of penetrating the armor of Russian T-34 tanks.

Nevertheless, employing the MK 103 as an air-to-air weapon by single-engine fighters had definite advantages in combating massed Allied bombers. When compared to the MK 108, the MK 103 was heavier by 185 lb (84 kg), nearly twice the overall length, had a slightly slower rate of fire (420 vs. 450 rpm), and a significantly higher muzzle velocity (2,822 vs. 1,600 ft/sec). It could also be synchronized but required a pitch of 8° 30.' Because of the weapon's longer shell trajectory, it was possible to effectively fire the weapon beyond the range of Allied counterfire.

One of the critical roles undertaken by the Fw 190 was that of a close support fighter-bomber — it was in this role the aircraft proved especially effective. Classified as a **Schlachtflugzeug**, this example owned by NASM, Fw 190 F-8/R1, W. Nr. 931884, KT+ZS, "White 7", is shown following its thorough restoration in 1983. It was anticipated the Ta 152 B-6, also a dedicated close support variant of the Ta 152, would ultimately replace the Fw 190 F series.

To adapt the MK 103 for single-engine fighter use, it was decided to install the weapon _within_ the wing, inboard at the wing root, where it would have less impact on the aircraft's flight characteristics. To test this arrangement, one of the early Dora 9 prototypes, the Fw 190 V53, W. Nr. 170003, DU+JC, was assigned to the program. Because this prototype was now to serve as a test bed for the MK 103, which required modification, this test aircraft was redesignated Fw 190 V68. It was flight cleared on 13 December 1944 and soon transferred to the _Luftwaffe's_ weapons proving ground at Tarnewitz.

Production of the Ta 152 B-5 was finally to commence in May 1945 at Erla and in July 1945 at Gotha. The principal production subtype was to have been the Ta 152 B-5/R11 _Schlechtwetterjagd_ (Bad Weather Fighter) equipped with various avionics to aid in IFR (Instrument Flight Rules) operations.

To speed development of the Ta 152 B-5, it was decided to transfer three prototypes (Ta 152 V19, V20, and V21) previously earmarked for the Ta 152 C-3 series, directly to the Ta 152 B-5/R11 program. The first two, the Ta 152 V19 and V20, were scheduled for completion during March 1945 with the V21 following in April 1945.

Before the collapse, two additional B series subtypes were advanced but neither variant progressed beyond the planning stage and, so far as is known, no development prototypes were allocated to either subtype. The Ta 152 B-6 _Schlachtflugzeug_ would have been essentially similar to the B-5 but reinstated cowl weapons and was powered by the Jumo 213 EB engine with high pressure MW 50 power boost. This engine lacked an intercooler and required the supercharged fuel/air mixture to be partially cooled by MW power boost in conjunction with B4 aviation fuel. The final B series subtype, the Ta 152 B-7 _Zerstörer_, would have been generally similar to

the B-6 but powered by the new 2,240 hp Jumo 213 J driving a wooden four-bladed VS 19 propeller. But the anticipated destabilizing influence of the Jumo 213 J with VS 19 was such that it would have been necessary to further enlarge the aircraft's fin and increase the size of the horizontal tailplane. In spite of the fact that only one prototype (Jumo 213 JV) of this advanced engine had been assembled by December 1944, the Air Ministry's Technical Office sanctioned production and approved its use in the Ta 152. Only certain engine components of further examples were finished before the end of the war. Unlike the Jumo 213 E, the Jumo 213 J had four valves per cylinder, instead of the usual three. It was also engineered to operate at increased engine RPMs while employing a three speed supercharger in conjunction with MW power boost.

ADDITIONAL Ta 152 C SERIES PROTOTYPES ARRIVE

By 5 January 1945, the Ta 152 V7, W. Nr. 110007, CI+XM, was flight cleared and three days later, on 8 January 1945, it was flown for the first time at Adelheide by Bernhard Märschel. Powered by the twentieth prototype of the DB 603 EC, W. Nr. 01300147, the V7 was completed to Ta 152 C-0/R11 standards. Among other things, this aircraft was to specifically test the FuG 16 and FuG 125 electronics and, on 25 January 1945, it was transferred to Siemens for installation of the LGW K23 autopilot. The following day, Hans Sander flew the aircraft back to Langenhagen without incident. Tank and his engineers were quite pleased with the V7 since it had the newly integrated engine fairings, resulting in higher speeds.

The previous October, the Air Ministry issued its "50 km/h _schneller_" (31 mph faster) edict whereby all aircraft under production contracts were to be redesigned, or modified, in order to attain the extra speed.

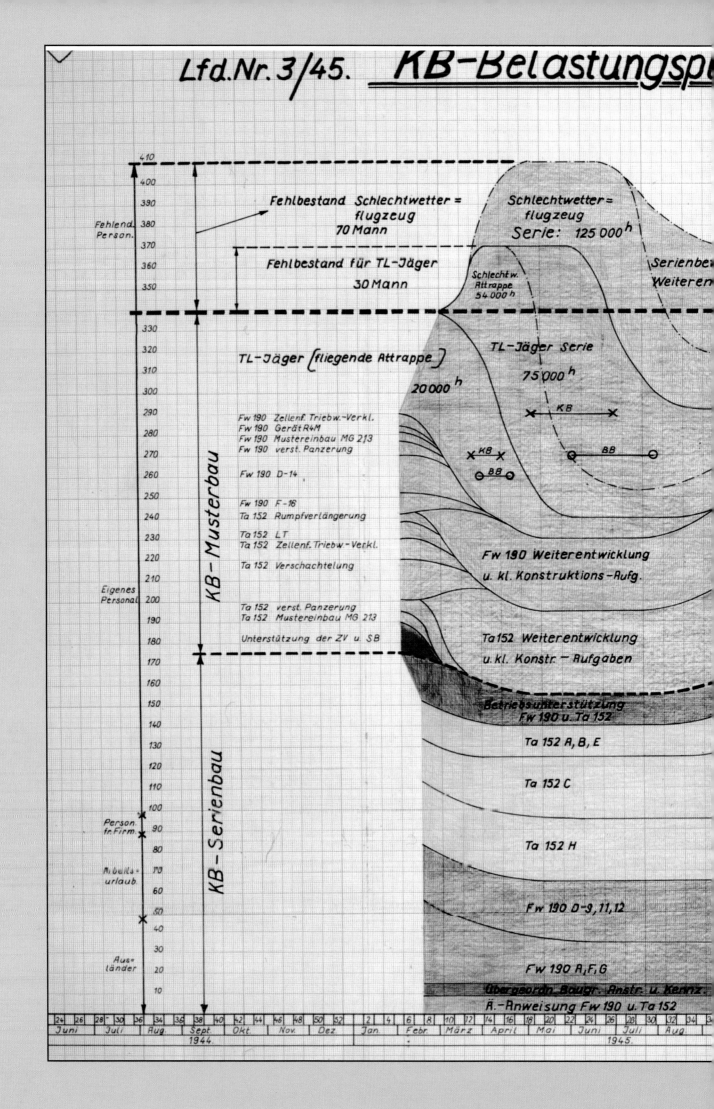

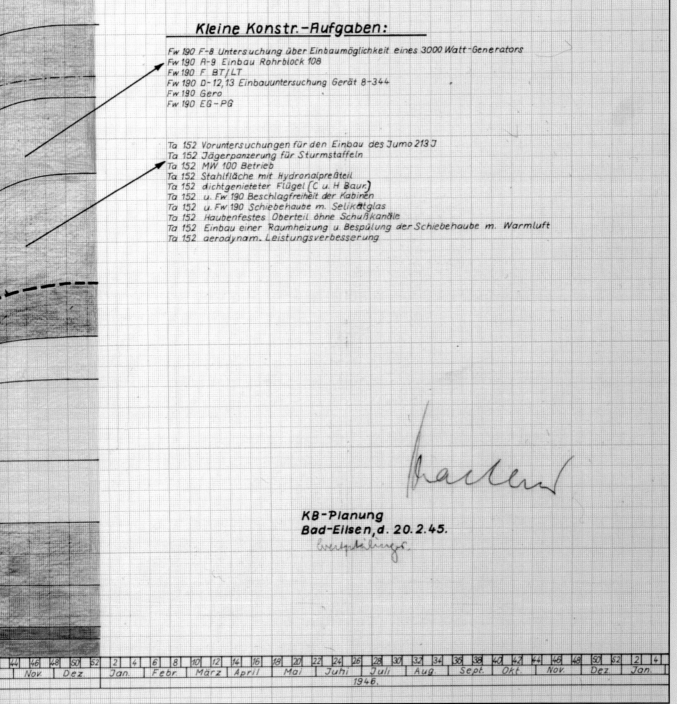

Lfd. Nr. 3/45 Konstruktion Büro – Work Load Plan / Bad Eilsen

This detailed document produced by the Focke-Wulf Planning Department at Bad Eilsen on 20 March 1945, gives a thorough picture of the company's plans for the Fw 190 and Ta 152 from February to December 1945.

The top most portion above the dotted line concerns itself with manpower issues relative to Focke-Wulf's entire production cycle.

The middle section, KB- Musterbau (Construction Bureau – Type Assembly), delineates the production cycle of various models and subtypes throughout 1945. Within this production cycle is a listing of Kleine Konstr.-Aufgaben (Small Construction to be Delivered) highly specialized Fw 190 and Ta 152 aircraft to be built only in small numbers.

The lower section below the next dotted line, KB-Serienbau (Construction Bureau – Series Construction), lists the principal Fw 190 and Ta 152 subtypes to enter production during the 10-month period. It is interesting to recognize the period in which this chart was created, Allied armies were poised to enter Germany itself and that within 90 days the war in Europe would be over.

Kleine Konstr.-Aufgaben:

Fw 190 F-8 Untersuchung über Einbaumöglichkeit eines 3000 Watt-Generators
Fw 190 A-9 Einbau Rohrblock 108
Fw 190 F BT/LT
Fw 190 D-12,13 Einbauuntersuchung Gerät 8-344
Fw 190 Gero
Fw 190 EG-PG

Ta 152 Voruntersuchungen für den Einbau des Jumo 213 J
Ta 152 Jägerpanzerung für Sturmstaffeln
Ta 152 MW 100 Betrieb
Ta 152 Stahlfläche mit Hydronalpreßteil
Ta 152 dichtgenieteter Flügel (C u. H Baur.)
Ta 152 u. Fw 190 Beschlagfreiheit der Kabinen
Ta 152 u. Fw 190 Schiebehaube m. Selikatglas
Ta 152 Haubenfestes Oberteil öhne Schußkanäle
Ta 152 Einbau einer Raumheizung u. Bespülung der Schiebehaube m. Warmluft
Ta 152 aerodynam. Leistungsverbesserung

KB-Planung
Bad-Eilsen, d. 20.2.45.

44	46	48	50	52	2	4	6	8	10	12	14	16	18	20	22	24	26	28	30	32	34	36	38	40	42	44	46	48	50	52	2	4
Nov.		Dez.			Jan.		Febr.		März		April		Mai		Juni		Juli		Aug.		Sept.		Okt.		Nov.		Dez.		Jan.			

1946.

The Fw 190 V68, W. Nr. 170003, DU+JC, was created to test the feasibility of installing the MK 103 aircraft cannon within the wing roots, an arrangement planned for the Ta 152 B-5. In reality, the V68 was essentially the modified Fw 190 V53 which, in the meantime, had served its initial purpose and was thus available for the Ta 152 Bertha program. When this photograph was taken, the wing root weapons change had not yet been completed.

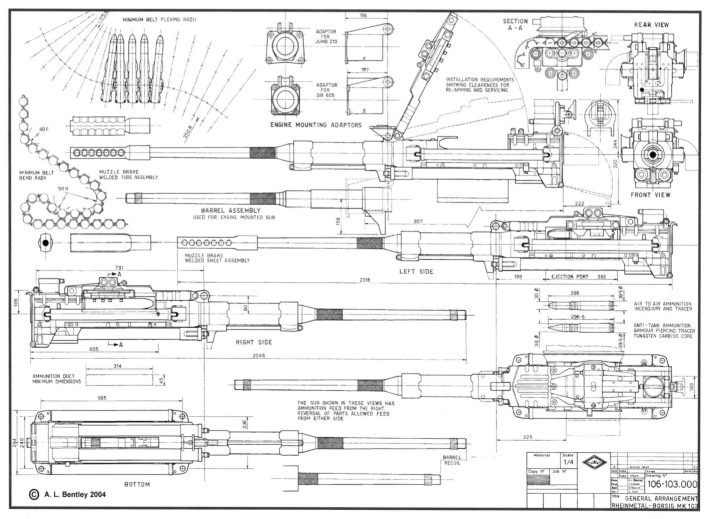

By January 1945, Focke-Wulf published a summary of the Fw 190 and Ta 152 programs to discuss how they might squeeze more speed out of the fighters through deviations in construction. In view of the war situation plus the fact that designers were already deeply involved in the quest for additional speed, such bureaucratic meddling was seen as counterproductive.

On 30 January 1945, the *Oberkommando der Luftwaffe* (OKL - Air Force High Command's Organizational Staff) held a planning conference during which *Oberst* Gollob outlined the current personnel and materials situation with a view to avoiding the *Reichsmarschall's* suggestions, which the OKL felt could not be realized. Among the aircraft under discussion were the jet fighters Me 262 and He 162, the Me 263 rocket interceptor and the Ta 152. It was stated that large scale introduction of the Ta 152 was not foreseeable at present due (in part) to "all wings being lost" at Posen; undoubtedly as a result of the large Allied bombing raid the previous May.

The third and last Adelheide-built Ta 152 prototype, the Ta 152 V8, W. Nr. 110008, GW+QA, equipped with the DB 603 EV19, W. Nr. 01300150 (DB 603 EC), was flight cleared on 14 January and flown by Märschel for the first time the next day, 15 January 1945. This prototype was generally similar to the V7 but fitted with the new EZ 42 gyro gun sight planned for the initial *Cäsar* production model, the Ta 152 C-1.

By 1 February 1945, after 18 flights with the Ta 152 V6,

totaling seven hours 41 minutes, test pilots were generally pleased with the DB 603. Compared to the Jumo 213, supercharger controls were much better. After a run-in time of two hours, the engine was run at full boost power (2,700 rpm and 1.96 atü boost) using MW 50 at 17,220 ft (5,250 m) to achieve a commendable speed of 426.9 mph (687 km/h). Testing further revealed that although some DB 603 supercharger problems reduced expected rated altitude to 34,110 ft (10,400 m), the climb rate at gross weight and combat power (2,500 rpm at 1.45 atü boost) was very good. However, with fully opened coolant flaps, oil and coolant temperatures were still too high.

Just as with the Ta 152 H, test pilots also encountered stability problems due to the aircraft's center of gravity being too far aft. By February 1945, fuel in the main fuselage tank amounted to 157 gal (594 liters) of B4 aviation fuel. This fuel source was supplemented by 36.9 gal (140 liters) of MW located in the rear fuselage tank. In an effort to alleviate this chronic problem, the aft tank holding the MW solution was left empty and 88 lbs of ballast, presumably as additional armor, were added to the engine compartment. Production examples of the Ta 152 C-1, C-3, and C-11, each with the R11 auxiliary apparatus and the DB 603 LA engine, were to have their MW tanks removed from the rear fuselage with the methanol-water relocated to the inboard port wing fuel tank as in the Ta 152 H-1. The remaining five wing-mounted fuel tanks carried B4 aviation fuel.

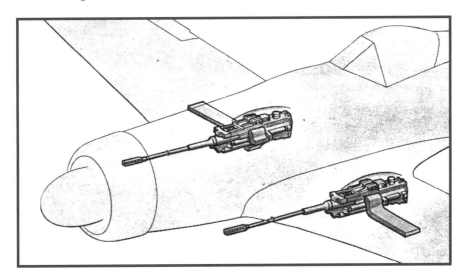

A schematic drawing showing installation locations of the MK 103 system.

A closeup of the 30 mm MK 103 evaluated on Fw 190 A-6/R3, W. Nr. 1903, RG+ZA, within an underwing gondola. This installation arrangement was forecast for the Ta 152 B-1 close support fighter whereas the later Ta 152 B-5 was to carry these powerful cannons buried within the wing roots. The MK 103 was over 7 feet in length, weighed 320 lbs, and relied upon a barrel recoil shell feeding system. Note the weapon's characteristic muzzle brake ports.

Three further images of the Fw 190 V68, the designated weapons test vehicle for the Ta 152 B-5. Shown is the aircraft's nose just prior to conversion, while the two closeup images below show the actual MK 103 internal conversion installation with the attendant ammunition feed belt illustrated on the previous page. After conversion work had been completed in December 1944, the prototype was flown to Tarnewitz for in-flight weapons testing and overall performance evaluation.

FOCKE-WULF Ta 152 SERIES PROTOTYPES

Series	Proto-type	W. Nr.	Stkz	Mission	Maker	Remarks
Ta 152 A	V1	250001	-	Fighter	Fw Cottbus planned	For Ta 152 A-1 but canceled
Jumo 213 C	V2	250002	-	"	Fw Cottbus planned	For Ta 152 A-1 but canceled
Ta 152 B	V19	110019	-	Zerstörer	Fw Sorau	Transferred from C-3 series and completed as Ta 152 B-5/R11. First flown 30 March 1945.
Jumo 213 E	V20	110020	-	"	"	Transferred from C-3 series and completed as Ta 152 B-5/R11. First flown 30 March 1945.
	V21	110021	-	"	"	Transferred from C-3 series and completed as Ta 152 B-5/R11. First flown 10 April 1945.
	V6	110006	VH+EY	Fighter	Fw Adelheide	First flight: 12 Dec 1944 as Ta 152 C-0 powered by the DB 603 EV21.
	V7	110007	CI+XM	"	"	First flight: 8 January 1945 as Ta 152 C-0/R11 powered by the DB 603 EV20.
	V8	110008	GW+QA	"	"	First flight: 15 January 1945 as Ta 152 C-0/EZ powered by the DB 603 EV19.
	V10	110010	-	"	Fw Sorau	For Ta 152 C-1 but canceled 18 October 1944
	V11	110011	-	"	"	For Ta 152 C-1 but canceled 18 October 1944
	V12	110012	-	"	"	For Ta 152 C-1 but canceled 18 October 1944.
	V13	110013	-	"	"	For Ta 152 C-1 but canceled 18 October 1944. Thereafter for strength tests.
	V15	110015	-	"	"	For Ta 152 C-1 but canceled 18 October 1944. Thereafter for strength tests.
Ta 152 C	V16	110016	-[2]	"	"	For Ta 152 C-3 forecast flight clear about April 1945
DB 603 L	V17	110017	-	"	"	For Ta 152 C-3 forecast flight clear about April 1945.
	V18	110018	-	"	"	Originally for Ta 152 C-2 and C-4 for LGW K23 + FuG 125 tests but canceled Dec 1944.
	V19	110019	-	"	"	Originally for Ta 152 C-3 then briefly for Ta 152 C-5 before transfer to Ta 152 B-5/R11.
	V20	110020	-	"	"	Originally for Ta 152 C-3 then briefly for Ta 152 C-5 before transfer to Ta 152 B-5/R11.
	V21	110021	-	"	"	Originally for Ta 152 C-3 then briefly for Ta 152 C-5 before transfer to Ta 152 B-5/R11.
	V22	110022	-	"	"	For Ta 152 C-4 but canceled 5 January 1945.
	V23	110023	-	"	"	For Ta 152 C-4 but canceled 5 January 1945.
	V24	110024	-	"	"	For Ta 152 C-4 but canceled 5 January 1945.
	V27	150027[1]	-	"	Fw Cottbus	Hybrid H-0 with 9-8603/B1/TEA + MK 103M only for Ta 152 C-3 but with 23,5 m² wing.
	V28	150028[1]	-	"	Fw Cottbus	Hybrid H-0 with 9-8603/B1/TEA + MK 103M only for Ta 152 C-3 but with 23,5 m² wing.
	V9	110009	-	Recon-Ftr.	Fw Sorau	For short span Ta 152 E-1 but canceled in favor of DB 603 LA powered Ta 152 C-11
Ta 152 E	V14	110014	-	"	"	For short span Ta 152 E-1 but canceled in favor of DB 603 LA powered Ta 152 C-11.
Jumo 213E	V26	110026	-	"	Mimetall Erfurt	For short span Ta 152 E-1 flight cleared February 1945.
	V3	260001	-	Hi-Alt Ftr.	Fw Cottbus planned	For Ta 152 H-1 but canceled.
	V4	260002	-	"	"	For Ta 152 H-1 but canceled.
	V5	260003	-	"	"	For Ta 152 H-1 but canceled.
	V18/U2	0040	CF+OY	"	Fw Adelheide	Replacement for Fw 190 V31, 0056, then replaced W. Nr. 110004. First flight: 19 Nov 1944.
Ta 152 H	V29/U1	0054	GH+KS	"	"	Replaced W. Nr. 110003. First flight: 24 September 1944.
Jumo 213 E	V30/U1	0055	GH+KT	"	"	Replaced W. Nr. 110002. First flight: 6 August 1944. Crashed 13 August 1944.
	V32/U2	0057	GH+KV	"	"	Replaced W. Nr. 110005. First flight: 1 October 1944.
	V33/U1	0058	GH+KW	"	"	Replaced W. Nr. 110001. First flight: 13 July 1944 but crashed following day.
	V25	110025	-	"	Fw Sorau	Built to Ta 152 H-1 std. as repl for V33/U1 but construct halted. Wings went to V32/U2.
Ta 152 S	C-1/U1	-	-	Trainer	Subcontracted	Conversions by Blohm & Voss in Apr 1945 + DLH Prague Aug 1945.
DB 603L						

1. The Ta 152 V27 and V28 were originally linked with W. Nr. 150027 and W. Nr. 150028 respectively, and officially tied to the Ta 152 C-3 series, yet this plan was altered when *Werknummern* 150027 and 150028 were completed as standard Ta 152 H-0s. The V27 and V28 were subsequently transferred respectively to W. Nr. 150030 and W. Nr. 150031. As in the first plan, this new V27 and V28 were to be hybrids… long span "Hs" but with DB 603 L engines.
2. *Stammkenzeichen* (Primary Identification) code for the V16 reportedly GW + QI but remains unverified.

Two views of the Ta 152 V7 during the prototype's early testing program in January 1945. Because the promised DB 603 LA was not ready in time, early examples of the DB 603 E (Triebwerk 9-8603B) were substituted in the first three Ta 152 C series prototypes. In addition, the V7 carried all of the equipment associated with Rüstsätze 11 (Auxiliary Apparatus 11) which included K23 directional control, FuG 125 "Hermine" VHF radio beacon signal receiver, heated windows and PKS 12 autopilot.

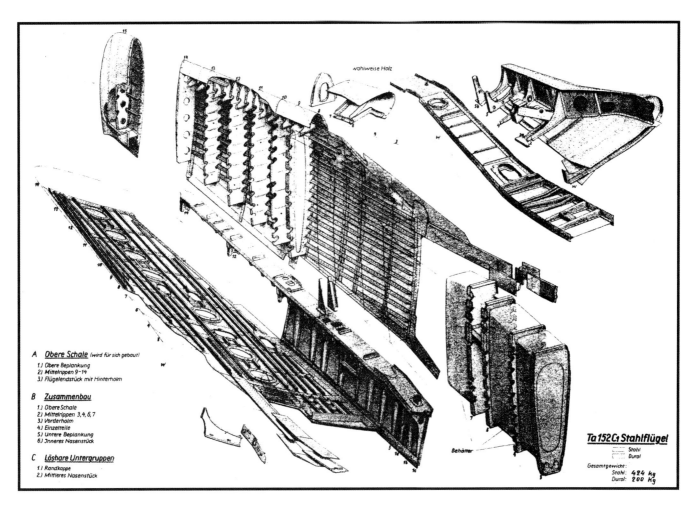

A *Obere Schale* (wird für sich gebaut)
1.) Obere Beplankung
2.) Mittelrippen 9-14
3.) Flügelendstück mit Hinterholm

B *Zusammenbau*
1.) Obere Schale
2.) Mittelrippen 3, 4, 6, 7
3.) Vorderholm
4.) Einzelteile
5.) Untere Beplankung
6.) Inneres Nasenstück

C *Lösbare Untergruppen*
1.) Randkappe
2.) Mittleres Nasenstück

Ta 152 C₁ Stahlflügel
▭ Stahl
▭ Dural

Gesamtgewicht:
Stahl: 424 kg
Dural: 200 kg

Exploded view of the Ta 152 C's starboard wing showing its main steel and Dural components including the three unprotected sack-type fuel cells. The Ta 152 C's wing had a span of 36 ft 6¼ in (11,000 mm) with an area of 209.9 ft² (19.5 m²). The plan view below shows the location of the dual spar, ribs, stringers, gear bay and wing tip cap.

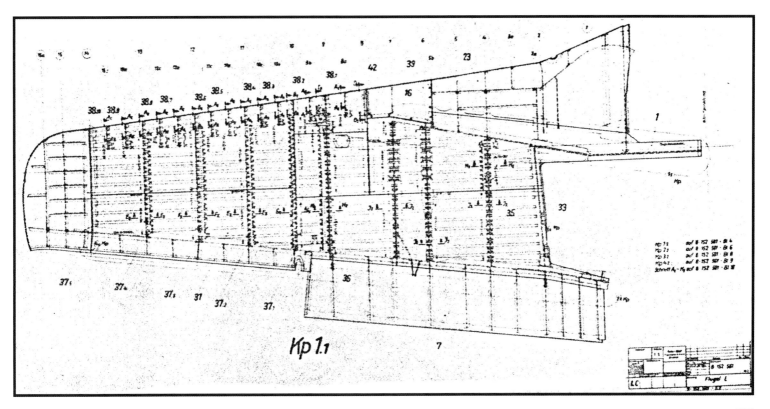

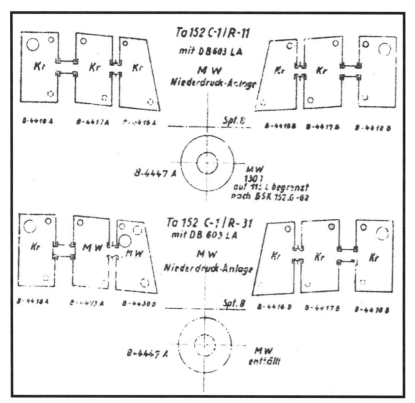

Left: A simplified Focke-Wulf diagram showing the distribution of wing fuel and power boosting tanks for the Ta 152 C-1/R11 (top) bad weather fighter, and the Ta 152 C-1/R31 which addressed center of gravity complaints. The top diagram depicts the six unprotected interconnected wing fuel tanks plus their respective part numbers for the Ta 152 C-1/R11 equipped with a DB 603 LA engine with low pressure MW power boost. Each tank, marked "Kr" was to be filled with C3 avgas of at least 96 octane. The concentric circles indicate the aft fuel tank containing 130 liters (34.3 gal) of MW 50 power boosting. The lower diagram for the Ta 152 C-1/R31, also with the DB 603 LA plus low pressure MW power boosting, is similar except the rear fuel tank (circles) was to be deleted or, if fitted, left empty with the MW being transferred to the port wing's inboard and middle fuel tanks. This arrangement reduced the aircraft's C3 fuel by 140 liters (37 gal). Presumably, this shortfall could have been made up by an external drop tank.

Below: An excellent comparison drawing showing the internal distribution of fuel and lubricants within the Ta 152 C and Ta 152 H to be virtually identical. The principal differences rest with the location of the power boosting chemicals. These were either contained in the port wing's in-board fuel tank, the protected aft circular fuselage tank or, in both locations as in the Ta 152 H requiring separate GM 1 and MW 50 systems. The two smaller tanks, shown forward in the plan view near the main wheels, were for engine oil (larger tank) containing 61 liters (16 gal) and hydraulic oil (small tank). Total internal fuel capacity for the Ta 152 C was between 1047 and 1050 liters (277 gal.) whereas the Ta 152 H carried slightly less at 977 to 980 liters (258 gal.).

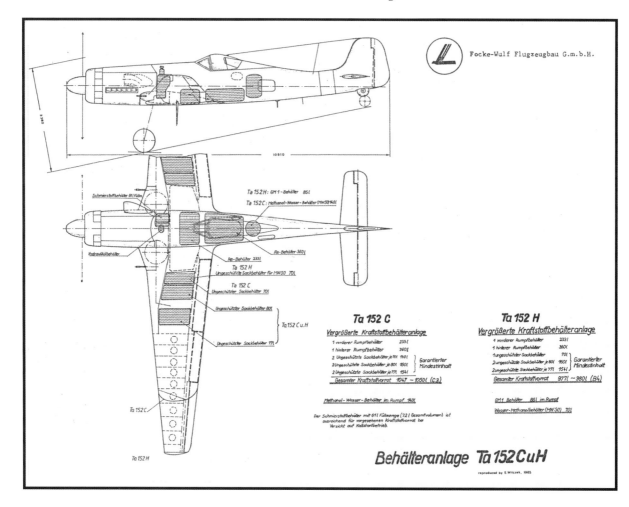

Two official company photographs of the Ta 152 V7 taken at Focke-Wulf's Adelheide branch early in 1945, are among the best surviving images of the Ta 152. Moreover, they reveal the design's unmistakable close affinity with the company's outstanding Fw 190. This prototype of the 'C' series, along with the V6 and V8, was initially powered by a DB 603 E since the anticipated DB 603 L and LA engines were not ready in time. Nevertheless, the performance of the 'E' engine was close enough to the 'L' for pilots to make a fair assessment of the aircraft's merits as well as its faults.

Ta 152 E SERIES PRODUCTION BEGINS

Early in March 1945, in fulfillment of the RLM order for a specialized reconnaissance version of the Ta 152, the workshops at Mitteldeutsche Metallwerke GmbH (Mimetall – MML) at Erfurt North began construction of a small number of Ta 152 E-0 machines concurrent with the first examples of the Ta 152 H-11 high altitude reconnaissance fighter. Following completion of approximately 40 aircraft of the original compliment of 115 Ta 152 H-0s in January 1945, it was decided to simultaneously cancel the Ta 152 H-10, reconnaissance fighter based on the H-0, in favor of the Ta 152 H-11, a dedicated reconnaissance fighter, which itself was based on the Ta 152 H-1 then entering production at Cottbus.

Presumably, as the designated prototype for the Ta 152 E-2/H-10 series, the Ta 152 V26, W. Nr. 150021, was ferried from Cottbus to Erfurt where it was to serve as a production template, although confirmation of its arrival and final disposition has not been determined. Ironically, the two short span, Jumo powered Ta 152 E-0/E-1 series prototypes, the Ta 152 V9 and V14, had both been canceled prior to construction of the first Ta 152 E-0. However, in spite of appearances, cancellation of these two prototypes did not impact, or cause cancellation of the E-1 program. But rather they were recognized as simply an unnecessary development step. The Air Ministry had apparently already decided that two dedicated short span reconnaissance versions of the Ta 152 should go forward simultaneously — specifically the Jumo 213 E powered Ta 152 E-1 and the Ta 152 C-11 equipped with the DB 603 L.

Although Mimetall succeeded in bringing a handful of Ta 152 E-0s and H-11s to an advanced stage of assembly, none were actually completed before V - E Day. Among the items recovered by American troops immediately after their arrival at Erfurt included approximately 40 Ta 152 fuselages in various stages of assembly.

Ta 152 C SERIES PLANNING

There can be no question about the Ta 152 C's potential for development. Its medium altitude capabilities were well documented and, had the type entered operational service, pilots would undoubtedly have been delighted and enthusiastic for its performance. However, so far as is known, only two examples of the Ta 152 C-1 were delivered for operations late in the war. Moreover, this duo appears to have ended their brief operational career without having flown a single combat mission.

Although no less than 17 Sorau produced C series prototypes were originally planned, by January 1945, most were deferred or canceled. When it was decided to rush the Ta 152 C-1 and C-3 into production without the customary testing phase, the Ta 152 V10, V11, V12, V13 and V15 were deemed unnecessary and summarily canceled. The Ta 152 V19, V20 and V21 were each pulled and transferred to the Ta 152 B-5 series where they were to be outfitted as *Zerstörer* aircraft. A contributing reason for series cancellation frequently rested with engine and equipment availability. C series prototypes falling into this category included the Ta 152 V18, V22, V23 and the V24. Each of these prototypes was earmarked for the Ta 152 C-4 series and dependent upon the DB 603 L engine.

In addition to the C-4 series, the DB 603 L equipped with an intercooler, was also the designated engine to power the Ta 152 C-0, C-2, C-5 and C-6. But, by 1945 deliveries of The DB 603 L remained questionable. In contrast, the simpler DB 603 LA (A – *Änderungs* / Alteration), which lacked the intercooler, appeared more certain and was therefore selected to power the initial production models, the Ta 152 C-1, C-3 and C-11.

Among the incomplete and damaged aircraft recovered by American troops at Mimetall's Erfurt facility, were a handful of Ta 152 E-0/E-1 short-range photographic reconnaissance fighters shown here in the company of a damaged Bf 109 G-10 on the far left, that appears to have made a forced landing with its engine still functioning. Instead of concentrating on one or two single-engine dedicated reconnaissance types, German industry chose to produce numerous versions within the Bf 109 and Fw 190 and Ta 152 series to fulfill this mission.

An American soldier relaxes soon after the war's end on the remains of a Ta 152 E-0 recovered at Mitteldeutsche Metallwerke GmbH, Erfurt Nord. Abbreviated as "Mimetall," this independent firm was awarded a contract to build dedicated photoreconnaissance versions of the Ta 152. Several examples of the Ta 152 E-0/E-1 were nearing completion when the facility was captured by American troops. Of these examples, some or most were purposely destroyed at MML before their capture. Apart from obligatory armament and cameras, the Ta 152 E-1 and Ta 152 B-5 would have had essentially identical airframes and powered by the same Jumo 213 E engine.

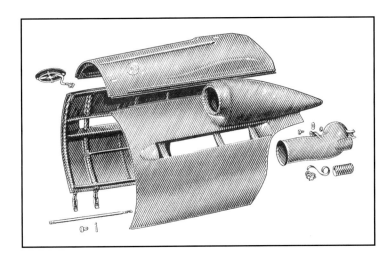

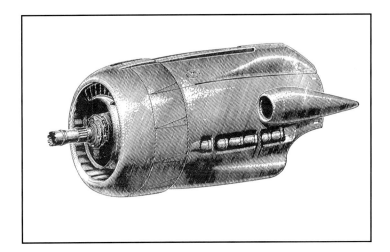

DB 603 cowl

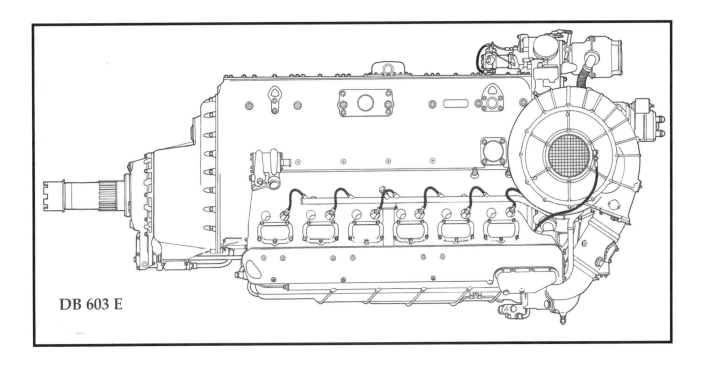

DB 603 E

Two additional 'C' series prototypes, the Ta 152 V27 and V28, were especially noteworthy hybrids. Each was officially intended solely as interim test aircraft for the Ta 152 C-3 series, yet their final configuration appears entirely consistent with two deferred Ta 152 H series proposals; namely the DB 603 L powered Ta 152 H-8/H-9! Surviving Focke-Wulf documents indicate these two Cottbus built prototypes, modified from Ta 152 H-0 airframes and retaining their long span wings, were supposedly linked to the Ta 152 C-3 program solely on account of their engine-mounted cannon (MK 103M). Yet, since the Ta 152 V16 and V17 were the officially established prototypes for the Ta 152 C-3 series and, inasmuch as the Ta 152 C-3 had already been ordered into production by the time the V27 and V28 were initiated, it would appear that Focke-Wulf was employing a sleight of hand in order to advance a "new" (and unauthorized) production model!

The projected series Ta 152 C-7, C-8, C-9 and C-10 are each provisionally defined and summarized on page 144. Each would have been powered by an engine holding the promise of greatly improved performance including the Jumo 213 J, BMW 801 R, Jumo 222 A-B/3 and the Jumo 222 E or C/D and the DB 603 E.

Another significant problem encountered with the Ta 152 C series prototypes concerned the engine mounts.

Daimler-Benz preferred steel mounts but the Air Ministry dictated a mixed alloy construction as a weight-saving measure. The result was poor aiming accuracy in air-firing tests due to the flexing nature of the alloy. Daimler-Benz was determined to either revert to all-steel mounts or adapt new mounts developed separately by Dornier for use in their Do 335. Additionally, because of differing engine mounting joints, similar engines of the same type were not necessarily interchangeable. For example, it is noteworthy that the engine 9-8603 C 1 (DB 603 E) was not interchangeable with engine 9-8603 C 2 (DB 603 LA).

Because of the worsening war situation, it had been decided that Focke-Wulf's Sorau facility would place a hold on additional Ta 152 C series prototypes until the supply situation improved. Instead, Sorau's manager, Heinz Gleschen, was ordered to completely focus the plant's limited resources toward accelerated production of the Fw 190 D-9. Although the entire Dora series, up to the last subtypes, were always considered "stop gap" fighters, to be phased out once production of the Ta 152 (both C and H series) had gained momentum, by 1945 this goal was simply unattainable. In the end, remarkably, Focke-Wulf's Sorau factory succeeded in producing over 600 examples of the Dora 9 before production ceased.

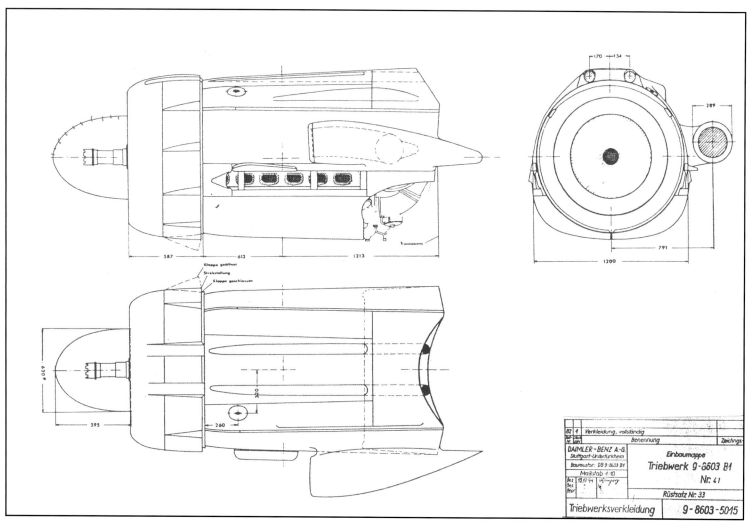

Below is presented a verbatim translation of a Daimler-Benz Development Office Internal memorandum, drafted two days after Christmas 1944, giving a particularly candid view of achievements and problems associated with the early examples of the firm's DB 603 Es as installed in the first three 'C' series prototypes. In keeping with established German practice, the engine's complete cowl assembly, including cooling radiators, (see previous page) and engine bearer arms were always considered integrated with the complete engine (**Triebwerk**), *and therefore were the responsibility of the engine maker.*

I. On my arrival at Adelheide, the aircraft Ta 152 C V6 with the DB 603 EV24 engine had already been flown to Langenhagen for further flight tests. No complaints regarding this engine. At Langenhagen, *Herr* Müllerschön had completed adjustment and testing for MW 50 special operation and increased engine output. On the scales, the aircraft showed a total weight of 60 kg (132 lbs.) less than calculated, including 35 kg (77 lbs.) ballast in the tail. The engine fitted still had the W 90 series supercharger. When the engine was changed, the certified supercharger was removed from the old engine and taken to Langenhagen, where it was available for replacement during a test pause. After about 2.5 hrs total engine running time, the oil cooler rips were found to leak (V2 version). For immediate repairs, the oil cooler from the DB 603 EV19 was removed in Adelheide and sent to Langenhagen by courier.

II. In the next aircraft, the Ta 152 CV7 fitted with the DB 603 EV20, the engine covers were firmly attached to the airframe as designated by Focke-Wulf. The DB 603 EV20 has the new engine with increased output, but still has the W 90 series supercharger. The exchange between the certified supercharger of the old engine will be arranged shortly. It should be ready for flight tests on 10 January 1945. The problem with the hand hole cover in the lower paneling between frames 1 and 1a, mentioned in internal memorandum Nr. 5611 was not followed through by Focke-Wulf because fuselage series production had already begun. In the interest of Daimler-Benz, hand hole cover should be mandatory. The automatic firing gear received was fitted to the Ta 152 V7. Two additional gears are to be provided for the Ta 152 V6 and V8 and are due to arrive by special courier.

III. Further firing tests are to be carried out with the DB 603 EV19 was therefore fitted outright with the new more powerful engine, the certified supercharger was exchanged, the automatic cowl flaps fitted, also the new reinforced flaps. Here it was discovered that the upper 3 flaps showed dimensional differences. Newly strengthened flaps similar to the old flaps in W 62 are being made for immediate replacement. Upon removal of the radiator head for the DB 603 EV19, it was found that the cooling air plate under the oil cooler at the crankcase was worn down by about 2 mm (1/16th in.), the plate will be cut down accordingly. The opening angle of the cooler exhaust flaps does not quite reach the calculated rated value, assuming the flaps are closed absolutely tight. If the 5 to 10 mm (1/4 to 3/8 in.) still lacking should become necessary at high outside temperatures, adjustment to larger opening angles will have to be made, thereby abandoning tight fitting when closed. Calculated and obtained results are being passed to W 62 for further checks.

DB Development Office - Internal Memorandum,

Signed: Holz, 27 Dec 1944

Three official photographs of the newly completed Ta 152 V7, W. Nr. 110007, CI+XM, photographed at Focke-Wulf's Adelheide shops early in 1945. This prototype was completed to Ta 152 C- 0 standards with bad weather **Rüstsatz 11** *(Auxiliary apparatus 11). It was flight cleared on 5 January 1945 flown for the first time by company test pilot, Bernhard Märschel three days later. Others also flew the prototype including Hans Sander who took a test hop at Langenhagen on 27 January 1945. During this period of exhaustive testing, the 'C' series prototypes displayed their unique 4-letter factory primary identification codes on their fuselages and the underwing.*

Ta 152 V8, (Ta 152 C-0)
W. Nr. 110008, GW+QA
January 1945

Ta 152 C- 0	Preproduction series was limited to the Ta 152 V6, V7 and V8 each powered by the DB 603 E because the 'L' engine was not ready. Each of these three examples was manufactured by Focke-Wulf at Sorau and flight cleared between 3 December 1944 and 12 January 1945. Equipped with the 19,5 m² wing without internal fuel storage. Armament consisted of one engine-mounted MK 108 and four MG 151/20 cannon with two each in the cowl and wing root positions. Provision was made for attaching two WGr 21 air-to-air rocket launchers beneath the outer wings. MW 50 power boosting fuel was contained in the cylindrical rear fuselage tank. Eligible for *Rüstsätze* (Auxiliary apparatus): R11, R33 and *Umrüst-bausätze* (Modification construction set): U1
Ta 152 C- 1	Primary series nonpressurized medium-altitude escort day fighter. Less than ten completed by Mimetall at Erfurt and ATG at Leipzig before the end of the war. This initial series was similar to the C-0 but equipped with the DB 603 LA (9-8603 B1), without intercooler, driving a 3-blade wooden VDM propeller. Avionics would have consisted of the FuG 16Zy, FuG 25a and FuG 125 and a LGW K23 autopilot. The series was eligible for the *Schloß* 503 An under-fuselage rack for either a 300 ltr. drop tank or a SC 500 bomb. Wing fuel stowage was divided between 6 interconnected fuel sacks. Eligible for *Rüstsätze*: R5, R11, R14, R15, R31.
Ta 152 C- 2	Virtually identical to the C-1 series but was to receive the DB 603 L and swap its FuG 16Zy radio for the newer (and still experimental) FuG 15. However, because the FuG 15 had not reached the degree of reliability, or availability, as originally planned, this series was deferred indefinitely on 15 December 1944. Eligible for *Rüstsätze*: R10, R11.
Ta 152 C- 3	A normal day fighter that was expected to be produced in numbers roughly equal to the C-1 beginning in June 1945. It was to be initially powered by the DB 603 LA (later with the DB 603 L) and would have been virtually identical to the C-1 but equipped with four MG 151/15 machine guns instead of the usual MG 151/20 cannons. Additionally, the MK 103 engine-mounted cannon replaced the MK 108. Production was to start with Siebel at Halle in June 1945 followed by ATG at Leipzig during July 1945. Eligible for *Rüstsätze*: R11
Ta 152 C- 4	A normal day fighter generally similar to the C-3 with the MK 103 engine-mounted cannon but also equipped with the newer FuG 15 radio. But, due to nonavailability of this advanced radio, the subtype was deferred indefinitely on 15 December 1944. Eligible for *Rüstsätze*: R11
Ta 152 C- 5	A heavy day fighter project scheduled to receive the DB 603 L (9-8603 B1/TL) with intercooler and armed with five MG 151/20 cannons in the engine, cowl and wing root positions. This version was to retain the proven FuG 16Zy radio. Eligible for *Rüstsätze*: R11
Ta 152 C- 6	A projected heavy day fighter version identical to the C-5 apart from its planned switch to the FuG 15 radio. This subtype was deferred indefinitely on 15 December 1944. Eligible for *Rüstsätze*: R11
Ta 152 C- 7	Provisionally: A normal day fighter project powered by the Junkers Jumo 213 J driving a Junkers VS 19 four-bladed propeller and otherwise, apart from its wing, generally similar to the high altitude Ta 152 H-7.
Ta 152 C- 8	Provisionally: A normal day fighter project powered by the BMW 801 R. This air-cooled radial engine project was loosely based upon the BMW 801 E but directly derived from the stillborn BMW 805. The BMW 801 R was equipped with a 2-stage, 4-speed supercharger requiring C3 fuel. With an overall length of 2,741 mm (8 ft - 11⅝ in) it was almost 29 inches longer than the standard BMW 801 A. Following American bombing raids on BMW facilities, the BMW 801 R was canceled in July 1944.
Ta 152 C- 9	Provisionally: A normal day fighter project powered by the Junkers Jumo 222 A-3 or C/D engine driving VS 19 four-bladed prop.
Ta 152 C- 10	Provisionally: A *Schlachtflugzeug* (close support) fighter-bomber powered by a DB 603 E and equipped with an ETC 503 under fuselage bomb rack plus four ETC 71 underwing bomb carriers. Armament restricted to three MG 151/20 cannons as an engine-mounted weapon plus two additional cannons in the wing root positions. A TSA 2D bomb sight was also included.
Ta 152 C- 11	A short range reconnaissance version powered by the DB 603 LA and based upon the Ta 152 C-1/R11 but carrying camera equipment originally intended for the Jumo powered Ta 152 E-1; a dedicated photoreconnaissance fighter equipped with an Rb 75/30 aerial camera or other similar smaller cameras that had been canceled earlier. Production was to be undertaken by Mimetall at Erfurt. Eligible for *Rüstsätze*: R1

Ta 152 C- Auxiliary Apparatus (*Rüstsätze*) Equipment
(Applicable for DB 603 equipped aircraft)

R10 - Provisionally: Additional armor plate for the engine and/or cockpit. Only for Ta 152 C- 2 subtype.

R11 - Bad weather fighter fitted with LGW K23 fighter directional control, FuG 125 "Hermine", VHF radio beacon signal receiver; heated windows and PKS 12 autopilot. The entire Ta 152 C- 1 production was to be equipped with R11 from the first aircraft.

R14 - A special torpedo fighter project fitted with an ETC 504 under-fuselage bomb rack capable of carrying one LT 1B or LT F5 airborne torpedo. Planned for operations during February 1945, but development was discontinued in favor of the Fw 190 D-12/R14 primarily because of the D-12's better torpedo suspension capability.

R31 - Modification to address center of gravity concerns. The cylindrical rear fuselage fuel tank containing MW 50 power boosting was deleted and the MW 50 transferred to the left wing's inner and middle fuel cells. The remaining four wing fuel cells carried B4 or C3 aviation fuel.

R33 - A special cowl assembly developed by Daimler-Benz for use in aircraft equipped with the DB 603 LA (9-8603 B1) engine. Effective 15 December 1944.

In addition to the above listed equipment options, a few novel anti-bomber weapons were planned or under test for eventual use by the Ta 152 C including:

(a) Wing-mounted vertically firing SG 500 *Jägerfaust* (Fighter's Fist) projectiles. Five of these 50 mm projectiles were installed vertically, in rifled barrels arranged in a line parallel to the fuselage and contained within the wing in the space normally occupied by the center fuel cell. The shells were fired by means of a photo-cell trigger when flying under a bomber.

(b) Similar to the SG 500 installation, was a device known as the *Rohrbock* 108 (Barrel Ram) which was comprised of two MK 108 gun barrels set vertically in the same location and manner as the SG 500 but fired by the pilot using a specially modified gun sight as the fighter flew beneath a bomber. Each of the two barrels per wing held only one 30 mm round.

(c) Two X-4 (Ru 344) air-to-air wire guided rockets mounted on underwing pylons and launched from a safe distance beyond a bomber's defensive fire. Their flight path was partially controlled by the pilot using a small joy-stick control whose signals were transmitted through a spool of wire that unwound when the missile was launched.

(d) The most successful anti-bomber projectile was the R4M air-to-air self-stabilizing rocket. Twelve R4Ms were to be carried on special launch rails beneath each wing and either fired individually or rippled off in one salvo. A number of Me 262s and Fw 190 D-9s successfully employed the R4M in operations during the closing weeks of the war.

(e) Four MG/MK 213 A cannons mounted at the cowl position and within the wing roots.

(f) Two WGr 21 air-to-air rocket projectiles mounted in special external "stove pipe" launchers attached to the underside of the wings.

(g) Clusters of *Panzerblitz* air-to-ground anti-tank missiles mounted on special rails attached to the underside of the wing's outer position.

Ta 152 C Modification Construction Set (*Umrüst-Bausätze*)
(Applicable for DB 603 LA equipped aircraft)

U1 - Two-seat trainer conversion which was to serve as a pilot model for the "production" Ta 152 S-1 and S-2 subtypes. Conversion sets were patterned after those successfully constructed for the Fw 190 F-8/U1, Fw 190 S-5 and S-8 subtypes.

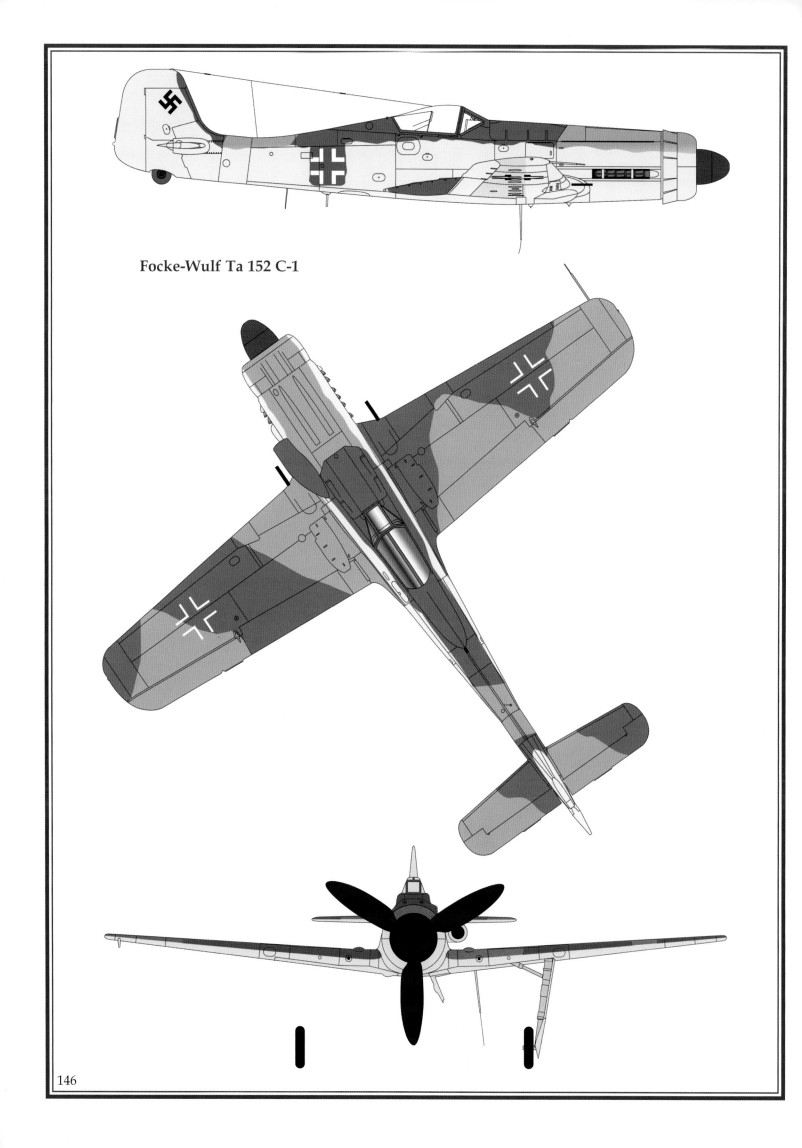

Focke-Wulf Ta 152 C-1

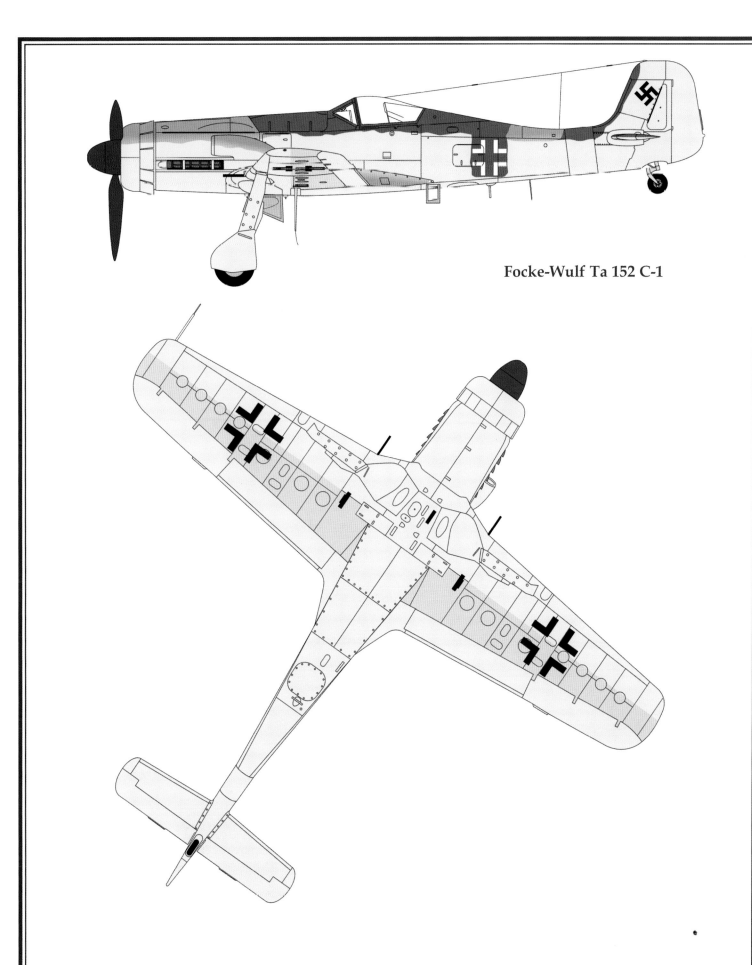

Focke-Wulf Ta 152 C-1

The Ta 152 C-1 would have been one of the more heavily armed single-engine, single-seat fighters in the Luftwaffe's inventory. With an armament of four 20 mm MG 151/20 cannon (2 x cowl at 150 rpg; 2 x wing roots with 175 rpg) plus one engine-mounted 30 mm MK 108 cannon with 90 rounds, it signaled a move from lesser caliber machine guns in favor of weapons packing a harder punch with fewer rounds. Additional weapons mounted internally or externally were theoretically optional but were limited by what they could achieve against specific targets. An example was early forms of guided and unguided air-to-air rockets, or missiles. These were primarily intended for use against massed enemy bombers. Their effectiveness was diminished due to their limited range and launch requirements. These optional weapon systems are listed in Appendix 3.

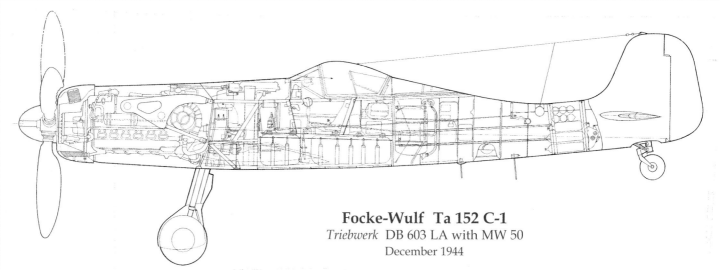

Focke-Wulf Ta 152 C-1
Triebwerk DB 603 LA with MW 50
December 1944

This sectional elevation clearly reveals many internal features and equipment. The Ta 152 C-1's fuselage contained two protected fuel tanks plus one unprotected tank in the rear fuselage. The forward-most tank, beneath the pilot's foot controls, contained 233 liters (62 gal) of C3 avgas of at least 96 octane. The second protected tank, immediately under the pilot's seat, was the largest tank having capacity for 360 liters (95 gal) of C3 fuel. The round drum-shaped tank mounted beneath the canopy's rear portion, had a capacity of 140 liters (37 gal) of power boosting fluid known as MW (Methanol-Water in equal amounts). However, due to center of gravity problems the amount of fuel carried in this aft mounted tank varied in an effort to correct the aircraft's corresponding adverse handling characteristics. A special under-fuselage rack was designed that would allow for a single 300 liter (79 gal) drop tank to be carried for extended missions. A larger, 600 liter (159 gal) drop tank was also planned for very long range missions, but there is no record of such a large tank being adapted to the Ta 152 C.

Junkers Jumo 222 C

Development of the Jumo 222 began in 1937, and over the next four years Junkers invested considerable time and resources endeavoring to bring their engine to a state of development whereby it would not only prove production reliable but would also consistently deliver its promised power. The task proved elusive and more difficult than expected. But by early 1942, Junkers made the decision to radically revamp the engine which included increasing the displacement to 49.9 liters by enlarging the bore and stroke to an almost square 145 x 140 mm (ca 5¾ x 5½ in). The exhaust manifold, ignition system and valveing were also revised. These and other changes resulted in the Jumo 222 C/D engine; the 'C' engine with right hand rotation while the 'D' was left hand rotation.

The Jumo 222 C/D was a liquid-cooled engine consisting of six engine blocks each with four cylinders, arranged about a central crankshaft. The intake and

exhaust manifolds were positioned close to one another and spaced evenly apart in clusters of three sets each having eight exhaust stacks. Each cylinder had two intake and one exhaust valve with fuel injectors positioned between the intakes adjacent to dual spark plugs.

Daimler-Benz's competitor, the 24-cylinder DB 604, was an X-type liquid-cooled monster that failed to progress beyond a small number of prototypes before being abandoned in September 1942. It was an interesting design but was substantially heavier than the Junkers and was not as powerful.

But as events unfolded, although the Jumo 222 C/D engine was more reliable and powerful than earlier models, it nevertheless failed to deliver its promised power and production was strictly limited to a small number of complete engines. As a consequence, the Ta 152 C-9 remained only a project without a future.

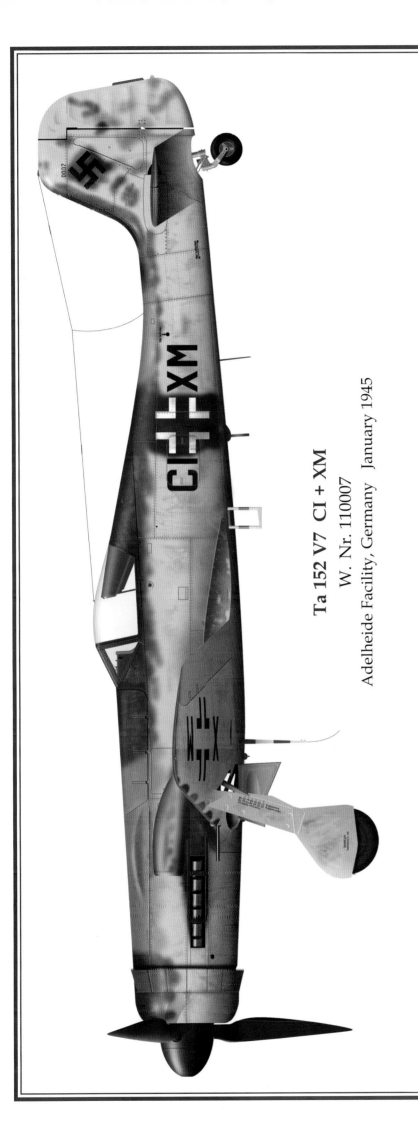

Ta 152 V7 CI + XM

W. Nr. 110007

Adelheide Facility, Germany January 1945

NOTABLE FEATURES

- No pressurized canopy
- All antennas intact
- Heated windscreen like Fw 190 D-9s

COLORS

UNDERSURFACES	RLM 76 Light Blue, underwing rear half unpainted except for ailerons and flap
UPPERSURFACES	RLM 75 Gray-Violet/RLM 83 Dark Green, Black exhaust panel; sawtooth camouflage on upperwing extends onto the underwing
PROP BLADES	RLM 70 Black-Green
SPINNER	RLM 70 Black-Green

NATIONAL MARKINGS

FUSELAGE	B5 600 mm White outline crosses
	H3 300 mm Black *Hakenkreuz*
WINGS	Upper: B6 600 mm White outline crosses
	Lower: B4 900 mm Black outline crosses

STENCILING

Standard; two line stencil on lower gear door

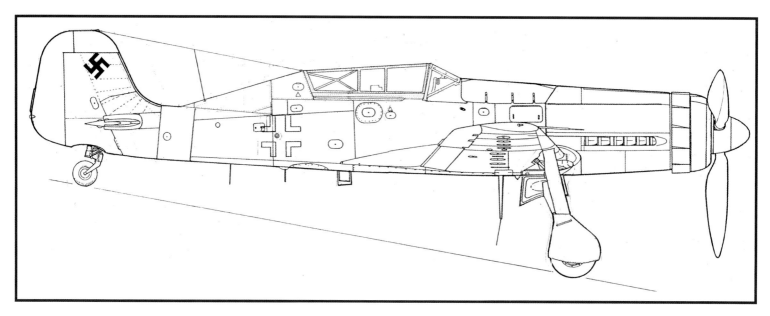

THE SIEGFRIED TWINS

One of the most important elements contributing to a successful fighter pilot is thorough training. By the time the Ta 152 became a reality, the need for qualified *Luftwaffe* fighter pilots had transitioned from critical to hopeless. This catastrophic situation had not only been reached through normal wartime attrition but also through relentless Allied bombing of fuel producing centers, which had the effect of severely curtailing available fuel stocks for training and other forms for non-combat flying. Nevertheless, Focke-Wulf had earlier envisioned a time when the venerable Fw 190 A and F series would be superseded by newer types such as the Fw 190 Dora series and the Ta 152. Inasmuch as the Dora series was considered by Prof. Tank to be only a transition model until the Ta 152 could attain full production, it was decided to skip over the Dora series and, instead, create a two-seat trainer version of the Ta 152; the S series (*Schulflugzeug* - School Aircraft).

Using the same modification template as used for the Fw 190 S-5 and S-8 (respectively modified A-5 and A-8 fighters), Focke-Wulf set forth similar conversion instructions for the Ta 152 C-1 and, in keeping with established tradition, the resulting alteration package resulted in the designation Ta 152 C-1/U1 (U1 – *Umrüst-Bausätze* – Modification Construction Set 1). Although no conversions were actually attempted

before the war's end, it was hoped that Blohm & Voss of Hamburg would be able to begin conversions in April 1945 with Deutsche Luft Hansa's workshops in Prague coming on line in August 1945. Both firms had considerable experience in converting single-seat fighters into two seat trainers.

The modifications included the installation of an elongated canopy hinged to open to the right, relocation of the rear fuselage fuel tank, various electronic sets and installation of a second seat with duplicate flight controls. Essential engine and flight instruments for the instructor seated aft would be mounted on a specially fabricated instrument panel. No armament or ordinance would be carried although an optional 300 liter drop tank was possible for extended range. In addition to advance flight training, the two-seat Ta 152 and Fw 190s would also serve as high-speed liaison aircraft.

Eventually, it was planned to construct a small number of two-seat trainers from the Ta 152 C-1. The first version, known as the Ta 152 S-1, was to be an unarmed two-seat trainer and liaison type equipped with a FuG 16Zy radio. The second model, the Ta 152 S-2, was based on the Ta 152 C-2 which itself was later canceled after it became clear the FuG 15 radio, which was destined for this variant, would not be forthcoming. Consequently, the proposed Ta 152 S-2, which was otherwise identical to the S-1, was canceled.

The planned two-seat trainer and high speed liaison aircraft Ta 152 C-1/U1, would have undergone the same conversion procedure as Fw 190 F-8/U1, W. Nr. 584219, "Black 38", shown here being run-up by Wing Commander Paul Brindley at RAF St. Athan in 1987. The designation Ta 152 S-1 (Schule – School) would have been applied to aircraft so modified in series whereas the "U1" designation suffix was generally applied to an individual modification construction set change. The Fw 190 shown here was converted to a two seater by R. Sochor Fabrik of Blanz-Blansko, Czechoslovakia, in 1944 and later captured at Grove by British forces.

CÄSAR AND THE AERIAL TORPEDO

By Christmas 1944, Focke-Wulf had completed detailed design drawings of the Ta 152 C-1/R14, a special *Torpedoflugzeug* (Torpedo Aircraft) employing auxiliary apparatus 'R14' which included an ETC 504 munitions rack with attendant electrical connections capable of carrying a single LT 1B or LT F5 aerial torpedo. The requirement for such an aircraft originated in response to an earlier effort to combat Allied coastal shipping.

In the summer of 1943, several Fw 190s were experimentally modified at Adelheide to carry the heavy *Lufttorpedo* (Airborne Torpedo). Initially two Fw 190 A-5s, W. Nr. 871, TD+SI, and W. Nr. 872, TD+SJ, were selected for modification, resulting in the Fw 190 A-5/U14. Both aircraft were later demonstrated before *Kriegsmarine* and *Luftwaffe* officers at Gotenshafen. The Air Ministry then requested Focke-Wulf to further modify aircraft for night torpedo operations realizing that the slow, low-flying torpedo-laden fighter would prove an easy target during daylight operations. Flight trials were protracted and disappointing. Moreover, it took a skilled pilot to handle the unwieldy aircraft, arm and activate the torpedo, and compute the correct release altitude.

In spite of poor results with the Fw 190, research continued; however, there was no getting around the fact that the *Luftwaffe* lacked a dedicated torpedo aircraft — a type that played such a pivotal role in the Pacific war. In addition, German torpedo research and development lagged behind American and Japanese advances. By December 1944, it had been finally recognized that the Fw 190 A and F series were simply unsuited as aerial torpedo carriers. Attention then shifted to the new Fw 190 D series, in particular the Fw 190 D-9/R14 and D-12/R14.

Concurrent with these developments, it was decided to investigate the possibility of adapting the Ta 152 C to carry an airborne torpedo. The model chosen was the Ta 152 C-1 equipped with a new multi-purpose ETC 504 munitions rack. This equipment was lighter and simpler than the ETC 502, tested on earlier aircraft and had the added advantage of allowing the aircraft to operate without the awkward tail wheel leg extension. Because of the increased take-off weight and center of gravity issues, it was further decided to delete the two cowl weapons and limit armament solely to the two wing root mounted cannons. However, after preliminary calculations with and without the extended tail wheel leg, indications were that this exotic version would have been inferior to the Fw 190 D-12/R14. All further work on the Ta 152 C-1/R14 was stopped. And since no documented evidence linking the Dora series with conversion aircraft has been discovered, it must be assumed that German efforts to develop a successful single-engine, single-seat, torpedo fighter failed to materialize leaving the requirement unfulfilled.

This closeup of an aerial torpedo mockup suspended beneath a specially modified Fw 190 A-5, illustrates the difficulty the Germans experienced in trying to adapt a light weight fighter to the torpedo carrying role. Ground clearance in relation to the torpedo's overall length coupled with center of gravity concerns, necessitated elevating the fuselage by resorting to significantly longer tail wheel legs. Later, the plan was resurrected when it was proposed that either the Fw 190 D or the Ta 152 C be considered as a torpedo carrying fighter. It was even suggested modifying the Ta 152 V7 to flight-test the scheme, but in the end it was decided the Fw 190 D was better suited and no further consideration was given to the Ta 152 C as a torpedo carrier.

Ta 152 C-9
Jumo 222 C

General Specifications for the Ta 152 C-9 with the Jumo 222 C

<u>Wingspan</u>: 11,000 mm (36 ft 1 1/8 in); <u>Wing area</u>: 19,5 m^2 (209.9 ft^2); <u>Length</u>: 10,670 mm (35 ft 3/4 in); <u>Height</u>: 4,200 mm (13 ft 9 3/8 in); <u>Stabilizer span</u>: 3,650 mm (11 ft 11 3/4 in); <u>Stabilizer area</u>: 2,82 m^2 (30.4 ft^2; <u>Wheel track</u>: 3,954 (12 ft 11 3/8 in); <u>Prop diameter</u>: 3,600 mm (11 ft 9 3/4 in); <u>Fuel grade</u>: B4 (87 octane); <u>Armament</u>: 4 X MG 151/20; <u>Weight Empty</u>: 4,075 kg (8,984); <u>Take off weight</u>: 4,900 kt (10,803 lb). *Provisional, see page 144.*

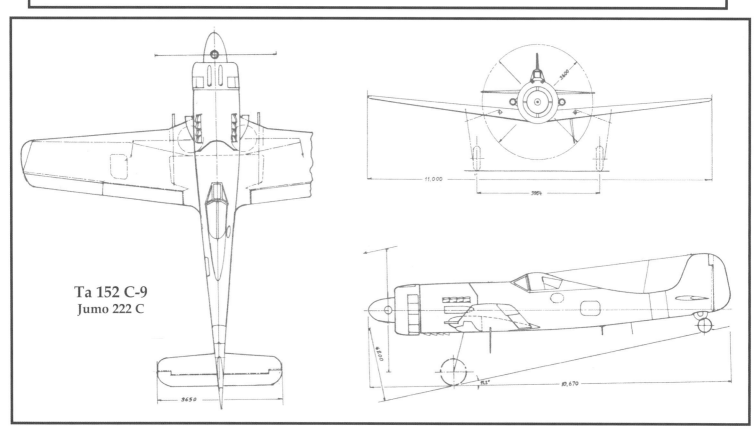

Ta 152 C-9
Jumo 222 C

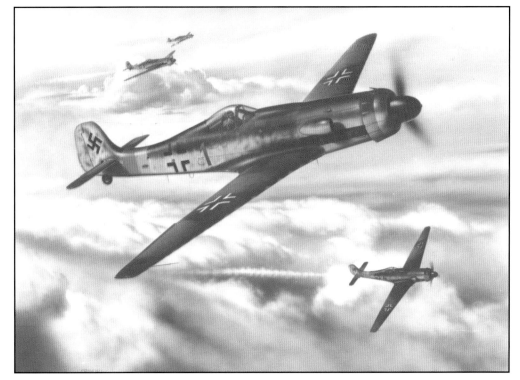

A splendid painting by noted aviation artist and publisher, Jerry Crandall convincingly depicts a flight of Ta 152 Hs in their natural environment. It is ironic that an aircraft so painstakingly designed to operate effectively at high altitude, should instead have ended up flying a great many successful missions at low altitude and even on the deck. It is little wonder then, that given this fighter's exceptional performance at any altitude, pilot Willi Reschke thought of the Tank fighter as his special life insurance policy.

JG 301 FLIES THE TANK FIGHTER IN COMBAT

On 1 February 1945, *Unteroffizier* Hermann Dürr of 12./JG 301 lost his life during a routine training flight near Alteno. Dürr was flying Ta 152 H-0, W. Nr. 150037. The cause of his crash is not recorded and was symptomatic of the chaotic conditions that existed within Germany at this period in the war.

A week later, on 9 February 1945, Hptm. Herbert Eggers was ferrying Ta 152 H-0, W. Nr. 150023, back to Rechlin following weapons trials at the *Luftwaffe*'s weapons testing base at Tarnewitz, when he too crashed while on final approach and was killed.

Most of the young Ta 152 pilots received only a 20 minute briefing at Cottbus, then made their first solo flight in a brand new fighter by ferrying the Ta 152 H a short distance to Alteno, where one or two practice flights were made before taking the aircraft directly into combat.

Oberfeldwebel Josef "Jupp" Keil, who had been previously awarded the *Deutsches Kreuz* in gold, managed to get in three training flights, totaling 1 hour 20 minutes, before his first *Feindflug* or combat flight on 7 February 1945, which lasted 40 minutes.

Whenever the weather was favorable, training flights were undertaken by the pilots of JG 301. Uffz. Julius "Jo" Berliner recalled the hectic nature of the transition program:

We received the first Ta 152 Hs at Luckau (Alteno), which we picked up ourselves at Cottbus. We then flew practice missions from Luckau in this machine. Simultaneously, however, we were flying ground-support missions against the east with our Dora 9s.

There was a big difference between the two. The

Dora 9 was good natured, robust. I could really take all-out flying with it, while the Ta 152 was much more sensitive; it let itself be flown, or so it seemed to me, almost like a sailplane. It had an enormous flight performance envelope which was especially marked at high altitudes. This was something completely new to us.

We basically had the order to take the Ta 152 H from delivery on into hard operational use with the combat troops and give reports of our experiences to Rechlin. We had to test the aircraft ourselves and had the order that, for example, we would not dive the plane over 496 mph [800 km/h]. However, we dived the Tank between 621 mph [1,000 km/h] and 746 mph [1,200 km/h]. In any event, the wings were induced to a crazy rocking motion but they nevertheless withstood these extreme dives.

The Ta 152 was easier to land than the Fw 190, which was relatively clumsy because of the twin-row radial engine. An advantage on take off was the more slender in-line engine of the Ta 152 when compared to the Fw 190's radial, which placed much greater restrictions on the view forward.

I had the impression that at altitudes around 39,360 ft [12,000 m] the Ta 152 H was still very maneuverable. A distinct advantage! Moreover, the Tank had excellent climb performance at altitude and was really superior to every opponent. Earlier, when flying the Me 109 or Fw 190, one tried to lure the enemy down since dogfight performance was much better with both these fighters at low altitude. That became superfluous with the Tank. It turned on a dime.

All of the JG 301 pilots who got to fly the Ta 152 H agreed it had a superb turn radius, but as Uffz. Rudolf Dieke

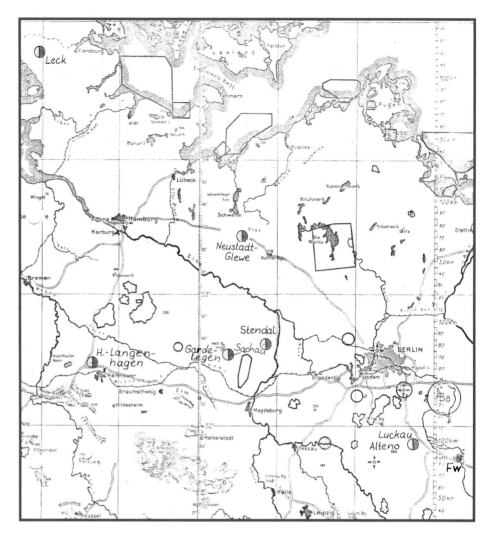

*Detail from a wartime **Luft-Navigationskarte** of the area near Berlin showing the location of important JG 301 bases identified by Red-Yellow circles. In the lower right hand corner, are the letters "Fw," which is the location of Focke-Wulf's important production facility at Cottbus (but given as Kottbus).*

remembered, "one's inclination was never to pull it through too quickly since we'd black out faster than with our other Focke-Wulf 190s due to the much lower wing loading."

Additionally, there was also a problem with aileron snatch in high speed turns, causing the aircraft to roll in the opposite direction.

Uffz. Rainer Michaelis thought:

The Ta 152 was substantially more maneuverable than the Fw 190. What was more significant and what surprised me in particular, was the incredible full manifold pressure height that the supercharger had, which was substantially higher than with the Fw 190. The full pressure height of the Fw 190 was 18,696 feet [5,700 m] with supercharger at 1:42 atü [42.5 in. Hg] and 2,700 rpm, which was War Emergency power. At 29,520 ft [9,000 m] the Fw 190 was very lame – if you tried a sharp turn you went into a spin. In the Ta 152 I couldn't find a trace of this characteristic. I climbed to 34,440 ft [10,500 m] without any difficulty but an oil line broke and the windshield was covered over completely – I was forced to head back to base immediately.

Although the Ta 152 H was designed with cabin pressurization as standard equipment, the problems encountered

in testing ultimately led Focke-Wulf to leave it inactivated. *Oberstleutnent* Fritz Auffhammer, *Kommodore* of JG 301, recalled that only one of the *Geschwader's* Ta 152 Hs had a functioning pressurized cockpit. As with so many of the other pilots who realized the performance potential of the new fighter, Auffhammer flew it as high as it would go, reaching 41,010 ft (12,500 m) without the cabin pressurization. Ironically, Auffhammer was later shot down while flying a mission in a Ta 152 H during combat near Neustrilitz.

On 2 February 1945, *Leutnant* A.W. Hagedorn, attached to the 9./JG 301, picked up a Ta 152 H at Cottbus and flew it to Alteno in the same *Schwarm* with Fw. Bubi Blum and Hptm. Benno Rühe. In spite of the fact the Ta 152 H Lt. Hagedorn flew out of Cottbus is recorded as "Yellow 2", it is likely this indicated a reconditioned aircraft of an earlier posting since all aircraft in the 9. *Staffel* routinely carried White numbers. Lt. Hagedorn recalls:

We reached the remarkable altitude of 43,290 ft (13,200 m). Our ground speed, which we worked out afterward with Obstlt. Siegfried Knemeyer, head of aircraft development of the Air Ministry's Technical Office, was somewhere around a good 508 to 515 mph [820 – 830 km/h]. I'd never had such a fast airplane under my behind in my life!

Up to 9,840 ft (3,000 m) we had a rate of climb on the variometer of about 3,936 ft/min (20 m/sec), and above 3,000 meters it began to drop off. In any case, for me this was a phenomenal development, with us hanging on the stick like ripe plums while the airplane kept pulling and pulling upwards – and the rudder never got sloppy.

Take off was incredible when you shove the throttle clear forward. The field at Luckau (Alteno), where I flew it, was 1,970 ft (600 m) long. The plane took off, and I mean really took off, in 984 to 1,312 ft (300 to 400 m)! I had never before seen such a thing, and above anything I had experienced in any other aircraft was its incredible maneuverability. It was known that even an Fw 190 would buffet very easily on the verge of spinning out in a dogfight if you pulled too hard. But we noticed in the Ta 152 that you could practically twist it around its tail. The plane really went 'round. Though others experienced aileron snatching, I managed this seemingly impossible turning radius without any problem at all with the ailerons."

Most *Luftwaffe* fighter units during this period had their *Gruppen* dispersed over a wide area and JG 301 was no exception. While the III. *Gruppe* trained with the Ta 152 at Alteno, the *Stabsschwarm* and I. *Gruppe* kept busy at Stendal while the II. *Gruppe* operated out of Welzow. But, on 16 February 1945, the III. *Gruppe* quit Alteno and relocated at Sachau.

As JG 301 continued operational flights with their Ta 152 Hs during February 1945, five of these aircraft were lost within a short time due to engine fires. According to the pilots, the fire usually started on the port side of the engine. Since each of the pilots successfully bailed out, all aircraft were total losses, making it difficult to precisely determine the cause. However, the probable cause was narrowed down to ruptured coolant lines. Coolant would flow onto the hot exhaust stacks, igniting the glycol. In all, 18 engines became unserviceable due to a number of problems, effectively grounding most of the unit's Ta 152s.

Obfw. Jupp Keil managed to squeeze in five more practice flights in a Ta 152 H before flying his second combat mission. Taking off from Sachau between 16:30 and 17:00 hours on 21 February 1945, Jupp claimed one B-17 shot down over Berlin. It is likely this was the first kill attributed to the Ta 152, but it is also likely the date was 22 February since there is no record of American heavy bombers over the *Reich's* capital the previous day. On 1 March 1945, Jupp Keil was up to his third combat mission in the Tank, taking off from Sachau at 10:25 hours in Ta 152 H "Number 1" (color unknown). This time he ran into a formation of P 51s and managed to shoot one down – the mission lasted one hour. Keil ended the war with five kills while flying the Ta 152 H. On 2 March 1945, Ofw. Keil and several other pilots scrambled to intercept a large formation (1,159 B-17s and B-24s) of approaching American Eighth Air Force bombers whose mission targets included the synthetic oil plants at Böhlen, Ruhland, and Magdeburg. Fortunately the German pilots failed to make contact with this massive force and each Ta 152 returned safely to Sachau.

A LAUNDRY LIST OF COMPLAINTS

During the last week in February 1945, Focke-Wulf's Technical Field Service Department had summarized JG 301's problems with their Ta 152 Hs. The following are the major points from numerous complaints:

- The pilot's seat, designed for the Fw 190, required the lowest possible position of adjustment due to the special high altitude parachutes worn by pilots. This pinches the hose of the small emergency oxygen bottle attached to the parachutes.
- The right landing gear leg continued to retract with great difficulty even after new fairing doors and higher hydraulic pressures were incorporated.
- The compressed air valves for the emergency landing gear and flap extension leaked in all aircraft – they were returned to the valve's manufacturers for testing.
- The guide pulley for the tail wheel retraction fitted on the stabilizer spar sprung from its track – all aircraft were to be flown with the tail wheel fixed in the extended position until the problem could be rectified.
- The ailerons could not be adjusted sufficiently to obtain acceptable control forces and the ball joint of the aileron tab linkage wore out quickly, resulting in aileron flutter.
- Upon landing, the wooden landing flaps were severely damaged by water thrown up from the runway. At each occurrence, they had to be replaced.
- On wet and muddy airfields, mud and dirt entered the wing through the two spar cutouts next to the wheel wells.
- The rudder jammed during landing and in the neutral position in flight – only repeated kicks on the rudder pedals freed the control surface.
- After the first few flying hours, loose rivets were found on all aircraft below the leading edge near the former for the wheel well.
- The hand wheel used to open and close the cooling flaps was still too hard to operate in flight since the proper position was not easily found. Pilots suggested replacing the wheel with a gearshift lever similar to that used on DKW automobiles.
- The windscreen washers were still spreading rather than removing glycol.
- On several aircraft, the radiator fairings were torn off, damaging the propeller, due to loose rivets and loose inner bolts.

Five days later, on 7 March 1945, The U.S. Army successfully seized and held the Remagen railway bridge despite fierce resistance and unsuccessful German attempts to destroy this vital structure. American troops and vehicles quickly exploited the opportunity and were the first Allied troops to

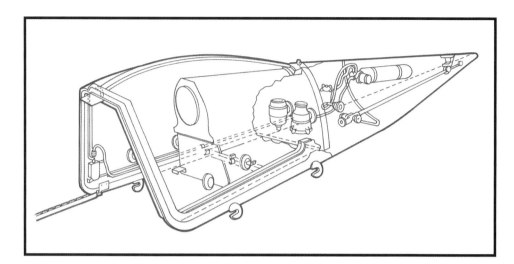

A detailed view of the Ta 152 H's aft-sliding canopy. Because the H series was pressurized, the Plexiglas portion was a double wall type sealed by means of inflatable rubber tubing fed by compressed air supplied by the cylinder shown beneath the rear cover with its fill point being located on the canopy's starboard side. Note the canopy's external locking lugs and circular leather head cushion attached to 20 mm armor plate and supported by a roll-over comb extending aft.

set foot on German soil. Soon thereafter the city of Köln surrendered. Now, with American troops firmly in Germany, many Americans felt the Germans would quickly surrender. Indeed, it could have happened had it not been for Hitler's obsession with "total victory or the death of the nation."

By mid-March 1945, the Ta 152 H had been in production for barely four months, yet during this period numerous alterations designed to correct all manner of mechanical gremlins, failed to remedy the most persistent complaint: Namely the key question of satisfactory flight stability.

REAPING THE FRUITS OF FRUSTRATION

From his headquarters in Berlin on 17 March 1945, no less a figure than *General der Jagdflieger Oberst* Gordon Gollob, took the unprecedented step of expressing his disappointment with the Tank fighter directly to the aircraft company's chief executive officer. The 32 year old Gollob was a highly decorated fighter pilot who assumed this title and post on 31 January 1945. He was one of a select few who wore the Knight's Cross of the Iron Cross with Oak Leaves, Swords, and Diamonds

after achieving 150 victories in 340 missions, almost all on the Eastern Front. Excerpts of Gollob's letter highlight how frustrated everyone had become to have such a high-performance fighter remain, for the most part, out of combat.

Dear Professor!

I have to point out in the strongest way possible that an aircraft with such negative flight characteristics is totally unacceptable for service duty. Yet the fighter service branch is greatly dependent on this aircraft.

I was informed that unexpected problems in pitch stability have arisen in the first production models as well as the test aircraft of type C (Ta 152 C Ed.). The chief of the TLR has proposed. as an emergency measure, a reduction in the amount of fuel stored in the fuselage by 75-80 liters and a loading of only 70 liters of MW 50 instead of the originally designated 140 liters. Also, a ballast of 58 kg should be installed in the compartment and the fuel capacity of the rear fuselage tanks must be reduced 380 to 280 liters…

A closeup view of the port side of an unpainted Ta 152 H's fuselage access hatch. This aircraft's hatch is made from aluminum but wooden examples were not uncommon (see page 166). Further aft, the open small rectangular port allowed access to the antenna matching lock. The circular aperture was the fuselage tie-down tube while the oval-shaped fixture below contained the aircraft's AZA 10 signal flares. Another set of four was fitted opposite on the aircraft's starboard side. The colored flares were signals used when landing especially when radio silence was observed. The fixed loop antenna and dipole antenna mounted beneath the fuselage were for direction finding and the FuG 25a radio respectively.

Oberst *Gordon Gollob, left, held the vital post of General of the Fighter Pilots and, besides being a highly decorated and accomplished fighter pilot, he was not a man to withhold his views. Utterly frustrated with the Ta 152's uncorrected shortcomings, Gollob took the bold step of communicating his displeasure directly to the airplane's designer, Kurt Tank.* **Reichsminister** *Albert Speer, right, was, among his many talents and duties, the respected Minister of Armaments and War Production. It was Speer who tried to protect the aircraft factories from radical Nazi policies during the final days of the war. He resisted those who promoted a scorched earth policy with mandatory labor transfers.*

Erprobungsstelle Rechlin stated that eight Ta 152 H aircraft exhibit barely acceptable stability around the yaw axis. Gunnery runs are impossible to initiate according to the gunnery school. Use of the K23 autopilot gives only slight improvement. Rechlin proposed to Focke-Wulf that the tail fin be enlarged

Stability around the aircraft's roll axis is also poor in the 8-152 H models as well as the 'C' model. Both models do not fulfil the expected minimum stability requirement.

Basically, the stability around the pitch axis could be eliminated through the non-installation of autopilot, the GM 1 power boost tank, the 115 liter fuel tank, FuG 125 radio ("Hermine" radio navigation equipment – Ed.) and a reduction in the fuel load of 135 liters. However, under no circumstances can the reduction of even the most minute amount of fuel be tolerated."

Gollob concluded by saying he feared this much tampering with the aft center of gravity problem would ultimately lead to extreme nose heaviness on landing.

On 29 March 1945, the technical staff of Focke-Wulf replied saying…"that they had been working on the problem for some time and that, in reality, only 7% fuel reserve was lost in the fuel reduction measures to improve stability. They also did not understand the non-installation paragraph since the autopilot and FuG 125 were included in the aircraft's empty weight. Moreover, the GM 1 equipment and the aft 115 liter fuel tank were not carried simultaneously."

The DB 603 LA and L engines were also being considered to replace the Jumo 213 in the Ta 152 H. They agreed that enlarging the vertical fin, which had already been done twice (Fw 190 V18/U1 and Fw 190 V32 – ed.), would improve the stability for gunnery. A redesigned fin was under development and would be flight-tested soon. They also noted that enlarging the horizontal stabilizer would solve some of the pitch stability problems.

During this chaotic period, Hitler issued his infamous "total scorched earth" edict and ordered the population to relocate into the center of the nation, but *Reichsminister* Speer, knowing this to be both unrealistic and unworkable and, at great personal risk, countermanded Hitler's order. The factories and labor force was to remain where they were. Those factories in danger of being over-run by the Allies were ordered to demolish anything of value before evacuating. However, compliance was not uniform and, thanks to Speer's efforts, many important and vital facilities were merely abandoned intact.

Nine days earlier, on 20 March 1945, *Oberst* Gollob and his staff finalized a plan for the re-equipment of the German day-fighter units. This plan called for equipping all Fw 190 A-8/A-9 units with the Dora 9, Dora 12, and possibly the Fw 190 D-13. JG 301 was still slated as the sole unit to fly the Ta 152. It is assumed that the first and second *Gruppen* were to operate either the Ta 152 C and/or H series while the third *Gruppen* was to be outfitted exclusively with the Ta 152 H. According to Gollob's plan the three *Gruppen* were to be thus equipped:

I./ JG 301
Current: Fw 190 A 9/R11
Proposed: Fw 190 D-9/R11 or Ta 152

II./JG 301
Current: Fw 190 A-9/R11
Proposed: Fw 190 D-9/R11 or Ta 152

III./JG 301
Current: Ta 152 H-1
Proposed: Ta 152 H-1

Major *Fritz Auffhammer.*

Certificate written by Fritz Auffhammer and Roderich Cescotti, authenticated with their signatures in September 2001, confirming the Orange-Red Ta 152.

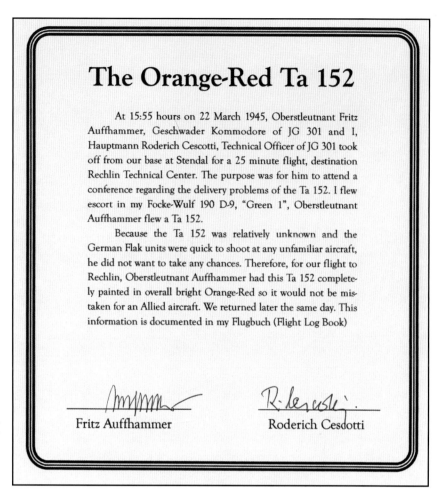

The Orange-Red Ta 152

At 15:55 hours on 22 March 1945, Oberstleutnant Fritz Auffhammer, Geschwader Kommodore of JG 301 and I, Hauptmann Roderich Cescotti, Technical Officer of JG 301 took off from our base at Stendal for a 25 minute flight, destination Rechlin Technical Center. The purpose was for him to attend a conference regarding the delivery problems of the Ta 152. I flew escort in my Focke-Wulf 190 D-9, "Green 1", Oberstleutnant Auffhammer flew a Ta 152.

Because the Ta 152 was relatively unknown and the German Flak units were quick to shoot at any unfamiliar aircraft, he did not want to take any chances. Therefore, for our flight to Rechlin, Oberstleutnant Auffhammer had this Ta 152 completely painted in overall bright Orange-Red so it would not be mistaken for an Allied aircraft. We returned later the same day. This information is documented in my Flugbuch (Flight Log Book)

Fritz Auffhammer   Roderich Cescotti

On 22 March 1945 the *Kommodore* of JG 301 Obslt. Fritz Auffhammer climbed into his all Orange-Red Ta 152 that he had been evaluating, in order to return it to the *Luftwaffe* proving ground at Rechlin. Because he felt uncomfortable flying a new type fighter that the trigger-happy Flak crews had not seen before, he ordered this Ta 152 to be painted a bright Orange-Red overall, including the spinner and over painting the JG 301 fuselage bands. The only thing not painted were the national markings necessary for identification.

On this flight, Hptm. Roderich Cescotti was asked to fly escort in a Fw 190 D-9 "Green 1". The purpose of the trip was to return the Ta 152 to Rechlin for adjustments, but more importantly to meet with engineers and officials from the Focke-Wulf factory to discuss the technical problems that were causing delivery delays in getting this new fighter to Auffhammer's JG 301. After hearing one excuse after another, Obslt. Auffhammer had heard enough. In a burst of anger and frustration he blurted out "I don't care about your problems, you can kiss my ass! I need these machines right now!"

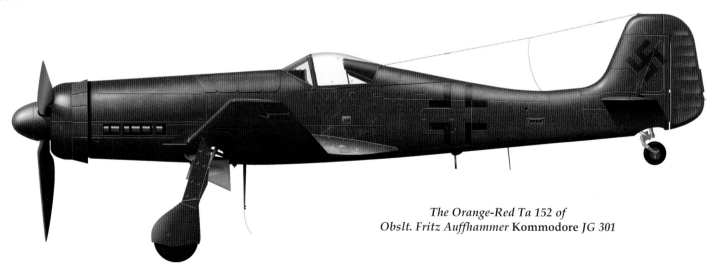

The Orange-Red Ta 152 of Obslt. Fritz Auffhammer Kommodore JG 301

At the end of March 1945, only the *Stabsschwarm* of JG 301 was equipped with the Ta 152 due to a lack of production aircraft and operational attrition. Though several pilots from III. *Gruppe* continued to fly the fighter, they did so with the *Geschwaderstab* aircraft. During March 1945, IV./JG 301, which then included 13., 14. and 15. *Staffeln* each flying the Bf 109 G-10, was formally disbanded. Ninety days earlier, in December 1944, 16./JG 301 had been disbanded with its aircraft and personnel being transferred to 15./JG 300.

On 25 March 1945, several pilots ferried their Ta 152s to the field at Langenhagen for operations. *Oberfänrich* Ludwig Bracht flew cover, along with Oblt. Heinz von Alven and Obfn. Hans Fay, in Fw 190s.

Bracht vividly remembered the transfer to Hannover-Langenhagen.

Continental (tire manufacturer – Ed.) was burning furiously. Smoke clouds up to 1,500 meters (4,920 ft) high, which I flew through, so thick that everything became dark in the cockpit.

Langenhagen field had received a carpet bombing just before our landing – holes and freshly filled bomb craters. Several Ta 152s crashed upon landing and two pilots were killed. Hptm Gerhard Posselmann, Gruppen Kommandeur, ripped off the landing gear of his Fw 190, "White 13". From here we would fly operations on the Western Front, though only the Stabsschwarm still had Ta 152s."

Bracht, along with several other III. *Gruppe* pilots, discovered what appeared to be newly completed Ta 152 Hs at Langenhagen seemingly unattended. Without asking questions, they repainted a few and began flying them. They also discovered several other Ta 152s and a Ta 154 at this location without engines. Because of the hopeless supply situation and the certainty of even tighter shortages, Bracht and his crew immediately stripped these airframes for their valuable and irreplaceable parts. The identity of the Ta 152 Hs at Langenhagen remains a mystery. Since this facility was not a production center but primarily a Focke-Wulf test and evaluation facility, it is likely that among the Ta 152 Hs appropriated by Bracht, one or more were prototypes.

An American serviceman poses next to "White 12, "an Fw 190 D-9, W. Nr. 500408, previously operated by the 5th **Staffel** *(White numbers) of the 2nd* **Gruppe** *(Red horizontal bar) of JG 301 (Yellow/Red tail band) written as 5./II./JG 301.*

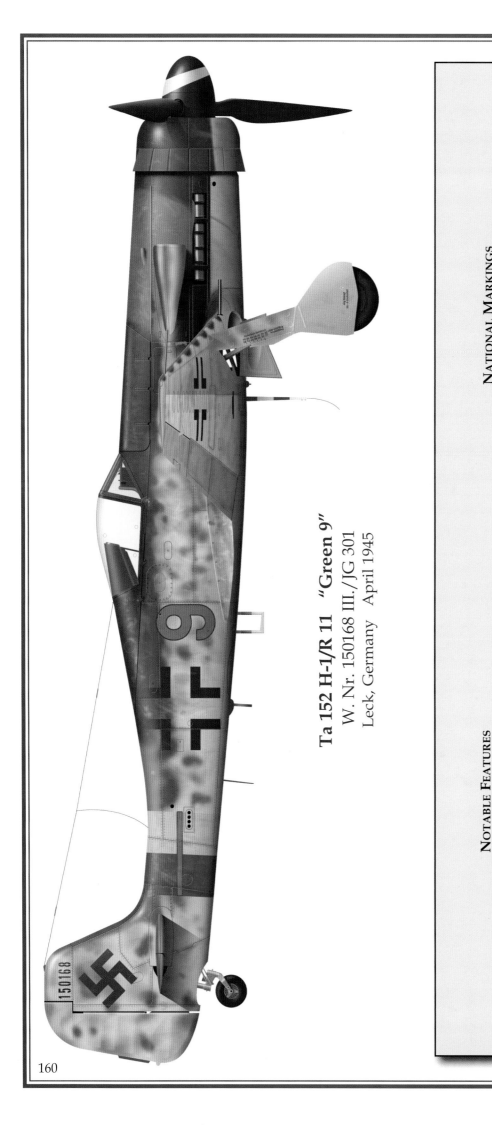

Ta 152 H-1/R 11 "Green 9"
W. Nr. 150168 III./JG 301
Leck, Germany   April 1945

NOTABLE FEATURES
- Pressurized canopy with pellets and hooks on base of canopy
- Small White square in corner of windscreen heating element
- All antennas intact
- No ETC rack or drop tank

COLORS

UNDERSURFACES	RLM 76 Light Blue, rear half of underwing is natural metal except for ailerons and flaps, some Green camouflage on upper gear doors
UPPERSURFACES	RLM 82 Bright Green/RLM 83 Dark Green,
PROP BLADES	RLM 70 Black-Green
SPINNER	Black with White spiral

NATIONAL MARKINGS

FUSELAGE	B4 800 mm Black outline crosses
	H3 500 mm Black *Hakenkreuz*
WINGS	Upper: B6 1000 mm White outline crosses
	Lower: B4 1000 mm Black outline crosses

STENCILING

Standard; Red and Yellow fuselage bands with Green bar over bands

Ta 152 H-1/R11 "Green 9"

W. Nr. 150168 III./JG 301

Leck, Germany   April 1945

The unit insignia of III. / JG 301 as it could have appeared on the Ta 152 H. Although there is no record of it ever being actually applied to a Ta 152, it is still considered official by all former pilots of the unit.

THE LAST 30 DAYS

On 6 April 1945, Focke-Wulf instructed their personnel at Langenhagen to evacuate those prototypes that could be flown to the relative safety of Reinsehlen airfield in northern Germany. Five aircraft successfully made the flight: Ta 152 H-0, W. Nr. 150004; Fw 190 V32/U2, W. Nr. 0057; Fw 190 V55, W. Nr. 170923, GV+CV (Fw 190 D-12 prototype); Fw 190 V18/U2, W. Nr. 0040 and the Fw 190 V73, W. Nr. 733705, TX+PQ (Fw 190 F-15 prototype).

On Sunday, 8 April 1945, the Staff flight of JG 301 received information that the Mimetall factory at Erfurt had succeeded in producing two new Ta 152s, which had just been flight cleared. When the pilots arrived to pick up their new mounts, they were surprised to see that the aircraft were DB 603 powered Ta 152 C-1/R31s. These two aircraft were, almost certainly, the sole production examples of the Ta 152 C series to be completed and accepted by the *Luftwaffe*. Both pilots successfully flew these brand new aircraft back to their base at Stendal. However, completely unknown to the members of JG 301, some 130 miles (209 km) to the southwest, at Bad Eilsen, a very different saga was unfolding.

At the stately Badehotel, one of the three large hotels in Bad Eilsen where Focke-Wulf's administrative offices were accommodated, the few employees who showed up for work were on edge. The previous night a few British artillery shells had landed in Bad Eilsen's park, causing little damage but signaling the closeness of Allied troops. In the morning, the sound of gunfire and armor could be heard in the distance. Eventually a contingent of British arrived at the front steps in a light tank and Jeeps. The hotel's doorman dutifully greeted the British officers, who immediately asked about Professor Tank. The evening before, most of the secret papers had been burned and the Focke-Wulf staff concealed the latest plans. Nevertheless, the British lost little time confiscating everything in sight. Two days later, on 10 April 1945, an RAF Regiment arrived and within 15 minutes Kurt Tank and his two principle assistants were placed under open arrest. The British wasted little time in taking charge.

Everything of significance was secured including the latest plans, drawings and files.

On the same day later in the evening, at 19:13 hours Jupp Keil was again airborne from Sachau, this time in Ta 152 H, "Green 3". North of Braunschweig, Keil became entangled in a fierce dogfight against no fewer than 15 Thunderbolts. After a number of passes, Keil managed to shoot down one of the P-47s. Three days later, Keil flew a mission from Stendal in Ta 152, number "15" (color unknown) encountering four Mustangs near Wittenberg. Neither side scored hits and, at 10:00 hours, Obfw. Keil landed safely at Neustadt-Glewe after 40 nerve-racking minutes in the air.

As of 12 April 1945, the operational status of the Ta 152 was defined by the *Luftwaffe's* I. *Jagd-Division* as follows:

Stabsstaffel JG 301 – 16 aircraft authorized; 7 on strength; 3 operationally ready. Six crew authorized; 6 on hand. Four combat crew available; 3 were combat ready.

III. *Gruppe* JG 301 – 52 aircraft authorized; 6 on strength; 3 operationally ready. Authorized crew stood at 36; 32 on hand. Combat crew stood at 19; 3 were combat ready.

The commander of II./JG 301, Hptm Roderich Cescotti, operated his Fw 190 D-9s and Bf 109 G-14s out of Welzow and Neustadt-Glewe, often alongside the *Stab's* Ta 152s. Cescotti witnessed a dramatic dogfight on 15 April 1945, between four Ta 152 H-1s and four RAF Tempests, which occurred from altitudes of 8,200 ft (2,500 m) down to 164 ft (50 m). During this melee, one of the Ta 152s, piloted by Obfw. Sepp Sattler dove out of the sun on a Tempest and immediately set it on fire, but to everyone's horror, the Tank continued to dive straight down, crashing into the ground at high speed. The Tempest crashed nearby, but the fate of its pilot is unknown. Hptm. Cescotti thought at the time that compressibility problems could have prevented Sattler from pulling out.

*Left: Ta 152 H pilot **Oberfeldwebel Willi Reschke** just after hostilities ceased in May 1945. Unlike American pilots whose ranks were entirely filled by officers, **Luftwaffe** pilots came from all ranks. Right: A lovely young lady flanked by two Luftwaffe knights of the air. Willi Reschke is to the lady's right while fellow Ta 152 H pilot **Oberfeldwebel Walter Loos** is to her left. Loss was posted to JG 301 in the final weeks of the war and was another highly valued pilot. He was credited with 38 aerial victories plus 8 unconfirmed and, in recognition of their achievements; both enlisted pilots were awarded their Knight's Cross of the Iron Cross at the same time barely two weeks earlier on 20 April 1945.*

Immediately after this combat, another British Tempest was engaged by a Ta 152 and destroyed, but not claimed as a victory. On this occasion, Obfw. Reschke, flying Ta 152 H, "White 1", was turning with a Tempest about 164 ft (50 m) above the ground when the Tank's cannon suddenly jammed. Reschke, no novice, reacted quickly. He had recently been awarded the Knight's Cross, and was officially credited with 26 victories in the West, including 18 B-17s shot down. He instinctively used the Tank's superior turning ability to make the Tempest pilot pull too tight a turn. In a second, the British fighter snap-rolled and hit the ground with an enormous explosion, instantly killing its hapless pilot. Obstlt. Auffhammer, who had led the *Stab's* Ta 152s that day, landed and soaked in perspiration, climbed out of his fighter. The supercharger of Auffhammer's Tank failed to shift, denying him the rated power when it was desperately needed.

Because JG 301 was based close to Berlin during the final month of the war in Europe, the *Geschwader* frequently encountered not only western Allied aircraft but Russian fighters operating from bases in the east. Ofw. Heinz Gassow's first combat mission with the Ta 152 was flown over Berlin. The *Geschwaderstab* flew the Ta 152 along with its three *Gruppen*, flying a mixed array of Fw 190s and Bf 109s. Gassow recalled that "the Ta 152 was so surprisingly good (compared to the Bf 109) that it surpassed the Mustang in every regard. Speed, climb and ceiling, as well as in general all-around performance."

Lt. Hagedorn recalled what it was like to operate the fighter during April 1945.

The Ta 152 was flown by a small group of us. Some Ta 152s were grounded anyway. Some of us tried to obtain replacement parts from the manufacturer but that was extremely difficult, considering the very small area we had under German control. Many Ta 152s were grounded by little details which could have been repaired easily through simple replacement if the supply system had been working.

We often said among ourselves, 'Why didn't we get the things (Ta 152s – Ed.) earlier?' Among the 'old hares' in our outfit, it was always said, 'When we have the thing, we won't be leery of the Spitfire anymore.

Flying from Neustadt-Glewe, the few JG 301 pilots who could get a Ta 152 into the air never doubted their mount's capabilities. Obfw. Walter Loos, after a brief stint as a flight instructor flying Arado Ar 96s, was transferred in March 1945, to the *Geschwaderstab* JG 301. Loos was a veteran pilot who ended the war with only 66 missions but 30 confirmed victories (22 four engine bombers, eight Soviet types plus another eight unconfirmed victories). Obfw. Loos flew his first combat mission in a Ta 152 H over the Soltau-Hannover area after only a single familiarization flight. On 24 April 1945, Loos was airborne in Ta 152 H, number '4' (presumably "Green 4" – Ed.) at 05:50 hours. Once over Berlin it was not long before he encountered what he identified as a formation of LaGG-9s, but which in reality were Yak-9s (there was no

"LaGG-9"-Ed.). Loos promptly downed two of the Russian fighters and safely returned to base at 07:05 hours.

On 25 April 1945, American and Soviet forces linked up at Torgau on the Elbe River south of Berlin. From this point on, Germany was split in two. Loos flew two more combat missions in the Ta 152 H, both in number '4,' on 25 April 1945, lasting one hour 15 minutes, and the second five days later on 30 April 1945, from 15:50 hours to 16:55 hours, and over Berlin. This tenacious fighter pilot downed another "LaGG-9" to finish the war as probably the most successful Ta 152 combat pilot.

On Monday, 30 April 1945, in the heart of Berlin as the Red Army encircled the city amid determined resistance, Adolf Hitler took his life deep within the *Führer's* bunker.

As of 30 April 1945, JG 301's strength comprised:

> *Stab* JG 301
> 2 serviceable Ta 152 C-1/R31 at Welzow
> All surviving Ta 152 Hs were unserviceable
>
> I./JG 301
> 36 serviceable Fw 190 D-9 at Finsterwalde
>
> II./JG 301
> 36 serviceable Fw 190 D-9s and Bf 109 G-14s at Welzow
>
> III./JG 301
> 36 serviceable Fw 190 G-3 at Alteno (disbanded)
> [The Fw 190 G-3, based upon the Fw 190 A-5, was classified as a *Jabo-Rei* – fighter-bomber with extended range.]

SEVEN FRANTIC DAYS TO THE END

By 1 May 1945, with Hitler dead and Germany cut in two, many surviving *Luftwaffe* units had retreated to northwest Germany and Denmark. During this time, JG 301 had relocated from Neustadt-Glewe and Hagenow to Leck in Schleswig-Holstein.

Ludwig Bracht remembered:

Whoever could still fly and had an airplane flew to Leck. Whoever didn't fly traveled in a pair of the remaining LKWs and VW Kübels. The column of land vehicles had been turned over to me by Posselmann. I crossed over the Elbe by ferry near Leuzen and brought the column back safe and sound through the middle between the Russians and the Americans, high up on the Elbe, via Lauenburg-Rabzenburg-Kiel.

At Leck we met again at the RAD (Reichsarbeitsdienst – Reichs Work Service) depot. Ta 152 H-1, "Green 6", stood on the airfield without a propeller as our last machine. The others we had already blown up at the perimeter of the field, in order not to give up these planes to the Tommies."

SUMMARY OF FOCKE-WULF Ta 152 PRODUCTION SERIES

Series	Engine	Motor K	Cowl	Wing Root	Outer wing weapons	Mission
A-1	9-213 A/C	MK 103	2 x MG 151	2 x MG 151	2 x MK 108 (R2 item)	Normaljäger - Canceled
A-2	9-213 A/C	MK 103	2 x MG 151	2 x MG 151	2 x MG 151/20 (R1 item)	Normaljäger - Deferred
B-0	9-213C	MK 108	2 x MG 151	2 x MG 151	Rüstsätze R1, R2	Schlachtflugzeug - Unverified but likely correct
B-1	9-213C	MK 108	2 x MG 151	2 x MG 151	Rüstsätze R1, R2	Schlachtflugzeug - Canceled
B-2	9-213C	MK 103	2 x MG 151	2 x MG 151	Rüstsätze R1, R2	Schlachtflugzeug - Canceled
B-3	9-213E	MK 108	2 x MK 108		Rüstsätze R1, R2	Schlachtflugzeug - Canceled
B-4	9-213E	MK 103	2 x MK 103		Rüstsätze R1, R2	Schlachtflugzeug - Canceled
B-5	9-213E-2	MK 103	2 x MK 103	-		Zerstörer
B-6	9-213EB	MG 151	2 x MG 151	-		Schlachtflugzeug like C-6, 1xETC 503 + 2x2xETC 71. Labeled Ta 152 B-1 13 Apr 45.
B-7	9-213J	MG 151	-	2 x MG 151	-	Zerstörer with VS 19 + 4/b prop otherwise like B-6. Labeled Ta 152 B-1 13/4/45
C-0	9-603L	MK 108	2 x MG 151	2 x MG 151	-	Normaljäger
C-1	9-603LA	MK 108	2 x MG 151	2 x MG 151	-	Normaljäger
C-2	9-603L	MK 108	2 x MG 151	2 x MG 151	-	Normaljäger – like C-1 but equipped with the FuG 15 - canceled
C-3	9-603LA	MK 103	2 x MG 151	2 x MG 151	-	Normaljäger – like C-1 but all four MG 151s were MG 151/15
C-4	9-603L	MK 103	2 x MG 151	2 x MG 151	-	Normaljäger – like C-3 but with the FuG 15 radio - canceled
C-5	9-603L	MK 103	2 x MG 151	2 x MK 103	-	Normaljäger - reverted to the FuG 16Zy radio
C-6	9-603L	MK 103	2 x MG 151	2 x MK 103	-	Normaljäger – like C-5 but with the FuG 15 radio
C-7	9-213J	MG 151	2 x MG 151	2 x MG 151	-	Normaljäger – with VS 19 + 4/b prop
C-8	9-801R	-	2 x MG 151	2 x MK 151	-	Normaljäger
C-9	9-222 AB	-	2 x MG 151	2 x MG 103	-	Normaljäger with wing tanks plus MW
C-10	9-222 E	-	2 x MG 151	2 x MG 151	-	Normaljäger with wing tanks plus MW
C-11	9-603LA	MK 108	2 x MG 151	2 x MG 151	-	Aufklärung of the C-1
E-0	9-213E	MK 108	-	2 x MG 151	-	Aufklärung/C series wing + 1 x Rb 75/30/ replaced by C 11
E-1	9-213E	MK 108	-	2 x MG 151	-	Aufklärung/C series wing + 1 x Rb 75/30/ replaced by C 11
E-2	9-213E	MK 108	-	2 x MG 151	-	Aufklärung/H-series wing + 1 x Rb 75/30/ replaced by H-10 mid Aug 1944
H-0	9-213E	MK 108	-	2 x MG 151	-	Höhenjäger – 115 ordered, approx. 40 completed
H-1	9-213E	MK 108	-	2 x MG 151	-	Höhenjäger – approx. 19 completed
H-2	9-213E	MK 108	-	2 x MG 151	-	Höhenjäger – FuG 15Zy canceled 15 Dec 44
H-3	9-603G	MK 108	-	2 x MG 151	-	Höhenjäger - canceled
H-4	9-603G	MK 103	-	2 x MG 151	-	Höhenjäger – maybe with FuG 15Zy and maybe with MK 108s - canceled
H-5	9-222E	-	2 x MG 151	2 x MG 151	-	Höhenjäger – new laminar wing without wing tanks or MW
H-6	9-222E	-	2 x MG 151	2 x MK 103	-	Höhenjäger – new laminar wing with wing tanks plus MW
H-7	9-213J	MK 108	-	2 x MG 151	-	Höhenjäger – equipped similar to H-1 with VS 19 4-bladed prop
H-8	9-603L	MK 108	-	2 x MG 151	-	Höhenjäger – equipped similar to H-1
H-9	9-603L	MK 108	-	2 x MG 151	-	Aufklärung version of the H-8
H-10	9-213E	MK 108	-	2 x MG 151	-	Aufklärung version of the H-0 but canceled March 1945
H-11	9-213E	MK 108	-	2 x MG 151	-	Aufklärung version of the H-1
H-12	9-213E	MK 108	-	2 x MG 151	-	Aufklärung version of the H-2 but canceled 15 Dec 1944
S-1	9-603LA	-	-	-	-	Schuleflugzeug based on C-1/U1 with FuG 16Zy radio
S-2	9-603LA	-	-	-	-	Schuleflugzeug as S-1 but with FuG 15 radio

When the Royal Canadian Air Force's 421 Squadron occupied Reinsehlen airfield, which was located some 50 miles south of Hamburg, they came upon the remains of the fourth Ta 152 prototype, the Fw 190 V18/U2 (see page 24), that had been purposely destroyed just prior to the field's occupation. Reinsehlen airfield was situated in a gently formed valley with just one runway. Other Focke-Wulf single-engine prototypes had been previously evacuated to this field by retreating German personnel, including the Fw 190 V32/U2, but their disposition and fate is unknown.

Before the surrender, JG 301 flew its last combat missions out of Leck on 4 May 1945, against what pilots identified as Spitfire Mk 22s, but most likely these were Mk 14s or Mk 18s instead, another of the late-model Griffon-engined versions since the Mk 22 did not see action during the war.

On 7 May 1945, the British took control of Leck and all of JG 301's personnel were interned by the British Army, whose officers wanted to lock them up in short order. On 20 May an RAF Spitfire unit had flown into Leck, commanded by a Canadian. Bracht recorded in his diary, "the Canadian commander sees in us an honorable and resourceful former foe of the RAF. This he tells us together with our commander, Hptm. Posselmann, before the entire assembled unit in the RAD depot. No barbed wire around us – Posselmann gave the Canadian his word that none of us would flee." Posselmann and his men kept their word and he was the last to be released on 2 August 1945, after laboring for the English work units.

Thus, with the end of the war in Europe, the Ta 152 passed from its frantic development, production, and combat operations, to its next but far less glamorous stage: captivity and exploitation.

The precise number of Ta 152s produced before V-E Day will probably never be known, but could not have exceeded 100 aircraft, including prototypes. Of these, many were lost through accidents, sabotage, Allied strafing and bombing operations, and in the end, by deliberate destruction at the hands of German troops. Acting on orders to deny the Allies flyable aircraft, complete and incomplete aircraft were deliberately blown up at their factories, airfields, and dispersal areas.

As Obfm. Bracht recalled, a number of pilots flew their Ta 152s to the relative safety of a *Luftwaffe* airfield near the Danish border at Leck, Germany. Located a short distance west of Flensburg, Leck was host to a mix of conventional and unconventional aircraft, including jet-propelled types. Among these was JG 1, equipped with the latest jet-powered fighter, the Heinkel He 162 *Volksjäger*. At least three known Ta 152 Hs arrived at Leck, including Ta 152 H-0, W. Nr. 150004 and Ta 152 H-1/R11, W. Nr. 150168 plus one additional Ta 152 H-0, the serial number of which remains unconfirmed. However, based on compelling circumstantial evidence (see p 110), it is the author's opinion that this third aircraft was W. Nr. 150010

built at Cottbus in December 1944, and transferred to Rechlin in January 1945, where its original metal tailplane was exchanged for one made from wood. In March 1945, it passed to JG 11 before being absorbed into JG 301.

This particular Ta 152 H-0 was next flown by its German pilot from Leck to Tirstrup, a small German-controlled airfield on Denmark's east coast, near the port city of Grenå. Not long afterward, the aircraft was formally surrendered intact to British forces, who promptly transported it to the larger airfield at Ålborg West for servicing. Its presence was reported to American authorities and, in accord with pre-existing American requirements, the British issued the identifier "USA 11" to this aircraft. Colonel Harold E. Watson, of Watson's Whizzers made arrangements to collect the prized Focke-Wulf as part of Project Lusty (*Luftwaffe* Secret Technology). Retired General Watson recalled:

...soon Captains McIntosh and Maxfield, along with some mechanics and crew and I climbed aboard our trusty C-47 and got to Ålborg at dusk. It was apparent that the engine in this Ta 152 had to be replaced. Captain

Edwin Maxfield took on this engine change task immediately along with some of our crew.

We had been picking up strange airplanes from airfields, farmers' hay fields, in all kinds of weather, from early sun-up until after sunset, on a steady diet of K-rations and much too much Spam (Single Portion Army Meal-Ed.). Captain McIntosh and crew searched for a decent meal. When dinner was announced, we were thrilled to see roast duck (liberated, tame or pet?) with all the extras including fresh strawberries and cream! All of this on an Army blanket under the wing of our C-47. The story of the Ålborg police searching for some missing pet ducks only confirmed the resourcefulness of my crew!

The next afternoon Capt. Fred McIntosh took off in our prize Ta 152 H for Melun, just south of Paris. From Melun, it was flown to Cherbourg where it, along with many other valuable German aircraft, was loaded aboard the British Navy's carrier HMS Reaper for shipment to the U.S. After unloading and reassembly at Newark Army Air Base, New Jersey, Capt. McIntosh flew the aircraft directly to the Army's Wright Field, at Dayton, Ohio.

Production of the Ta 152 H-1/R11 had begun in March 1945 at Focke-Wulf Bremen but although one aircraft (left) had reached an advanced stage of assembly and, at least one additional machine was in final assembly (above), none are known to have been completed prior to American occupation. Ta 152 Hs built at Bremen were assigned **Werknummern** *within the 200000 serial number block. Note the wooden fuselage access hatch.*

Two views of Ta 152 H-1/R11, W. Nr. 150167, recovered by American troops at Bremen where it served as an instructional production template. Manufactured early in 1945 at Cottbus, it was completed with Auxiliary Apparatus R11 that included bad weather equipment LGW K23 fighter directional control, FuG 125 "Hermine" VHF radio beacon signal receiver; heated windows; and Siemens PKS autopilot. Typical of German fighter aircraft during this period, the aircraft's complete engine assembly including its pre-painted cowling arrived at the final assembly point as finished components thus explaining the seemingly mismatched camouflage paint scheme between fuselage and engine.

FOREIGN EQUIPMENT 112

When the aircraft arrived in the States, it was assigned Foreign Equipment identifier FE-112, and possibly test flown by American pilots, but this last point is unconfirmed. By 1948, with the creation of the Air Force as a separate service branch, FE-112 became T2-112 (T2 was USAF's Air Technical Intelligence division). Also, by this time, the Ta 152 was declared no longer of interest and was relegated to the Air Force's inactive classification (see pages 110, 111). Eventually, in the early 1950s, it was assigned to the proposed National Aviation Museum. But in 1960, it was finally passed to the Smithsonian Institution. Today, this Ta 152, the sole surviving example, is in storage at the National Air and Space Museum's Paul E. Garber restoration facility at Silver Hill, Maryland. Presumably, at some future date, it will be restored.

AIR MINISTRY NUMBER 11

As recounted above, at least two additional Ta 152s were surrendered to the British at Leck. Ta 152 H-0, W. Nr. 150004, "Green 6", was determined to be in flyable condition, and was issued British Air Ministry number AM 11. It was slated for eventual transfer to England, but before this occurred, it was decided to reassign AM 11 to Ta 152 H-1/R11, W. Nr. 150168. The reason for this swap is unknown, but presumably it was based on the fact that the H-1/R11 was probably in better airworthy condition and/or better equipped.

Ta 152 H-0, W. Nr. 150004, the fourth preproduction H-0 series completed, sat at Leck for some period before being transported in January 1946, by road to Schleswig, south of Flensburg, to "await disposal." Presumably it was scrapped at Schleswig as no further record of the aircraft can be found.

Ta 152 H-1/R11, W. Nr. 150167, a Cottbus-built machine, was captured intact by British and Canadian troops at Bremen where it is thought to have served as a production template for Focke-Wulf's newly created Bremen Ta 152 H assembly line. When American troops decided this example was worthy of further study, it was disassembled and transported to Kassel, pending final disposition .

Ta 152 H-1/R11, W. Nr. 150168, "Green 9", of *Stab*/JG 301, Air Ministry 11, was flown from Leck to Schleswig where it was maintained. On 3 August 1945, it was flown to RAE Farnborough by RAF Flying Officer Lawson. Two weeks later, on 18 August 1945, it was flown by Lieutenant Commander Eric Brown to No. 6 MU at Brize Norton and, on 22 October 1945, it returned to Farnborough to be exhibited to the public

One of two additional views of Ta 152 H-1/R11, W. Nr. 150167, as it was found by American forces soon after troops occupied Bremen, where it served as a production template.

Interesting top view of Ta 152 H-1/R11, W. Nr. 150167, as it was found by American forces. This aircraft was equipped with two 20 mm MG 151/20 cannon each having 175 rounds plus one 30 mm MK 108 cannon with provision of between 85 and 100 rounds. It also differed from the preproduction H-0 series by having six unprotected wing fuel cells with a total capacity of 384 liters (101 gal) of 87 octane B4 avgas.

at the "German Aircraft Exhibition" held between 29 October and 12 November 1945. Lt/Cdr Brown recalled:

> *...take off of the Ta 152 H-1 was shorter than that of the Spitfire 19 and the climb was steeper albeit somewhat shorter than that of the British fighter, but once the 30,000 feet (9,145 m) mark had slipped past the altimeter, the Tank fighter gave the impression of holding its rate of climb better than its British counterpart. Insofar as maneuverability was concerned, the story was very much the same... but, about 35,000 feet (10,670 m), the Ta 152 H-1 enjoyed a decided edge.*

As advanced as the Ta 152 H was, it, like many German aircraft of the period, suffered from woefully inadequate brakes as Eric Brown discovered.

He continued...

> *The flight was uneventful, but once I touched down on Farnborough's main runway and began to apply the foot brakes I immediately realized that these were very weak indeed. In fact they faded away rapidly to zero effectiveness. A slight swing started to develop and I let this go enough to steer me onto the grass in order to slow the aircraft. I then applied full opposite rudder to prevent a ground loop developing. After a few adrenalin pumping seconds, the Ta 152 H slowed gently to a standstill. I can doubt this hydraulic fault ever being rectified as I cannot recollect the fighter ever flying again.*

Some thirteen months after the exhibition closed, this Ta 152 H was recorded at the scrap area of Farnborough. Eric Brown's assessment of the Tank fighter was to the point:

> *...In my view, the Ta 152 H was every bit as good as any of its Allied piston engined counterparts and, from some aspects, better than most. It was unfortunate for the Jagdflieger but undoubtedly fortunate for the Allies that it arrived on the scene too late to play any serious role in the air war.*

Above and below: American Army mechanics are shown in the process of dismantling Ta 152 H-1/R11, W. Nr. 150167, preparatory to its transfer to the main American aircraft collection point at Kassel — normally, a straightforward job for qualified personnel, but sometimes made interesting, if not downright dangerous, by the presence of cleverly hidden booby traps.

Owing to their simplicity of design, changing or removing German reciprocating engines was a relatively easy task, one that could be accomplished within an hour by trained mechanics having the right equipment. Here, Ta 152 H-1/R11, W. Nr. 150167, is about to have its Jumo 213 E engine removed and crated for transfer to Kassel.

Above and below: Flanked by other captured German aircraft, the fuselage to W. Nr. 150167 rests at Kassel awaiting disposition. Apparently this Ta 152 H-1/R11 never left this American collection point for no subsequent record of this aircraft can be found. In all probability it was declared surplus and scrapped when it was ascertained that at least one additional airworthy Ta 152 H had already been acquired by Col. Watson's team. The exception to this scenario could be W. Nr. 150167's nearly new Jumo 213 E engine. In this regard, it is not beyond the realm of possibility to suggest its Jumo may be the same engine shown on page 104. Of special interest is the damaged fuselage of Fw 190 D-9, W. Nr. 500666, "Yellow 15", which was previously operational with 3./JG 301.

Two views of Ta 152 H-1/R11, W. Nr. 150168, after its capture by British forces. Interestingly, it was the next production machine built at Cottbus, after the Ta 152 H shown on the four preceding pages. The top image was taken on the continent prior to its transfer to England. The lower image dates from November 1945 when it was on public exhibit at Farnborough. Unfortunately, no photographs have been discovered showing this particular fighter in its original German national aircraft insignia and unit markings. Nevertheless, it is known to have been originally "Green 9" having the distinctive Yellow-Red tail band with a narrow horizontal bar in

Green superimposed. These markings reveal this was originally a **Geschwader** headquarters aircraft of JG 301. Once in captivity, the RAF wasted little time in overpainting the machine's original insignia and markings as shown here. This German fighter also featured the usual White spiral motif on its spinner but there is a question regarding the base color. A British eyewitness reporter described the aircraft's camouflage in some detail stating the spinner was Black with the White spiral, but it was repainted Red with White spiral for the display at Farnborough.

Ta 152 H-1/R11, W. Nr. 150168, photographed during the summer of 1946 with British Air Ministry 11 abbreviated along its rear fuselage. The first Ta 152 H to be "AM 11" was another example, W. Nr. 150004, which was abandoned and reassigned to W. Nr. 150168. Nineteen months after capture, W. Nr. 150168 was broken up at Farnborough.

The only known photograph of Ta 152 H-0, W. Nr. 150010, "Green 4" while it was still on the continent. It is shown here in RAF insignia being readied for its flight to Melun, France by Capt. McIntosh of Col. Watson's group. This particular aircraft is today's sole surviving Ta 152 presently in storage at NASM. The identity of the captured Do 217 N in the background is unknown but it may have been among the aircraft destined for the United States.

Ta 152 H-0, W. Nr. 150010, "Green 4", is greeted by interested Army Air Corps personnel upon its arrival at Wright Field's Base Operations building following its flight from Newark airfield. It is questionable if it was ever subsequently flown since no flight records have been discovered and the aircraft did not appear to have ever been adorned with American national aircraft insignia. The H-0 preproduction series was originally scheduled to include 115 aircraft, but after approximately 40 had been completed, it was decided to move directly into the initial full production model, the H-1. Normally, the so-called preproduction series constituted fewer than 20 aircraft, but because time was critical and the obligatory flight testing program had to be greatly accelerated, coupled with delays in delivering H-1 wings, the Air Ministry approved the order for a large number of preproduction aircraft.

This image has been airbrushed to include German insignia. Nevertheless, it shows W. Nr. 150010 secured off the flight line at Wright Field. By this time the wing-mounted cannons had long since been removed and the ports sealed.

These images were taken at Wright Field during the autumn of 1945 while the W. Nr. 150010 was still mainly in its original factory camouflage colors. After 1947, with the creation of the Air Force as a separate service branch, the Tank fighter then bore the Air Force Intelligence Code "T2-112" and an inventive camouflage paint scheme.

"FE-112" is shown here without its armament at Wright Field autumn 1945. Note the distinctive oval supercharger scoop.

Frontal view of Ta 152 H-0, W. Nr. 150010, FE-112, as it appeared at Wright Field in September 1945. Several sources have suggested this Ta 152 H-0 was initially flown to Freeman Field, Seymour, Indiana, but the author can find no official confirmation of this claim. Freeman Field was a first class facility approximately 100 miles southwest of Wright Field. In March 1943, it officially became Freeman Army airfield and later served as the Foreign Aircraft Evaluation Center. It boasted four 5,500 foot long active runways plus some 413 buildings and was home to an advanced twin-engine aircraft training school. But after the war, its evaluation role was transferred to Wright Field which contained all the necessary support facilities for a large controlled aircraft evaluation program. Freeman Field was eventually deactivated late in 1948.

These images, taken at Wright-Patterson Air Force Base sometime after formation of the U.S. Air Force as a separate service branch in September 1947, show the Ta 152 H-0 now as T2-112 (the "T2" signified Air Force Intelligence). By this time too, the aircraft had been repainted and was displayed without its propeller and spinner. It shares the hardtop with another former enemy aircraft, a Japanese Nakajima J1N1-S Gekko "Irving", T2-700. This Japanese naval twin-engine night fighter has subsequently been meticulously restored to its original condition and is on public display at the NASM.

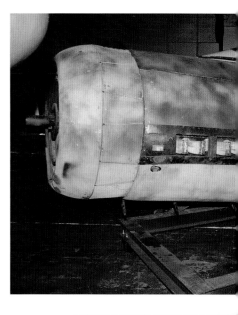

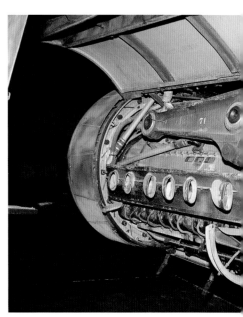

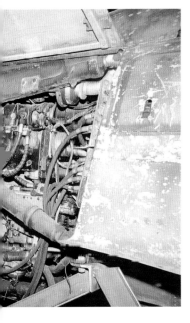

Epilogue

In the Foreword, veteran Ta 152 pilot, Willi Reschke laments the fact that of all of the Ta 152s that survived the war, only one remains. Even with all of its development difficulties, this historically significant warplane was nevertheless a masterful creation. Accordingly, it would not have been unreasonable to assume the Allies would have exercised restraint in the disposition of such noteworthy aircraft. Yet in the halcyon days following the war, a pervasive mind set existed that proved unfavorable to the long term preservation of vanquished Axis aircraft—regardless of how significant such aircraft may have appeared in 1945. Therefore, it is all the more remarkable that one example of the Ta 152 still survives, albeit in an unrestored condition.

The adjacent detail images, taken at the National Air and Space Museum's Silver Hill facility during the summer of 2005, depict something of the sole surviving Ta 152's present condition. Museum staff has performed selected color sanding and other tasks in an effort to establish not only the aircraft's overall condition, but to learn something of its original colors and markings. Preliminary results have been fruitful and encouraging.

As recounted in Chapter 4, page 110, it is the author's belief this particular aircraft, an early example of the Ta 152 H-0 preproduction series, is in fact W. Nr. 150010. Throughout its career it has worn no less than seven distinct marking identities. These include:

1) The original camouflage scheme applied when the aircraft was built at Cottbus with its metal tail unit.
2) Its original factory primary identification code, CW+CJ was applied to the air frame for the first time upon its transfer to Rechlin where it received its present wooden tail.
3) After being accepted for active duty with 11./JG 301 it became "Yellow 4" with a Yellow/Red tail band, divided horizontally, by a narrow Yellow bar.
4) Reassigned to *Stab* /JG 301, it ended its active duty with the *Luftwaffe* as "Green 4" with a narrow horizontal Light Green bar replacing the previous Yellow bar.
5) It received British national aircraft insignia shortly after its capture.
6) In American hands at Wright Field it became "FE-112" with rudimentary German insignia.
7) Finally ending its career as "T2-112" and receiving its present paint scheme in 1947.

During its time at Rechlin, where it received its wooden tail assembly (for test purposes), field personnel would have painted the aircraft's primary identification code on both sides of the rear fuselage and beneath the wings. For security purposes, after November 1944, this four-letter identification code, CW+CJ, unique to this aircraft, would only be applied to the airframe if the aircraft was assigned to experimental test or evaluation duties. Prior to this date, four-letter codes routinely appeared on almost all German military aircraft for easy identification. The photographs appearing on pages 175, of FE-112, clearly reveals traces of the distinctive German font for the letter 'J' adjacent to the Green '4'. Again, according to regulations, an operational unit such as 11./JG 301 would have immediately removed, or overpainted the aircraft's unique primary identification code before it was accepted for operations. Whether or not further color sanding of the fuselage and under side of the wings will reveal traces of this code remains to be determined.

The top left and bottom photographs on the opposite page give a sense of the aircraft's long wing span. In the bottom image, the long wooden landing flaps are extended to reveal American applied zinc chromate paint. Normally, the inside of these wooden surfaces would have been treated with a clear varnish. The size, style and location of the American applied German national insignia is incorrect and inconsistent for the Ta 152.

The top right and bottom right photographs reveal details around the aircraft's nose, cowling and unmolested engine compartment. In his interview with the author, General Watson made mention of an engine swap having been carried out before the aircraft could be flown out of Denmark, but there is some question this was actually under taken. Note the preserved engine serial number and maker identification plates attached to the block just above the engine exhaust stacks.

The two middle photographs show starboard and port sides of the vertical tail revealing the original German swastika, traces of the RAF Red, White, and Blue fin flash as well as the bogus American applied swastika at the top. Also evident is the Red and Yellow rear fuselage tail band with a narrow Light Green horizontal bar indicating this aircraft belonged to the staff flight of JG 301.

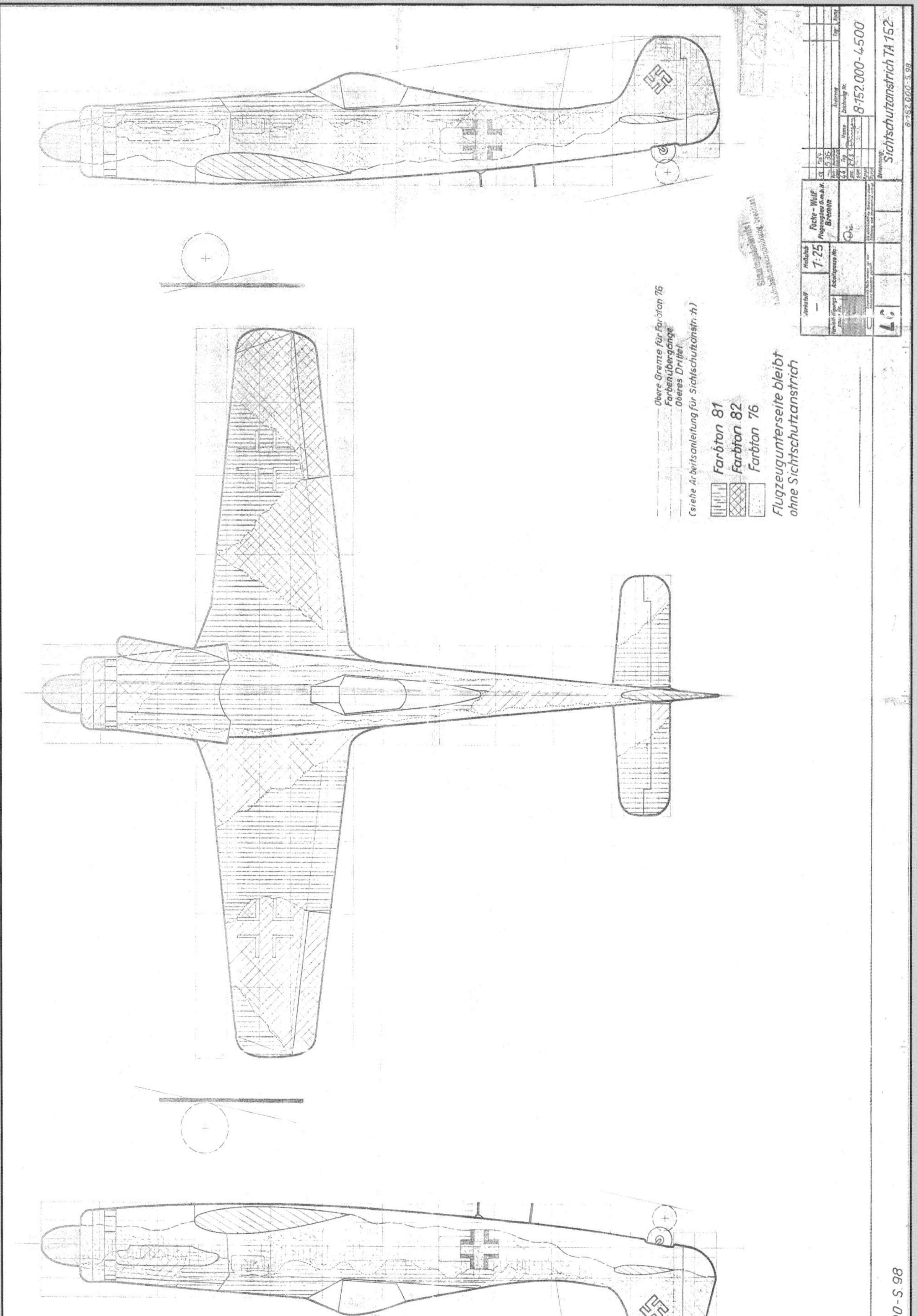

Obere Grenze für Farbton 76
Farbenübergänge
Oberes Drittel
(siehe Arbeitsanleitung für Sichtschutzanstrich)
Farbton 81
Farbton 82
Farbton 76
Flugzeugunterseite bleibt ohne Sichtschutzanstrich
Focke-Wulf
Bremen
1:25
8-152.000-4.500
Sichtschutzanstrich TA 152
8-152.000-S.98

This November 1944 aircraft camouflage instruction drawing was for the proposed Ta 152 A-1 but was also applicable to the Ta 152 C-1 insofar as its pattern delineation was concerned. Note **Farbon 76** *was restricted to the fuselage and tailplane's vertical surfaces. The aircraft's undersurfaces were not to be camouflaged.*

Appendix 1
Camouflage, Insignia & Markings

CAMOUFLAGE

When the first Ta 152 prototype took to the air in July 1944, it was painted in the standard German day fighter camouflage colors then extant. Four months later, when the first production Ta 152 emerged, its upper surface camouflage coloring reflected changes dictated by shifting wartime necessities. Moreover, during the last six months of the war in Europe, further painting changes occurred which were the direct result of strenuous German efforts to increase aircraft production through decentralization and labor saving programs.

Ta 152 PROTOTYPES

As recounted in Chapter 4, the first five Ta 152 prototypes were not newly built aircraft as originally planned, but instead, each test machine was created from existing Focke-Wulf Fw 190 research and development aircraft. The first two of these modified aircraft to serve as substitute Ta 152 prototypes, resulted in the Fw 190 V33/U1 and V30/U1 (see p 90-91). Each retained their original standard German day fighter camouflage coloring. Not surprisingly, their camouflage pattern remained essentially unchanged albeit with obvious accommodation for their extended noses and elongated wings. Their camouflage consisted of a prescribed segmented pattern of the standard upper surface colors RLM 74 Gray-Green and RLM 75 Gray-Violet. The fuselage side and lower surface color was a uniform RLM 76 Light Blue. Mottling composed of three colors; RLM 02 Gray, RLM 70 Black-Green and RLM 74 Gray-Green were sprayed in equal amounts in soft alternating patches along the fuselage flank and vertical tailplane. Lastly the spinner and metal and wooden propeller blades were painted RLM 70 Black-Green

PAINTING CHART OF 21 MARCH 1944

When first published in March 1944, the official Focke-Wulf camouflage directive, *Sichtschutzanstrich TA 152, Zeichnung* Nr. 8-152.960-02, stipulated the use of the standard trio of German day fighter camouflage colors of 74, 75, and 76. It also prescribed RLM 02 Gray for the soft mottle applied narrowly along the length of the fuselage at the terminus of the two top colors. In addition, mottle patches of RLM 02 were to be softly sprayed on the vertical tailplane in conjunction with equal amounts of colors 74 and 75 over the Light Blue base. Lastly, the chart indicated the aircraft's spinner was to be finished in RLM 70 Black-Green.

Eight months later, in November 1944, this camouflage chart was updated to reflect changes in the prescribed camouflage colors. This amendment, *Zeichnung* Nr. 8-152.000-4500 (see facing page) was released barely a month prior the first flight of the first production Ta 152. Moreover, this document depicts the Jumo-powered Ta 152 A 1 with its distinctive flared cowl. Although the camouflage colors were changed, the segmented pattern was not. Thus, the new colors 81 and 82 merely replaced 74 and 75 respectively. RLM 02 was no longer

specified. The soft mottling on the vertical tailplane was to be in equal amounts of 81 and 82 over a base of 76. Though not mentioned on the amendment, undoubtedly the aircraft's spinner would have remained RLM 70.

Of particular significance is the statement *"Flugzeugunterseite bleibt ohne Sichtschutzanstrich"* (Aircraft under surfaces remain without camouflage). Apart from the specified top surface camouflage colors and allowance for its engine, the actual placement and pattern of colors shown in this document, was not markedly different from the pattern specified for the Fw 190 A-8/A-9.

A few months earlier, on 1 July 1944, the RLM directed that: "all new aircraft types whose mission would have required the use of colors 70 and 71, are from now on to be painted in colors 81 and 82." Thus, by this date, the use of RLM colors 81 and 82 appeared to have been restricted to aircraft other than single-engine day fighters. Apart from isolated instances, single-engine day fighters had not used the dark Green camouflage colors 70 and 71 as part of their approved camouflage since the early days of the war in Europe.

Forty-five days later, on 15 August 1944, the Air Ministry issued its Summary Report Nr. 2 calling for the gradual elimination of camouflage colors RLM 65 Bright Blue, 70, 71 and 74 while introducing dark RLM color 83 (shade unspecified but almost certainly Dark Green).

For normal single-engine day fighters, this meant the upper surface camouflage color 74 Gray-Green was to be phased out and replaced with the new dark camouflage color RLM 83. Whether or not the resulting combination of Gray-Violet and Dark Green over Light Blue, was considered a transition, or the definitive scheme for the short span Ta 152, is unknown.

THE Ta 152 H CAMOUFLAGE

When the first Ta 152 H-0 appeared in November 1944, it was camouflaged in accord with Air Ministry instructions governing single-seat high altitude fighters. The illustration (p 160-161), of Ta 152 H-1, W. Nr. 150168, "Green 9", is instructive and representative of the so-called late war defensive camouflage colors. Based on an eye-witness description published in the 29 November 1945, issue of the British bi-weekly, The Aeroplane Spotter, the reporter stated this aircraft "...is camouflaged on the upper surfaces of the wings, fuselage and tailplane and the fuselage sides in various shades of Green. On the fuselage the effect is mottled, but on the wings two Greens make a zigzag pattern. The whole of the underside of this particular machine W. Nr. 150168, is Sky Blue, while the Black spinner is enhanced by a White spiral."

Undoubtedly, this reporter's mention of "various shades" of Green implied the two new upper surface camouflage colors RLM 82 Bright Green and RLM 83 Dark Green. The other new late-war upper surface camouflage color, RLM 81 Brown-Violet, could have been paired with either 82 or 83, but in the case of W. Nr. 150168, The Aeroplane Spotter's reporter made no mention of a "Brown." Nevertheless, because this particular H series aircraft represented the 51st

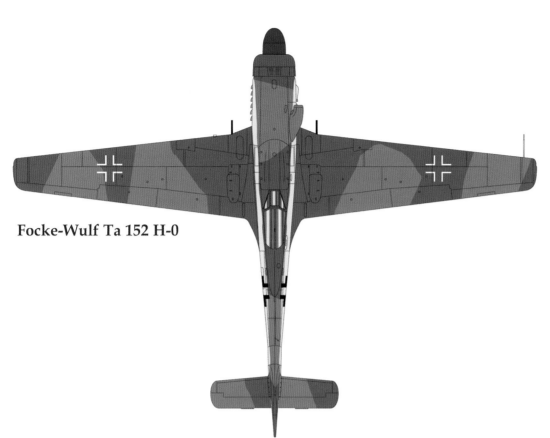

Focke-Wulf Ta 152 H-0

and was applied in roughly equal amounts of colors 75 and 83 over the RLM 76 Light Blue base coat. Fuselage sides as well as portions of the underside were sprayed in 76 Light Blue. In each case, color intersections were irregular and soft edged in which color overspray of up to 100 mm was permitted. In accordance with paint and labor conservation directives, only a portion of the wing undersurface was to be painted. As applied to the Ta 152 V6 and V7, only the forward half of the wing undersurface, plus gear covers, ailerons and flaps, were painted. The remaining aft portion of the wing under surface was left in natural metal. Aircraft spinners and metal VDM propeller blades were uniformly finished in color RLM 70 Black-Green with the blades receiving an additional coat of RLM 00 Waterbright (clear coat) which afforded a slight sheen to the surface.

production example, by this time period, cowls were pre-painted in decentralized locations differently from early production machines. Instead of a continuous and unified flow of camouflage colors over the entire upper fuselage (see page 160); W. Nr. 150168's coloration is interrupted at the cowl leading to an impression of mis-matched parts. A good example of prepainted parts (cowls), painted in dark Green, can be viewed on page 104.

Undoubtedly, a detailed camouflage chart expressly for the long span Ta 152 H was created but has not yet been discovered. The illustration above graphically displays the approximate placement of the two upper surface camouflage colors RLM 82 Bright Green and 83 Dark Green. Mottling of the fuselage and vertical tailplane was achieved by lightly spraying equal amounts of RLM 82 and 83. Frequently, the long narrow rectangular panel at the engine exhaust was painted Black. When the H series entered production, the aircraft's spinners were normally sprayed RLM 70 Black-Green, but RLM 22 Black was also permitted. Wooden propeller blades were also finished in the requisite RLM 70 Black-Green.

THE Ta 152 C CAMOUFLAGE

Although the Ta 152 C series was properly classified as a single-seat day fighter, it was not considered a high altitude aircraft. Possibly, because of this distinction, its camouflage colors, as evidenced by the two Adelheide-built prototypes, the Ta 152 V6 and V7, which differed significantly from the Ta 152 H, were finished in camouflage colors 75, 76 and 83. The plan view on the right illustrates the placement of the two uppersurface camouflage colors RLM 75 Gray-Violet and RLM 83 Dark Green. Mottling was restricted to the vertical tailplane

LAYING OUT THE COLORS

Upper surface color patterns for single-engine propeller driven day fighters were frequently laid out according to a precise plan involving grid blocks superimposed over the aircraft's plan and side elevations developed by the manufacturer with Air Ministry approval.

The fuselage plan view is divided symmetrically into

Focke-Wulf Ta 152 C-1

five rectangular blocks whose combined width equals the fuselage's widest point. The fuselage's overall length, running from the tip of the spinner to the vertical tailplane's starting point, is divided equally into ten which forms the length of each rectangular block.

The wing plan was similarly divided into ten long blocks running from tip to tip across the fuselage. Five rows begin where the wing meets the fuselage. The horizontal stabilizer was laid out in a similar fashion as are the two fuselage side elevations. Interestingly, in each side elevation the aircraft's top reference point is the highest point of the fuselage excluding the cockpit.

The aircraft's vertical tailplane elevation was also divided into equal blocks of five beginning where the tailplane meets the fuselage and extending to the tip of the rudder. Vertically, the reference point for the five blocks begins at the point of intersection between the fuselage's underside and the underside of the tailplane and runs vertically to the top of the fin.

The aircraft's camouflage plan pattern is then established within the resulting grid pattern. In this, each of the two top surface colors was apportioned in alternating irregular shapes. The aircraft's fuselage plan pattern was also divided in alternating irregular color areas. The degree to which the fuselage top colors were allowed to flow down the fuselage side was not fixed but was usually sufficient for 95 percent of the surface area, seen in plan, to be covered by the top surface colors.

It must be stressed that such apparent precision in the application of camouflage paint was not an idle exercise but, nor was it inexorably "carved in stone." Colors and their patterns were occasionally reversed, as in a mirror image and, by 1945, due in part to production decentralization; it became common practice for individual components to be prepainted either in a solid or, complementary color shade or pattern to that of its adjacent component. By 1945, such seeming irregularities resulting in what resembled mismatched color schemes were deemed acceptable.

NATIONAL AIRCRAFT INSIGNIA

The Focke-Wulf document, reproduced on page 180, not only set forth the Ta 152's official camouflage pattern, but also the style, size and placement of German national aircraft insignia. By November 1944, the style of German national aircraft insignia had been reduced to its simplest form. The six *Balkenkreuz* insignia displayed on both sides of the fuselage together with those above and below each wing represented an abbreviated form of the traditional German Black and White cross. This simplified single color rendition was such that the aircraft's camouflage color, or natural metal, served as the insignia's interior background field. The *Hakenkreuz* centered on the aircraft's fin, also an integral part of the German national aircraft insignia, was a simple solid Black outline variety in which its center was the color of the fin.

INSIGNIA OF THE Ta 152 A

Represented by the Fw camouflage chart on page 182, the White top wing cross (B6 style) measured 600 mm, the underwing Black cross (not shown but B4 style) measured 900 mm while the Black fuselage cross (also B4 style) measured 600 mm. The swastika (H5 style) measured 300 mm.

INSIGNIA OF THE Ta 152 C

Based on the examination of surviving photographs of the Ta 152 V7, German national aircraft insignia was similar in size and placement to the Focke-Wulf chart on page 182. The top wing cross was unchanged at 600 mm while the fuselage *Balkenkreuz* was a simple 600 mm White outline (B5 style). The fuselage top surface camouflage color, RLM 83 Dark Green, extended downward to frame the background field for the cross. The fin's solid Black swastika (H3 style) of 300 mm was centered on the fin against an area which had first been sprayed RLM 83 forming a framed background field.

INSIGNIA OF THE Ta 152 H

German national aircraft insignia of the Ta 152 H was similar in style to the C series, and noted for its simplicity. The upper surface *Balkenkreuz* (B6 style) and the underwing cross (B4 style) each measured 1000 mm. In contrast to the C series, the Black fuselage cross (B4 style) of the Ta 152 H was larger at 800 mm. The aircraft's swastika (H3 style) was also larger at 500 mm. In each location, the insignia background field merely consisted of the aircraft's normal camouflage without any special framing.

MARKINGS

Markings are defined as letters, numbers, symbols and colors having reference to individual aircraft identification and/or operating unit identification. Markings also apply to cautionary or instructional information applied to facilitate ground handling and to ensure proper servicing of the aircraft.

THE *STAMMKENNZEICHEN* CODES

German military aircraft employed a masterfully simple yet effective system of individual aircraft identification known as the *Stammkennzeichen* - stkz (primary identification) system. Essentially, this provided the manufacturer and operator with a nearly faultless means for quickly identifying individual aircraft.

The stkz code was usually applied using a washable, yet waterproof, Black distemper that could be easily removed with solvents without damage to the aircraft's underlying paint. The main purpose of this primary identification system, insofar as fighters was concerned, was to aid in identifying and tracking individual aircraft from manufacturer to frontline unit. However, the codes also served to identify individual aircraft assigned to testing and experimental stations or, involved in other specialized roles. Once a fighter aircraft arrived at its operational duty station, ground crew quickly removed all external traces of the code from the airframe. If washable solvents were not readily available, the stkz code was simply overpainted. All German military aircraft were assigned a stkz code including liaison types, trainers, twin-engined fighters, multi-engined aircraft and even non-powered types.

These four letter codes, beginning with consonants, were applied at the point of manufacture and repeated on the aircraft's service card. To avoid duplication, a special RLM command, the *Generalluftzeugmeisters/Prufstelle für Luftfahrtzeug* - Berlin (General Aviation Chief/Aviation Auditor

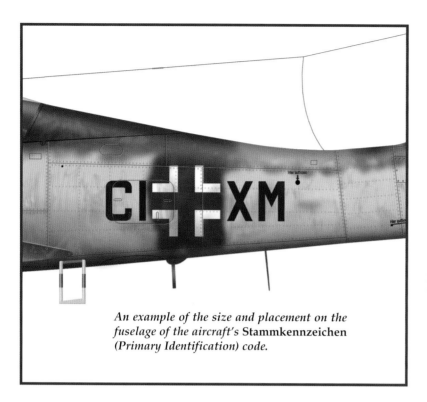

*An example of the size and placement on the fuselage of the aircraft's **Stammkennzeichen** (Primary Identification) code.*

both sides of the fuselage, just ahead of the Black national cross. The color of these tactical numbers was significant inasmuch as it identified individual, squadrons and head-quarters aircraft within the fighter wing.

According to usual German practice, four aircraft were assigned to the *Geschwader Stab* and these bore Green numbers ranging from 1 to 4. By 1944, JG 301 was comprised of four groups, each having up to 16 aircraft, plus each group's own headquarters flight amounting to an additional four aircraft; thus making a total of up to 68 air-craft for each group.

In addition to the group's headquarters flight (e.g. *Stab* III./JG 301), each of the four groups was further broken down into four *Staffeln* identified with Arabic numerals (1. – 4./JG 301 with I./JG 301 and 5. – 8./JG 301 within II./JG 301). The first eight *Staffeln* (evenly divided between I. and II./JG 301) were identified by colored numbers thus:

1./JG 301 + 5./JG 301	(White 1 to White 16)
2./JG 301 + 6./JG 301	(Red 1 to Red 16)
3./JG 301 + 7./JG 301	(Yellow 1 to Yellow 16)
4./JG 301 + 8./JG 301	(Blue 1 to Blue 16)

Station Berlin) maintained tight control over the distribution of all code allocations. Although stkz prefixes (i.e. the first two letters) were distributed from the authority, code suffixes were usually assigned sequentially by the final assembly facility. By 1940, it was usual practice for manufacturers to assign suffix letters in an alphabetic sequence beginning with the fourth letter. For example, when the Fw 190 V29 was manufactured it received the stkz "GH+KS", with the next aircraft, the Fw 190 V30, being the coded "GH+KT" while the Fw 190 V31 became "GH+KU." However, there were inevitable breaks in letter sequencing brought about by security concerns, a switch in aircraft production, or other special circumstances. On 1 July 1944, the Air Ministry issued instructions to all aircraft manufacturers forbidding factories from physically applying the stkz code to the aircraft's exterior on all newly produced or pre-existing front-line aircraft. A code was still issued, just not applied externally. This explains why the Ta 152 H-0 and H-1s produced by Focke-Wulf's factory at Cottbus did not display their stkz codes.

Test aircraft or prototypes, such as the Ta 152 V6, V7, V8 and others, were handled differently and were exempt from this regulation.

The code consisted of four letters in an approved font with two letters appearing on either side of the fuselage *Balkenkreuz*. These four letters were repeated, slightly larger in size, on the wing's underside with their tops facing the direction of flight. The first two letters appeared beneath the starboard wing separated equidistant from the under wing cross insignia to which they were aligned. The remaining two letters were similarly positioned under the port wing.

Not surprisingly, the proper size and positioning of *Stammkennzeichen* codes on the aircraft's airframe was clearly delineated by the manufacturer in detailed drawings.

TACTICAL NUMBERS AND THEIR COLORS

The primary *Luftwaffe* operator of Ta 152 was JG 301. Ta 152s assigned for operational duty with this unit routinely carried one or two-digit identification numbers painted on

The third group of JG 301 (III./JG 301), was the only group to be equipped with the Ta 152 and to fly the aircraft operationally. The four *Staffeln* employed a similar sequence of color-coded numbers:

9./JG 301: White 1 up to White 16
10./JG 301: Red 1 up to Red 16
11./JG 301: Yellow 1 up to Yellow 16
12./JG 301: Black 1 up to Black 16

For unknown reasons the 12th *Staffel* broke with tradition and, instead of Blue numbers, they chose Black identifying numbers running from 1 up to 16.

The fourth group, IV./JG 301, was comprised of the 13th through 16th *Staffel*, and was each color coded in the same sequence as III./JG 301. But it must be remembered that groups I., II. and IV./JG 301 flew single-engine fighters other than the Ta 152.

The four aircraft of the headquarters flight of III./JG 301, (*Stab* III./JG 301) like the aircraft of the unit's *Geschwader* headquarters flight, employed Green numbers but these ran from 21 to 24. Though relatively rare, some *Luftwaffe* squadrons occasionally used numbers from 17 to 20. Aircraft with numbers higher than 24 were also recorded but these were almost always assigned for very specific purposes.

In the final weeks of the war in Europe, because III./JG 301 suffered Ta 152 losses that could not be made up; the unit was hastily reorganized into a single fighting element known as the *Stabsstaffel* /JG 301. Surviving Ta 152s flying under this final command employed Green numbers (1 up to at least 9). Not surprisingly, some surviving Ta 152s, culled from the group's four *Staffeln*, are known to have retained the colored numbers of their last squadron posting.

TACTICAL TAIL BANDS AND *GRUPPE* COLORS

In February 1945, all four *Gruppen* of JG 301 carried the now mandatory color coded fighter wing recognition tail band. JG 301 was assigned two 450 mm Yellow and Red bands. Throughout the war, fighter units employed a system of geometric symbols to aid in *Gruppe* identification as well as *Geschwader* and *Gruppen* headquarters flights. For unknown reasons, JG 301 instituted a unique system to differentiate their four *Gruppen* and *Geschwader*. This was cleverly accomplished by superimposing a narrow horizontal colored bar over the Yellow and Red tail band that effectively cut the band in half.

JG 301's horizontal bar colors were allocated thus:

Geschwader Stab:	Green bar	(a hybrid bright Green)
I. *Gruppe*:	White bar	RLM Color 21 *Weiss*
II. *Gruppe*:	Red bar	RLM Color 23 *Rot*
III. *Gruppe*:	Yellow bar	RLM Color 04 *Gelb*
IV. *Gruppe*:	Blue bar	RLM Color 24 *Blau*

After 13 March 1945 the promised 30 to 50 Ta 152s were never delivered to III./JG 301 as production delays plagued the Focke-Wulf factories. Because of this, Obslt. Fritz Auffhammer pulled the few Ta 152s from III. Gruppe, reassigned them into a small unit designated the **Stabsschwarm** *and changed the Yellow III. Gruppe horizontal bar to Green. There is some photo evidence of* **Gruppenstab** *aircraft also utilizing Green numbers.*

Where the horizontal bar color was Red or Yellow (i.e. the II. or III. *Gruppe*), that portion of the bar that crossed into the adjacent band of the same color (i.e. Red or Yellow), the bar was usually enhanced by the addition of a very narrow accenting stripe of the adjacent band's color.

UNIT OR PERSONAL EMBLEMS FOR THE Ta 152?

Although the unit emblem illustrated below is documented as belonging to JG 301, there is no evidence this, or any other emblem, was ever actually placed on the Ta 152.

Stab/JG 301

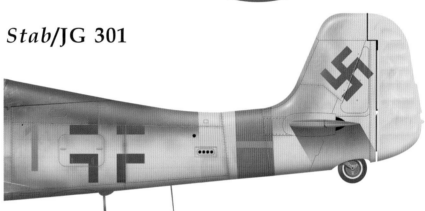

A rare color image of an abandoned JG 301 aircraft photographed at Salzwedel shortly after the war. It depicts an Fw 190 A-9/R11, "Yellow 8" that was formerly attached to 3./Staffel (Yellow numbers) of I./ Gruppe (White horizontal bar on the tail band) of JG 301 (Yellow/Red tail band). Because of paint overspray, the aircraft's original **Werknummer** *is not readable. Note the burnt-out remains of a Bf 109 G to the left.*

Although of indifferent quality, the photograph above is historically significant because it is one of the few surviving images of the Ta 152 in operational markings taken during the war. It shows Ta 152 H-0, W. Nr. 150007, "White 7", of JG 301 in the company of one of this unit's Fw 190 D-9s "White 16". The images below taken on 14 March 1945 at Stendal airfield, also reveal the same "White 7" on the occasion of a visit by **Generalmajor Dietrich Peltz**, the 31 year old commander of IX. **Fliegerkorps**. Peltz flew "White 7" shown above and on page 147 of *The Focke-Wulf Fw 190 Dora Volume One* by Jerry Crandall published by Eagle Editions Ltd. Over the Red and Yellow fuselage bands is the Green **Stab** horizontal bar as well. After April 1944, all the Ta 152s in JG 301 were grouped together as part of JG 301 **Stabschwarm**. Peltz, holder of the Knight's Cross with Oak Leaves and Swords was actually a skilled bomber pilot, but in late 1944 was controversially assigned to take command of II. **Jagdkorps**.

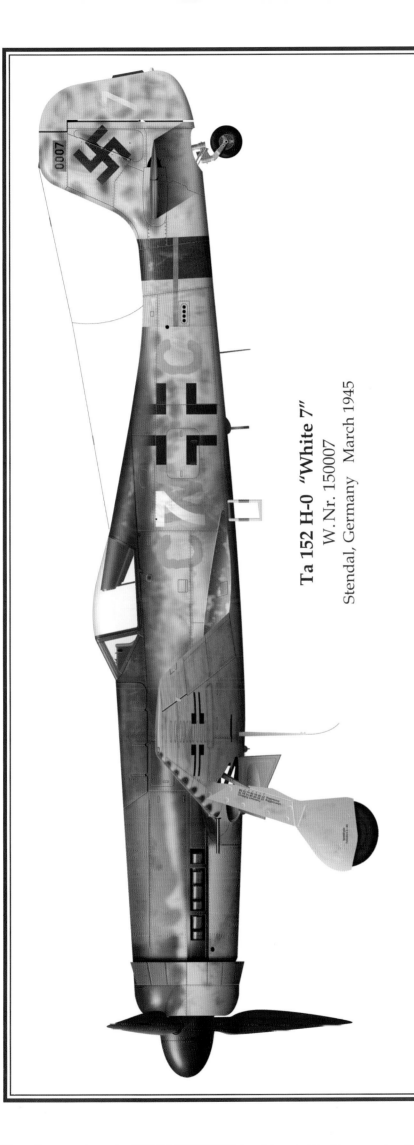

Ta 152 H-0 "White 7"
W. Nr. 150007
Stendal, Germany March 1945

Notable Features
- No pressurized canopy
- All antennas intact
- No ETC rack or drop tank

Colors
Undersurfaces	RLM 76 Light Blue,
Uppersurfaces	RLM 82 Bright Green/RLM 83 Dark Green,
	Black exhaust area; Sawtooth camouflage
	on upperwing extends onto the underwing
Prop blades	RLM 70 Black-Green
Spinner	RLM 70 Black-Green, No spiral

National Markings
Fuselage	B4 800 mm Black outline crosses
	H3 500 mm Black *Hakenkreuz*
Wings	Upper: B6 1000 mm White outline crosses
	Lower: B4 1000 mm Black outline crosses

Stenciling
Standard; overpainted factory codes CW + CG

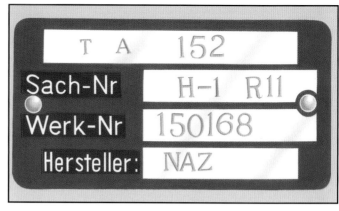

*A Ta 152's serial number would have been customarily recorded in two or three locations on the airframe. The most visible means of recording the aircraft's serial number was atop the fin in Black stenciled numbers. In addition to this location, a small rectangular aluminum plate, similar to the rendering above for W. Nr. 150168, measuring about 60 mm in length, was usually riveted to the port side of the rear fuselage next to the lower right arm to the national aircraft insignia, **Balkenkreuz**. Although no examples of such an ID plate are known to exist, the above representation is based on plates recovered Fw 190 D-9s produced at the same Cottbus factory that produced the Ta 152 H-1. The four lines identify the aircraft type, the model number, the aircraft's serial number and a 3-letter code (e.g. naz) identifying the producer.*

Three successive Focke-Wulf confidential production reports, spanning a period just under 60 days, detailing their vast network of suppliers and final assembly plants dedicated to the production of many diverse variants of the Fw 190 and Ta 152. Such reports give a vivid picture of ever changing production resources during the last weeks of 1944.

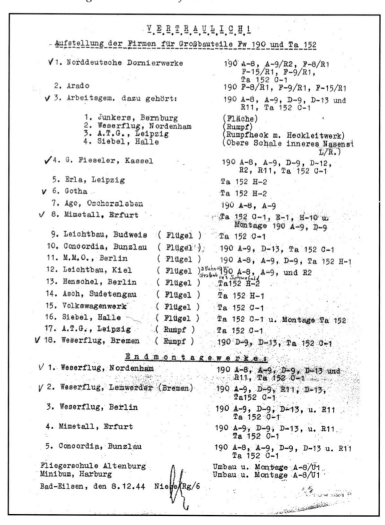

Appendix 2

Production

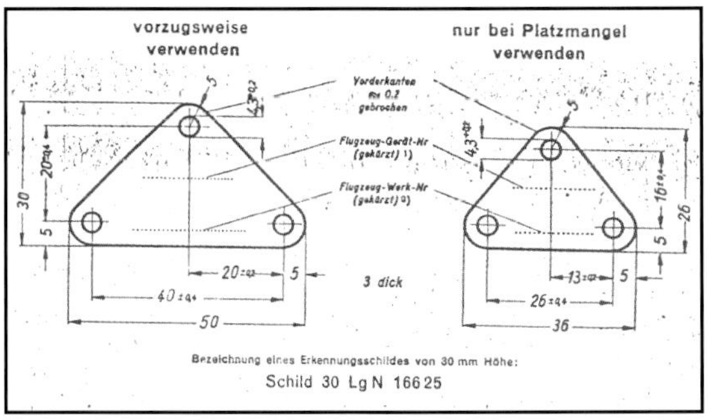

In June 1944, a third location for a **Werknummer** *plate was devised whereby a small triangular tab was riveted to the inside vertical metal of the fin at the rudder hinge. This location was selected as being the most likely place on the airframe to survive a devastating crash and still prove readable. Location of data plate is shown in illustration below.*

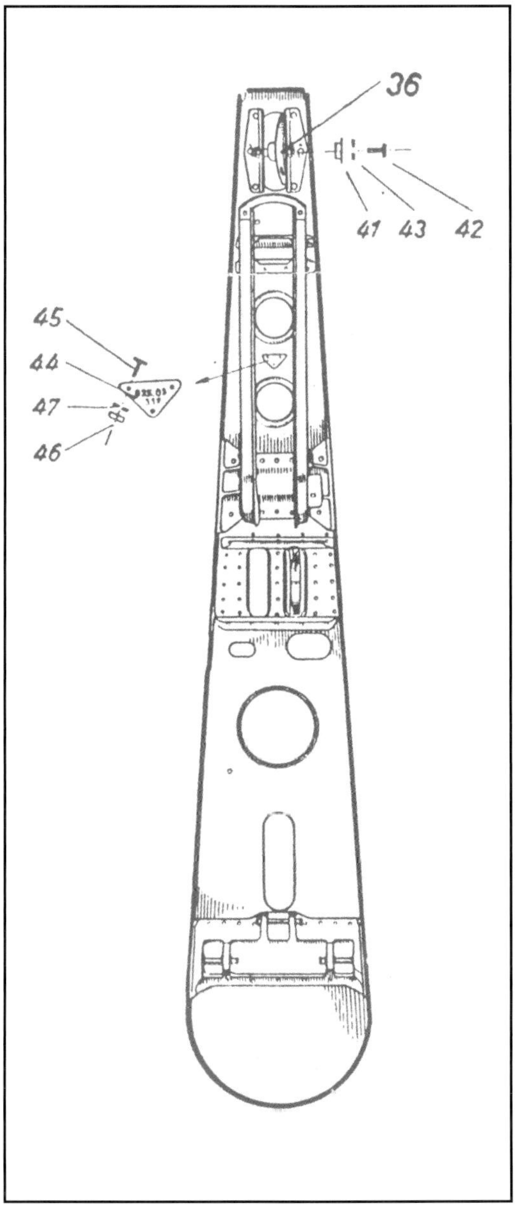

DECENTRALIZATION & LABOR

From the beginning, because the Ta 152 was so heavily based upon the Fw 190, apart from its wings and powerplants, it was assumed the anticipated production transition from the radial-powered Fw 190 to the new fighter would be handily accommodated within the numerous existing Focke-Wulf facilities. Focke-Wulf's sprawling production network was actively involved in the manufacture of large and small military aircraft including the Fw 200, Fw 189 and Fw 190.

By the time the first prototypes of the Ta 152 had flown, American and British forces were well established on the continent. Moreover, Russian operations in the east were clearly on the offense. Against this backdrop, thousands of German workers, foreign laborers and forced labor inmates toiled to produce ever greater quantities of fighter aircraft, including the Ta 152.

Much of the astonishing German production success achieved in 1944 was the direct result of decentralizing aircraft production. Not only was this done to minimize exposure to Allied bombing, but it was also skillfully orchestrated so as to enlist as many German manufacturing firms as possible. In concert with this program was the deliberate policy of exploiting the captive labor resource represented by tens of thousands of inmates locked in prisoner of war camps, *Zivilarbeiter* (civil servants) camps, and the infamous death camps. The scope of this operation was immense. No less than 2,500 German firms benefited directly from forced labor. To meet the government's demand, companies such as Concordia AG, Dornier, Henschel, Junkers, Daimler-Benz and Vereinigte Deutsche Metallwerke AG, were dependant upon labor provided by the Nazi Lagersystem. Some firms even actively solicited the camps themselves while others were ordered to accommodate forced laborers within their ranks. Insofar as the Ta 152 is concerned, there is no question but many Focke-Wulf suppliers were dependent upon forced labor even though the main Focke-Wulf assembly centers did not directly rely on this labor pool.

During this period of aircraft production in 1944, *Reichsministers* Albert Speer and Karl Saur oversaw a vast expansion of aircraft production especially of singe-seat fighters. Strict regulations were enacted throughout the industry in an attempt to streamline and coordinate production. Approximately 300 Focke-Wulf employees were directly involved in this monumental task. The work was divided according to the aircraft's major components. These included the fuselage, engine housing, tail assemblies, and wings. In addition, a host of suppliers produced all manner of parts and systems common to fighter planes: propellers, engines, radiators, fuel, oil and coolant tanks, instruments, weapons, munitions, Plexiglas windscreens and canopies, wheels, tires, and electrical components. Focke-Wulf periodically published a list of firms participating in the decentralized production of Fw 190 and Ta 152 (see three reports on opposite page). As a result of Allied bombing and other factors, these lists had to be continually adjusted.

Ta 152 FINAL ASSEMBLY SITES

As recounted in the text, Focke-Wulf's plant at Sorau was originally to have been responsible for the construction of the first 25 prototypes (Ta 152 V1 - V25) with corresponding *Werknummern* 110001 through 110025. But after it was decided to cancel the first five machines (W. Nr. 110001 - 110005), the first all new prototype was actually built at Adelheide and was the sixth machine, the Ta 152 V6, W. Nr. 110006. In addition, six further scheduled prototypes were eventually canceled. Thus the Sorau factory's involvement with the Ta 152 was to conclude with completion of the last of 14 prototypes. Almost all of the Sorau-built aircraft were to serve the Ta 152 C series.

Focke-Wulf's Cottbus plant was responsible for the manufacture of 115 preproduction Ta 152 H-0s plus two to three times that figure of full production Ta 152 H-1s. But in reality the Cottbus assembly lines succeeded in producing not less than 40, but not more than 55 examples of the H-0, plus approximately 17 complete H-1s. In sum, the Cottbus factory managed to produce between 57 and 72 Ta 152 H series fighters before the war's end.

Mitteldeutschen Metallwerke Erfurt (Mimetall or MML), at Erfurt North, emerged in 1944 from the former Reparaturwerk Erfurt (REWE) to become a full-fledged aircraft production center. This firm was charged with producing the Ta 152 C-1, but as events unfolded, only two were completed and hastily delivered to JG 301. MML was also responsible for photoreconnaissance versions of the Ta 152—namely the short span Ta 152 E-0/E-1 and the long span Ta 152 H-11 (after the Ta 152 H-10 was canceled in March 1945, MML began construction of the H-11). When American troops captured MML in April 1945, they discovered that less than a dozen Ta 152 E-0/E-1s plus only two Ta 152 H-11s were in an advance stage of assembly.

Similarly, at least one Ta 152 H-1/R11 was nearly fin-ished by Focke-Wulf at Bremen while ATG at Leipzig had several Ta 152 C-1/R11s nearing completion by May 1945.

FINAL PRODUCTION PLAN

The chart below lists the final ten principal assembly centers, their preassigned aircraft *Werknummern* batches, and the subseries each was to manufacture. Included are Focke-Wulf at Bremen, Siebel at Halle, Ago at Oschersleben, Fieseler at Kassel, Erla at Leipzig, Gotha Waggonfabrik at Gotha, Mimetall at Erfurt, Norddeutsche Dornier Werke (NDW) at Wismar, and Allegemein Transportanlage GmbH (ATG) at Leipzig. Also included was the Arbeitsgemeinschaft Roland (Labor Partnership Roland) linked to Weser Flugzeugbau GmbH located at Nordenham, Lemwerder and Berlin-Templehof.

Although not delineated by manufacturer, the reader is encouraged to examine the chart on pages 128 and 129 in which Focke-Wulf's Construction Bureau forecast their anticipated work load plan for a multitude of production and development Fw 190s and Ta 152s for the 11 month period between February and December 1945.

Ta 152 PLANNED PRODUCTION AND FINAL ASSEMBLY FACILITIES			
Facility	**Makers Code**	**Variant**	***Werknummern***
Fw Sorau	ncc	Ta152 V1-V25	110001-110025
Fw Cottbus	naz	Ta 152 H-O/R11	150001-150040
		Ta 152 H-1/R11	150158-150174
Fw Bremen	gwy	Ta 152 H-1/R11	200000
Ago-Oschersleben	jhe	Ta 152 C-O	380000
		Ta 152 C-1	380000
ATG-Leipzig	hlr	Ta 152 C-1/R11	830000
		Ta 152 C-3	920000
Erla-Leipzig	mcu	Ta 152 B-5/R11	510000
		Ta 152 H-1/R11	640000
		Ta 152 H-2	canceled
Fieseler-Kassel	hps	Ta 152 C-1/R11	480000
		Ta 152 C-2	canceled
Gotha Waggonfabrik	csx	Ta 152 B-5/R11	580000
		Ta 152 C-1/R11	720000
		Ta 152 C-2	canceled
		Ta 152 C-4	canceled
		Ta 152 H-1/R11	
		Ta 152 H-2	canceled
Mimetall-Erfurt	mct[1]	Ta 152 C-1/R11	600000
		Ta 152 C-2	canceled
		Ta 152 C-11/R11	
		Ta 152 E-O/E-1	870000
		Ta 152 H-10	Based on H-O, canceled March '45
		Ta 152 H-11	Based on H-1
NDW-Wismar	hmw	Ta 152 C-1	710000
		Ta 152 C-2	canceled
		Ta 152 C-4	canceled
Arb.Gem.Roland-WFG	mdl	Ta 152 C-1/R11	790000
		Ta 152 C-2	canceled
		Ta 152 C-4	canceled
Siebel-Halle	jbn	Ta 152 C-11/R11	360000
		Ta 152 C-3	440000

1. Mimetall used the same manufacturing code as the former REWE company.

FOCKE-WULF Ta 152 SERIES PRODUCTION AIRCRAFT

W. Nr.	Stkz	Versuch	Series	Mission	Maker		Remarks
150001	CW+CA		H-0	Höhenjäger	Fw Cottbus	naz	First flown 21 Nov 44 by Hans Sander, forced off-field landing. To Rechlin in Dec, later transferred to III./JG 301, 27 Jan 45.
150002	CW+CB		H-0	"	"		First flown 29 Nov 44 by Hans Sander. To Rechlin 3 Dec 44, test flown by Heinrich Beauvais.
150003	CW+CC		H-0	"	"		First flown 3 Dec 44 by Hans Sander. Flown at Rechlin by Harry Böttcher and H. Beauvais. MW 50 drop tank. Received wooden tail at Rechlin. With E.Kdo. 152.
150004	CW+CD		H-0/R11	"	"		First flown 17 Nov 44 by H. Sander to Langenhagen for modified fuselage-mounted engine cowl. Handed over to III./JG 301, "Green 6". Found at Leck 6 Apr 1945.
150005	CW+CE		H-0	"	"		First flown early December then transferred to Junkers for engine development, fate unk.
150006	CW+CF		H-0	"	"		First flown in December and later transferred to Rechlin where it was flown by Heinrich Beauvais on 2 Feb 45. Later sent to E.Kdo. 152 for operational service.
150007	CW+CG		H-0	"	"		First flown in December. Delivered to 12./JG 301, "Black 13". Transferred to Stab/JG 301. Flown by Generalmajor Dietrich Peltz in March. Flown operationally by Obfw. Reschke.
150008	CW+CH		H-0	"	"		First flown in December and transferred to Rechlin where it was flown by H. Beauvais on 20 Feb 45. Later to operational service with E.Kdo 152.
150009	CW+CI		H-0	"	"		First flown in December 1944. Transferred to E.Kdo. 152 then to Stab/JG 11. Fate unknown.
150010	CW+CJ		H-0	"	"		Flown Dec. To Rechlin in Jan, flown by H. Beauvais. Second "H" modified with wooden tail unit. To E.Kdo. 152 then 11./JG 301, "Yellow 4", then Stab/JG 301, "Green 4". Now in storage for the NASM.
150011	CW+CK		H-0/R11	"	"		Built in Dec. 1944. Fitted with aux. apparatus R11 plus first Ta 152 with GM1. Transferred to E.Kdo. 152 for operational duty. Fate unknown.
150012	CW+CL		H-0	"	"		Completed early in Jan. 1945. Transferred to E.Kdo. 152. Ultimate fate unknown.
150013	CW+CM		H-0	"	"		First flown on 2 Jan 45. Pilot and aircraft fate unknown.
150014	CW+CN		H-0	"	"		First flown 23 Dec by Werner Bielefeld. Fate unknown.
150015	CW+CO		H-0	"	"		First flown 23 Dec 1944 but ultimate assignment unknown.
150016	CW+CP		H-0	"	"		First flown 29 Dec 1944. No additional information.
150017	CW+CQ		H-0	"	"		No information
150018	CW+CR		H-0	"	"		No information
150019	CW+CS		H-0	"	"		No information
150020	CW+CT		H-0	Höhenjäger	Fw Cottbus	naz	First flown in January and transferred to Rechlin in February.
150021	CW+CU		H-0	"	"		First flown in December 1944
150022	CW+CV		H-0	"	"		First flown in January and delivered to III./JG 301.
150023	CW+CW		H-0	"	"		First flown in December and later transferred to III./JG 301.
150024	CW+CX		H-0	"	Fw Cottbus	naz	First flown in December and later transferred to III./JG 301.
150025	CW+CY		H-0	"	"		First flown in December and later transferred to III./JG 301.
150026	CW+CZ		H-0	"	"		First flown in December. No additional information known.
150027		V27 (first)	H-0	"	"		Completed in January as H-0. Originally to be a hybrid prototype for Ta 152 "C-3" but canceled. With long span wings and DB 603 L, it was closer to the Ta 152 H-8/H-9.
150028		V28 (first)	H-0	"	"		Completed in January as H-0. Originally to be a hybrid prototype for Ta 152 "C-3" but canceled. With long span wings and DB 603 L, it was closer to the Ta 152 H-8/H-9.
150029			H-0	"	Fw Cottbus		First flown 7 Jan 45 and later transferred to III./JG 301.
150030		V27	H-0	"	Fw Langenhagen		Hybrid development a/c with DB 603 E and long span wings. Prototype for unofficial Ta 152 H-8/H-9. Lost in crash at Langenhagen 2 Feb 45 piloted by Hans Sander.
150031		V28	H-0	"	Fw Langenhagen		Companion hybrid a/c to V27 scheduled to be flight cleared in Mar 45. Uncertain if it was completed or flown.
150032			H-0	"	Fw Cottbus		First flown 17 Jan 45 and delivered to III./JG 301.
150033			H-0				Reportedly finished with a Ta 152 H-10 fuselage as a production template for MML who was to build the H-10 reconnaissance fighter.
150034			H-0	"	"		First flown 20 Jan 45 and delivered to III./JG 301.
150035			H-0				First flown in January 1945 and operational with III./JG 301.
150036			H-0				First flown in January 1945 and operational with III./JG 301.
150037			H-0				First flown 16 Jan and delivered to III./JG 301. Uffz. Hermann Dürr crashed and was killed while on training flight at Alteno (SW of Terpt) 100% loss.
150038			H-0				Delivered to III./JG 301 late in January 1945. Fate unknown.
150039			H-0				Delivered to III./JG 301 late in January 1945. Fate unknown.
150040			H-0		"		Last H-0 completed. Produced late in January 1945. Reportedly captured intact at war's end and later shipped to Farnborough. No other details known.
150158			H-1/R11	Höhenjäger	Fw Cottbus		Reportedly captured by U.S. troops on 8 May 45. No further details.
150159			H-1/R11	"	"		
150160			H-1/R11	"	"		
150161			H-1/R11	"	"		
150162			H-1/R11	"	"		Flown to Flugzeugwerk Eger GmbH (now Cheb, Czech Republic) and found by U.S. Army on 19 Apr 45. No further details.
150163			H-1/R11	"	"		
150164			H-1/R11	"	"		
150165			H-1/R11	"	"		
150166			H-1/R11	"	"		
150167			H-1/R11	"	"		Captured by British and American forces at Fw Bremen – Served as H-1 production model and later declared as surplus by U.S. Army and scrapped at Kassel.
150168			H-1/R11	"	"		Stab/JG 301, "Green 9". Flown by Willi Reschke. Reportedly captured by RAF at Leck and flown to Farnborough as AM 11. Scrapped in 1946.
150169			H-1/R11	"	"		Stab/JG 301, reportedly captured by British forces at Leck. No further details.
150170			H-1/R11	"	"		
150171			H-1/R11	"	"		
150172			H-1/R11	"	"		
150173			H-1/R11	"	"		
150174			H-1/R11	"	"		Stab/JG 301, "Green 5", reportedly captured by British forces at Leck. Possibly the last H-1 produced at Cottbus. Fate unknown.
600001[2]			C-1/R31	Jäger	Mimetall-Erfurt	mct	Delivered to Stab/JG 301, further details are unknown.
600002[2]			C-1/R31	"	"	"	Delivered to Stab/JG 301, further details are unknown.

1) Previous page: Reported here is the original code for Reparaturwerk Erfurt, which was expanded early in the war and renamed Mitteldeutsche Metallwerke (MML) Erfurt, or Mimetall Erfurt for short. It is the belief of the author that the original REWE's 3-digit code (mct) would have continued in use by MML which possibly explains why historians cannot locate a new code for MML.

2) The precise Werknummern for these two C series aircraft are unknown. The six-digit examples listed above are speculative based on the allocation of known number blocks. It is entirely possible the end digit sequence could have commenced with numbers other than '1' or '2' since such a precedent had already been firmly established by Focke-Wulf. For example, the aircraft's beginning Werknummer could just as easily have been something such as 600024.

An overall aerial view of the Mimetall works, taken by a U.S. Army photographer soon after the war at Erfurt North, shows largely intact hangars, specialized structures, runways and aircraft recovered by American troops. The cluster of aircraft shown at the bottom of the image and enlarged below are the same Ta 152 Es shown at the bottom of page 138.

Close up view showing several Ta 152 aircraft at Erfurt.

Appendix 3
Specifications, Weights, Performance and Equipment

By January 1945, the RLM had decided that seven of the eight Ta 152 subtypes listed on the following pages were to be placed in production as soon as possible. The eighth, the Ta 152 A-2, though enthusiastically supported by Kurt Tank, was not favored by the Air Ministry. Nevertheless, it was never officially removed from the "do not produce" list thereby fostering Focke-Wulf's notion that it would eventually enter series production.

The data contained on the following pages is self explanatory but in a few instances contains dimensions which are at variance with certain Focke-Wulf documents. These are cited in the footnoes located at the base of the chart. Specifically, there are two sets of dimensions given for the Ta 152 H-0 and H-1. The initial set was established during 1944 at a time when the aircraft's wing, with rounded tips, was to have been 380 mm longer (15 inches) while the overall length of the aircraft was some 110 mm 4 3/8 inches) greater than the final figure. By the time the H series entered preproduction, the rounded wing tips were eliminated together with subtle fuselage changes.

Throughout its career, the Ta 152 became eligible for certain modifications and additional equipment depending on the aircraft's intended mission and mission requirements. As with other German fighters produced during the Third *Reich*, these modifications fell within four categories:

1. Complex modifications initially undertaken by a production center,
2. Modifications carried out by *Luftwaffe* units in accordance with established mission requirements,
3. Modifications endorsed by *Luftwaffe* testing sites and ad hoc operational units, and lastly
4. Modifications carried out and adopted on the aircraft assembly lines.

The first modification category resulted in the so-called *Umrüst-Bausätze* (Modification Construction Sets) which, in the case of the Ta 152, resulted in conversion of single-seat fighters into two-seat liaison and training aircraft. The letter 'U' followed by a number (without a hypen) identified aircraft so modified, e.g., the Ta 152 C-1/U1. Following a trial period in which the modification was approved for series production, an entirely new series designation was generated. For example, the Ta 152 C-1/U1 led the way toward creation of the Ta 152 S series.

The second modification category centered on the so-called *Rüstsätz* (Auxiliary Apparatus) classification. Changes to the standard equipment of production aircraft enabling the pilot to carry out a specific mission with different equipment resulted in this category. Usually written as 'R' followed by a number (without a hyphen), these changes were theoretically performed at the unit level. For example, the Ta 152 C-1/R14 would have been modified by *Luftwaffe* units to enable the aircraft to carry out torpedo attacks. During the manufacturing cycle, it was common for aircraft to be "prewired" to facilitate anticipated changes to the aircraft's standard equipment in order to more easily facilitate such changes within the field.

Further, duplications within *Rüstsätze* for a single aircraft series were not uncommon (as shown below); by 1944 each manufacturer took steps to avoid duplication of 'R' numbers. For example, the R14 modification was specific not only for the Ta 152, but also for the Fw 190.

RÜSTSÄTZE FOR THE Ta 152:

R1 - 2 X MG 151/120 with 140 rpg within the out wings. Only applicable for the Ta 152 A-1, A-2, B-1, B-2, B-3 and B-4.

R2 - 1 X Rb 50/18 aerial reconnaissance camera obliquely mounted within the rear fuselage with a camera angle 10 degrees below the horizon. Only for the Ta 152 E-1.

R2 - 2 X MK 108 cannon with 55 rpg mounted within the outer wings. Only for the Ta 152 A-1, A-2, -1, B-2, B-3 and B-4.

R3 - 2 X MK 103 cannon with 40 rpg within a gondola-mounted outboard under the wing. Applicable for the Ta 152 A-1, A-2, B-1, B-3, B-3 and B-4.

R5 - 2 X 2 X ETC 71 underwing racks capable of carrying a total of 8 SC 50 bombs (thereby 4 on an ER4 adapter 50) or 4 X SC 50 plus 1 X AB 250 for close support missions. Also included within this equipment was a TSA 2D bomb sight. Only for the Ta 152 C-1.

R10 - Listed, but not defined, within a British postwar report dealing with Ta 152 armament. According to the report, only one Ta 152 subtype was eligible for this unknown equipment: the Ta 152 C-2/R10.

R11 - Bad weather fighter equipped with LGW K2 fighter directional control, FuG 125 *Hermine* VHF radio beacon signal receiver, heated windows, and PKS 12 autopilot. Delivery of the entire B-5, C-1 and H-1 series to be equipped with R11 from the first aircraft. Only two H-0s are known to have been completed with this equipment.

R14 - Proposed torpedo fighter for the Ta 152 C-1 with an ETC 504 bomb rack intended to carry an LT 1B or LT F5 airborne torpedo. Suspension tests found the device was better suited for the Fw 190 D-13/R14.

R21 - Special version equipped with either the Jumo 213 E-1 or EB engines in conjunction with high pressure MW 50 carried in the left inboard wing fuel tank; PKS 12 autopilot; FuG 125 "Hermine". GM 1 power boost not installed. Only for the Ta 152 H-1.

R25 - High pressure MW 50 carried in the left inboard wing fuel tank similar to the system to be employed by the Fw 190 D-12. Only for the Ta 152 B-5.

R31 - Modification to address center of gravity concerns. For the Ta 152 C-1/R31 and probably the C-3/R31, the fuselage tank containing MW 50 was deleted. Instead, MW 50 was relocated to the left wing inner and middle tanks. The remaining four wing tanks held either B4 or C3 aviation fuel. The fuselage fuel supply was unchanged. For the Ta 152 H-2/R31, the designated engine was the Jumo 213 E-1 or EB with high pressure MW injection. The pressurized GM 1 propellant bottles were removed from the engine area. In their place, ballast of steel plates was added. The standard 85 ltr. tank for GM 1, installed in the rear fuselage aft of seam was unchanged. The standard rear fuselage fuel tank, with a capacity of 360 ltr. was restricted to only 280 ltr.

R33 - Special engine cowl for the Ta 152 C-1 and C-3 employing *Triebwerk* 9-8603 B1 (complete cowled engine DB 603 LA).

The third modification category included an array of conventional and unorthodox weapon systems for the Ta 152 C/U without special designators including: wing mounted, vertcally firing *Rohrbock* 108 or SB 500 projectiles installed in place of the wing's center fuel tank; and two X-4 (Ru 344) air-to-air wire-guided rockets mounted on underwing pylons.

For the C series, R4M air to air rockets were to be installed beneath each wing. Two WGr 21 air to air mortar rockets were briefly considered.

The C series was also to utilize the astonishing MG 213A once it became available.

Finally other modifications were planned directly for the assembly line including special performance enhancing cowls with rigid casings, increased pilot armor and special windshield armor for ground attack versions, additional aircraft turning displays, more wood components and the simplified Mansfeld landing gear.

Ta 152 Specifications, Weights, Performance and

Role			Ta 152 A-2 Fighter	Ta 152 B-5 Zerstörer	Ta 152 C-1 Fighter
Seating			1	1	1
Wing span	mm	(ft - in)	11,000 (36' 1 1/8")	11,000 (36' 1 1/8')	11,000 (36' 1 1/8')
Wing area	m²	(ft²)	19.6 (210.9)	19.5 (209.9)	19.5 (209.9)
Length	mm	(ft - in)	10,784 (35' 4 5/8")	10,810 (35' 5 1/2")	10,820 (35' 6")
Height	mm	(ft - in)	3,360 (11' 2 7/8")	3,360 (11' 2 3/8")	3,360 (11' 11 3/8")
Stabilizer span	mm	(ft - in)	3,650 (11' 11 3/4")	3,650 (11' 11 3/4")	3,650 (11' 11 3/4")
Stabilizer area	m²	(ft²)	2.89 (31.1)	2.82 (30.4)	2.82 (30.4)
Wheel track	mm	(ft - in)	3,954 (12' 11 3/4")	3,954 (12' 11 3/4")	3,954 (12' 11 3/4")
Main wheel size	mm		740 X 210	740 X 210	740 X 210
Tail wheel size	mm		380 X 150	380 X 150	380 X 150
Engine type			Jumo 213 C	Jumo 213 EB/E-2	DB 603 LA
Take off power	hp-rpm		2,000 at 3,300 rpm	2,000 at 3,300 rpm	2,100 at 2,700 rpm
Climb to altitude and combat	hp-rpm		1,580 at 3,000 rpm	1,580 at 3,000 rpm	1,675 at 3,000 rpm
Propeller type			VS 9	VS 9	VDM - VP
Diameter/blade number/material	mm	(ft - in)	3,600 (11' 9 3/4") 3 blade wood	3,600 (11' 9 3/4") 3 blade wood	3,600 (11' 9 3/4") 3 blade wood
Fuel supply			B4	B4	B4
Electronics			FuG 16 ZS, FuG 25a FuG 125	FuG 16 zy, FuG 25a FuG 125	FuG 16 zy, FuG 25a FuG 125
Cameras			1XRobot II in port wing	1XRobot II in port wing	1XRobot II in port wing
Empty weight	kg	(lb)	3,704 (8,166)	4,270 (9,414)	4014 (8,849)
Equipped weight	kg	(lb)	4,465 (9,844)	4,325 (9,535)	4,207 (9,171)
Crew weight	kg	(lb)	100 (221)	100 (221)	100 (221)
Fuel weight	kg	(lb)	440 (970)	833 (1,836)	833 (1,836)
MW fuel	kg	(lb)	— —	127 (280)	127 (280)
GM 1 fuel	kg	(lb)	140 (309)	— —	— —
Lubricants weight	kg	(lb)	40 (88)	55 (121)	55 (121)
Ammunition	kg	(lb)	181 (399)	65 (143)	193 (426)
Take off weight	kg	(lb)	4,846 (10,683)	5,450 (12,015)	5,322 (11,733)
Maximum combat speed:					
at sea level	km/h-km	(mph-ft)		529-0 (329-0)	560-0 (347-0)
at altitude	km/h-km	(mph-ft)	678-8.0 (421-26,247)	683-10.7 (424-35,105)	730-10.4 (454-34,119)
at max. altitude	km/h-km	(mph-ft)	671-10.9 (416-35,761)		663-12.3 (412-40,355)
Service ceiling	m	(ft)	10,500 (34,449)	11,600 (38,058)	12,200 (40,022)
Climb to 8 km (26,247 ft) altitude	min				10.2
Rate of climb	m/s	(ft/sec)	14.8 (48.60)		16.0 (52.49)
Normal cruising range	km-km	(miles-ft)		1,165-660 (723-2165)	1,100-675 (684-2,215)
Landing speed	km/h	(mph)			170 (106)
Take off distance	m	(ft)			605 (1,985)
Armament (standard)	Engine position		1XMK 103 with 70 rds	1XMK 103 with 80 rds	1XMK 108 with 90 rds
	Cowl position		2XMK 151/20 -150 rds	none	2XMG 151/20-150 rds
	Inner wing position		2XMG 151/20-50 rds	2XMK 103 w/44 rds	2XMG 151/20-175 rds
	Outer wing position		*Rüstsätze*	none	none
Modification construction sets (*Umrüst-Bausätze*)	U1		—		2 seat trainer conversion-pilot model for S-1 & S-2 series. None converted or completed
Auxiliary apparatus (*Rüstsätze*)	R		R1, R2, R3	R11, R25	R5, R11, R14, R31, R33

Ta 152 C-3 Fighter	Ta 152 E-1 Photoreconn.	Ta 152 H-0 High Alt. Fighter	Ta 152 H-1 High Alt. Fighter	Ta 152 H-10 High Alt. Photo Reconn.
1	1	1	1	1
11,000 (36' 1 1/8")	11,000 (36' 1 1/8")	14,440[1] (47' 4 1/2")	14,440[1] (47' 4 1/2")	14,440[1] (47' 4 1/2")
19.5 (209.9)	19.5 (209.9)	23.5 (252.9)	23.5 (252.9)	23.5 (252.9)
10,820 (35' 6")	10,810 (35' 5 5/8")	10,710[2] (35' 1 3/4')	10,710[2] (35' 1 3/4")	10,810[2] (35' 5 5/8")
3,360 (11' 2 3/8")	3,360 (11' 2 5/8")	3,360 (11' 2 3/8")	3,360 (11' 2 3/8")	3,360 (11' X 2 3/8")
3,650 (11' 11 3/4")	3,650 (11' 11 3/4")	3,650 (11' 11 3/4")	3,650 (11' 11 3/4")	3,650 (11' 11 3/4")
2.82 (30.4)	2.82 (30.4)	2.82 (30.4)	2.82 (30.4)	2.82 (30.4)
3,954 (12' 11 3/4")	3,954 (12' 11 3/4")	3,954 (12' 11 3/4")	3,954 (12' 11 3/4")	3,954 (12' 11 3/4")
740 X 210	740 X 210	740 X 210	740 X 210	740 X 210
380 X 150	380 X 150	380 X 150	380 X 150	380 X 150
DB 603 LA	Jumo 213 E/E-1	Jumo 213 E	Jumo 213 E/E-1	Jumo 213 E
2,100 at 2,700 rpm	2,000 at 3,300 rpm	1,750 at 3200 rpm	1,750 at 3,200 rpm	1,750 at 3,200 rpm
1,675 at 2,500 rpm	1,580 at 3,000 rpm	1,580 at 3,000 rpm	1,580 at 3,000 rpm	1,580 at 3,000 rpm
VDM - VP	VS 9	VS 9	VS 9	VS 9
3,600 (11' 9 3/4")	3,600 (11' 9 3/4")	3,600 (11' 9 3/4")	3,600 (11' 9 3/4")	3,600 (11' 9 3/4")
3 blade wood	3 blade wood	3 blade wood	3 blade wood	3 blade wood
B4	B4	B4	B4 (later C3)	B4 (later C3)
FuG 16zy, FuG 25a FuG 125	FuG 15, FuG 25 a FuG 125	FuG 16zy, FuG 25a FuG 125	FuG 16zy, FuG 25a FuG 125	FuG 15, FuG 25a FuG 125
1XRobot II in port wing	1XRobot II in port wing	1XRobot II in port wing	1XRobot II in port wing	1XRobot II in port wing 1XRb 75/30 in fuselage
4,109 (9,059)	4,110 (9,061)	3,920 (8,642)	4,031 (8,887)	4,031 (8,887)
4,302 (9,484)	4,300 (9,480)	4,514 (9,952)	4,625 (10,196)	4,675 (10,307)
100 (221)	100 (221)	100 (221)	100 (221)	100 (221)
833 (1,836)	833 (1,836)	440 (970)	736 (1,623)	440 (970)
127 (280)	127 (280)	— —	64 (141)	64 (141)
— —	— —	— —	104 (229)	104 (229)
55 (121)	55 (121)	55 (121)	55 (121)	55 (121)
218 (481)	127 (280)	127 (280)	127 (280)	127 (280)
5,442 (11,991)	4,675 (10,306)	4,727 (10,421)	5,217 (11,501)	5,228 (11,526)
560-0 (347-0)		563-0 (350-0)	563-0 (350-0)	
730-10.4 (454-34,119)	710-10.5 (442-34,449)	752-12.4 (467-40,682)[4]	752-12.4 (467-40,682)[4]	
663-12.3 (412-40355)		737-13.8 (457-45,276)[4]	737-13.8 (457-45,276)[4]	
12,200 (40,022)	12,900 (42,329)	13,500 (44,289)	13,500 (44,289)	Similar to H-0
10.2	10.9	12.6	12.6	
16. 0 (52.49)	13.0 (42.65)	17.5 (57.42)[3]	17.5 (57.42)[3]	
1,100-675 (684-2,215)		1,140-585 (708-364)	1,140-585 (708-364)	
170 (106)		155 (96)	155 (96)	
605 (1,985)	595 (1,952)	500 (1,640)	500 (1,640)	
1XMK 103 w/ 80 rds	1XMK 108 w/90 rds	1XMK 108 w/85-100 rds	1X MK 108 w/85-100 rds	1XMK 108 w/85-100 rds
2XMG 151/15 w/150 rds	none	none	none	none
2XMG 151/15 w/175 rds	2XMG 151/20 w/ 175rds	2X MG 151/20 w/175 rds	2XMG 151/20 w/175 rds	2XMG 151/20 w/175 rds
none	none	none	none	none
—	—	—	—	—
R5, R11, R31, R33	R1 (oblique camera)	R11 (only fitted to two)	R11, R21, R31	none recorded

1. wing span with rounded tips was 14,820 mm (48' 7 3/8")
2. original length without external tab was 10,810 mm (35' 5 5/8")
3. with MW 50 power boost 4. with GM 1 power boost

Based on the Ta 152 H-0, the H-10 was canceled March 45 in favor of the Ta 152 H-11 which was based on the Ta 152 H-1.

Appendix 4
Pilot Operating Instructions
for the Ta 152 H-1 and Ta 152 H-1/R11*

I. GENERAL
Airplane Components

The cabin is pressurized and has a jettisonable sliding canopy. Air is supplied by dynamic pressure or compressor. The armoring consists of head, back and front plate and bulletproof glass, inside and out; and both visibility windows are heated electrically inside; full windshield rinsing. The pilot's seat and the rudder pedals can be adjusted on the floor. The stabilizer is adjusted electrically. A pressure oil system operates retracting and lowering of landing gear and landing flaps. The emergency operation of the landing gear and landing flaps is by compressed air.

Engine

The engine is a Jumo 213 E, with a two-stage supercharger and a three-speed change gear with boost cooler installed in the engine's radiator circuit.

The critical altitude is 10,000 m (32,808 ft). The propeller is of the VS 9 type with wooden blades and control is automatic by means of oil pressure, cooling and lubricant temperatures are regulated automatically by oil pressure. The rated power control is operated by hand.

The engine is not suited for inverted flying, but brief upside-down positions are permissible during flight maneuvers.

Radio Installation

The radio system consists of one FuG 16 ZY ultra short wave set for inter-airplane, as well as ground communication, homing and Y-conducting. A radio FuG 25a, recognition radar, and an additional radio set, FuG 125 plus an automatic pilot K23 is also included (only for H-1/R11).

Armament

The installation consists of one automatic MK 108 engine cannon of 30 mm (1.181 in) caliber, with electric pneumatic loading and electric firing; 85 rounds. Two wing root MG 151/20 E with electric loading, electric trigger and firing 135 rounds each.

Rescue and Safety Equipment

One-man rubber boat pack for back-type parachute.
Back type parachute with perlon harness, oxygen apparatus, altitude release and air vent.
Optional reversible oxygen apparatus with automatically controlled supplementary air or with an air regulator mounted airtight.
Breathing air compressor, pressure check and relief valve, rotary slide valve, internal cabin pressure indicator and altitude warning signal

Mission and Stress Group III

Disposal fuel load:
Front fuselage tank: 230 ltr (60.76 gal)
Rear fuselage tank: 360 ltr (92.10 gal)
ETC 503 A-1 tank: 300 ltr (79.25 gal)

Wing Tanks

Left and right inside tanks: 75 ltr (19.81 gal) each
Left and right center tanks: 85 ltr (22.45 gal) each
Left and right outer tanks: 80 ltr (21.13 gal) each

Special Fuel Load

GM 1 system in aft tank: 85 ltr (22.45 gal)

* Document Source:
8-152 H-1, H-1/R11
Bedienungsvorschrift-Fl. Teil 1
Bedienungskarte für den
Flugzeug-führer, Ausgabe 1945.

MW system: 75 ltr (19.81 gal) in inside left wing tank, or optionally B4 fuel.

Fuel Consumption Values

Power Output	RPM	Ltrs(gals) / hour
At Start	3,250 + 50	640 (169.1)
At climb and combat	3,000	555 (147.6)
Cont. power output I	2,700	375 (99.1)
		to 14.5 (3.83)
Cont. power output II	2,400	285 (75.3)
Cont. power output III	2,100	215 (56.8)

II. PREPARATION FOR STARTING
Airplane Components
1. Adjust the pilot's seat and rudder controls to the pilot's size (cross lines in the reflector sight are at eye level).
2. Close the sliding canopy.
3. Test maneuverability of the rudder.

Engine

Turn the hand wheel operating the rated power output of the cooling flaps toward the "on" (*auf*) position (functioning test).

Radio Installation

Connect the wireless headset.

Armament

Press the automatic switch on the right instrument console controlling the weapons in the wing root and engine cannon.

Rescue and Safety Equipment
1. Put on oxygen mask and test for tightness.
2. The supply on the oxygen apparatus supplying the rescue parachute should register "full" (*voll*).
3. Connect the mask to the parachute's breathing tube.
4. Connect the aircraft system's breathing tube to the elbow on the automatic disconnect point.
5. Hook the emergency valve's snap hook to the pilot's seat.
6. Open the oxygen stop valve. The pressure indicator should show 150 atm (2,633 psi) above atm. pr.
7. Check the functioning of oxygen supervision by breathing
8. Operate the oxygen jet to check the functioning of oxygen supervision.
9. Remove the oxygen mask.

III. STARTING
A. Starting when engine is cold
1. Ignition "off" (*aus*).
2. Press the automatic ignition and starting system (*Zünd-und Anlassanlage*) switches, generator and tank pump (*Behälterpumpen*) switches When starting the aircraft's battery, press the automatic battery (*Sammler*) switch.

3. Make sure that the landing gear indicator "down" (*aus*) indicator is located at the landing gear control grip; otherwise pull (*ziehen*) the landing gear operating grip.
4. Set the power output lever in starting position.
5. Make sure that the safety cock lever is open (*auf*). Check the fuel pressure gauge.
6. Press (*drücken*) the starter switch for 10 seconds.
7. Pull (*ziehen*) out the starter switch and at the same time inject starting fuel with the atomizer pump.

(a) When outside temperature is above 0° C (32° F)
8. The engine servicing unit should be set to operate automatically, the hand pull pressed down.
9. Set the throttle about 5 mm (¼ in) from the idling stop.
10. Ignition "On" (*ein*).
11. Press (*drücken*) the starter switch for 10-20 seconds.
12. Pull (*ziehen*) the starter switch when the clear (*frei*) signal is given.
13. Directly after starting, the oil pressure should register on its gauge, otherwise immediately shut off the engine [throttle in stop position (*stopsellung*)].
14. Push the throttle slightly forward.
15. After starting by means of an external source, (*aussenbord*) press down on the automatic battery (*Sammler*) switch.

(b) When the outside temperature is below 0° C (32° F)
8. Pull the emergency for the engine servicing unit.
9. Set the throttle about 40 mm (1.5 in) from idling stop.
10. Ignition on (*Ein*).
11. Press (*drücken*) the starter switch for about 10-20 seconds.
12. Pull (*ziehen*) the starter switch when the clear (*frei*) signal is given.

13. Directly after starting, the oil pressure should register on this gauge; otherwise immediately shut the engine off [throttle in stop position (*stopsellung*)].
14. Set the throttle in the idling position (*leerlauf*).
15. Turn the servicing unit's emergency pull 90° to the right and press it back to neutral position.
16. After starting by means of external source, (*aussenbord*) press down the automatic battery (*Sammler*) switch.
Regardless of the outside temperature the engine will usually start by pulling the emergency.

B. Starting with warmed-up engine
This cancels A.1, 4, 6 and 7. Automatic start or, start by pulling the emergency is possible.

C. Warming up
1. After opening the radiator flaps, set the hand wheel for radiator flap control at 100° C (212° F).
2. Run the engine at 1,000 to 1,200 rpm until the lubricant temperature registers 20° C (68° F).
3. Increase the rpm gradually to 2,000 until the coolant temperature registers 70° C (158° F).
4. When starting with a cold engine accelerate according to oil pressure (maximum 11 atm. or, 156.42 psi above atm. pr.)

IV. TEST RUNNING
1. Pull the elevator fully and hold it. The stabilizer should be fully compensated for the heaviness.
2. Set the throttle in take-off position.
Caution!
Anchor or weigh down the fuselage tail, otherwise do not exceed 2,800 rpm.
Speed: 3,050 ± 75 rpm at INA standard day.
Fuel pressure: 1.7 ± 0.1 atm. (24.2 ± 1.4 psi) above atm. pr.
Lubricant pressure to 13 atm. (184.9 psi) above atm. pr. Boost pressure according to coolant and outside temperature.

Change in boost pressure:
For each 10°C (18°F) increase in outside temperature + 0.015 atm. (.213 psi).

3. Test the magneto starting ignition. A decrease of 100 rpm is permissible by a smoothly running engine.
4. Slowly pull back the throttle.

V. TAXIING TO TAKE OFF
1. Unlock the skid by pressing down (*drücken*) on the control grip. Do not apply the brake while unlocking as it would tie-up the locking bolt.
2. Set the stabilizer in "0" position.
3. Set the hand wheel for rated power output in open (*auf*) position.
4. Do not increase the coolant temperature; 120°C (248°F) is temporarily permissible. Keep within short taxiing runs.
5. Test the brakes.

VI. TAKE OFF
Radio system
1. Press the automatic switch for the radio FuG 16 ZY and FuG 25a. The units should be ready for operation after 2 minutes.
2. When pressing the automatic switch for the FuG 16 ZY, set the operating switch for general use of the AD 18 Ya at "FT" (wireless telegraph).

Airplane and engine
1. Set the landing flaps in flight position.
2. Adjust the hand wheel for radiator flap control to "100°" position.
3. Push throttle to starting position (3,250 rpm).
4. After take-off apply the brakes lightly.
5. Push the safety flap on the landing gear control grip to the right and press (*drücken*) the landing grip to the stop. Release the grip; the safety flap snaps back.
6. The red landing gear signals should be visible; otherwise press the landing gear control grip once more.
7. The mechanical landing gear indicator rods on the wings should have retracted.
8. Compensate any load variation by trim.

VII. CLIMB
1. The best climbing speed is 270-250 km/h (168 – 155 mph) indicated air speed.
2. Change from 1st to 2nd gear at 2,500 ± 200 m (8,200 ± 656 ft) altitude.

VIII. CRUISING
Airplane
1. Clean the oiled visibility panes by opening the cock for window rinsing.
2. When there is danger of ice formation, immediately heat the outside pitot tube and heating disk.
3. Ventilate the cockpit up to 8,000 m (26,246 ft) altitude.

Values at outside temperatures of + 15°C (59° F):						
Coolant Temperature	80°C (176° F)	90°C (194°F)	100° (212°F)	110° (230°F)	120° (248°F)	Tolerance
Boost pressure Atm. (psi)	1.57 (22.32)	1.58 (22.47)	1.60 (22.75)	1.61 (22.89)	1.63 (23.18)	± 0.02 (.284)

From the port side of the NASM Ta 152 H-0 looking into the cockpit.

a. At high outside temperatures:
   Set rotary valve at fresh air supply (*Frischluft*).
b. At low outside temperatures:
   Fill the airtight tube.
   Set the rotary air supply valve at pressure operation (*Druckbetrieb*).

Engine

1. Fly according to rpm reading:

Performance	Time allowance	RPM
Take off	up to 30 min	3,250
Climb and combat	continuous	3,000
Continuous power output	I continuous	2,700
Continuous power output	II continuous	2,400
Continuous power output	III continuous	2,100
Idling (flight)	-	1,200 – 1,500

Fuel consumption is high at continuous use for climb and combat.

2. Operating values
   Fuel pressure: 1.7± 0.1 kg/cm²
                   (24.2 ± 1.4 lb/in²)
   Lubricant pressure: 3.5 to 13 kg/cm²
                   (49.8 to 184.7 lb/in²)
   Lubricant temp: max. 135°C (275°F)
   Coolant temp: 100°C (212°F) at all altitudes.
   During take-off and taxiing, temp may temporarily rise to 120°C (248°F) (speed less than 1,800 rpm).

Fuel System Operation:

(a) Fuel supply gauge
1. A supply indicator with selector switch for the front and rear fuselage tanks is located on the lower instrument panel. The regular switch is on the rear tank.
2. There are no fuel supply gauges for the six wing tanks. Supplementary fuel flows into the rear fuselage tank.
3. When the wing tanks are empty, the fuel supply gauge, which is switched to the rear tank, drops below 260 ltr (68.7 gal).
4. The under fuselage drop tank has no supply gauge. Supplementary fuel flows into the rear fuselage tank.
5. When the drop tank is empty the supply gauge, which is switched on to the rear tank, drops below 200 ltr (52.8 gal).
6. The white warning light on the instrument panel flashes when the rear tank supply has dropped to about 10 ltr (2.6 gal).
7. A red warning light flashes when the supply in the front tank has dropped to about 80 ltr (21.1 gal). This fuel supply suffices for 15 minutes flying time at 2,400 rpm.

Special Fuel System
   See servicing instructions for GM 1 – supplement Ta 152 H-1
   See servicing instructions for MW – supplement Ta 152 H-1 (see note at end)

(b) Fuel tank switching

	Condition	Cause	Remedy	Result
NORMAL OPERATION	Indicator for rear tank is stationary with no residual warning supply.	All tanks filled	Open (*auf*) safety cock lever	Suction and pressure action from front tank pump from rear tank into front tank.
	Supply indicator for the rear tank drops below 260 ltr (68.7 gal).	Wing tanks empty	ditto	ditto
	Supply indicator for the rear tank drops below 200 ltr (52.8 gal).	Drop tank empty	ditto	ditto
	White light shows	Rear tank empty	Switch the supply gauge to front tank. Open (*auf*)	Suction and pressure action from front tank.
	Red light shows	Front tank has only 80 ltr (21.1 gal)	Only 15-min. flying time remaining. Open (*auf*)	Suction and pressure action from front tank.
SPECIAL	Red light shows before white light	No fuel flow from rear to front tank	Emergency (*Not*)	Suction action from rear tank
	Supply gauge in rear tank shows more rapid decline	Loss of fuel from rear tank	Emergency (*Not*) When the residual warning flashes white, open safety cock	Suction action from rear tank. Suction and pressure action from front tank
	Red light shows. No supply indication in front. Decline in fuel pressure. Engine fails.	Front tank fails suddenly	Emergency (*Not*)	Suction action from rear tank

Radio Installation

(a) Radio Telephone Communication
1. Set the frequency selector switch at the stipulated stop.
2. Set the operating selector switch at "FT" (radio telephone).
3. Adjust the volume.
4. Press the telephone button and speak.
5. Adjust the frequency to the best reception by tapping.

(b) Approaching on a Beam
(Homing is only possible at stops II, Δ, Í.)
1. Frequency selector switches on II, Δ or Í.
2. Take up radio telephone communication with ground (see a). The ground station will then switch on the radio beam.
3. Set the operating selector switch at intermediate frequency ("ZF"). The needle on AFN 2 (indicator for radio navigation) deflects when off course (a vibrating tone is also heard in the ear phones).
4. The distance indicator on the AFN 2 responds.
5. Adjust the course until the course indicator stays in the middle position (a constant tone is audible).
6. Sensing through a brief change of course to the left results in a deflection to the left on the instrument at approach.
Caution! If the pointer deflects to the right (left) by a change in course to the left (right), then there is a deviation from the transmitter. The AFN 2 is an indicator instrument and not a master control.

(c) Ground-to-Air Direction Finding
(The ground set is an ultra short wave d/f, for instance the Tornado direction finder.)
1. Set the frequency selector switch at the stipulated stop (usually stop Δ).
2. Pick up radio telephone communication (see a).
3. Upon request from the R/T ground station, press the microphone button and speak (count, say "Tuba").
4. The bearing is returned from the ground station. Various ground-to-air D/F types are possible (qdm, qte, qdr, qtf, etc.).

(d) Y- Conducting – only possible at stop I.
1. Pick up radio communication with the control station at stop II (see a).
2. Upon request from the Control Officer, switch to stop I.
3. Upon request from the Control Officer, set the operating switch to Y, test sound 3000 or 300 cps audible.
4. Simultaneous radio telephone communication with ground station is also possible with the switch in the Y position, after pressing the microphone switch at the control grip.

(e) Egon Conducting (see note at end)
1. Select the stipulated identification stop 1, 2 or center stop on operating unit BG 25a.
2. When the switch is in position 1 or 2 and connection has been established through the radar unit, a control light will flash synchronous with the radiated beam.
3. The test button will be temporarily out of order.
4. Radio telephone communication is established by means of radio set FuG 16 ZY (see a). Comply with special instructions. No specifications are available for radio set FuG 125.

Automatic Pilot - H-1/R11 only
Throw the automatic switch. The direction indica-
tor, built as a grip ring, and dome switch are mounted on the control column. For a right turn, turn the grip ring to the right (viewed from above).

Armament
1. Test the brightness of the reflector sight.
2. Throw the safety switch on the instrument panel for weapons to load the MG 151/20 E.
3. Indication of completed loading:
   Left cannon – left closing control signal.
   Right cannon – right closing control signal.
4. Number of rounds indicator: For the left cannon only (175 rounds per gun).
5. Press the loading button to load the automatic engine cannon MK 108 with priming device.
6. Shift the firing lever on the control stick.
7. Firing: The MG 151/20 E is fired by means of the A-button (firing lever), the automatic MK 108 cannon is fired by the B or C button.
8. Safety: Before the firing lever is shifted, the safety switch should be off (aus).

IX. HIGH ALTITUDE FLYING
Rescue and Safety Equipment
(a) At 4,000 m (13,123 ft) altitude begin breathing oxygen and continue at altitudes above 4,000 m.
1. Open the remote oxygen control valve. Watch the pressure gauge and oxygen supervision.
(b) At 8,000 m (26,246 ft) altitude, switch the pressure operation on.
1. Turn the rotary slide for breathing air supply to "pressure operation" (Druckbetrieb).
2. Fill the airtight hose by pressing the valve 15 to 20 seconds.
3. Watch the cockpit's internal pressure indicator occasionally. The internal pressure should be equal to that at 8 km (26,247 ft).

X. DIVING
1. Maximum permissible diving speeds:

Altitude		Speed	
km	ft	km/h	mph
9	(29,528)	500	(310.685)
7	(22,966)	600	(372.822)
5	(16,404)	700	(434.959)
4-0	(13,123)	750	(466.027)

2. Pull the throttle back. Do not exceed 3,300 rpm as short time limit.

XI. GLIDING
1. The coolant temperature should not go below 60°C (140°F).
2. Push the throttle forward several times during longer glide (to clean the spark plugs).

XII. LANDING
Aircraft
1. Slow to about 300 km/h (186 mph).
2. Pull (ziehen) the landing gear control grip and release.
3. The visual signal on the electric landing gear indicator must show green; otherwise pull the landing gear control again.
4. The mechanical landing gear indicator should be visible (red rod protruding on top of the wings).
5. Lower the landing flaps completely. The speed should be between 320 and 220 km/h (199 and 137 mph). Equalize changes in load by trim.
6. Approach at about 190 km/h (118 mph).
7. Touch down at about 155 km/h (96 mph) according to gross loading.
8. Set the radiator flap's control hand wheel at open (auf) position.
9. Retract the landing flaps after the landing run.

Engine
Set the throttle only to the idling stop.

Radio System
Leave the radio switched on until the landing run.

XIII. STOP
Airplane
1. De-aerate the airtight hose.
2. Left – unlock the sliding canopy.
3. Right – crank the handle to open the sliding canopy.

Engine
1. Allow the engine to cool at 1,800 rpm. The maximum permissible coolant temperature is 90°C (194°F) below 1,000 rpm.
2. Set the throttle in the stop position.
3. Shut off (aus) the ignition and remove the key.
4. Close (zu) the fire cock.

Electrical System
1. Press the circuit cut-off switch.
2. Switch off the pressed down automatic switch.

XIV. CRITICAL FLYING CONDITION
Scramble take-off
1. Zoom with fully lowered landing flaps.
2. Retract the landing gear.
3. Trim the aircraft.
4. Retract the landing flaps at sufficient altitude and speed.

Emergency Landing
1. Be firmly strapped.
2. When at low altitude zoom up immediately until the speed is slowed to 300 km/h (186 mph).
3. Jettison the drop tank.
4. Set the throttle for quick stop (schnellstop).
5. Shut off (aus) ignition.
6. Press down the circuit cut-out switch.
7. Close (zu) the fire cock.
8. Crank the handle of the sliding canopy to the last notch. Set the handle.
9. Only lower the landing gear for an airfield; otherwise make a belly-landing.
10. Lower the landing flaps completely. Compensate the aircraft for tail heaviness.

Landing in water
1. Same as for emergency landing outside an airfield, but with loosened straps.
2. Jettison the canopy.
3. Leave the aircraft as soon as possible after setting it down.

Parachuting
1. Slow the speed if possible (pull up). When parachuting from high altitudes it is necessary to have the oxygen mask fit tightly. Oxygen mask 10-6704 is recommended. The maximum speed at which a parachute with air vent can be deployed is about 550 km/h (342 mph). The minimum parachuting altitude is 150 m (492 ft).
2. Loosen the microphone disconnect point at the neck.
3. Disconnect the break coupling.
4. Unstrap the safety harness.

When the canopy is not sealed:

5. Bend the upper portion of the body forward; press the canopy's emergency jettison lever (the canopy is hurled off). If there is sufficient time and the speed is below 300 km/h (186 mph), uncrank the canopy entirely.

6. Give the control stick a strong kick forward with the feet; the pilot is catapulted out.

At altitudes above 8,000 m (26,246 ft) with sealed canopy:

5a. Exhale completely.

6a. Press the canopy's emergency jettisoning lever (de-aerate the airtight hose). After 3 to 5 seconds press the lever down completely. (The canopy is hurled off.) Bend the upper part of the body forward.

7a. Give the control stick a strong kick forward with the feet; the pilot is catapulted out.

8a. At altitudes below 4,000 m (13,123 ft) remove the oxygen mask.

Landing gear emergency operation

1. Pull (ziehen) the landing gear control grip.
2. At a speed below 240 km/h (149 mph) try to lower the landing gear by strong pushing. If unsuccessful:
3. Open the compressed air valve for landing gear emergency (Fahrwerk Not).
4. Watch the electrical and mechanical indicators.
5. Do not close the compressed air valve.

Landing flap emergency operation

1. Open the compressed air valve for landing flap emergency (Landeklappen Not).
2. Watch the electrical and mechanical indicators.
3. Do not close the compressed air valve.

Engine trouble caused by disruption of the automatic control servicing the engine; stalled or uneven running engine

1. Set the throttle back.
2. Pull (ziehen) the emergency for the engine operating unit.
3. Do not exceed boost pressure of 1.55 atm (22.0 psi).

Other Irregularities

(a) Altitude warning light flashes:
Dive immediately to altitudes below 11,000 m (36,080 ft).

(b) Oil or fuel fumes, fire, etc. in the pressure cabin at 8,000 – 11,000 m (26,246 – 36,080 ft):

1. Exhale completely.
2. De-aerate the airtight hose.
3. Open the canopy as much as needed.

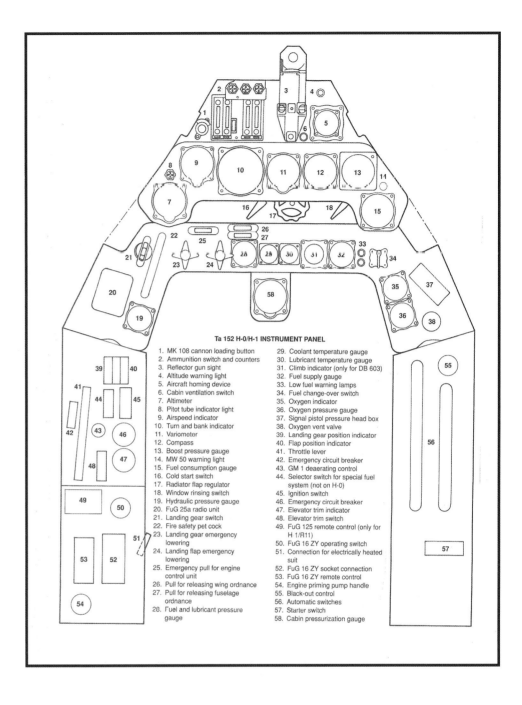

Ta 152 H-0/H-1 INSTRUMENT PANEL

1. MK 108 cannon loading button
2. Ammunition switch and counters
3. Reflector gun sight
4. Altitude warning light
5. Aircraft homing device
6. Cabin ventilation switch
7. Altimeter
8. Pitot tube indicator light
9. Airspeed indicator
10. Turn and bank indicator
11. Variometer
12. Compass
13. Boost pressure gauge
14. MW 50 warning light
15. Fuel consumption gauge
16. Cold start switch
17. Radiator flap regulator
18. Window rinsing switch
19. Hydraulic pressure gauge
20. FuG 25a radio unit
21. Landing gear switch
22. Fire safety pet cock
23. Landing gear emergency lowering
24. Landing flap emergency lowering
25. Emergency pull for engine control unit
26. Pull for releasing wing ordnance
27. Pull for releasing fuselage ordnance
28. Fuel and lubricant pressure gauge
29. Coolant temperature gauge
30. Lubricant temperature gauge
31. Climb indicator (only for DB 603)
32. Fuel supply gauge
33. Low fuel warning lamps
34. Fuel change-over switch
35. Oxygen indicator
36. Oxygen pressure gauge
37. Signal pistol pressure head box
38. Oxygen vent valve
39. Landing gear position indicator
40. Flap position indicator
41. Throttle lever
42. Emergency circuit breaker
43. GM 1 deaerating control
44. Selector switch for special fuel system (not on H-0)
45. Ignition switch
46. Emergency circuit breaker
47. Elevator trim indicator
48. Elevator trim switch
49. FuG 125 remote control (only for H 1/R11)
50. FuG 16 ZY operating switch
51. Connection for electrically heated suit
52. FuG 16 ZY socket connection
53. FuG 16 ZY remote control
54. Engine priming pump handle
55. Black-out control
56. Automatic switches
57. Starter switch
58. Cabin pressurization gauge

ENEMY AIRCRAFT INTERCEPT SYSTEMS

Y System

During mid-1943 the *Luftwaffe* installed a network of ground control stations throughout Germany and the Low Countries to coordinate fighter defenses. Known as the 'Y' system, it enabled ground control to bring fighters on an intercept course. The intercepting fighters would have one or more aircraft with the 'Y' system. These aircraft would receive continuous ground transmissions informing the pilot of the target's position, course and altitude, in addition to other factors. The 'Y' aircraft pilot would then transmit this information on a different frequency to others within the flight.

EGON System

EGON was a long-range guidance system for fighters and was intended as a replacement for the complicated 'Y' system. It involved the *Weitling* FuSAn 730 ground unit oper-
ating as a purely secondary radar, with separate transmitting and receiving frequencies, and was developed from the *Freya-LZ* FuMG 401 by removal of the 125 Mhz receiver with reception antenna field, and by inserting a direction aerial for the identification signal receiver *Gemse* on 156 MHz. There were no interfering ground echoes with this pure two-frequency operation, but enemy aircraft could no longer be identified by type. Replacing the 'Y' system with EGON was never fully implemented. By the spring of 1945, fewer than 150 EGON fighter guidance centers had become operational.

Power Boosting Systems

Specifically, power boosting systems can be divided generally into two broad categories; liquid injection and direct air injection. The first, liquid injection, involves the delivery under pressure of a fluid that, upon reaching the airstream of the engine's supercharger, is immediately atomized and combined with the fuel/air mixture. The second category, direct air injection, is accomplished by boosting the pressure of the supercharger's incoming air by means of turbo charging. As applied to the Ta 152, all power boosting systems involved liquid injection. Although turbo supercharging was considered, there is no evidence this form of power boosting was actually incorporated within a Ta 152. Its bulk and complexity alone were enough to discourage its application.

Nitrous Oxide Power Boosting

Nitrous oxide, refered to as GM 1(Gas *Mischung* 1 – Gas Mixture 1), also known as "ha ha gas" (laughing gas) or derisively as *Göring Mischung*, was employed by injecting the mixture directly into the fuel air stream at the supercharger's intake.

Nitrous oxide is an odorless, colorless gas composed of two atoms of nitrogen attached to one oxygen atom. Two forms of liquefying the nitrous oxide gas for use are possible. The gas can be transformed into a liquid by compression to 760 psi at 70 degress F (865 psi at 80 degrees F), or by lowering its temperature to –127 F. When applied to fighter aircraft, the former method had the disadvantage of requiring heavy pressurized propellant bottles and the ever present danger of explosion from enemy fire. The latter system required substantial thermal insulation for the holding tank and fluid delivery pipe.

Nitrous oxide allowed the pilot to fly above the rated altitude of the engine. By pushing the throttle past its limit, to a maximum of 110 percent, at a predetermined altitude, the pilot automatically activated GM 1 injection. Nitrous oxide by itself does not provide power. It will not burn, nor is it a fuel. Instead, when the gas is heated to approximately 572 degrees F on the compression stroke, it breaks down and releases its oxygen. Thus, it provides the engine with additional oxygen which allows fuel to burn at a faster rate than normal thereby permitting greater power for approximately 40 to 50 minutes at emergency boost pressure. By burning more fuel, higher cylinder pressures are encountered which, in turn creates most of the additional power. As pressurized GM 1 is injected, it changes from a liquid to a gas or boils, and this boiling effect actually reduces the temperature of the gas to –127 degrees F. The resulting charge cooling also significantly reduces intake temperature by approximately 70 degrees F and increases power. In this way, GM 1 also acts as an antidetonant (engine knocking resulting from fuel exploding within

the cylinder instead of burning). The nitrogen, which was released during the engine's compression stroke, served to dampen the greatly increased cylinder pressures leading to a controlled combustion. Nevertheless, since nitrous oxide is only activated at full throttle, the pilot had to exercise caution not to over-run the engine beyond its ability to absorb the resulting increased forces. In the case of the the Ta 152, this usually meant restricting the application of GM 1 to a maximum of 10 minutes continuous operation.

Aircraft equipped with GM 1 were not required to burn high octane fuel.

MW Power Boosting

The MW 50 power boosting system was composed of a special fuel that contained 50 percent methanol, 49.9 percent tap water plus 0.5 percent *Schutzöl* 39, an anti-corrosion fluid. Alternatively, MW 30, containing 30 percent methanol, 69.5 percent tap water, and 0.5 percent *Korrosionsschutzöl* 39 was an optional blend. A third choice, known as EW 50, consisted of 50 percent Ethanol (ethyl alcohol), 49.9 percent tap water plus 0.5 percent *Schutzöl* 39.

The MW 50 power boosting system was used to obtain extra power below the rated altitude of the supercharger and it also acted as an anti-detonant, providing charge cooling and allowing greater boost pressure. A 4 percent power increase could be obtained for a maximum of 10 continuious minutes, with five minute lapse time between use periods. Spark plug life was cut to 15-30 hours while fuel consumption rose by 40 percent during take off. Boost pressure from the supercharger was used to apply the necessary propellant, which brought the solution to the supercharger intake, where it was injected directly into the eyelet. The MW system was controlled by a solenoid valve, actuated by an automatic throttle, when the throttle was pushed beyond its normal limit to the 110 percent position.

For the Ta 152, all variants were eligible for MW power boosting. In addition the Ta 152 E-2 (high altitude reconnaissance fighter) and the entire Ta 152 H series were also to be equipped with GM 1 power boosting. Simultaneously installing both power boosting systems within one aircraft was not unique to the Ta 152, but it was clearly unusual. As stated above, one system provided extra power below the engine's rated altitude (MW), while the other (GM 1) provided extra power above the engine's rated altitude.

Bibliography

The reader will be aware that this volume does not contain footnotes within the text. However, every citation or event can be referenced to a source. Because many of the principals mentioned in the narrative are no longer living, or are infirm octogenarians…and beyond, clarification of personal events that occurred six decades earlier has proven virtually hopeless. Often contradictory information contained in contemporary official memoranda, production tables, correspondence and post-war interviews only serve to further cloud events. Occasionally, postwar statements are found which are clearly "revisionist" or, are imbued with an obvious bias. Often impeccable sources can not agree on the basic question of dates. Even such events as the precise date a prototype first flew, or the date of an important air raid, differ from source to source. There are also ample examples of unsolved mysteries. The cause of an accident, the fate of a particular pilot, seemingly often went unreported during the closing months of the war. In contrast, and as if in self-indulgence, certain pedestrian events were documented in the most excruciating detail.

Source Documents:
Rechlin Partial Report 15 f Development Order 1661 and 1603, E 2c, secret, 15 Oct 1941.
F-TS-542-RE; Operating Instructions for Pilots 8-152 H-1, H-1/R11; T-2, Wright Field, Dayton, Ohio; 29 Apr 1946.
A-I-2 (G) Report N°. 2383; German Aircraft New and Projected Types, January 1946.
Air Documents Research Center, US Strategic Air Forces in Europe A-2 various documents contained in the following microfilm reels: 120, 206, 2009, 2025, 2040, 2059, 2076, 2264, 2277, 2281,2306, 2325, 2357, 2370, 2447, 2707, 2727, 2742, 2748, 2749, 2758, 2770, 2775, 2786, 2858, 2861, 2876, 2887, 2888, 2896, 2966, 3214, 3237, 3275, 3282, 3287, 3328, 3492, 3606, 3624 3953, 3954, 3970, 3971, 3972, 3973, 3974, 3975, 3996, 8001, 8011, 8022, 8038, 8066, 8055, 8083, 8084, 8159, 8280
Other miscellaneous German wartime documents including:
Verstellschraubenübersich (nach Flügetzahl geordnet), Junkers OMW, Kobü-Luftschrauben, Fläming, 30 Jan 45.
Fw 190 Ausführungs-Übersichslist 0003, Stand Nov 1942
Fw 190 Muster u. Serienflugzeug Nr. 9, March 1944; Nr. 10a, May 1944; Nr. 16, Oct 1944.
Fw 190 mit Einheitstriebwerk Jumo 213A, Nov. 1943
Baumuster-Uebersicht Ta 152 mith DB 603, Jumo 213, January 1945
OKL, TLR/Fl.E 2 III, March 1945

Correspondence:
Amtmann, Hans H. (†) (former engineer with Blohm u Voss) various 1989 - 1997
Kappus, Peter G. (†) (former Flugbaumeister for BMW) various 1978 – 1984.
Sander, Hans Dipl. Ing. (†) (former Focke-Wulf test pilot) various 1980 – 1983.
Smith, J. Richard (published aviation author) various 1985 – 2007.

Internet Sources:
Wikipedia plus various postings from "12 O'Clock High!" Luftwaffe Discussion Forum, Luftwaffe Experten Forum.

Select Bibliography:
Aders, Gebhard (1986) Monogram Close-Up 8, Fw 190 F. Boylston, MA: Monogram Aviation Publications.
Angolia, John R., LTC (1979), On The Field Of Honor, Volume 1, San Jose, California, R. James Bender Publishing.
Baeuvais, Heinrich; Kössler, Karl; Regel, Christoph (1998) Die deutsche Luftfahrt, Flugerprogungs stellen bis 1945. Bonn, Germany: Bernard & Graefe Verlag.
Boog, Horst H. (1982) Die deutschen Luftwaffenführung 1935-1945. Stuttgart, Germany: Deutsche Verlags-Anstalt.
Brown, Eric (1977) Wings of the Luftwaffe. London, England: MacDonald and Jane's Publishers Ltd.
Carter, Kit C. & Mueller, Robert (1973) Combat Chronology 1941-1945. Washington DC: Center for Air Force History.
Conradis, Heinz (1960) Design for Flight, The Kurt Tank Story. London, England: Macdonald & Co. Ltd.
Ethell, Jeffrey L. (†) (1990) Monogram Close-Up 24, Ta 152. Sturbridge, MA: Monogram Aviation Publications.
von Gersdorff, Kyrill, Grasmann, Kurt (1981) Die deutschen Luftfahrt Flugmotoren und Strahltriebwerke: München, Germany: Bernard & Graefe Verlag.
Green, William (1970) Warplanes of the Third Reich. Garden City, New York: Doubleday and Company, Inc.
Griehl, Manfred & Dressel, Joachim (1995) Focke-Wulf Fw 190 / Ta 152. Stuttgart, Germany: Motorbuch Verlag.
Hitchcock, Thomas H. (1980)The Official Monogram Painting Guide to German Aircraft 1935-1945. Boylston, MA: Monogram Aviation Publications.
Hoffschmidt, Edward J. (1969) German Aircraft Guns WWI – WWII. Old Greenwich, CT: We Inc.
Irving, David. (1973)The Rise and Fall of the Luftwaffe. Boston, MA: Little, Brown and Company.
Jablonski, Edward (1974) Double Strike, The Epic Air Raids on Regensburg / Schweinfurt. New York, NY: Doubleday & Company, Inc..
Lang, Bruno (1986) Die deutschen Luftfahrt Typenhandbuch der deutschen Luftfahrttechnik: Koblenz, Germany: Bernard & Graefe Verlag.
Nowarra, Heinz J. (†) (1988) Aircraft & Legend Focke-Wulf Fw 190 & Ta 152, Newbury Park, California, Haynes Publications, Inc.
Raitt, D.I. (1969) Catalogue of Enemy Aircraft Reports 1939-1946, London, UK, RAE Ministry of Technology.
Schmid, Walter (2003) Die Entwicklungsgeschichte der Mauser-Flugzeugbordwaffe MG/MK 213C. Blaufelden, Germany: DWJ Verlags GmbH.
Smith, J. Richard; Creek, Eddie J. (1986) Monogram Close-Up 10, Fw 190 D. Boylston, MA: Monogram Aviation Publications.
Spenser, Jay P. (1983) Monogram Close-Up 22, Moskito. Boylston, MA: Monogram Aviation Publications.
United States Strategic Bombing Survey (1947) Aircraft Division Industry Report, Washington DC, United States Government Printing Office.
United States Holocaust Memorial Museum (1996), Historical Atlas of the Holocaust, New York, NY. Macmillan Publishing USA.
Vajda, Ferenc A. & Dancey, Peter (1998) German Aircraft Industry and Production 1933-1945. Shrewsbury, UK: Airlife Publishing Ltd.
Wagner, Wolfgang (1980) Die deutsche Luftfahrt, Kurt Tank- Konstrukteur und Testpilot bei Focke-Wulf. München, Germany: Bernard & Graefe Verlag.

Credits

PHOTOGRAPHIC – AGENCY
Champlin Fighter Museum: 104T, 104B; Dornier GmbH: 88; Imperial War Museum: 27, 172B; Messerschmitt-Bölkow-Blohm GmbH: 71; National Air and Space Museum: 127; Public Record Office: 142, 147; United States Air Force: 74, 175, 176, 177; United States Army: 89, 192; Vereinigte Flugtechnische Werke: 32T, 45, 46, 52, 58, 91, 92, 94, 101T, 102, 105B, 106, 130, 131, 132, 134B, 137T, 167, 168, 169.

PHOTOGRAPHIC – INDIVIDUALS
Robert Bracken: 96T; Philip Butler: 111B; S. Butte: 124, 172T; J.C. Carbonel: 15B; Peter W. Cohausz: 196-197; Jerry Crandall: 158, 162; James V. Crow: 6TL, 159, 171M; Eddie J. Creek: 34, 150; F. Dölling: 119; Walter Frentz: 157TR; Harry Gann (†): 26B; Raymond Goggans (†): 97, 138, 139; Jean-Michel Goyat: 76; Malcolm V. Lowe: 103, 134T, 166B; Norman Malayney: 166T, 170, 171T; Frederick B. McIntosh (†): 111T, 173B; Brian Nicklas: 107BL, 180, 181, 198, 199; Heinz J. Nowarra (†): 31, 36, 151, 114; H. Osterwald: 22T; Willi Reschke: 5; Robert Rinder: 171B; Hanfried Schliephake: 80; Brian M. Silcox: 8,87BR. 105T; F. Wagner: 22BL, 22BR; Günter Sengfelder: 7TR, 35T, 113; J. Richard Smith:14, 157TL; Anthony Speir: 50; Harold E. Watson, Maj-Gen (†): 174T; Michael Wolski: 75; Gordon S. Williams: 26T. All other photographs are from the author's private collection.

DRAWING AND ILLUSTRATION
Arthur L. Bentley: 98-99, 118, 130; Jean-Marc Berthe: 85, 152; Jerry Crandall: 153; Dennis Davison: 143; Juanita Franzi: 57; Marco Gueli: 120B, 121B, 149B; Gareth Hector: cover illustration, 3, 90, 208; Lloyd S. Jones: 17, 42, 43TR; Sonny Schug: 188; Thomas A. Tullis: 8, 108-109, 122, 123, 146-147, 149T, 151, 158, 160, 161, 179, 184, 185, 187, 202; Keith Woodcock: 53, 75, 88, 201. All others are from the author's private collection.